HISTORICAL DICTIONARIES OF RELIGIONS, PHILOSOPHIES, AND MOVEMENTS
Edited by Jon Woronoff

1. *Buddhism,* by Charles S. Prebish, 1993
2. *Mormonism,* by Davis Bitton, 1994. *Out of print. See No. 32.*
3. *Ecumenical Christianity,* by Ans Joachim van der Bent, 1994
4. *Terrorism,* by Sean Anderson and Stephen Sloan, 1995
5. *Sikhism,* by W. H. McLeod, 1995
6. *Feminism,* by Janet K. Boles and Diane Long Hoeveler, 1995
7. *Olympic Movement,* by Ian Buchanan and Bill Mallon, 1995
8. *Methodism,* by Charles Yrigoyen Jr. and Susan E. Warrick, 1996
9. *Orthodox Church,* by Michael Prokurat, Alexander Golitzin, and Michael D. Peterson, 1996
10. *Organized Labor,* by James C. Docherty, 1996
11. *Civil Rights Movement,* by Ralph E. Luker, 1997
12. *Catholicism,* by William J. Collinge, 1997
13. *Hinduism,* by Bruce M. Sullivan, 1997
14. *North American Environmentalism,* by Edward R. Wells and Alan M. Schwartz, 1997
15. *Welfare State,* by Bent Greve, 1998
16. *Socialism,* by James C. Docherty, 1997
17. *Bahá'í Faith,* by Hugh C. Adamson and Philip Hainsworth, 1998
18. *Taoism,* by Julian F. Pas in cooperation with Man Kam Leung, 1998
19. *Judaism,* by Norman Solomon, 1998
20. *Green Movement,* by Elim Papadakis, 1998
21. *Nietzscheanism,* by Carol Diethe, 1999
22. *Gay Liberation Movement,* by Ronald J. Hunt, 1999
23. *Islamic Fundamentalist Movements in the Arab World, Iran, and Turkey,* by Ahmad S. Moussalli, 1999
24. *Reformed Churches,* by Robert Benedetto, Darrell L. Guder, and Donald K. McKim, 1999
25. *Baptists,* by William H. Brackney, 1999
26. *Cooperative Movement,* by Jack Shaffer, 1999
27. *Reformation and Counter-Reformation,* by Hans J. Hillerbrand, 2000
28. *Shakers,* by Holley Gene Duffield, 2000

Historical Dictionary of the Olympic Movement

Second Edition

Ian Buchanan and Bill Mallon

*Historical Dictionaries of Religions,
Philosophies, and Movements, No. 39*

The Scarecrow Press, Inc.
Lanham, Maryland, and London
2001

SCARECROW PRESS, INC.

Published in the United States of America
by Scarecrow Press, Inc.
4720 Boston Way
Lanham, Maryland 20706
www.scarecrowpress.com

4 Pleydell Gardens, Folkestone
Kent CT20 2DN, England

British Library Cataloguing in Publication Information Available

Library of Congress Cataloging-in-Publication Data

Buchanan, Ian.
    Historical dictionary of the Olympic movement / Ian Buchanan and Bill Mallon.—2nd ed.
        p. cm.—(Historical dictionaries of religions, philosophies, and movements ; no. 39)
    Includes bibliographical references (p.).
    ISBN 0-8108-4054-5 (alk. paper)
        1. Olympics—History—Dictionaries. 2. Olympics—Records. I. Mallon, Bill. II. Title.
    III. Series.

GV721.5 .B83 2001
796.48'03—dc21   2001034224

First edition by Ian Buchanan and Bill Mallon. Historical Dictionaries of Religions,
Philosophies, and Movements, No. 7, Scarecrow Press, 1995. ISBN 0-8108-3062-0

Contents

Editor's Foreword

Of the many movements included in this series, there is nothing quite like the Olympic movement in scope. The original Olympic Games were held nearly three millennia ago and the next Olympic Games are never more than two years away. The flame from the old to the new Games was carried by dedicated individuals, Pierre de Coubertin and other pioneers, and is now borne by tens of thousands of organizers, athletes, trainers, sponsors, and fans, and observed by a public that numbers in the hundreds of millions. Whereas only Greeks participated in the original Olympic Games, participation has now spread around the world, including persons of every race, religion, and nationality. Despite a need for organization and the creation of institutions, this remains a people's movement more than any other.

But the Olympic movement is also often something more and occasionally something less. The participants are not only competing in their own interest or that of the country they represent, to win highly coveted prizes, but to show how sport can enrich humanity. They are imbued, to some extent at least, with the ideals of the Olympics and even the spectators somehow come away better than they arrived. But these ideals, some so lofty that they simply cannot be fulfilled, contrast with the institutional side of the Olympics: which city and country to choose, which sports to include, how to make the athletes abide by the rules, how to organize and run the biggest show on Earth, and how to have that show cover its costs and perhaps turn a profit. Even the more ordinary day-to-day activities of what has become a vast and complex set of organizations are less than inspiring. Thus, on occasion, there is a pressing need for reform.

Given the vast scope of the Olympic movement, this book had to cover an unusually broad range of persons, places, and events as well as an extended time horizon. It has done so extremely well with a helpful chronology and concise recapitulation of the modern Olympic Games and with entries on Olympic bodies, significant pioneers, organizers and athletes, the various sporting events and associations, and a multitude of countries. These are all updated and expanded to produce a more complete dictionary. And, for this new edition, further entries were added on the problems and, indeed, scandals that have seriously tarnished the Olympic movement but fortunately also induced major reforms. The appendices provide handy information on leading figures in the movement and the outstanding athletes. An extensive bibliography suggests further reading.

This second edition of the *Historical Dictionary of the Olympic Movement* was written by the same exceptional team of authors as the first, Ian Buchanan and Bill Mallon. Both have an abiding interest in sports and have actively supported the Olympic movement. Among other things, they helped found the International Society of Olympic Historians (ISOH), of which Ian Buchanan is the former and first president and Bill Mallon is the current president. They have already written a number of significant works on the Olympic Games and again combine their knowledge and insight in a book that is informative and readable, and will be an excellent guide for countless readers who wish to know more.

Jon Woronoff
Series Editor

Authors' Preface

Since 1896, the Olympic Games have become one of the most watched and publicized spectacles in the world. It has been noted that they now constitute the largest peacetime gathering of humanity in the history of the world. One former U.S. Olympic competitor, Elliott Denman (a walker), reflected on the Olympic Games: "[The Olympics] bring the world together. They are a remarkable cause for the good of mankind. In a planet beset with divisiveness, the Games continue to promote both the magnificent diversity of mankind, and the commonality of all." (Program at 60th Anniversary of Shore Athletic Club, *Asbury Park Press,* 30 October 1994)

Although the world watches the Olympic Games every four years and wonders at the feats of the athletes, the Olympic movement and its philosophy of Olympism go on daily and are the cornerstones of the work of the International Olympic Committee (IOC). The Olympic movement does not receive the publicity received by the Games themselves, but it has the ability to serve and has served as a major force for international goodwill. Former U.S. Vice President Al Gore correctly pointed out that "the IOC is the oldest multi-national, non-governmental continuous organization in the world." *(Olympic Review, XXV(1):* 43, February–March 1995)

The first edition of *Historical Dictionary of the Olympic Movement* was published by Scarecrow Press in 1995. We have been gratified by the response to the book and pleased that this response has allowed us to update the first edition. This second edition is greatly expanded from the first. We have added biographies of more than 60 Olympic athletes. The introductory section has been significantly enlarged, discussing many of the current problems of the Olympic movement. Many new entries have been added, notably a long one relating to the Olympic Bribery Scandal of 1999, and many of the previous entries have been lengthened.

When we began the original work, we thought it might be a rehashing of work we had done together on earlier projects. Quickly, we realized it was not, and that the need for a complete dictionary of the Olympic movement was real. Though we have both studied the Olympic Games and Olympic movement extensively, we do not think a comparable work exists that allows the student of the Olympics to find background references on all aspects of the Olympic Games and Olympic movement in one source. This book is not intended to be an encyclopaedic study of the Olympic movement and Olympic Games, but an introductory text allowing readers to gain insight into the history, politics, and fascinating events that have surrounded the Olympics since their inception in Ancient Greece and their modern resurrection in 1896. To this end, we hope we have been successful.

Since the first edition of this book, a great deal has happened in the Olympic world. Specifically, in 1999, the International Olympic Committee was rocked by scandal relating to the process of selecting host cities for the Olympic Games. Reports of bribery were rampant and revelations relating to this scandal were in the media almost daily during 1999. We have dealt with this problem in some detail in this new edition. But we hope to emphasize that the Olympic movement is related to much more than just the holding of sports events, and the publicity engendered by the scandal should not blind people to all the good that is done by the Olympic movement and the International Olympic Committee. And we hope that the recent Sydney Olympics, an exemplar of Olympic Games, will help people realize this.

We would like to thank Jon Woronoff, the series editor of Scarecrow's Historical Dictionaries of Religions, Philosophies, and Movements. We have been helped in our research particularly by Karel Wendl of the IOC, who first suggested our names to Jon Woronoff. We would also like to thank Wolf Lyberg (SWE), Joachim K. Rühl (GER), Ture Widlund (SWE), and David Young (USA). Lyberg, Rühl, Wendl, Widlund, and Young are all members of a relatively new organization devoted to studying the Olympic Games and Olympic movement. We also extend special thanks to IOC and ISOH member Dick Pound (CAN), who wrote the foreword to the first edition and also carefully edited many sections of that book.

We again thank the many loyal Olympic followers worldwide who have assisted us in our researches. We thanked many of them in the preface to the first edition, but our thanks go out especially to the almost 300 members of the International Society of Olympic Historians (ISOH), many of whom have lent their knowledge. ISOH members continue to be at the forefront of the study of the Olympic Games and Olympic movement, and we are both proud to be involved in the organization.

We hope you like it.

Ian Buchanan
Burgh Next Aylsham, Norwich, England

Bill Mallon
Durham, North Carolina, USA
February 2001

Abbreviations and Acronyms

Three-Letter Sport Abbreviations

ARC	Archery
ASK	Alpine Skiing
ATH	Athletics (Track & Field)
BAS	Basketball
BDM	Badminton
BIA	Biathlon
BOB	Bobsledding
BOX	Boxing
BSB	Baseball
CAN	Canoe & Kayaking
CUR	Curling
CYC	Cycling
DIV	Diving
EQU	Equestrian Events
FEN	Fencing
FKL	Freestyle Skiing
FSK	Figure Skating
FTB	Football, Association (Soccer)
GYM	Gymnastics
HAN	Team Handball
HOK	Hockey (Field)
ICH	Ice Hockey
JUD	Judo
LAX	Lacrosse
LUG	Luge
MOP	Modern Pentathlon
MSP	Military Ski Patrol

MTB	Motorboating
NSK	Nordic Skiing
POL	Polo
ROW	Rowing & Sculling
RUG	Rugby Football
SAI	Sailing
SHO	Shooting
SKE	Skeleton
SSK	Speed Skating (Long-Track)
STK	Short-Track Speed Skating
SWI	Swimming
TEN	Tennis (Lawn Tennis)
TOW	Tug-of-War
TTN	Table Tennis
VOL	Volleyball
WAP	Water Polo
WLT	Weightlifting
WRE	Wrestling
YAC	Yachting

Three-Letter National Abbreviations

AFG	Afghanistan
AHO	Netherlands Antilles
ALB	Albania
ALG	Algeria
AND	Andorra
ANG	Angola
ANL	Antilles (West Indies)
ANT	Antigua and Barbuda
ARG	Argentina
ARM	Armenia
ARU	Aruba
ASA	American Samoa
AUS	Australia
AUT	Austria
AZE	Azerbaijan

BAH	The Bahamas
BAN	Bangladesh
BAR	Barbados
BDI	Burundi
BEL	Belgium
BEN	Benin
BER	Bermuda
BHU	Bhutan
BIH	Bosnia-Herzegovina
BIR	Burma
BIZ	Belize
BLR	Belarus
BOH	Bohemia
BOL	Bolivia
BOT	Botswana
BRA	Brazil
BRN	Bahrain
BRU	Brunei
BUL	Bulgaria
BUR	Burkina Faso
CAF	Central African Republic
CAM	Cambodia (Kampuchea)
CAN	Canada
CAY	Cayman Islands
CEY	Ceylon
CGO	Congo
CHA	Chad
CHI	Chile
CHN	China
CIS	Commonwealth of Independent States (aka EUN)
CIV	Côte d'Ivoire (Ivory Coast)
CMR	Cameroon
COK	Cook Islands
COL	Colombia
COM	Comoros Islands
CPV	Cape Verde
CRC	Costa Rica
CRO	Croatia

CUB	Cuba
CYP	Cyprus
CZE	Czech Republic
DEN	Denmark
DJI	Djibouti
DMA	Dominica
DOM	Dominican Republic
ECU	Ecuador
EGY	Egypt
ERI	Eritrea
ESA	El Salvador
ESP	Spain
EST	Estonia
ETH	Ethiopia
EUN	Unified Team (Équipe Unifié) (aka CIS)
FIJ	Fiji
FIN	Finland
FRA	France
FRG	Federal Republic of Germany
FSM	Federated States of Micronesia
GAB	Gabon
GAM	The Gambia
GBR	Great Britain
GBS	Guinea-Bissau
GDR	German Democratic Republic
GEO	Georgia
GEQ	Equatorial Guinea
GER	Germany
GHA	Ghana
GRE	Greece
GRN	Grenada
GUA	Guatemala
GUI	Guinea
GUM	Guam
GUY	Guyana
HAI	Haiti
HKG	Hong Kong
HUN	Hungary

INA	Indonesia
IND	India
IOP	Independent Olympic Participant
IRI	Iran
IRL	Ireland
IRQ	Iraq
ISL	Iceland
ISR	Israel
ISV	U. S. Virgin Islands
ITA	Italy
IVB	British Virgin Islands
JAM	Jamaica
JOR	Jordan
JPN	Japan
KAZ	Kazakstan
KEN	Kenya
KGZ	Kyrgyzstan
KOR	Korea (South)
KSA	Saudi Arabia
KUW	Kuwait
LAO	Laos
LAT	Latvia
LBA	Libya
LBR	Liberia
LCA	Saint Lucia
LES	Lesotho
LIB	Lebanon
LIE	Liechtenstein
LTU	Lithuania
LUX	Luxembourg
MAD	Madagascar
MAR	Morocco
MAS	Malaysia
MAW	Malawi
MDV	Maldives
MEX	Mexico
MGL	Mongolia
MKD	Macedonia

MLD	Moldova
MLI	Mali
MLT	Malta
MON	Monaco
MOZ	Mozambique
MRI	Mauritius
MTN	Mauritania
MYA	Myanmar
NAM	Namibia
NCA	Nicaragua
NED	The Netherlands
NEP	Nepal
NFL	Newfoundland
NGR	Nigeria
NIG	Niger
NOR	Norway
NRU	Nauru
NZL	New Zealand
OMA	Oman
PAK	Pakistan
PAN	Panama
PAR	Paraguay
PER	Peru
PHI	The Philippines
PLE	Palestine
PLW	Palau
PNG	Papua-New Guinea
POL	Poland
POR	Portugal
PRK	Democratic People's Republic of Korea (North)
PUR	Puerto Rico
QAT	Qatar
RHO	Rhodesia
ROM	Romania
RSA	South Africa
RUS	Russia
RWA	Rwanda
SAM	Samoa (Western)

SCO	Scotland
SEN	Senegal
SEY	Seychelles
SIN	Singapore
SKN	St. Kitts and Nevis
SLE	Sierra Leone
SLO	Slovenia
SMR	San Marino
SMY	Smyrna
SOL	Solomon Islands
SOM	Somalia
SRI	Sri Lanka
STP	São Tomé and Princípe
SUD	The Sudan
SUI	Switzerland
SUR	Suriname
SVK	Slovakia
SWE	Sweden
SWZ	Swaziland
SYR	Syria
TAN	Tanzania
TCH	Czechoslovakia
TGA	Tonga
THA	Thailand
TJK	Tajikistan
TKM	Turkmenistan
TOG	Togo
TPE	Chinese Taipei
TRI	Trinidad and Tobago
TSL	Thessalonika (Thessaloníkí)
TUN	Tunisia
TUR	Turkey
UAE	United Arab Emirates
UGA	Uganda
UKR	The Ukraine
URS	Soviet Union
URU	Uruguay
USA	United States

UZB	Uzbekistan
VAN	Vanuatu
VEN	Venezuela
VIE	Vietnam
VIN	St. Vincent and the Grenadines
VOL	Upper Volta
YAR	Yemen Arab Republic (North)
YEM	Yemen
YMD	Yemen Democratic Republic (South)
YUG	Yugoslavia
ZAI	Zaire
ZAM	Zambia
ZIM	Zimbabwe

Other Abbreviations Used

AAU	Amateur Athletic Union (USA)
ACNO	Association des Comités Nationaux Olympiques
ACNOA	Association des Comités Nationaux Olympique d'Afrique
AGFIS	Association Générale des Fédérations Internationales de Sports
AIBA	Association Internationale de Boxe Amateur
AIOWF	Association of the International Olympic Winter Sports Federations
ANOC	Association of National Olympic Committees
ARISF	Association of the IOC-Recognized International Sports Federations
ASOIF	Association of Summer Olympic International Federations
CAS	Court of Arbitration for Sport
CMAS	Confédération Mondiale des Activités Subaquatiques
CMSB	Confédération Mondiale des Sports de Boules
COJO	Comité d'Organisateur des Jeux Olympiques
EOC	European Olympic Committees
FEI	Fédération Équestre Internationale
FIA	Fédération Internationale de l'Automobile

FIBA	Fédération Internationale de Basketball
FIBT	Fédération Internationale de Bobsleigh et de Tobogganing
FIC	Fédération Internationale de Canoë
FIDE	Fédération Internationale des Échecs
FIE	Fédération Internationale d'Éscrime
FIFA	Fédération Internationale de Football Association
FIG	Fédération Internationale de Gymnastique
FIH	Fédération Internationale de Hockey
FIL	Fédération Internationale de Luge de Course
FILA	Fédération Internationale de Luttes Associées
FIM	Fédération Internationale de Motocyclisme
FINA	Fédération Internationale de Natation Amateur
FIPV	Fédération Internationale de Pelote Basque
FIQ	Fédération Internationale de Quilleurs
FIRS	Fédération Internationale de Roller-Skating
FIS	Fédération Internationale de Ski
FISA	Fédération Internationale des Sociétés d'Aviron
FIT	Fédération Internationale de Trampoline
FITA	Fédération Internationale de Tir à l'Arc
FIVB	Fédération Internationale de Volleyball
GAISF	General Association of International Sports Federations
GANEFO	Games of the New Emerging Forces
IAAF	International Amateur Athletic Federation
IBA	International Baseball Federation
IBF	International Badminton Federation
IBF	International Boxing Federation
IBU	International Biathlon Union
IF(s)	International Federation(s)
IFBB	International Federation of Body Builders
IHF	International Handball Federation
IIHF	International Ice Hockey Federation
IJF	International Judo Federation
IKF	International Korfball Federation
IOA	International Olympic Academy
IOC	International Olympic Committee
IOF	International Orienteering Federation
IPC	Institut Pierre de Coubertin
IPC	International Paralympic Committee

ISA	International Surfing Association
ISAF	International Sailing Federation
ISF	International Softball Federation
ISOH	International Society of Olympic Historians
ISSF	International Shooting Sport Federation
ISU	International Skating Union
ITF	International Tennis Federation
ITTF	International Table Tennis Federation
ITU	International Triathlon Union
IWF	International Weightlifting Federation
IWSF	International Water Ski Federation
IWUF	International Wushu Federation
NBA	National Basketball Association (USA)
NOA(s)	National Olympic Academy(ies)
NOC(s)	National Olympic Committee(s)
OCA	Olympic Council of Asia
OCOG	Organizing Committee of the Olympic Games
ODECABE	Organización Deportiva Centroamericana y del Caribe
ODEPA	Organización Deportiva Panamericana
ONOC	Oceania National Olympic Committees
PASO	Pan American Sports Organization
q.v.	*quod vide*, literally "which see," meaning "See also"
qq.v.	*quae vide*, literally "which see," meaning "See also (several)"; plural of q.v.
TOP	The Olympic Programme
TWIF	Tug of War International Federation
UCI	Union Cycliste Internationale
UIAA	Union Internationale des Associations d'Alpinisme
UIM	Union Internationale Motonautique
UIPM	Union Internationale de Pentathlon Moderne
UN	United Nations
WADA	World Anti-Doping Agency
WBA	World Boxing Association
WBF	World Bridge Federation
WCF	World Curling Federation
WSF	World Squash Federation
WTF	The World Taekwondo Federation
YMCA	Young Men's Christian Association

Chronology of the Olympic Movement

776 B.C. First recorded Ancient Olympiad celebrated in Olympia on the Peloponnesus Peninsula in Ancient Greece. The Olympic Games initially consist of a single race of about 190 meters in length, termed a *stadion race*. The first winner is Coroebus, a cook from the city-state of Elis.

582 B.C. The first Pythian Games are held at Delphi in Ancient Greece.

582 (581?) B.C. The first Isthmian Games are held at the Isthmus of Corinth in Ancient Greece.

573 B.C. The first Nemean Games are held at Nemea in Ancient Greece.

393 A.D. The Ancient Olympic Games end after 12 centuries when they are prohibited by the imperial decree of Roman Emperor Theodosius I.

1612–1642 Robert Dover's Games, an early attempt at revival often called the Cotswold Olimpick Games, are held annually in the Cotswolds (England) on Thursday and Friday of Whitsun Week. They stop shortly after Dover's death in 1641 but are revived during the reign of King Charles II in the 1660s.

22 Oct 1850 The Much Wenlock Olympian Games, the brainchild of British sports enthusiast Dr. William Penny Brookes (1809–1895), are held for the first time in Much Wenlock, England, a small town in rural Shropshire. The Much Wenlock "Olympics" are a major influence on Pierre de Coubertin, who visits them in 1889.

15 Nov 1859 The 1st Zappas Olympic Games, an early attempt at revival of the Olympics, are held in Athens. The Games were initiated and financed by a wealthy grain dealer, Evangelis Zappas (1800–1865).

1 Jan 1863 Pierre Frédy, the Baron de Coubertin, is born in Paris, France, to Charles Louis Frédy, the Baron de Coubertin, and the former Agathe Marie Marcelle Gabrielle de Grisenoy de Mirville.

15 Nov 1870   The 2nd Zappas Olympic Games are held in Athens. They are considered the most successful of the Zappas Olympics.

18 May 1875   The 3rd Zappas Olympic Games are held in Athens.

18 May 1889   The 4th Zappas Olympic Games are held in Athens.

1891   The 1st Panhellenic Gymnastic Society Games, modeled after the Zappas Olympics, are held in Athens.

25 Nov 1892   Meeting of sports dignitaries at the Sorbonne celebrating the fifth anniversary of the Union des Sociétés Françaises de Sports Athlétiques (USFSA), at which Coubertin first broached the idea of the revival of the Olympic Games. His speech ended with the now famous summons, "Let us export rowers, runners, and fencers; there is the free trade of the future, and on the day when it is introduced within the walls of old Europe the cause of peace will have received a new and mighty stay. This is enough to encourage your servant to dream now about the second part of his program; he hopes that you will help him as you have helped him hitherto, and that with you he will be able to continue and complete, on a basis suited to the conditions of modern life, this grandiose and salutary task, the restoration of the Olympic Games."

1893   The 2nd Panhellenic Gymnastic Society Games, modeled after the Zappas Olympics, are held in Athens.

16–24 Jun 1894   The Paris International Athletic Congress is organized by Coubertin at the Palais de la Sorbonne in Paris. Although it was purported to be a congress with amateurism as its main theme, the program lists 10 points to be discussed, the last three of which concern the re-establishment of the Olympic Games. This is later regarded as the 1st Olympic Congress.

23 Jun 1894   The International Olympic Committee is formed at the end of the Sorbonne Congress and consists mostly of sports dignitaries who had attended the Congress.

23 Jun 1894   Demetrios Vikelas of Greece elected as the first President of the International Olympic Committee at the end of the First Session of the IOC.

6–15 Apr 1896   Athens, Greece—Celebration of the Games of the Ist Olympiad of the modern era.

10 Apr 1896   Baron Pierre de Coubertin of France elected as the second President of the International Olympic Committee at the Second Session of the IOC.

23–31 Jul 1897   Le Havre, France—2nd Olympic Congress celebrated at the Town Hall of Le Havre with "Sports Hygiene and Pedagogy" as the theme.

20 May–28 Oct 1900   Paris, France—Celebration of the Games of the IInd Olympiad.

1 Jul–23 Nov 1904   St. Louis, Missouri, USA—Celebration of the Games of the IIIrd Olympiad.

9–14 Jun 1905   Brussels, Belgium—3rd Olympic Congress celebrated at the Palais des Académies with "Sport and Physical Education" as the theme.

22 Apr–2 May 1906   Athens, Greece—Intercalated Olympic Games are held in Athens during the interim between the celebrations of the Olympiad.

23–25 May 1906   Paris, France—4th Olympic Congress celebrated at the Comédie Française et Touring Club with "Art, Literature, and Sport" as the theme.

27 Apr–31 Oct 1908   London, England—Celebration of the Games of the IVth Olympiad.

5 May–27 Jul 1912   Stockholm, Sweden—Celebration of the Games of the Vth Olympiad.

7–11 May 1913   Lausanne, Switzerland—5th Olympic Congress celebrated at the Palais de l'Université with "Sports Psychology and Physiology" as the theme.

15–23 Jun 1914   Paris, France—6th Olympic Congress celebrated at the Palais de la Sorbonne with "Olympic Regulations" as the theme.

Dec 1915–Feb 1917   Baron Godefroy de Blonay of Switzerland is appointed interim IOC president by Coubertin, who enlists to help the French war effort. Coubertin felt that the IOC should not be headed by a soldier.

Summer 1916 The Games of the VIth Olympiad, scheduled to be held in Berlin, Germany, are canceled due to World War I.

Feb 1917 Baron Pierre de Coubertin resumes his post as President of the International Olympic Committee.

23 Apr–12 Sep 1920 Antwerp, Belgium—Celebration of the Games of the VIIth Olympiad.

2–7 Jun 1921 Lausanne, Switzerland—7th Olympic Congress celebrated at the Casino de Montbenon with "Olympic Regulations" as the theme.

25 Jan–4 Feb 1924 Chamonix, France—Celebration of the "Semaine internationale des sports d'hiver" (International Winter Sports Week), which was later designated retroactively as the 1st Olympic Winter Games.

4 May–27 Jul 1924 Paris, France—Celebration of the Games of the VIIIth Olympiad.

28 May 1925 Count Henri de Baillet-Latour of Belgium elected as the third President of the International Olympic Committee at the 24th Session of the IOC in Prague.

29 May–4 Jun 1925 Prague, Czechoslovakia—8th Olympic Congress celebrated at the Prague Town Hall with "Sports Pedagogy and Olympic Regulations" as the theme. The Congress is notable for Coubertin's retirement as IOC President.

11–19 Feb 1928 St. Moritz, Switzerland—Celebration of the 2nd Olympic Winter Games.

17 May–12 Aug 1928 Amsterdam, The Netherlands—Celebration of the Games of the IXth Olympiad.

25–30 May 1930 Berlin, Germany—9th Olympic Congress celebrated at the Aula of the Friedrich Wilhelm University with "Olympic Regulations" as the theme.

4–15 Feb 1932 Lake Placid, New York, USA—Celebration of the 3rd Olympic Winter Games.

30 Jul–14 Aug 1932 Los Angeles, California, USA—Celebration of the Games of the Xth Olympiad.

15 Sep 1935   At a rally in Nuremburg, Hitler announces the enactment of the Nuremburg Laws, stripping Jews of their German citizenship and their rights under German law. This gives new impetus to consideration to boycott the 1936 Olympics, both to be based in Germany.

6–16 Feb 1936   Garmisch-Partenkirchen, Germany—Celebration of the 4th Olympic Winter Games.

7 Mar 1936   Hitler orders three battalions of the German army into the Rhineland, violating the Treaty of Versailles. In response, France considers the possibility of a boycott of the 1936 Olympics.

1–16 Aug 1936   Berlin, Germany—Celebration of the Games of the XIth Olympiad. Despite calls for a boycott from many nations, almost all IOC member nations participate at Berlin.

2 Sep 1937   Pierre de Coubertin dies while walking through Lagrange Park in Geneva, Switzerland.

26 Mar 1938   At a ceremony in Ancient Olympia, the heart of Pierre de Coubertin, which had been removed from his body shortly after his death, is placed for perpetuity in a marble stele at the base of the Kronos Hill, near the Ancient Olympic stadium.

Winter 1940   The 5th Olympic Winter Games are canceled due to World War II. The Games were originally awarded to Sapporo, Japan, which withdrew on 16 July 1938. They were reassigned to St. Moritz, Switzerland, which withdrew as host on 9 June 1939. The Games were then reassigned to Garmisch-Partenkirchen, Germany.

Summer 1940   The Games of the XIIth Olympiad, originally scheduled to be held in Tokyo, Japan, and later (after the withdrawal of Tokyo on 16 July 1938) awarded to Helsinki, Finland (awarded 3 September 1938), are canceled due to World War II.

6 Jan 1942   IOC President Count Baillet-Latour dies. The International Olympic Committee presidency will remain vacant during the remainder of World War II, although Sweden's J. Sigfrid Edström assumes the position of *de facto* President.

Winter 1944   The 5th Olympic Winter Games, tentatively scheduled for Cortina d'Ampezzo, Italy, are canceled due to World War II.

Summer 1944 The Games of the XIIIth Olympiad, originally scheduled to be held in London, England, are canceled due to World War II.

4 Sep 1946 J[ohannes] Sigfrid Edström of Sweden elected as the fourth President of the International Olympic Committee at the 40th Session of the IOC in Lausanne.

30 Jan–8 Feb 1948 St. Moritz, Switzerland—Celebration of the 5th Olympic Winter Games.

29 Jul–14 Aug 1948 London, England—Celebration of the Games of the XIVth Olympiad.

14–25 Feb 1952 Oslo, Norway—Celebration of the 6th Olympic Winter Games.

16 Jul 1952 Avery Brundage of the United States elected as the fifth President of the International Olympic Committee at the 48th Session of the IOC in Helsinki.

19 Jul–3 Aug 1952 Helsinki, Finland—Celebration of the Games of the XVth Olympiad.

26 Jan–5 Feb 1956 Cortina d'Ampezzo, Italy—Celebration of the 7th Olympic Winter Games.

10–17 Jun 1956 Stockholm, Sweden—Celebration of the Equestrian Games of the XVIth Olympiad. The Equestrian Games were made necessary because of Australia's highly restrictive animal quarantine restrictions.

29 Oct 1956 Israel invades the Sinai Peninsula, a part of Egypt. Egypt, Lebanon, and Iraq withdraw from the Melbourne Olympics in protest.

4 Nov 1956 Soviet troops enter Budapest, Hungary in an effort to stop rising political insurgency. This eventually leads to boycotts of the Melbourne Olympics by Spain, Switzerland, and the Netherlands, protesting the Soviet action.

22 Nov–8 Dec 1956 Melbourne, Victoria, Australia—Celebration of the Games of the XVIth Olympiad. In an attempt to solve the problem of the two Germanys, a unified German team representing both East

(GDR) and West (FRG) Germany competes at the International Olympic Committee's behest.

18–28 Feb 1960 Squaw Valley, California, USA—Celebration of the 8th Olympic Winter Games.

25 Aug–11 Sep 1960 Rome, Italy—Celebration of the Games of the XVIIth Olympiad.

Nov 1963 GANEFO—the Games of the New Emerging Forces—are held in Djakarta, Indonesia. GANEFO refuses to admit athletes from Israel or Taiwan (Chinese Taipei), and the international federations for track & field athletics, swimming, and shooting ban all athletes who competed at GANEFO from competing at the Tokyo Olympics in 1964. The IOC did not support this as a blanket ban on all athletes competing at GANEFO.

29 Jan–9 Feb 1964 Innsbruck, Austria—Celebration of the 9th Olympic Winter Games.

10–24 Oct 1964 Tokyo, Japan—Celebration of the Games of the XVIIIth Olympiad.

6–18 Feb 1968 Grenoble, France—Celebration of the 10th Olympic Winter Games.

2 Oct 1968 Student protests against the Mexico City Olympics come to a head in the capital city. On this day, student protesters hold a rally in the Plaza of Three Cultures, and government troops open fire, killing almost 300, with thousands injured and imprisoned.

12–27 Oct 1968 Mexico City, Mexico—Celebration of the Games of the XIXth Olympiad.

3–13 Feb 1972 Sapporo, Japan—Celebration of the 11th Olympic Winter Games.

21 Aug 1972 Sir Michael Morris, the Lord Killanin of Dublin and Spiddal (Ireland), elected as the sixth President of the International Olympic Committee at the 73rd Session of the International Olympic Committee in Munich.

26 Aug–11 Sep 1972 Munich, Federal Republic of Germany—Celebration of the Games of the XXth Olympiad.

5 Sep 1972   Terrorists representing the Black September group forever change the Olympic Games when they take hostage and then savagely murder 11 members of the Israeli Olympic team. The deaths occur at Fürstenfeldbruck airport on the outskirts of Munich.

30 Sep–4 Oct 1973   Varna, Bulgaria—10th Olympic Congress, the first in 43 years, celebrated at the Sports Palace with "Sport for a World of Peace—The Olympic Movement and Its Future" as the theme.

4–15 Feb 1976   Innsbruck, Austria—Celebration of the 12th Olympic Winter Games.

17 Jul–1 Aug 1976   Montreal, Quebec, Canada—Celebration of the Games of the XXIst Olympiad.

25–26 Nov 1979   The two-China question is finally resolved. On 25 November 1979, mainland China, the People's Republic of China, is recognized officially by the IOC. The next day, the Chinese Taipei Olympic Committee is given official International Olympic Committee recognition under that name, agreeing to compete using only that name, and not as the Republic of China. This clears the way for both Chinese Olympic Committees to compete together at the Olympic Games.

25–27 Dec 1979   The Soviet Union invades Afghanistan, precipitating an eventual boycott of the Moscow Olympics.

4 Jan 1980   In retaliation for the Soviet invasion of Afghanistan, U.S. President Jimmy Carter announces, for the first time, the possibility of a U.S. boycott of the 1980 Moscow Olympics.

13–24 Feb 1980   Lake Placid, New York, USA—Celebration of the 13th Olympic Winter Games.

16 Jul 1980   Juan Antonio Samaranch [Torello] elected as the seventh President of the International Olympic Committee at the 83rd Session of the IOC in Moscow.

19 Jul–3 Aug 1980   Moscow, USSR—Celebration of the Games of the XXIInd Olympiad. Approximately 60 countries boycott the Olympics in protest of the Soviet Union's invasion of Afghanistan.

23–28 Sep 1981   Baden-Baden, Federal Republic of Germany—11th Olympic Congress celebrated at Baden-Baden's Kurhaus with "United

By and For Sport" as the theme, with three sub-themes: 1) The Future of the Olympic Games; 2) International Cooperation; and 3) The Future Olympic Movement.

8–19 Feb 1984   Sarajevo, Yugoslavia—Celebration of the 14th Olympic Winter Games.

8 May 1984   The Soviet Union announces it will not attend the Los Angeles Olympic Games, citing concerns over the safety of its athletes in Los Angeles, and because of "anti-Communist activities" in the United States.

28 Jul–12 Aug 1984   Los Angeles, California, USA—Celebration of the Games of the XXIIIrd Olympiad. Fourteen invited countries join the Soviet-inspired boycott. Of the Soviet-bloc nations, only Romania defies the boycott and competes.

13–28 Feb 1988   Calgary, Alberta, Canada—Celebration of the 15th Olympic Winter Games.

17 Sep–5 Oct 1988   Seoul, Republic of Korea—Celebration of the Games of the XXIVth Olympiad. A small boycott of six nations occurs, because certain countries support only North Korea and do not recognize South Korea, refusing to compete in that nation.

8–23 Feb 1992   Albertville, France—Celebration of the 16th Olympic Winter Games.

25 Jul–9 Aug 1992   Barcelona, Spain—Celebration of the Games of the XXVth Olympiad. For the first Olympics since 1960, no politically inspired boycott or other serious political problems mar the Games.

12–27 Feb 1994   Lillehammer, Norway—Celebration of the 17th Olympic Winter Games.

23 Jun 1994   The 100th Anniversary of the founding of the Modern Olympic Games is celebrated with a ceremony at the Sorbonne, where Coubertin held the First Olympic Congress that re-established the Modern Olympic Games.

29 Aug–3 Sep 1994   Paris, France—12th Olympic Congress celebrated with four main themes: 1) The Olympic Movement's Contribution to Modern Society; 2) The Contemporary Athlete; 3) Sport in Its Social

Context; and 4) Sport and the Media. The 12th Olympic Congress is held in celebration of the 100th Anniversary of the Olympic Movement.

19 Jul–4 Aug 1996 Atlanta, Georgia, USA—Celebration of the Games of the XXVIth Olympiad, the Centennial Olympic Games.

27 Jul 1996 During the Atlanta Olympics, a bomb explodes in Centennial Olympic Park, killing two people and injuring many more. As of April 2001, the perpetrator(s) has(ve) not been found.

7–22 Feb 1998 Nagano, Japan—Celebration of the 18th Olympic Winter Games.

24 Nov 1998 Salt Lake City television station KTVX revealed that the Salt Lake Bid Committee had been paying tuition and expenses for the daughter of an IOC Member. The Olympic Bribery Scandal begins.

8 Feb 1999 First report related to the Olympic Bribery Scandal released by the Board of Ethics of the Salt Lake Organizing Committee for the Olympic Winter Games of 2002.

1 Mar 1999 Release of the Mitchell Commission Report.

17–18 Mar 1999 Extraordinary Session of the IOC relating to the Olympic Bribery Scandal. The Pound Commission Report was released during this meeting. At the end of the Session, 10 IOC Members had either resigned or been expelled relating to findings of the various commissions.

11–12 Dec 1999 IOC Session in Lausanne, Switzerland, at which the 50 recommendations of the IOC 2000 Commission were discussed and, eventually, implemented in full.

16 Sep–1 Oct 2000 Sydney, New South Wales, Australia—Celebration of the Games of the XXVIIth Olympiad.

8–24 Feb 2002 Salt Lake City, Utah, USA—Scheduled celebration of the 19th Olympic Winter Games.

13–29 Aug 2004 Athens, Greece—Scheduled celebration of the Games of the XXVIIIth Olympiad.

11–26 Feb 2006 Turin (Torino), Italy—Scheduled celebration of the 20th Olympic Winter Games.

Chronology of the Olympic Games and Olympic Winter Games

The Games of the Ist Olympiad (1896) The Games of the Ist Olympiad were held in Athens, Greece, from 6 through 15 April 1896. (At the time, Greece recognized the Julian Calendar, not the Gregorian Calendar used by much of the world then and now used universally. In Greek terms, the Games were held from 25 March to 3 April 1896.) London was initially to have been the site but the Sorbonne Congress of 1894 elected Athens as the host city by acclamation. The only other city seriously considered was Paris.

Fourteen nations competed at Athens, with approximately 220–250 athletes—it cannot be determined with certainty. No women competed. The first Olympic champion of the modern era was James Connolly of the United States who won the hop, step, and jump in track & field athletics (now called the triple jump). Greece won the most medals with 50, while the United States won the most gold medals with 11, including most of the track & field athletics events. The highlight of the Games was the marathon victory of Spiridon Loues of Greece. When he neared the stadium, messengers came into the ancient stadium and cried out, "Hellas! Hellas! (A Greek! A Greek!)," sending the crowd into a frenzy. The Olympic pride based on millennia of Olympic tradition was then realized by the home crowd, which had been rather disappointed by the results of the Greek athletes. Loues won the race and became a hero, offered gifts and riches by many different Greek merchants. But he asked only for a cart to help him carry and sell his water and he returned to being a shepherd in his small town of Amarousi.

Many people wanted the Games to remain permanently in Athens, and in 1896 the American athletes wrote a letter to *The New York Times* asking that this be done. But Coubertin insisted that the Games be spread to various countries to emphasize the international flavor of the Olympic Games.

The Games of the IInd Olympiad (1900)   The Games of the IInd Olympiad were held in Paris, France, from 20 May through 28 October 1900. They were a disaster. If one had to nominate the "worst modern Olympics" ever, 1900 and 1904 would surely lead the voting.

In 1900, Paris hosted a great World's Fair, the Exposition Universelle Internationale de 1900 à Paris. Coubertin made plans to hold the Olympics as part of the fair and planned to organize the events. But the organizers of the Fair relegated Coubertin to a relatively minor administrative position and took over the organization of the sporting events connected with the Fair. Most of the events we today consider "Olympic" were not even labeled as such in 1900, often being called the "Championnats d'Exposition," or "Championnats Internationaux." Years later, many athletes did not know that they had competed in the Olympic Games, believing that their sport had been only a part of the World's Fair. Only the athletics (track & field) events were really publicized in the media as being part of the Olympics.

The Games were stretched out over five months (May through October) and formal opening and closing ceremonies were not held. It is difficult to know, because of the confusion over titles, and the many, many events held at the Fair, what events should actually be considered "Olympic" and which should not. The IOC had no real control over this and thus one sees various listings. Many unusual sports and events were contested such as motorboating, balloon racing, underwater swimming, and an obstacle swimming race. So the number of nations and athletes competing is completely conjectural.

Women made their Olympic début, with the first known competitors being a yachtswoman, Countess Hélène de Pourtalès of Portugal, and two croquet players listed only as Mme. Brohy and Mlle. Ohnier. Charlotte Cooper (GBR) won the first championships by a woman, in tennis singles and mixed doubles. Margaret Abbott (USA) won the "Olympic" golf championship in early October. Neither of those two sports was labeled as Olympic by the organizers. Years later, Abbott's relatives did not know for certain that the title she won that day had been for the Olympic championship. In many sports, medals were not awarded. Most of the listed prizes were cups and other similar trophies. In several sports, notably fencing and shooting, professional events were held and yet were considered later by the IOC to be of "Olympic" stature.

The Games of the IIIrd Olympiad (1904)   The Games of the IIIrd Olympiad were held in St. Louis, Missouri, USA, from 1 July through 23 November 1904. After the debacle of 1900, Coubertin was hoping for better from the United States in 1904, but did not see his hopes realized. The Games were awarded to Chicago. However, St. Louis was to host a major world's fair in 1904, the Louisiana Purchase International Exposition, and the St. Louis organizers wanted the Olympics as part of the fair. They threatened to hold competing Olympics if Chicago did not allow them to have the Games. Chicago eventually acquiesced.

The Games were very similar to 1900—they lasted almost five months, many of the events were not labeled as Olympic but only as championships of the Fair, it is difficult to know which sports and events were definitely on the Olympic program, a number of unusual sports and events saw their way to the program, and the Games were mostly an afterthought to the Fair. Again, the number of competing nations and athletes cannot be determined with any accuracy.

Coubertin vowed after 1904 that he would never again hold the Olympics as a sideshow to a fair. Notably, he did not even attend the Olympics in 1904, sending two IOC delegates from Hungary and Germany in his place. He was appalled when he heard of the happenings in St. Louis, but never more so than when he heard about the "Anthropological Days." The Fair organizers included several days of "Olympic" competitions among several so-called primitive tribes, which were being exhibited at the Exposition. Among these were Pygmies, Patagonians, Filipinos, Native American Indian tribes, Japanese Ainus, and certain Asian tribes. Events included throwing bolos, mud fighting, and climbing a greased pole.

Again, only the athletics (track & field) received any great publicity as being an Olympic sport. These events were virtually an American club championship, and, in fact, Albert Spalding donated a trophy to be awarded to the American club scoring the most points in the event. Though surpassed by athletes in other sports, the American foursome of Archie Hahn, Harry Hillman, James Lightbody, and Ray Ewry won three gold medals each in track & field and received the bulk of the media attention. In other sports, American dominance was almost as complete, owing to the fact that only a few other countries attended the Games, and very few foreign athletes competed.

Two black Tswana tribesmen who were part of the Boer War exhibition at the fair, Len Tau and Jan Mashiani, also competed in the marathon. Ironically, they are considered to be the first Olympic competitors from South Africa.

The Intercalated Olympic Games of 1906 The Olympic Games of 1906 were held in Athens, Greece, from 22 April through 2 May 1906. Twenty nations attended with 826 athletes competing (820 men and 6 women). (Fifteen Danish women also gave a gymnastics exhibition in 1906.)

Today, the IOC and some historians do not consider the 1906 Intercalated Olympics to be "true" Olympic Games. By doing so, they neglect the Games that may have helped save the Olympic Movement. After the debacles of 1900 and 1904, the Olympics were in desperate straits. The Greeks had wanted to host more Olympics and they proposed holding "interim" Olympics, every four years in the even year between the Olympics. The first of these was scheduled in 1906. The Greeks later scheduled interim Olympics for 1910 and 1914 but political and economic events in Greece prevented those from being held.

The Games of 1906 were not of the caliber of many Olympics of later years, but they were the best Olympics to that date. Again, many of the facilities were not of the highest quality. However, as in 1896, the Greeks approached their responsibility with enthusiasm and the most international field to date competed in these Olympics. A true opening ceremony was conducted for the first time, with the athletes marching with their teams following a flag bearer from their own country.

The newspapers considered these Games to be the Olympics and labeled them as such. Coubertin, at first opposed to the idea, subsequently embraced them as Olympics when he saw that the Greeks were organizing the best "Olympics" of the modern era. The IOC made no official determination of the status of these events at first, but in 1948 declared them not to be official based on the findings of the Brundage Commission. The Olympics of 1906 deserve that title much more so than do the farces that were 1900 and 1904. They resurrected the flagging Olympic Movement.

The Games of the IVth Olympiad (1908) The Games of the IVth Olympiad were held in London, England from 27 April through 31 October 1908. Twenty-two nations attended with 2,035 athletes competing (1,999 men and 36 women). The Games were originally awarded to

Rome, Italy, which was chosen over Berlin, Germany, at the 6th IOC Session in London on 22 June 1904. Historically, it has usually been stated that the Italians relinquished the 1908 Olympics because of the 1906 explosion of Mt. Vesuvius, which erupted near Naples, and the Italians felt that they needed the money to rebuild the area around the volcano. However, it is now established that the Italians were preparing to give up their rights to the IVth Olympiad even before the explosion. London gladly accepted to host the 1908 Olympics after the Italians told the IOC of their plans.

These Olympics were easily the best organized to date. They also had the most international flavor of any Olympics yet held. By now the Olympics were becoming "known" to the world and athletes everywhere wanted to compete, and managed to find ways to do so. Still, the Games, though superbly run, are best known for multiple political arguments and other bickering that occurred.

The problems began at the Opening Ceremony. The Swedish and United States flags did not fly over the stadium, as the organizers stated that they could not find them. This so infuriated the Swedes that when a dispute arose over wrestling rules later in the Games, they threatened to withdraw from the competition. The Finns marched in the ceremony without a flag. Finland was a territory of Russia in 1908, but Russia allowed them to compete separately, provided they did so under the Russian flag. The Finns, in protest, marched under no flag. The United States later protested the officiating in multiple track & field athletics events.

Two of the best-known controversies involved the 400-meter race and the marathon. In the 400 meters, American John Carpenter won the initial running of the final, but was disqualified when it was ruled that he had run out of his lane in the final straight to impede Britain's Wyndham Halswelle. The other two Americans in the final, William Robbins and John Taylor, refused to run in the second final and Halswelle walked over to the gold medal. In the tug-of-war, the Americans pulled a team of London policemen in the first round and were easily defeated. But the Americans protested the footwear of the London constables, stating that they were specially prepared to give them better traction during the pull. The protest was disallowed.

The final controversy and the most memorable event of the 1908 Olympics was the marathon. The race was to start at Windsor Castle so that Queen Alexandra's grandchildren could watch the beginning. The distance from there to the finish line at the Shepherd's Bush stadium was 26 miles, 385 yards. This was the first time this distance was chosen for a marathon and it later became the standard.

The leader for most of the second half of the race was Dorando Pietri, a candymaker from Capri, Italy. But when Pietri entered the Stadium, he was totally exhausted. Like a drunken sailor, he staggered and fell several times before the finish line. He also turned in the wrong direction twice during the last lap. Officials, urged on by sympathetic fans, helped him to his feet and directed him to the finish line. He finished the race first and was declared the winner. A few hundred meters behind him finished Johnny Hayes of the United States. An immediate protest was lodged and Pietri was disqualified, with Hayes winning the gold medal.

The Games of the Vth Olympiad (1912)   The Games of the Vth Olympiad were held in Stockholm, Sweden, from 5 May through 27 July 1912. After the problems and controversies of 1908, the pseudo-Olympics of 1900 and 1904, and the meager international participation of 1896 and 1906, Stockholm should be credited with the first truly modern Games of Olympic proportions. No other city was seriously considered as host for 1912 and Stockholm was elected by acclamation at the 10th IOC Session in Berlin on 28 May 1909. Twenty-seven nations attended, with 2,383 athletes competing (2,330 men and 53 women).

The Games were marvelously organized. The only significant political problems concerned the entries of Finland and Bohemia. Both nations wished to compete as independent nations, but in 1912, Finland was a part of Russia, and Bohemia was a part of the Austro-Hungarian Empire. As in 1908, both were allowed to compete but were not allowed to use their own flags.

But probably more than any other Olympics, the 1912 Games belonged to one person, Jim Thorpe. Jim Thorpe was a Sac-and-Fox Indian from Oklahoma who had attended the Carlisle Indian School. In 1912, Thorpe decided to compete in the two new Olympic events testing the all-around abilities of the track & field athletes—the decathlon of 10 events, and pentathlon of five events. He won by enormous margins. When awarded his prizes by King Gustav V, the King reportedly said, "Sir, you are the greatest athlete in the world." Thorpe's reply was supposedly, "Thanks, King." But, in 1913, it was discovered that

Thorpe had played minor league professional baseball in 1909 and 1910, and he was stripped of his medals. Seventy years later, in 1982, the IOC finally relented and restored the medals to Thorpe's family — he had died in 1953.

Hannes Kolehmainen of Finland, the first of the great Flying Finn distance runners, also made his début at the 1912 Olympics. He won four medals: three gold in the 5,000 meters, 10,000 meters, and individual cross-country, and a silver in the team cross-country. When Kolehmainen won, the Russian flag was raised because of Finland's subjugation to the Russians at that time. "I would almost rather not have won, than see that flag up there," he said. (Lord Killanin and John Rodda, *The Olympic Games 1984,* p. 77. Salem, New Hampshire: Michael Joseph, 1983.)

One tragedy did occur at the 1912 Olympic Games when the Portuguese marathoner Francisco Lazaro collapsed during the race and died early the next morning. He was the first Olympic athlete to die during the competition. This has occurred only one other time, in 1960, when the Danish cyclist Knut Enemark Jensen died during the cycling road race.

The 1912 Olympics were also noteworthy for the first swimming events for women. Previously, women had competed at the Olympics to any degree only in tennis, with minor appearances in archery, golf, yachting, and croquet in 1900, 1904, and 1908. There were only two swim events for women in 1912, a 100-meter freestyle and a freestyle relay, as well as a high diving event, but they were important as they were the first truly "athletic" events in which women were allowed to compete at the Olympics. The list of events in which women compete would increase with each Olympiad.

The Games of the VIth Olympiad (1916) The Games of the VIth Olympiad were originally awarded to Berlin, Germany, which was chosen at the 14th IOC Session in Stockholm on 4 July 1912 over Budapest, Hungary. Other cities that expressed an interest to host the 1916 Olympics were Alexandria, Egypt; Amsterdam, The Netherlands; Brussels, Belgium; and Cleveland, Ohio, USA. Because of World War I, the Games were not celebrated.

The Games of the VIIth Olympiad (1920) The Games of the VIIth Olympiad were held in Antwerp, Belgium, from 23 April through 12 September 1920. Other cities which had expressed an interest in hosting the 1920 Olympic Games were Amsterdam, The Netherlands; Atlanta, Georgia, USA; Budapest, Hungary; Cleveland, Ohio, USA; Havana, Cuba; and Philadelphia, Pennsylvania, USA. An offer from Lyon, France, was seriously considered during World War I when Belgium was being ravaged by the effects of the War, but Antwerp was officially chosen at the 17th IOC Session in Lausanne on 5 April 1919. However, 29 nations eventually attended the Games in Antwerp, with 2,670 athletes competing (2,593 men and 77 women).

The War was only over a year when the 1920 Olympics were finally awarded to war-ravaged Belgium. Coubertin decided that, although the war would be over less than two years, the VIIth Olympiad should be celebrated as scheduled. Although the Games were decidedly austere, the Belgian people and organizing committee did an amazing job in preparing for the Games on such short notice.

The opening ceremonies were notable for the first use of the Olympic flag at the Olympics, the first time the Olympic Oath was taken by a competitor (Victor Boin), and the first release of homing pigeons as a symbol of peace. Of the 29 countries competing, Germany, Austria, Hungary, and Bulgaria were missing as the IOC barred them because they were aggressor nations in World War I.

The Olympics were most notable for the début of Paavo Nurmi of Finland, probably the greatest distance runner ever. Nurmi competed in four events, losing only in the 5,000 meters. His countryman, Hannes Kolehmainen, returned eight years after his Stockholm victories in the 5,000 and 10,000 meters, and won the marathon. The shooting program contained 20 events, including 10 team events, allowing Willis Lee and Lloyd Spooner of the United States to win seven medals, and Carl Osburn (USA) to win six. Nedo Nadi (ITA) was also much decorated as he won five gold medals in fencing.

The Antwerp Olympics helped the world recover from the Great War. Coubertin summarized them in the Antwerp Town Hall when he addressed the IOC in the presence of King Albert of Belgium:

> This is what the seventh Olympiad has brought us: general comprehension; the certainty of being henceforward understood by all . . . These festivals . . . are above all festivals of human unity. In an incomparable synthesis the effort of muscles and of mind, mutual help and competition, lofty patriotism and intelligent cosmopolitanism, the personal interest in the champion and the abnegation of the team-member, are bound in a sheaf for a common task.

The 1st Olympic Winter Games (1924)   The 1st Olympic Winter Games were held in Chamonix, France, from 25 January through 4 February 1924. Sixteen nations attended with 258 athletes competing (245 men and 13 women).

In June 1922, the French Olympic Committee held a congress in which representatives of skiing, skating, and ice hockey were present. They arranged to hold an International Winter Sports Week in Chamonix in early 1924. The contests were not originally called the *Olympic Games*, but the opening speech, while not using the word Olympic in their title, did state that they were under the "high patronage of the International Olympic Committee." Their original official title was the "Semaine internationale des sports d'hiver" (International Winter Sports Week). On 27 May 1925, the IOC amended its charter to begin a cycle of Olympic Winter Games. The Chamonix events were never officially mentioned as the 1st Olympic Winter Games in this proclamation. It is felt, however, that this was an error of the secretary taking the minutes as the IOC has long since recognized the 1924 Chamonix events as the 1st Olympic Winter Games.

The politics of declaring these as Olympic Games may have been more interesting than the Games themselves. The 1924 Winter Olympics saw Clas Thunberg and Thorleif Haug crowned as multiple champions in skating and skiing, respectively. Gillis Grafström repeated his title in men's figure skating that he had won at the Summer Games in Antwerp in 1920. In women's figure skating, Herma Planck-Szabó of Austria won the title but the eighth, and last, place finisher would later become the greatest women's figure skater ever, Sonja Henie.

The Games of the VIIIth Olympiad (1924)   The Games of the VIIIth Olympiad were held in Paris, France, from 4 May through 27 July 1924. Other cities considered as hosts were Amsterdam, The Netherlands; Barcelona, Spain; Los Angeles, California, USA; Prague, Czechoslovakia; and Rome, Italy. Forty-four nations attended the 1924 Olympics, with 3,092 athletes competing (2,956 men and 136 women). After the difficulties of the 1900 Olympics in Paris, Coubertin fervently desired to see his home city host another Olympics. Paris was elected to host the 1924 Olympics at the 19th IOC session in Lausanne on 2 June 1921 and redeemed itself nicely.

The 1924 Olympics are today most famous as the Olympics of Harold Abrahams and Eric Liddell, the Olympics of *Chariots of Fire*. In

1981, the movie *Chariots of Fire* was made, celebrating the lives of Abrahams and Liddell and their route to the 1924 Olympic Games. The movie won the Academy Award for Best Picture of the Year. It was an excellent movie, but much of the story was apocryphal, with ample use of poetic license.

Besides its heralded stars, the 1924 Olympics unveiled several other notable firsts. The Olympic motto—"Citius, Altius, Fortius"—was used for the first time at the Olympic Games themselves, although Coubertin had used it as early as 1894 in the *Revue Olympique*. And at the closing ceremony, the practice of raising three flags—one for the IOC, one for the host nation, and one for the succeeding host nation—was instituted for the first time. For the first time, there was also a small Olympic Village at Paris in 1924.

In swimming, Johnny Weissmuller (USA) made his first Olympic appearance and showed why he would someday become known as the world's greatest swimmer. He later competed in the 1928 Olympics as well, and then turned to Hollywood where he became famous as Tarzan, portraying that character in 19 movies.

The Games themselves were the personal playground of Paavo Nurmi, who took up where he left off in 1920. Nurmi won five gold medals and could have won more had the schedule allowed him time to compete in more events.

The 2nd Olympic Winter Games (1928)   The 2nd Olympic Winter Games were held in St. Moritz, Switzerland, from 11 through 19 February 1928. Other cities considered by the IOC as possible hosts were Davos, Switzerland, and Engelberg, Switzerland, but St. Moritz was awarded the Games at the 27th IOC Session in Lausanne on 10 April 1929. Twenty-five nations attended with 464 athletes competing (438 men and 26 women). The 1928 Olympic Winter Games were highly successful but the organizers had to contend with poor weather. The föhn, a strong wind coming down the leeward side of a mountain and carrying warm weather with it, postponed several events and forced the cancellation of one. On the morning of the 50-kilometer cross-country skiing, the temperature was about 0° C. (32° F.) but during the competition, the föhn came in and temperatures rose to 25° C. (77° F.) by midday, playing havoc with the snow and waxing conditions.

Later that night, the warm weather brought rain that poured down and ruined the ski courses. Fortunately snow and frost over the next few days rescued the organizers. But the föhn affected several other events as well. In the 10,000-meter speed skating, the United States' Irving Jaffee had the best time after the first few runs. But the föhn was bringing in warm weather and melting the rink, so the event was halted because of the conditions and it was never restarted. Jaffee is listed by some American sources, incorrectly, as having won the event, but it actually was never contested to a conclusion. The five-man bob race also suffered the wrath of the föhn, when the bob course thawed and the four-run contest was shortened to only two runs.

The individual stars of the Games were Clas Thunberg, who won two more golds in speed skating; Johan Grøttumsbråten, who won two Nordic skiing golds; Gillis Grafström, who won his third consecutive figure skating title; and Sonja Henie, who won her first of three Olympic figure skating championships. But perhaps the real star of the 1928 Winter Olympics was the Canadian ice hockey leviathan, which in the absence of American participation, was unchallenged in winning the title with a goal margin of 38–0.

The Games of the IXth Olympiad (1928) The Games of the IXth Olympiad were held in Amsterdam, The Netherlands, from 17 May through 12 August 1928. The only other city seriously considered as a host was Los Angeles, California, USA. Amsterdam was chosen as host of the 1928 Olympics at the 19th IOC Session in Lausanne on 2 June 1921. Forty-six nations attended with 3,014 athletes competing (2,724 men and 290 women).

The 1928 Olympic Games were remarkable for the return of Germany to the Olympic Games for the first time since 1912, after the country had not been invited in 1920 or 1924. In addition, an Olympic flame burned at the Olympic stadium for the first time ever. It burned atop the marathon tower, although it was not lit at the end of a torch relay.

The 1928 Olympics were an unusual event in that no single athlete dominated. Paavo Nurmi was back and he won three more medals, but only one of them was gold. Johnny Weissmuller was back and again won two gold medals. But the biggest story of the 1928 Olympics was probably the emergence of women.

The Ancient Olympic Games did not allow women as competitors, or even as spectators. If they were found to be watching they were supposedly put to death. Baron de Coubertin did not want women in the

Olympics and he explicitly said so several times in his writings. In the modern Olympics, probably because of Coubertin's opposition, women were admitted slowly and only grudgingly.

Women had competed at the Olympics since 1900 but in small numbers and never in the showcase sport of track & field athletics. Women were not allowed to compete in this sport until the 1928 Olympics. Track & field is governed by the IAAF (International Amateur Athletic Federation) and it did not initially support the admission of women's track & field to the Olympics. So the women formed a separate organization, the FSFI (Fédération Sportive Féminine Internationale). The FSFI held its own events, the Women's "Olympics" in 1922 in Paris, and the 1926 "2nd International Ladies' Games" in Göteborg, Sweden.

It was only after these games proved the success of women's athletics that the IAAF acquiesced and allowed the sport into the Olympics. However, in 1928, only five events were held for women. The 1928 Olympic track & field events were so few and in such varied disciplines that no single woman could dominate. They were marred when several women finalists were on the verge of collapse after the 800 meters, which was also a common sight among men. The IOC reacted by barring women from running distances over 200 meters, and this was not changed until 1960.

The 1928 Olympics were one of the last truly peaceful and fully attended Olympics. The depression had not yet occurred, which would mar the 1932 Olympics. Hitler was still in prison and the post–World War II boycotts had not yet occurred. They were missing the single standout athlete and one other thing. Because of illness, Coubertin missed his first Olympics since 1906. He did not get to see women compete in track & field.

The 3rd Olympic Winter Games (1932)   The 3rd Olympic Winter Games were held in Lake Placid, New York, USA, from 4 through 15 February 1932. Seventeen nations attended with 252 athletes competing (231 men and 21 women). Several other U.S. cities also submitted candidatures to the IOC as well as Montreal, Quebec, Canada, but Lake Placid was chosen to host at the 27th IOC Session in Lausanne on 10 April 1929.

The biggest news of these Games was the controversy over the manner in which the speed-skating events were contested. For the first time in Olympic history, the European method of skating time trials in pairs was not used. Instead the American method of pack racing was used to determine the Olympic champions. (It became a separate indoor discipline of the sport again in 1992 at Albertville.) The Europeans, unaccustomed to the style, fared badly, and the great Clas Thunberg, still a viable competitor at age 39, refused to compete in protest of the change. Norway's Ivar Ballangrud did compete, but managed only a silver medal in the unfamiliar style.

One innovation that débuted at the Olympics in 1932 was the use of the three-level victory podium for presentation of the medals. It had first been used at the 1930 British Empire Games in Hamilton, Ontario, Canada.

The pack style did make heroes of two U.S. skaters. Hometown boy Jack Shea returned from Dartmouth College and won the 500- and 1,500-meter races. He also delivered the oath of the athletes and, in 1980, would be a member of the organizing committee when the Winter Olympics returned to Lake Placid. Irving Jaffee won the other two events, the 5,000 and 10,000 meters. A few years later, during the depths of the depression, he pawned the gold medals and never saw them again.

In figure skating, Gillis Grafström competed again but was finally defeated as Austrian Karl Schäfer won the title with Grafström second. Sonja Henie repeated in the women's competition. In bobsledding, U.S. teammates Billy Fiske and Clifford Grey repeated as gold medalists from 1928.

The Games of the Xth Olympiad (1932) The Games of the Xth Olympiad were held in Los Angeles, California, USA, from 30 July through 14 August 1932. It was the only city that applied to host the Olympics, as the world was in the midst of a terrible economic depression. Los Angeles was awarded the Games by acclamation at the 21st IOC Session on 8 April 1923. Only 37 nations attended, the first time the number of competing nations had not increased at an Olympics. There were 1,408 competing athletes (1,281 men and 127 women). The depression and the travel distance from Europe kept the international turnout low. Less then half as many athletes competed as in 1928, as many nations sent only small squads.

The 1932 Olympics also saw the unveiling of a woman to rival the feats of Jim Thorpe. Mildred Ella "Babe" Didrikson was a 21-year-old Texas tomboy in 1932. She was from Dallas and was heralded even before the Olympics. Restrictions on women's participation prevented Babe from showing her true colors. She was allowed to enter only three events, though no such restriction existed for men. She won the javelin throw, and the 80-meter hurdles, but in a virtual dead-heat with Evelyne Hall [USA]. Babe was second in the high jump, losing in a jump-off after she tied for first with Jean Shiley. Had she been able to compete in more events, it is likely that Didrikson could have won several more medals. After the Olympics, Babe Didrikson took up golf and became the greatest women's player in that sport.

Paavo Nurmi also attempted to compete at the 1932 Olympics but was not allowed to do so. Shortly before the Games the IOC declared him a professional for having received money for a tour of Germany. He had planned to run the marathon in 1932 and it is almost certain that he would have won that race, had he been allowed to compete.

The United States dominated what was close to a domestic Olympics, winning 41 gold medals and 103 medals in all. This was more than the winning totals of the next four best nations combined.

The 4th Olympic Winter Games (1936)   The 4th Olympic Winter Games were held in Garmisch-Partenkirchen, Germany, from 6 through 16 February 1936. Garmisch-Partenkirchen was chosen by the IOC at its 31st Session in Vienna on 8 June 1933. Other candidate cities were Montreal, Quebec, Canada, and St. Moritz, Switzerland. Twenty-eight nations attended with 668 athletes competing (588 men and 80 women).

The 1936 Olympic Winter Games were held under the Nazi regime of Adolf Hitler. When IOC president, Henri de Baillet-Latour, was traveling to Garmisch to see the Games, he was astonished to see road signs en route declaring "Dogs and Jews not allowed." Baillet-Latour demanded an audience with Der Führer and demanded that the signs be taken down. Hitler replied that he thought it usual, when a guest entered a person's home, that the guest followed the wishes of the host. Baillet-Latour responded that when the flag of Olympia flew over the area, he became the host and Hitler was only an invited guest. Hitler acquiesced and had the signs removed.

The Games were opened in a blinding snowstorm. They ended with the ski jump being watched by a record attendance of 150,000 people. In between, Ivar Ballangrud won three more gold medals in speed skating. Sonja Henie won her third consecutive gold medal in figure skating but the victory was a bit controversial. Henie had become a favorite of Der Führer, and it was thought that he wished her to win. She was not undeserving, but Britain's Cecilia Colledge was much improved and some thought that her second place finish was less than it could have been.

The biggest upset of the 1936 Olympic Winter Games occurred in ice hockey when the British team defeated the Canadians. The victory was aided by the scheming of J. F. "Bunny" Ahearne, general secretary of the British Ice Hockey Federation. Ahearne had a "mole" working in the Canadian Amateur Hockey Association and by 1934 had a complete list of all Canadian registered players who had been born in the British Isles. He contacted many of them and the team that won in Garmisch was led by eight ersatz Brits, several of whom had been imported from Canada. The Canadians howled in protest but to no avail.

The Games of the XIth Olympiad (1936*)*** The Games of the XIth Olympiad were held in Berlin, Germany, from 1 through 16 August 1936. The IOC considered at least 11 other cities as possible hosts, but Berlin was chosen in the final vote over Barcelona, Spain, by 43–16 at the 29th IOC Session in Barcelona on 26 April 1931. Forty-nine nations attended, with 4,066 athletes competing (3,738 men and 328 women).

Because of Nazi policies against Jews and their aggressive national tendencies, there were many protests against the Olympics being held in Berlin in 1936. The Americans came the closest to boycotting in protest, although the British and French both considered the option. At the IOC Session in Vienna on 7 June 1933, the membership discussed the discrepancy between Nazi doctrine and Olympic Principles, with two American members questioning the German members about their country's policies. At the 33rd IOC Session in Athens on 15 May 1934, Lord Aberdare, a British member, then expressed concerns about reports from Germany. He pointedly asked the German IOC members if their government's pledges were trustworthy. In September 1934, future IOC President Avery Brundage traveled to Germany to inspect the country and its policies. He later recommended that the Games go on in Germany, but calls for a boycott continued, although they were never realized.

And the Games were magnificently staged, as Hitler spared no expense and used them as a propaganda tool to demonstrate the beauty and efficiency of the Third Reich. He had Leni Riefenstahl, a renowned German filmmaker, produce a wondrous movie, *Olympia*, to ensure that the propaganda would not end at the closing ceremonies.

No other Olympics belonged to a single non-competitor as much as the 1936 Olympics with Adolf Hitler. But these Olympics were actually dominated by Jesse Owens. He showed up Hitler's Aryan supremacy theories and ruled the Berlin Olympic Games. Owens, a black American, won four gold medals in track & field athletics, winning the 100 meters, the 200 meters, the long (broad) jump, and the 4 x 100-meter relay. He was the most heralded and popular athlete of the 1936 Olympics.

The greatest innovation of the 1936 Olympics was conceived by Dr. Carl Diem, head of the organizing committee. He proposed that a torch relay be instituted to carry a flame from Ancient Olympia to the Berlin Stadium and then to light the Olympic flame at the stadium. On 20 July 1936, 15 Greek maidens clad in short, belted smocks representing the robes of priestesses, gathered on the plain at Ancient Olympia and the flame was lit there by the rays of the Greek sun off a reflector. The high priestess presented the flame to Kyril Kondylis, the first Greek runner, to begin a torch relay. After several thousand miles, the flame arrived in Berlin where it was lit in the stadium by Fritz Schilgen. It is sad to think that the first flame of Olympia burned over a Reich that later used flames to incinerate millions of Jews, and other "undesirables," in World War II.

The 1940 Olympic Winter Games   The 5th Olympic Winter Games, scheduled for 1940, were originally awarded to Sapporo, Japan, at the 36th IOC Session in Warsaw on 9 June 1937. Sapporo withdrew on 16 July 1938, and the Games were awarded to St. Moritz at the IOC Executive Board meeting in Brussels on 3 September 1938. St. Moritz withdrew on 9 June 1939 at the 38th IOC Session in London and the 1940 Olympic Winter Games were then awarded to Garmisch-Partenkirchen, which eventually also withdrew. The Games were not held because of World War II.

The Games of the XIIth Olympiad (1940)   The Games of the XIIth Olympiad were to have been held in 1940, but did not take place because of the onset of World War II. At the 35th IOC Session in Berlin on 31 July 1936, the Games were awarded to Tokyo, Japan, in a vote of 36–27 over Helsinki, Finland. Other cities that had expressed interest in hosting the 1940 Olympics were Alexandria, Egypt; Buenos Aires, Argentina; Dublin, Ireland; Athens, Greece; Rio de Janeiro, Brazil; Barcelona, Spain; Budapest, Hungary; and either Toronto or Montreal, Canada. On 16 July 1938, Tokyo withdrew as host. On 3 September

1938, at the IOC Executive Board meeting in Brussels, the Games were awarded to Helsinki, but the Games were canceled late in 1939.

The 1944 Olympic Winter Games   Although the 1940 Olympic Winter Games were not held, the 5th Olympic Winter Games were scheduled for 1944 and were awarded to Cortina d'Ampezzo, Italy (16 votes in round two), which was chosen over Montreal, Quebec, Canada (12 votes in round two); and Oslo, Norway (2 votes in round two) at the 38th IOC Session in London on 9 June 1939. The Games were not celebrated because of World War II.

The Games of the XIIIth Olympiad (1944)   The Games of the XIIIth Olympiad were to have been held in 1944, but did not take place because of World War II. The Games had been awarded to London, England, which won the IOC nomination with 20 votes over Rome, Italy (11 votes); Detroit, Michigan, USA (2 votes); and Lausanne, Switzerland (1 vote) at the 38th IOC Session in London on 9 June 1939.

The 5th Olympic Winter Games (1948)   The 5th Olympic Winter Games were held in St. Moritz, Switzerland, from 30 January through 8 February. Twenty-eight nations attended with 669 athletes competing (592 men and 77 women). The only candidate that opposed St. Moritz for 1948 was Lake Placid, New York. St. Moritz was chosen by the IOC Executive Board, which met in Lausanne on 4 September 1946 and made its decision.

St. Moritz hurriedly put together excellent arrangements for the Games that were again disturbed, though less severely, by the föhn. Ice hockey matches (held outdoors) and the 10,000 meters speed skating had to be delayed but no events were canceled this time.

Alpine skiing made its true Olympic début. A few combined events had been held in 1936 but this time there were three events for both men and women. Two athletes won a second "St. Moritz" Olympic medal, as "Bibi" Torriani played on the Swiss ice hockey team to match his bronze from 1928; and John Heaton (USA) also repeated his silver medal from the skeleton race in 1928. The skeleton race, a form of tobogganing unique to the St. Moritz resort, was held at the Olympics for the second time to date. Skeleton will return to the Olympic Program in 2002 at Salt Lake City.

The Games of the XIVth Olympiad (1948)   The Games of the XIVth Olympiad were held in London, England, from 29 July through 14 August 1948. For the only time in Olympic history, the Games were awarded by a postal vote after the IOC recommended London as the site to its members. The vote was confirmed by the IOC membership at its 39th Session in Lausanne on 4 September 1946. Other candidate cities were Baltimore, Maryland, USA; Lausanne, Switzerland; Los Angeles, California, USA; Minneapolis, Minnesota, USA; Philadelphia, Pennsylvania, USA. Fifty-nine nations attended with 4,099 athletes competing (3,714 men and 385 women).

As in 1920, the IOC decided that it was necessary to resurrect the Olympic Movement at the earliest scheduled time. Thus, although England had been ravaged by Hitler's air raids, the Games of the XIVth Olympiad were awarded to London in 1948. In spite of years of difficulties caused by rationing of food, clothes, and other essential materials, the English organizing committee did an outstanding job.

No great innovations accompanied the Games themselves, as most of the protocols of the opening, closing, and victory ceremonies were by now established. However, these Games were significant as they were televised for the first time, although only to small local audiences. Television sets were still quite rare.

One country that was missed was the Soviet Union. The USSR had competed in 1946 at the European Championships in track & field athletics and it was thought that perhaps it would return to the Olympics in 1948. This was not to be and the reasons for its failure to compete have never been fully revealed.

As a very popular sport in England, track & field was truly the focus of these Olympics, as it is so often. Three athletes stood out in the athletics stadium. "Fanny" Blankers-Koen (NED), a 30-year-old mother of three children in 1948, won the 100 meters, 200 meters, 80-meter high hurdles, and helped win gold in the 4 x 100-meter relay. Bob Mathias (USA), a 17-year-old schoolboy, won the decathlon despite a torrential downpour throughout much of the two-day event. In the next few years he would prove that it was not a fluke. He would win again in 1952 at Helsinki and was never defeated in his decathlon career. Finally, Emil Zátopek (TCH) won the 10,000 meters and finished second in the 5,000. It was only a prelude to his heroics of 1952.

The 6th Olympic Winter Games (1952) The 6th Olympic Winter Games were held in Oslo, Norway, from 14 through 25 February 1952. Thirty nations attended with 694 athletes competing (585 men and 109 women). At the 40th IOC Session in Stockholm on 21 June 1947, Oslo was chosen by the IOC with 18 votes over Cortina d'Ampezzo, Italy (9 votes), and Lake Placid, New York, USA (1 vote).

The Olympic Winter Games were finally held in a Nordic country and an Olympic Flame was first lit at the Olympic Winter Games. Unlike the summer flame, however, this flame was originally lit from the hearth of the house in Morgedal, Norway, where Sondre Norheim, the pioneer of modern skiing, was born. At the end of a ski relay, Eigil Nansen, grandson of the explorer Fridtjof Nansen, lit the flame in the Bislett Stadium.

Norway's athletes dominated the events, especially Hjalmar Andersen, who won three gold medals in speed skating. In Alpine skiing, the handsome Stein Eriksen of Norway seemed the embodiment of a modern ski hero. He won the giant slalom and was second in the slalom. Dick Button of the United States won his second consecutive men's figure skating championship. In women's skiing, Andrea Mead-Lawrence (USA) won two events by upsetting the European women.

In bobsledding, Germany won both the two-man and four-man events. Its "athletes" in this event were so large that their momentum helped them win by increasing their speed. This caused the International Bobsleigh Federation to change its rules to place a weight limit on bobsled teams.

The Games of the XVth Olympiad (1952)   The Games of the XVth Olympiad were held in Helsinki, Finland, from 19 July through 3 August 1952. At the 40th IOC Session in Stockholm on 21 June 1947, Helsinki won the vote in the second round over Los Angeles, California, USA; Minneapolis, Minnesota, USA; Amsterdam, The Netherlands; Detroit, Michigan, USA; Chicago, Illinois, USA; and Philadelphia, Pennsylvania, USA. Sixty-nine nations attended with 4,925 athletes competing (4,407 men and 518 women).

In 1952, the biggest news from Helsinki was that the Soviets were there. After the Bolshevik Revolution of 1917, the USSR had not competed in the Olympics until the Helsinki Games. The world braced for the athletic battles between the Soviet Union and the United States—in effect, a cold-war Olympics. The Soviets were accorded one rather unusual allowance. They were housed in a separate Olympic Village, and stayed only with athletes from the Eastern Bloc countries of Hungary, Poland, Bulgaria, Romania, and Czechoslovakia.

It is always an exciting moment when the Olympic torch enters the stadium. In 1952, the excitement was palpable when the Finnish crowd realized that the torchbearer was the Finnish hero of heroes, Paavo Nurmi. Although by then 55 years old, Nurmi carried the torch on high and still had his very familiar stride. Not only the crowd, but even the athletes were excited. They broke ranks to run to the side of the track to get closer to the distance running legend. Some Finnish football players then brought the torch from the track to the top of the tower, handing it to Hannes Kolehmainen, second only to Nurmi in the Finnish pantheon of sporting heroes. The 62-year-old Kolehmainen lit the Olympic flame at the top of the tower.

Given that the Games were opened by two of the greatest distance runners ever, it was fitting that the 1952 Olympics were dominated by a distance runner who even surpassed a few of their feats. Emil Zátopek, the Czech who had won the 10,000 meters in 1948, was by now the greatest distance runner in the world. He entered the 5,000 and 10,000 meters and won both of them rather easily. He then entered the marathon, a race he had never before run. Still, the extra distance did not deter Zátopek. He was running with the favored Jim Peters of Great Britain for the first half of the race when he turned to Peters and asked him if the pace wasn't a bit slow. With no reply, Zátopek took off and was never seen again by Peters. Zátopek won the race by more than 2½ minutes, while Peters failed to finish.

The Americans and the Soviets met several times in these Olympics, most notably in the boxing ring. In 1952, the Americans had the best of it, though the Soviets would improve in the coming years. The press made a big thing out of the medal counts, which were led early by the Soviet Union, although the United States eventually won the most medals and gold medals. This, too, would change in later Olympics.

The 7th Olympic Winter Games (1956) The 7th Olympic Winter Games were held in Cortina d'Ampezzo, Italy from 26 January through 5 February 1956. Thirty-two nations attended with 820 athletes competing (688 men and 132 women). Cortina d'Ampezzo was chosen at the 43rd IOC Session in Rome on 28 April 1949 with 31 votes over Montreal, Quebec, Canada (7 votes); Colorado Springs, Colorado, USA (2 votes); and Lake Placid, New York, USA (1 vote).

The Cortina Olympics began ominously when the torch bearer at the opening ceremonies, speed skater Guido Caroli, tripped over a microphone wire and fell. However, he was not harmed and the torch did not go out. After that initial difficulty, the Games were a wonder.

The big news was the entrance of the Soviets into the Winter Olympics. The Soviet Union immediately excelled at speed skating and, in an upset, began its domination of ice hockey when its team defeated the Canadians.

The hero of the Cortina Olympics was movie idol–handsome Toni Sailer of Austria, "The Blitz from Kitz" (Kitzbühel). Sailer won all three Alpine skiing events by large victory margins each time. In ski jumping, the Finns introduced a new aerodynamic style when they placed their arms against their sides rather than forward in front of their heads. With the new method Antti Hyvirinen and Aulis Kallakorpi took first and second, respectively. The figure skating competitions saw two very close contests as Americans swept the men's medals, with Hayes Alan Jenkins winning. Among the women, Tenley Albright barely defeated Carol Heiss. Heiss and Jenkins would later marry.

The 1956 Equestrian Olympic Games   After the IOC awarded the Games of the XVIth Olympiad to Melbourne, Australia, they learned that Australian quarantine laws would not allow the importation of horses for the equestrian events without an extended quarantine period. This precluded Melbourne from being able to host the equestrian events at the 1956 Olympic Games. It was decided, actually in violation of the *Olympic Charter*, to contest separate Equestrian Olympic Games in Stockholm, Sweden, from 10 through 17 June 1956. At the 49th IOC Session in Athens on 13 May 1954, Stockholm was chosen with 25 votes over Paris, France (10 votes); Rio de Janeiro, Brazil (8 votes); Berlin, Germany (2 votes); and Los Angeles, California, USA (2 votes).

The Equestrian Games of 1956 were held without major incidents and were contested by 29 nations and 158 athletes (145 men and 13 women). The opening ceremony was quite unusual as all competitors came in on their mounts, including the flag bearers. Hans Wikne brought the Olympic Flame into the stadium on horseback and lit the main torch. Karin Lindberg and Henry Eriksson held lighted torches, ran toward the stadium tower with the torches, and lit flames there. Sweden's Henri Saint Cyr recited the oath of the athletes while on his horse, and later won two gold medals in individual and team dressage. This was matched by Germany's Hans Günter Winkler, who won gold medals in the individual and team show jumping events. The only controversy of the 1956 Equestrian Games came in the three-day event when one horse broke his leg and had to be destroyed. The SPCA (Society for the Prevention of Cruelty to Animals) was very upset and a lengthy debate followed.

The Games of the XVIth Olympiad (1956)   The Games of the XVIth Olympiad were held in Melbourne, Victoria, Australia, from 22 November through 8 December 1956. At the 43rd IOC Session in Rome on 28 April 1949, Melbourne was awarded the Olympics by a single vote in the fourth round over Buenos Aires, Argentina. Other candidate cities were (with round of elimination from voting): Los Angeles, California, USA (third round); Detroit, Michigan, USA (third round); Mexico City, Mexico (second round); Chicago, Illinois, USA (first round); Minneapolis, Minnesota, USA (first round); and Philadelphia, Pennsylvania, USA (first round). Sixty-seven nations and 3,184 athletes eventually competed in Melbourne (2,813 men and 371 women).

This was the first time that the Games were held in the Southern Hemisphere and necessitated the Olympic Games being held very late in the year to take advantage of the early part of the Australian summer. Because of Australian quarantine laws, it was decided, in violation of the *Olympic Charter*, to contest separate Olympic Equestrian Games in Stockholm, Sweden from 10 to 17 June 1956. (See above: The 1956 Equestrian Olympic Games)

But between June and the Melbourne Olympics, the world was thrown into turmoil. On 29 October, Israel invaded Egypt's Sinai peninsula. Then on 4 November 1956, 200,000 Soviet troops entered Budapest, Hungary, to quell political uprisings in that country. Egypt, Lebanon, and Iraq withdrew in protest at Israel's action. The Netherlands, Spain, and, somewhat surprisingly, Switzerland withdrew in protest at the Soviet action. Switzerland kept alive its record of competing in every modern Olympics only because it had already been represented by athletes in Stockholm. These protests constituted the first true boycott in modern Olympic history, though the scene would be repeated many times in the coming decades.

With that background, water polo had the unusual distinction of being perhaps the most awaited event of the Olympics. In a final round match, the Soviet Union met the Hungarians, usually a water polo power. The athletes from both countries wasted no time in breaking all known rules and niceties of water polo. The water was literally blood red in several areas during the match and several players had to be helped out of the water because of bleeding. Hungary achieved some measure of revenge for the invasion of their country when it won, 4–0.

The Games were less well attended than those of other years because of the travel distance to Australia. Still, all the major sporting countries were represented. In a precursor of problems to come, the People's Republic of China (Beijing, then Peking) withdrew because the Republic of China (Taiwan) was allowed to compete. The question of the two countries' representation would not be resolved for 28 years.

The 8th Olympic Winter Games (1960) The 8th Olympic Winter Games were held in Squaw Valley, California, USA, from 18 through 28 February 1960. Thirty nations attended with 665 athletes competing (522 men and 143 women). At the 50th IOC Session in Paris on 14 June 1955, Squaw Valley won a close contest by two votes over Innsbruck, Austria (32–30 in the second round). Garmisch-Partenkirchen, Germany, and St. Moritz, Switzerland, were also candidate cities, but were eliminated in the first round of voting.

When the 1960 Olympic Winter Games were awarded to Squaw Valley, all that existed there was a hotel. The ski village was the dream of Alexander Cushing and he succeeded in convincing the IOC to hold the Olympics based on his dream. After the award the Europeans verbally attacked the site for various reasons. The ski courses were not up to FIS caliber in the Alpine competitions, while in the Nordic races, the altitude (2,000 meters [6,650 feet]) was felt to be too stressful for the competitors. The Squaw Valley organizers polled the Winter Olympic nations and found that only nine would send a bobsled team so they elected to save the expense by not building a run and not contesting the sport. In all, despite the initial misgivings about the site, the Games were well run with few problems. And U.S. television was present, showing the events to the American people for the first time.

Biathlon was introduced as a sport for the first time. Women's speed skating also made its Olympic début and saw the arrival of Lidiya Skoblikova (URS) who won two gold medals. In figure skating, Hayes Alan Jenkins' brother, David Jenkins, won the men's titles, while David Jenkins' future sister-in-law, Carol Heiss, avenged her 1956 defeat to easily win the women's title. In the Nordic combined event, Georg Thoma (FRG) became the first non-Scandinavian to win a Nordic Olympic event. In ice hockey, the United States pulled a major upset when it defeated the

Soviet Union in the semi-final match. The U.S. went on to defeat Czechoslovakia in the finals and win the gold medal. Not as well publicized as the miracle of 1980, the U.S. victory in 1960 was equally astonishing.

The Games of the XVIIth Olympiad (1960)   The Games of the XVIIth Olympiad were held in Rome, Italy, from 25 August through 11 September 1960. At the 50th IOC Session in Paris on 16 June 1955, Rome was awarded the Games in the third round over Lausanne, Switzerland, by a vote of 35–24. The other candidate cities (with round of elimination from voting) were Detroit, Michigan, USA (second round); Budapest, Hungary (second round); Brussels, Belgium (first round); Mexico City, Mexico (first round); and Tokyo, Japan (first round). Eighty-three nations attended the Games, with 5,346 athletes competing (4,736 men and 610 women).

Rome had been awarded the 1908 Olympics but eventually relinquished its right to host them. Fifty-two years later the Olympics would return to the eternal city. Never before, and possibly never again, were the ancient and modern civilizations so intertwined at an Olympics. The 1960 Olympics were a wonder. With the boycotts, massacres, and political problems that were to come, many Olympic afficionados would later yearn for the glory that was Ancient Greece and the grandeur that was Modern Rome.

Many of the events took place in settings thousands of years old. Wrestling was held in the Basilica of Maxentius, where similar competitions had taken place two millennia previously. Gymnastics events were contested in the Terme di Caracalla. The marathon began in front of the ancient Roman capitol, on Capitoline Hill, and finished along the Appian Way beneath the Arch of Constantine. For modern facilities the Italians provided Stadio Olimpico, a beautiful track & field complex, the Sports Palace for boxing, and the Velodrome for cycling.

A number of heroes emerged from the Games. In women's athletics, the Italians and the world thrilled to the feats of Wilma Rudolph, an American sprinter from Tennessee. Long-legged and attractive, she was dubbed by the European press as "La Gazelle Noire"—the black gazelle. She won the women's 100 meters, 200 meters, and anchored the sprint relay.

In basketball and boxing, two of the greatest ever practitioners of those sports were on display. In basketball, the U.S. men's team won very easily as the team was led by Oscar Robertson, Jerry West, Jerry

Lucas, Walt Bellamy, and Terry Dischinger. Certainly the greatest amateur team ever, it rivals many of the great NBA teams. In boxing, the light-heavyweight gold medal was won by Cassius Marcellus Clay, who as Muhammad Ali would thrill the world for the next two decades as "The Greatest."

The 1960 Olympics were the first Summer Olympics televised in the United States, although all events were shown on tape delay after the film was flown from Rome to New York. And also for the first time since the 1912 marathon (Portuguese runner Francisco Lazaro), the Olympics saw the death of a competitor. In the cycling road race, Knut Enemark Jensen (DEN) collapsed and later died. He was found to have taken amphetamines and his death was partially responsible for the institution of drug testing in the mid-1960s.

The 9th Olympic Winter Games (1964)   The 9th Olympic Winter Games were held in Innsbruck, Austria, from 29 January through 9 February 1964. Thirty-six nations attended with 1,091 athletes competing (891 men and 200 women). At the 55th IOC Session in Munich, Germany, on 26 May 1959, Innsbruck (49 votes) was chosen over Calgary, Alberta, Canada (9 votes); and Lahti, Finland (0 votes).

Innsbruck was an almost unanimous choice to host the 1964 Olympic Winter Games, and the IOC has made few better choices. Innsbruck became the first Olympic host city since World War II, winter or summer, to spread the Olympic events around geographically a bit, with some events being held 30 kilometers (20 miles) from Innsbruck center. Because of this and the central location of the city, well over a million spectators saw these Olympics. In addition, television now transmitted them to more than a billion viewers. Computers were also present for the first time at the Olympics, as the electronic age came to Olympia.

With all this, there were a few problems. The organizing committee forgot to order snow for the events. In the last few days, the Austrian army hauled 20,000 cubic meters of snow to the ski courses so they would be well packed. In practice before the Games, two athletes were killed—Ross Milne, an Australian skier, and Kazimierz Skrzypecki, a Polish-born British luger.

Soviet women were the biggest winners at Innsbruck. Lidiya Skoblikova produced one of the great performances of the Olympic Winter Games when she won all four women's speed-skating gold medals in four days. In women's cross-country skiing, Klavdiya Boyarskikh won gold medals in all three women's events. The Soviets also ensured there would be no repeat of 1960 and won the ice hockey title easily. But in bobsledding, both events produced big upsets. Britain's Tony Nash and Robin Dixon won the two-man title, while Vic Emery drove the four-man champion sled from Canada. Neither country had a bobsled run in 1964.

The Games of the XVIIIth Olympiad (1964) The Games of the XVIIIth Olympiad were held in Tokyo, Japan, from 10 through 24 October 1964. At the 55th IOC Session in Munich, Germany, on 26 May 1959, Tokyo (34 votes) won the final vote in the first round over Detroit, Michigan, USA (10 votes); Vienna, Austria (9 votes); and Brussels, Belgium (5 votes). Ninety-three nations attended with 5,140 athletes competing (4,457 men and 683 women).

For the first time, the Olympic Games were celebrated in an Asian country. The Japanese were eager to prove that they had recovered from the horrors of World War II and, to emphasize the point, they chose as the final torchbearer Yoshinori Sakai, who had been born in Hiroshima on the day the atomic bomb immolated that city.

Before the Games began there was a minor controversy when Indonesia and North Korea withdrew because several of their athletes were declared ineligible. The affected athletes had competed in the Games of the New Emerging Forces (GANEFO) in Jakarta, Indonesia, in November 1963. Indonesia did not allow Taiwan or Israel to compete at those Games, so the international federations for athletics, swimming, and shooting banned any athlete from the Tokyo Olympics who had competed at GANEFO. Because this affected several of their athletes, Indonesia and North Korea withdrew from Tokyo in protest. The only significant athlete missing was Dan Sin-Kim of North Korea, the women's world record holder in the 400 and 800 meters.

In athletics, Billy Mills of the United States pulled off one of the biggest upsets in Olympic history when he won the 10,000-meter run. The most decorated hero of the Games was swimmer Don Schollander who won four gold medals in men's swimming. Schollander could have won a fifth gold medal but the U.S. coaches left him off the medley relay team, although he was America's fastest freestyler.

The Japanese were gracious hosts but they were helped in their own efforts by two new Olympic sports: judo and volleyball. In volleyball, the Japanese women, coached by the martinet-like Hirofumi Daimatsu, were easily victorious. In judo, the Japanese won three of the four gold medals. But the one they lost, in the open class to Holland's Anton Geesink, was a crushing blow to the hosts.

The Games were beautifully run and the minor boycott had no effect. The 1964 Olympics were the last Olympics to be held for 28 years without major political overtones and boycotts.

The 10th Olympic Winter Games (1968)   The 10th Olympic Winter Games were held in Grenoble, France, from 6 through 18 February 1968. Thirty-seven nations attended with 1,158 athletes competing (947 men and 211 women). At the 62nd IOC Session in Innsbruck on 28 May 1964, Grenoble was chosen on the third ballot over a large field of candidate cities which included Calgary, Alberta, Canada (third round); Lahti, Finland (second round); Sapporo, Japan (first round); Oslo, Norway (first round); and Lake Placid, New York, USA (first round).

The controversy so often associated with the Olympic Games began to reach Winter Olympia in 1968 at Grenoble. Though the Games went fairly well, there were many problems. It began before the Olympics when the IOC decided it wished to curb advertising on skis and clothing by the Alpine skiers. They threatened to expel certain skiers, while the skiers threatened to withdraw *en masse* in revolt if that were done. A compromise was eventually reached in which the skiers agreed to remove all equipment with advertising prior to being photographed or interviewed.

The 1968 Winter Games' hero of heroes was Jean-Claude Killy, who had grown up and learned to ski in the neighboring mountains. He was favored in all three alpine events, and all of France expected Killy to duplicate Toni Sailer's 1956 feat and win the three Alpine skiing gold medals. He succeeded, but not without a major controversy in the slalom. The race was held in fog and both Karl Schranz (AUT) and Håkon Mjøn (NOR) initially posted faster times, but both were disqualified for missing gates. Schranz appealed, stating that he had been interfered with and replays showed that he had. He was allowed a restart and again posted a winning time. But he was then disqualified when further investigation revealed that the interference on the first run occurred after Schranz had missed his gates. And Killy had his third gold medal and France had its hero.

In the bobsled events, held on l'Alpe d'Huez, the site of so much heroism and suffering during the Tour de France, Eugenio Monti of

Italy finally succeeded in winning an Olympic gold medal. In fact he won two. In pairs figure skating, the almost lyrical team of Lyudmila Belousova and Oleg Protopopov won their second consecutive championship.

The Games of the XIXth Olympiad (1968)   The Games of the XIXth Olympiad were held from 12 through 27 October 1968 in Mexico City, Mexico. At the 60th IOC Session in Baden-Baden, Germany, on 18 October 1963, Mexico City had been awarded the Games on the first ballot in 1963 with 30 votes over Detroit, Michigan, USA (14 votes); Lyon, France (12 votes); and Buenos Aires, Argentina (2 votes). One hundred twelve nations attended with 5,530 athletes competing (4,749 men and 781 women).

In 1963, the IOC awarded the Olympics to Mexico, despite warnings about the effects of competing at the altitude (2,134 meters) of Mexico City. The warnings would prove prophetic, both for good and bad, but also prominent at Mexico City was the first large-scale incursion of politics into the Olympic scene since 1936.

Political problems first manifested themselves as protests by Mexican students before the Games. The students were upset that so much money was spent on the Olympics in the face of such widespread poverty in their own country. As the protest movement gathered momentum leading up to the Games, the Mexican Army took charge on the night of 2 October. When 10,000 people demonstrated in the Square of the Three Cultures in Mexico City, the army surrounded the crowd and opened fire. More than 300 people were killed and over a thousand were injured.

In the United States, Harry Edwards, a professor at San Jose State University, urged American blacks to boycott the Olympics to protest the rampant racism of American society. The boycott never materialized. However, his efforts came to fruition in the victory ceremony of the 200 meters. The race was won by Tommie Smith (USA) with the bronze medal going to John Carlos (USA). On the victory platform, as "The Star-Spangled Banner" played in the background, almost unheard, the two black Americans stood barefoot, heads bowed, and raised a single black-gloved fist in their own form of protest. The IOC banned the two from future Olympic participation and ordered them to leave the Olympic village immediately.

On a positive political note, the Federal Republic of Germany (West Germany) and the German Democratic Republic (East Germany) entered separate national teams for the first time, although they competed wearing the same emblems and flag, and using a joint anthem for medal ceremonies.

The altitude severely affected many track & field events. Bob Beamon used the lesser gravity to set a stunning world record in the long jump of 8.90 meters (29'2½"). It would not be broken for 23 years. In the 100-, 200-, 400-, 400-meter hurdles, 4 x 100 relay, 4 x 400 relay, and the triple jump, all sprint events not requiring much oxygen, and aided by the lessened pull of gravity, new world records were set by the men. Many of these records would last for years. But the distance running events saw very slow times, as the runners gasped for the oxygen that was not there.

The 11th Olympic Winter Games (1972)   The 11th Olympic Winter Games were held in Sapporo, Japan from 3 through 13 February 1972. Thirty-five nations attended with 1,006 athletes competing (800 men and 206 women). At the 64th IOC Session in Rome on 26 April 1966, Sapporo was chosen on the first ballot (32 votes) over Banff, Alberta, Canada (16 votes); Lahti, Finland (7 votes); and Salt Lake City, Utah, USA (7 votes).

The controversy that had started in Grenoble four years earlier continued and erupted at the beginning of the Games. Avery Brundage insisted on ending commercialization by skiers and singled out Austrian star, Karl Schranz, who was expelled from the Games.

Another controversy occurred when Canada refused to send its ice hockey team, protesting professionalism by the Soviets. The USSR won that gold medal quite easily, though it is unlikely the Canadians would have made a difference, as by 1972, the Soviets were showing that they could now play well against the NHL (National Hockey League).

Ard Schenk (NED) was the best publicized athlete at these Olympics as he won three championships in speed skating. His triple was matched in women's cross-country skiing by Galina Kulakova (URS), though a bit more surreptitiously to the world's media. The Japanese, not usually a winter sports power, were exultant when three of their ski jumpers, led by Yukio Kasaya, swept the medals in the 70-meter ski jumping.

The Games of the XXth Olympiad (1972)   The Games of the XXth Olympiad were held in Munich, Germany (Federal Republic/West) from 26 August through 11 September 1972. At the 64th IOC Session in Rome in 1966, Munich had been awarded the Games on the second ballot (31 votes) over Montreal, Quebec, Canada (15 votes); Madrid, Spain (13 votes); and Detroit, Michigan, USA (eliminated after round one). One hundred twenty-one nations attended with 7,123 athletes competing (6,065 men and 1,058 women).

The Munich Olympics began as The Games of Joy, in which the West German government attempted to atone for the militaristic Nazi image so associated with the 1936 Berlin Games. They ended as The Games of Terror and Tragedy.

The first 11 days of the 1972 Olympics were beautiful. But on the morning of 5 September, stark reality hit when the Games were interrupted by eight Arab terrorists, representing the militant Black September group. They entered the Olympic Village and took 11 members of the Israeli Olympic team as hostages. While the world watched on television and waited, the terrorists occupied the building of 31 Connollystraße, and demanded freedom for several Arabs held in Israeli prisons. The Israeli government refused this as a day of tense negotiations ensued.

Late in the evening of 5 September, the terrorists took their hostages to Fürstenfeldbruck, an Army air base near Munich. There, in a few quick minutes of fighting as the Germans tried to save them, all the Israelis were murdered by a bomb the terrorists had set in the helicopter that was to take them to freedom. Several of the terrorists were killed, but most escaped. A few were later captured but none ever came to trial.

The murdered Israeli athletes and coaches were David Marc Berger, Zeev Friedman, Yossef Gutfreund, Eliezer Halfin, Yossef Romano, Amitzur Shapira, Kehat Shorr, Mark Slavin, Andrei Spitzer, Yacov Springer, and Moshe Weinberg.

The day after the murders, a memorial service was held in the Olympic Stadium, and the Olympic Games were halted for a single day. Many people called for the cancellation of the remainder of the Olympics in memoriam. At the memorial service, International Olympic Committee President Avery Brundage incensed many when he compared the Israeli murders to the political problems that the International Olympic Committee had had with the African nations who wished to expel Rhodesia prior to the Olympics. During the service, Brundage made the now famous statement, "The Games must go on."

There were some marvelous athletic performances at the 1972 Olympics, notably Mark Spitz winning seven gold medals, and setting seven world records, but they seemed of little consequence. The Olympic Games would never be the same again.

The 12th Olympic Winter Games (1976)   The 12th Olympic Winter Games were held in Innsbruck, Austria, from 4 through 15 February 1976. Thirty-seven nations attended with 1,123 athletes competing (892 men and 231 women). Innsbruck was not originally even a candidate city for the 1976 Olympic Winter Games. At the 69th IOC Session in Amsterdam on 13 May 1970, the original choice of the IOC was Denver, Colorado, USA, which won out on the third ballot (39 votes) over Sion, Switzerland (30 votes in round three); Tampere, Finland (second round); and Vancouver, British Columbia, Canada (first round). In November 1972, the citizens of Colorado, in a referendum, indicated that they did not wish the Olympics to be held in Denver, fearing a negative impact on the environment. Denver officially withdrew as host on 12 November 1972. Innsbruck, which had held the Games so successfully in 1964, was able to step in on short notice, after being selected over hastily arranged bids from Lake Placid (USA), Chamonix (FRA), and Tampere. And once again Innsbruck demonstrated how well an Olympic Winter Games could be staged.

The competitions were well-contested though no single athlete could be said to dominate, as in years past. Rosi Mittermaier (FRG) was perhaps the best publicized Olympian in 1976. She won the downhill and slalom early in the Games and had a chance to equal the feats of Toni Sailer and Jean-Claude Killy by winning the giant slalom. Older than many of the competitors, close to retirement, and born nearby, just across the German border at Reit im Winkl, she was a heavy sentimental favorite. But it was not to be. Canada's Kathy Kreiner defeated Mittermaier by 12/100ths of a second in the giant slalom. In men's skiing, Austria's Franz Klammer electrified fans and the television audience with a spectacular run, in which he skied to the edge and was on the verge of falling several times, to win the downhill gold medal over Switzerland's Bernhard Russi.

In figure skating, Irina Rodnina (URS) again won a pairs gold medal, but with a different partner than in 1972. In men's figure skating, Britain's John Curry and Canada's Toller Cranston introduced a more balletic style than in years past. Among the women, Dorothy Hamill of the United States became a media favorite with her ability and style, her wholesome looks, and pixie-like hairdo.

The Games of the XXIst Olympiad (1976) The Games of the XXIst Olympiad were held in Montreal, Quebec, Canada, from 17 July through 1 August 1976. At the 69th IOC Session on 13 May 1970, Montreal had been awarded the Games in the second round of balloting (41 votes) by the IOC over Moscow, USSR (28 votes), and Los Angeles, California, USA (eliminated after round one). Ninety-two nations eventually competed in the Montreal Games, with 6,026 athletes participating (4,779 men and 1,247 women).

The city of Montreal spent extravagantly to host the Games, leaving the citizens of Canada and Quebec with a tax debt they would be repaying for years, and the Games were dubbed the billion-dollar circus by the Canadian press. In 1994, the debt still remaining to the Quebec citizenry was estimated at $304 million (US). Much of the debt, however, was incurred to finance infrastructure that Montreal would have eventually built.

Shortly before the 1976 Olympics were to start, they were marred by a boycott of 22 African countries, Guyana, and Chinese Taipei (then Taiwan). The African/Guyanan boycott was in protest of a recent tour of South Africa by the New Zealand national rugby team. As South Africa was ostracized from international sporting competition, the African nations demanded that New Zealand not be allowed to compete at Montreal. But the IOC had little control over this problem, as rugby had no current affiliation with the Olympic Movement. New Zealand competed and most of Africa did not.

The Taiwan boycott occurred when Canada at first considered refusing to allow the team to enter the country, as the Canadian government did not recognize the island nation. This was in direct violation of their agreement as host country to admit all eligible nations in honoring the *Olympic Charter*. The Canadians acquiesced and were going to allow the Taiwanese to compete, but they refused to allow them to do so under the title of the Republic of China, their official national name. Several other countries protested and threatened withdrawal, notably the United States, if the Taiwan athletes were not allowed to compete. However, these protests were short-lived and the IOC finally gave in to the Canadian government. Taiwan withdrew and did not compete.

Twenty-six nations eventually boycotted the Montreal Olympics. Twenty-two of these did not compete at all and are as follows: Algeria, Central African Republic, Chad, People's Republic of Congo, Ethiopia, The Gambia, Ghana, Guyana, Iraq, Kenya, Libya, Malawi, Mali, Niger,

Nigeria, Sudan, Swaziland, Tanzania, Togo, Uganda, Upper Volta, and Zambia. In addition, Egypt, Cameroon, Morocco, and Tunisia also boycotted, although they are listed as competing nations, because some of their athletes competed on the first two days of the Olympics before they officially withdrew.

After all this the Olympics began. Despite the absence of some top African track athletes, they were well run and the boycotts had minimal effect on competition. The fans thrilled to the exploits of Romania's Nadia Comăneci in gymnastics as she dominated the competition, scoring the first perfect 10s ever awarded at the Olympics. The major effect of the boycott on track & field athletics was in the 1,500 meters, in which John Walker (ironically of New Zealand) and Filbert Bayi (Tanzania) were to compete. They were the two best milers in the world by far, but in Bayi's absence, Walker had only himself to beat, and he managed a comfortable gold medal victory. The most spectacular athlete on the track was probably Cuba's Alberto Juantorena, who won the 400- and 800-meter runs.

The 13th Olympic Winter Games (1980)   The 13th Olympic Winter Games were held in Lake Placid, New York, USA, from 13 through 24 February 1980. Thirty-seven nations attended with 1,072 athletes competing (839 men and 233 women). Lake Placid was unopposed in its bid and was chosen by the IOC at its 75th Session in Vienna on 23 October 1974.

Lake Placid, like St. Moritz and Innsbruck before it, was given a second chance to host the Olympic Winter Games. In the era of spiraling costs, Lake Placid promised a simpler Olympics. But the complexity of television and millions of spectators proved almost too much for the small upstate New York village. Transportation and communication were difficult and the IOC vowed never to return the Games to such a small venue.

As if these were not enough problems, shortly before the Olympics, the Soviet Union invaded Afghanistan. President Jimmy Carter promptly called for a U.S.-led boycott of the Moscow Olympics. And he used Secretary of State Cyrus Vance to lecture the IOC at its session in Lake Placid days before the Games started, which greatly offended the International Olympic Committee.

But Lake Placid had two great redeeming features—Eric Heiden and the U.S. ice hockey team. In speed skating, Heiden was the greatest skater in the world and pre-Games predictions had him possibly winning five gold medals, though few believed he could actually win all five. But he did. He ended his Olympic dominance with a gold medal in the 10,000 meters. Racing in the second pair with Viktor Lyoskin (URS), Heiden set a world record by six seconds and earned his fifth gold medal.

In ice hockey, the Soviet Union was by now conceded the gold medal at all Olympics. A week before the Olympics, the USA and the USSR played an exhibition game in Madison Square Garden and the Soviets won, 10–3. But the U.S. team had more fortitude than anyone suspected and were led by a coach, Herb Brooks, who brought more out of them than they knew they had. The Americans could not, and would not, be intimidated.

In the semi-finals they faced the Soviets. The score was tied in the third period when captain Mike Eruzione scored to put the U.S. ahead, 4–3. As time ran out with that same score, Al Michaels, ABC television announcer, echoed every American's thoughts when he asked, "Do you believe in miracles?" Two nights later, the Americans came from behind to defeat Finland and win the gold medal.

The Games of the XXIInd Olympiad (1980) The Games of the XXIInd Olympiad were held in Moscow, Russian Republic, USSR, from 19 July through 3 August 1980. At the 75th IOC Session in Athens on 18 May 1978, Moscow was awarded the Games by a vote of 39–20 over Los Angeles, the only other city that bid for the Olympics. Eighty countries eventually competed in Moscow, with 5,217 athletes competing (4,092 men and 1,125 women).

In late December 1979, Soviet tanks invaded Afghanistan. After the Soviet invasion of Afghanistan, United States' President Jimmy Carter called for a boycott of the Moscow Olympics if the Soviets did not withdraw before 20 February 1980. They did not. Carter pressed his efforts, attempting to enlist other countries to join his boycott. But American allies Britain, Finland, France, Ireland, Italy, New Zealand, Spain, and Sweden all competed at Moscow. Carter made his announcement public to the IOC via Secretary of State Cyrus Vance, who rather rudely addressed the IOC at the Lake Placid Games in February.

Approximately 63 countries eventually boycotted the Moscow Olympic. Notable among these were the United States, Canada, West Germany, Japan, China, Kenya, and Norway (a full list follows at the end of this section). Several countries that did not boycott protested at the Olympic ceremonies in various ways. Ten countries elected not to march at the opening ceremonies, while six other nations marched behind flags of their National Olympic Committees, or the Olympic Flag, rather than their national flags. Several countries chose not to have their national anthems played at victory ceremonies, substituting instead the Olympic Hymn. Finally, at the closing ceremony President Carter refused to allow the American flag to be raised as the host country of the next Olympics. The flag of Los Angeles was raised instead.

The Games suffered in level of competition but they were marvelously run, although spectators spoke often of the military atmosphere as Soviet soldiers were on every street corner with automatic weapons. The most awaited races matched two British athletes in the 800 and 1,500 meters in the track and the boycott had no effect on them. Sebastian Coe was favored in the 800 and Steve Ovett in the 1,500. They each won a gold medal, but in the "other man's" event. The athlete winning the most medals in Moscow was Soviet gymnast Aleksandr Dityatin, who won medals in all eight gymnastics events, three of them gold, setting a record for the most medals won at a single Olympics.

It is almost impossible to be certain how many nations boycotted or chose not to attend the 1980 Olympic Games in response to the Soviet invasion of Afghanistan. The United States' Government dogmatically stated numerous times that 65 nations joined the U.S.-led boycott, but that number is almost certainly wrong and too high. Because of political repercussions, many nations simply stated that they could not attend because of financial or other reasons, when in likelihood they were joining the boycott. On the other hand, among the non-participating nations, it is likely that a few were not boycotting, but did not compete for other reasons. No definitive further conclusions can be drawn concerning the number of boycotting nations.

For the record, the following 63 nations did not compete in Moscow but were IOC members, and eligible to compete in the Olympics, as of 27 May 1980, the date due for acceptance of invitations to the 1980 Olympic Games: Albania, Antigua, Argentina, Bahamas, Bahrain, Bangladesh, Barbados, Belize, Bermuda, Bolivia, Canada, Cayman Islands, Central African Republic, Chad, Chile, China, Egypt, El Salvador, Federal Republic of Germany, Fiji, Gabon, The Gambia, Ghana, Haiti, Honduras, Hong Kong, Indonesia, Israel, Ivory Coast, Japan,

Kenya, Korea, Liberia, Liechtenstein, Malawi, Malaysia, Mauritania, Mauritius, Monaco, Morocco, Netherlands Antilles, Niger, Norway, Pakistan, Panama, Papua-New Guinea, Paraguay, Philippines, Saudi Arabia, Singapore, Somalia, Sudan, Suriname, Swaziland, Thailand, Togo, Tunisia, Turkey, United States, U.S. Virgin Islands, Upper Volta, Uruguay, and Zaire.

As stated, the deadline for responding to the Moscow invitation to compete at the Olympic Games was 27 May 1980. The above nations can be separated into three categories based on this deadline—1) declined the invitation, 2) did not respond to the invitation, and 3) accepted the invitation but eventually did not compete.

Twenty-eight nations declined the invitation to compete, as follows: Albania, Argentina, Bahrain, Bermuda, Canada, Cayman Islands, China, Federal Republic of Germany, The Gambia, Honduras, Hong Kong, Indonesia, Israel, Kenya, Liechtenstein, Malawi, Malaysia, Mauritania, Pakistan, Paraguay, The Philippines, Saudi Arabia, Singapore, Thailand, Tunisia, Turkey, United States, and Uruguay.

Twenty-nine nations did not respond to the invitation to compete by 27 May 1980, as follows: Antigua, Bahamas, Bangladesh, Barbados, Belize, Bolivia, Central African Republic, Chad, Chile, Egypt, El Salvador, Fiji, Ghana, Haiti, Ivory Coast, Japan, Korea, Liberia, Monaco, Morocco, Netherlands Antilles, Norway, Papua-New Guinea, Somalia, Sudan, Swaziland, Togo, U.S. Virgin Islands, and Zaire.

Six nations accepted the invitation to compete, but eventually chose not to, as follows: Gabon, Mauritius, Niger, Panama, Suriname, and Upper Volta. The reasons for these nations' eventually choosing not to participate are not clear.

There were two further categories of "IOC-member" nations in 1980. Both Chinese Taipei and Iran had been member nations of the IOC but at the time of the Moscow invitation they were in suspension and were not eligible to compete at the 1980 Olympic Games.

Finally, three nations were accepted into IOC membership at the IOC Executive Board Meeting in Lausanne on 9–10 June 1980, after the due date for acceptances to the Moscow invitation. These were Mozambique, Qatar, and the United Arab Emirates. These nations were, therefore, not technically eligible to compete at Moscow. However, Mozambique did compete, although Qatar and the United Arab Emirates did not. It is likely that, because of the boycott, late invitations were extended to these three nations to fill out the list of competing nations in

Moscow, and Mozambique was able to field a team in time, and chose to do so.

The 14th Olympic Winter Games (1984)   The 14th Olympic Winter Games were held in Sarajevo, Bosnia-Herzegovina Province, Yugoslavia, from 8 through 19 February 1984. Forty-nine nations attended with 1,274 athletes competing (1,000 men and 274 women). At the 80th IOC Session in Athens on 18 May 1978, Sarajevo was chosen in the second round of balloting (39 votes) over Sapporo, Japan (36 votes); and Göteburg, Sweden (eliminated after round one).

After the controversy, problems, and excitement that were Lake Placid, Sarajevo's Winter Olympics were much quieter, in marked contrast to the Yugoslavian civil war that would come to Sarajevo within the next decade. The only difficulties were early weather problems. An initial concern about lack of snow was alleviated when a blizzard hit shortly after the opening ceremonies, forcing the men's downhill to be postponed twice.

In Nordic skiing, Marja-Liisa Hämäläinen (FIN) won three cross-country skiing gold medals. But Nordic skiing rarely captures the press notices of figure skating, Alpine skiing or ice hockey, and Hämäläinen's feat was noted with little fanfare outside Finland.

In ice hockey, the Soviets restored the status quo when they easily won the gold medal. The Canadians, having returned to Olympic ice hockey in 1980, were thought to have a chance as some professionals could now be used. But the USSR played seven games, won seven games, and won the gold medal.

In ice dancing, the British couple, Jayne Torvill and Christopher Dean, was heavily favored based on past performances. Their final program was quite controversial, however, as it probably violated ice dancing protocol by being based on a single piece of music, Ravel's "Bolero." Their performance to "Bolero" was mesmerizing, building to an almost orgiastic finish that brought the crowd to a frenzy. The judges awarded the British pair the highest scores ever seen in figure skating, with 12 perfect 6.0s out of 18 marks.

In singles figure skating, Scott Hamilton (USA) and Katarina Witt (GDR) won gold medals. Hamilton was expected to win as he had been nonpareil since the 1980 Olympics. Witt was not as well known and was not favored, but her stunning beauty helped to make her a crowd favorite.

Sarajevo had been a beautiful Olympic city, but within a decade it would lie in ruins, as would many of the sports facilities, destroyed by the senseless war in the Balkans. They were victims of ethnic cleansing.

The Games of the XXIIIrd Olympiad (1984) The Games of the XXIIIrd Olympiad were held in Los Angeles, California, USA, from 28 July through 12 August 1984. Los Angeles was awarded the Olympics by acclamation at the 80th IOC Session in Athens on 18 May 1978. No other candidate city bid for these Olympics. One hundred forty nations attended the Los Angeles Olympics with 6,797 athletes competing (5,230 men and 1,567 women).

In May 1984, the Soviet Union announced that it would not attend the Olympics in Los Angeles, citing concerns over the safety of its athletes because of the "anti-Soviet and anti-Communist activities" in the Los Angeles area. Most people considered the boycott one of retribution for the United States' refusal to compete in Moscow. Most of the Eastern European countries joined in the Soviet-bloc boycott, notably East Germany (GDR), and it was joined by Cuba. Although only 14 invited countries did not compete in Los Angeles, the absence of the USSR, Cuba, and the GDR made many of the events mere shadows of what was anticipated.

Still, more countries and athletes competed at Los Angeles than in any previous Olympics. However, what the 1984 boycott lacked in numbers relative to the 1980 boycott, it made up for in its impact on the competition. Boxing, weightlifting, wrestling, gymnastics, and, to a certain extent, track & field would have been dominated by the boycotting nations. The nations which did not compete were: Afghanistan, Bulgaria, Cuba, Czechoslovakia, Ethiopia, German Democratic Republic, Hungary, Laos, Mongolia, North Korea, Poland, South Yemen, Vietnam, and the U.S.S.R. Bravely, Romania defied the boycott and competed at the Olympics, receiving an ovation at the opening ceremonies second only to that of the United States.

China also returned to the Olympic Games at Los Angeles in 1984, after an absence of 32 years (China had competed at the Olympic Games of 1932, 1936, 1948, and 1952). It had competed at the 1980 Olympic Winter Games in Lake Placid, but China's appearance at the opening ceremonies was greeted warmly by the American crowd, especially in light of the Soviet boycott. Yugoslavia, not Soviet dominated, was the only other country from Eastern Europe to compete.

After all that, the Olympics were very well run, although the Europeans had numerous complaints, mostly about customary American methods of doing business. American television concentrated on U.S. athletes, which infuriated the Europeans. For the first time ever, the Games were managed in an entrepreneurial fashion. Organizing committee President Peter Ueberroth insisted that the Olympics be designed to break even or even provide a profit. Again, the Europeans, used to the simon-pure idealistic image of the Olympics for the Olympics' sake, rebelled against this philosophy. But Ueberroth was determined that the Games would be financially independent and he succeeded admirably in that regard. Ueberroth's marketing methods, though initially vilified by the Europeans, have since been copied by all organizing committees and even the IOC itself.

As to the sports themselves, the competition was good, though diluted in many ways because of the boycott. Carl Lewis emerged as the American men's star, equaling Jesse Owens' 1936 feat of winning four gold medals in track & field. But Lewis did not have Owens' appeal to the American public and his image, almost obsequiously nurtured by his manager, failed to live up to his deeds on the track.

Failing Lewis, the American public reached instead to Mary Lou Retton, who became the first American gymnast to win the all-around individual gold. To win, she needed a perfect 10 on her last event, the horse vault. Given two vaults, she achieved the 10, not once, but twice.

After the difficulties of Munich and Montreal, Los Angeles had been the only bidder for the Games of 1984. But Los Angeles, despite its problems, revitalized the Olympic Movement to some degree. Having shown that the Olympics did not need to be a "loss-leader" and could, in fact, produce an operating profit, many cities now were interested in hosting the Olympics. Shortly after the 1984 Olympics, six cities would submit official bids to host the 1992 Games.

The 15th Olympic Winter Games (1988) The 15th Olympic Winter Games were held in Calgary, Alberta, Canada, from 13 through 28 February 1988. Fifty-seven nations attended with 1,423 athletes competing (1,110 men and 313 women). At the 84th IOC Session in Baden-Baden, Germany, on 30 September 1981, Calgary was chosen on the second round (48 votes) over Falun, Sweden (31 votes); and Cortina d'Ampezzo, Italy (eliminated after round one).

In ice hockey, the Soviets again were dominant. The speed-skating hero was the unlikely Yvonne van Gennip of The Netherlands. All attention was focused on the GDR's quartet of Karin Kania, Andrea Ehrig, Christa Rothenburger, and Gabi Zange, and the United States' Bonnie Blair. They skated well, with Blair winning the 500 and Rothenburger the 1,000, and between them, those five won 12 of the available 15 medals. But the other three were won by van Gennip, who won the 1,500, 3,000, and 5,000 meters, defeating the favored Ehrig and Zange in the long-distance races.

One of the media heroes was Italian Alpine skier Alberto Tomba, who won two gold medals, and delighted the press with his nightly antics. He attempted to date the GDR's Katarina Witt, who won her second consecutive figure skating gold medal, but he got nowhere, which further delighted the media. Witt's top competitor was the American, Debi Thomas, who had been World Champion in 1987, but Thomas skated relatively poorly and finished third. Her bronze medal was the first ever won by a black athlete at the Olympic Winter Games.

In men's speed skating, the real hero was probably a man who never finished a race at Calgary. Dan Jansen was a favorite in the 500 meters, and in the 1,000, he was thought to have a chance to win. But on the morning of the first race, the 500, he found out that his sister, who had been ill with leukemia, had died. He elected to skate that night, but fell on the first turn. A few days later, he hoped to redeem himself in the 1,000 meters and through 600 meters, he had the fastest pace. But he fell again. The world watched and suffered with him, but Dan Jansen offered no excuses. He was gracious and magnanimous throughout. Years of effort were lost, certainly by the emotions of the moment, but he responded with the grace so often requested of our athletes, and yet so rarely offered.

The Games of the XXIVth Olympiad (1988)   The Games of the XXIVth Olympiad were held in Seoul, Republic of Korea, from 17 September through 5 October 1988. One hundred fifty-nine nations attended the Olympics with 8,465 athletes competing (6,279 men and 2,186 women).

On 30 September 1981, the IOC elected Seoul as the host city over Nagoya, Japan, by a vote of 52–27 at the 84th IOC Session in Baden-Baden, Germany. The choice was highly controversial as many prominent nations in the Olympic Movement, notably the Soviet-bloc nations, did not have diplomatic relations with the Seoul government. There was widespread concern that another boycott would ensue because of this.

The problem became more complicated in July 1985 when North Korea demanded that it be allowed to co-host the Games with the Republic of Korea. Over the next three years, the IOC negotiated with North Korea and offered to allow it to stage several events. However, no IOC concession was ever enough for the North, which wanted equal co-host status and an equal number of events. It demanded this despite the fact that the Games were close at hand and it had no possible hope of building the necessary facilities in time. When the IOC would not acquiesce further to the North's demands, North Korea announced that it would definitely boycott the Seoul Olympics.

By then, however, most of the Soviet-bloc countries had agreed to compete in Seoul, making 1988 the first Summer Olympic competition in 12 years between the United States, the Soviet Union, and the German Democratic Republic. After the North Korean's official boycott announcement, Cuba and Ethiopia also made it official that they would not attend the Olympics, out of solidarity with North Korea. Nicaragua, Albania, and the Seychelles also did not attend the Olympics, although their reasons were less clear and may not have been directly related to any boycott.

Thus, although there was a boycott of the 1988 Olympics, it encompassed only six nations and had minimal effect on the Games themselves. The Seoul Games went on and saw the largest participation in Olympic history. There were more nations and athletes represented than ever before. The Games themselves were excellent and were very well run. Controversies and political intrusions, unlike the Games of the last 20 years, were relatively few and comparatively minor.

Three swimmers and one female track & field athlete dominated the sporting events. In the pool, the GDR's Kristin Otto broke all sorts of records by winning six gold medals, an unmatched performance by a woman at the Olympics. Her only rival for swimming supremacy was America's Janet Evans, who won three distance swimming gold medals. On the men's side of the pool, Matt Biondi was attempting to equal Mark Spitz's record of seven gold medals. He failed in his first two events, taking a silver and a bronze, but won gold medals in his last five events.

On the track, the world was stunned by the performances of sprinter Florence Griffith Joyner. At the Olympics, she won the 100 and 200, setting a world record in the 200 finals, and helped the American women win a gold medal in the 4 x 100 relay. She also ran anchor on the 4 x 400 relay team, adding a silver medal to her three golds, in the best race of the 1988 Olympics, as the Soviet Union narrowly defeated the American relay team.

The biggest media event of the 1988 Olympic Games was the disqualification of sprinter Ben Johnson, after he had won the 100 meters in a world record time of 9.79, defeating Carl Lewis. Johnson tested positive for an anabolic steroid (stanazolol) and was disqualified, with Lewis receiving the gold medal. After the uproar of the scandal, the Canadians organized an investigation into drug use in international athletics, the Dubin Inquiry. At the inquiry, Johnson admitted that he had used steroids for several years.

The 16th Olympic Winter Games (1992)   The 16th Olympic Winter Games were held in Albertville, France, from 8 through 23 February 1992. Sixty-four nations attended with 1,801 athletes competing (1,313 men and 488 women). At the 91st IOC Session in Lausanne on 17 October 1986, Albertville was chosen by the IOC on the fifth round of voting over a large field of candidate cities: Sofia, Bulgaria (fifth round); Falun, Sweden (fifth round); Lillehammer, Norway (fourth round); Cortina d'Ampezzo, Italy (third round); Anchorage, Alaska, USA (second round); and Berchtesgaden, Germany (first round).

This was the third Olympic Winter Games to be held in France, and the second to be held in the French Savoie, after the 1924 Games in Chamonix in the Haute-Savoie. The 1968 Games in Grenoble (Isère), were in the Dauphiné area of the French Alps. The Games were awarded to Albertville but they were actually spread over several small towns and villages of the French Savoie in the French Alps. Expected problems with transportation between the villages did not materialize and the Games were extremely well run.

Another innovation was the introduction of a number of new Olympic sports and events to the Winter Games. Women competed in biathlon for the first time. Men and women competed in short-track speed skating skated in a pack style. Freestyle skiing, which had been a demonstration sport in 1988, returned with moguls débuting as a full medal sport. Speed skiing and the other two freestyle disciplines, ballet and aerials, were demonstration events.

The biggest news was the Olympic appearance of several new teams because of the political upheavals that had occurred in the past two years. Germany competed as a single team and independent nation for the first time since 1936. Because of the break-up of the Soviet Union, the Baltic States of Estonia and Latvia competed for the first time since 1936, and Lithuania for the first time since 1928. Two newly independent nations that had been former states of Yugoslavia, Croatia and Slovenia, competed at the Olympics as independent nations. The Soviet Union, which no longer existed, was represented instead by the Unified Team (Équipe Unifé), representing a portion of the Commonwealth of Independent States. Russia, Belarus (formerly Byelorussia), the Ukraine, Kazakstan, and Uzbekistan made up the states of the Unified Team at Albertville.

Athletically, the biggest winners were two male cross-country runners from Norway and two female cross-country runners from the Unified Team. Yelena Välbe and Lyubov Yegorova won five medals in the women's events while Vegard Ulvang and Bjørn Dæhlie won four medals in the men's events.

The Games of the XXVth Olympiad (1992) The Games of the XXVth Olympiad were held in Barcelona, Spain, from 25 July through 9 August 1992. At the 91st IOC Session in Lausanne on 17 October 1986, Barcelona (47 votes) was awarded the Games on the third ballot over Paris, France (23 votes); Brisbane, Australia (10 votes); and Belgrade, Yugoslavia (5 votes). Other candidate cities that were eliminated earlier in the voting were Birmingham, England, Great Britain (second round); and Amsterdam, The Netherlands (first round). One hundred sixty-nine nations attended the Games with 9,367 athletes competing (6,659 men and 2,708 women).

The Barcelona Olympics were the Games of the New World Order. They were the most highly attended Olympics in history, both in terms of countries and athletes attending. After four consecutive Olympics with some form of protest or boycott, the Barcelona Olympics were boycott-free.

Since Seoul in 1988, the world had taken on a new face. The Soviet Union no longer existed, but the Commonwealth of Independent States did. Estonia, Latvia, and Lithuania were once again free countries. East and West Germany were no more, replaced again by a unified Germany; Yugoslavia was now split into several republics; and North and South Yemen had merged into one. All of these new national groupings appeared at Barcelona. South Africa had eliminated, at least constitutionally, apartheid, and competed at the Olympics for the first time since

1960. The Commonwealth of Independent States competed as a "Unified Team" for the last time, representing all the former republics of the Soviet Union, save for the Baltic States.

The Games were opened beautifully and dramatically as archer Antônio Rebollo lit the Olympic Flame via bow and arrow. The drama and beauty of Catalonia continued on stage throughout the 16 days of the Olympics. There was concern about terrorist activity because the area was home to some terrorist groups, but heightened security and vigilance helped avoid any problems.

The competition was excellent. For the first time since 1972, all the major nations of the world attended. The most publicized athletes were the American basketball players. The U.S. was allowed to use professional players from the NBA (National Basketball Association) because all the other nations were by now using professionals. The NBA All-Star team, nicknamed "The Dream Team," did not disappoint, putting on a clinic for all nations and winning the gold medal unchallenged. It was led by professional greats Magic Johnson, Michael Jordan, and Larry Bird.

Many East European countries and the former Soviets continued to dominate certain sports, such as gymnastics and weightlifting. There were many great athletic performances but, other than the Dream Team, no one athlete seemed to capture these Games like so many had in the past. It was probably fitting, for then no athlete seemed larger than the Games themselves; fitting for Barcelona was possibly the finest manifestation yet seen of the Olympic Movement.

The 17th Olympic Winter Games (1994)   The 17th Olympic Winter Games were held in Lillehammer, Norway, from 12 through 27 February 1994. Sixty-seven nations attended with 1,737 athletes competing (1,217 men and 520 women). At the 94th IOC Session in Seoul on 15 September 1988, Lillehammer was chosen on the third round (45 votes) over Östersund, Sweden (39 votes, third round); Anchorage, Alaska, USA (second round); and Sofia, Bulgaria (first round).

For the first time, the Olympic Winter Games were not scheduled for the same year as the Games of the Olympiad. The International Olympic Committee had decided to hold the Olympic Winter Games in the second year after the Olympic Games, thus shortening the cycle so that an Olympic Games or Olympic Winter Games would be held in a rotation every two years. The decision was ostensibly because this would result in greater advertising and sponsorship money.

Before the Lillehammer Olympics began, they were haunted by the Nancy Kerrigan-Tonya Harding story, in which Harding's bodyguard and ex-husband admitted to attacking Kerrigan prior to the U.S. Olympic Trials, a story that was ubiquitous in the U.S. press and television. Eventually, both Kerrigan and Harding made the U.S. Olympic figure skating team. Kerrigan skated well, winning a silver medal behind The Ukraine's Oksana Bayul. Harding eventually pleaded to having knowledge of the attack on Kerrigan and her figure skating effectively ended after her eighth-place finish at Lillehammer.

But even The Kardigan Saga would not mar what was a fairy-tale-like two weeks, which ended all thoughts of the problems that had preceded them, and reminded us again of what the Olympics and sport can bring to the world. There were many great athletic feats at the Lillehammer Games. Manuela Di Centa won five medals in cross-country skiing. Norway's Johann Olav Koss won three speed-skating gold medals in world record time. Dan Jansen won the hearts of sports fans everywhere when he finally won a gold medal in the 1,000-meter speed skating. But through it all, the champions seemed to be the small town of Lillehammer and the people of Norway itself.

There were also many poignant memories of Sarajevo, which had hosted the 1984 Olympic Winter Games, and which lay in ruins because of the senseless war in the Balkans. Katarina Witt skated her long program to "Where Have All the Flowers Gone?" in memory of the citizens who had lost their lives in that war. On the next-to-last night, at the figure skating exhibition, Jayne Torvill and Christopher Dean skated "Bolero" as they had done so hauntingly in 1984 at Sarajevo. Koss donated a major portion of his Olympic bonus (about $33,000 [U.S.]) to Olympic Aid for the citizens of Sarajevo. And during the Lillehammer Olympics, IOC President Samaranch visited Sarajevo, seeing in person the stark contrast between the Olympic City and the Sarajevo of 1994. At the Closing Ceremonies, Samaranch also spoke movingly about the war-torn city.

It was said of the Lillehammer Olympics: "The XVII Winter Olympics did not exist. Norway did not exist. These were the fairy-tale Games, drawn from the imagination, staged in the pages of a children's book. They could not exist. Reality cannot be this good." (*Sports Illustrated,* 7 March 1994, p. 90)

The Games of the XXVIth Olympiad (1996)   The Games of the XXVIth Olympiad were held in Atlanta, Georgia, USA, from 19 July through 4 August 1996. Atlanta won the IOC nomination at the 96th IOC Session on 18 September 1990 in the fifth round (51 votes) over Athens, Greece (35 votes). Other candidate cities were Toronto, Ontario, Canada (fourth round); Melbourne, Australia (third round); Manchester, England, Great Britain (second round); and Belgrade, Yugoslavia (first round). For the first time ever, all IOC member nations competed at the Olympics, with 197 nations present, with 10,301 athletes competing (6,797 men and 3,513 women).

Atlanta was a highly controversial choice, as Athens was favored. Athens had not been an Olympic host since 1906, or officially 1896, and the Greeks seemed to feel that the 1996 Olympics belonged to them as a birthright. When they lost the bid, the Greeks were irate, feeling that the games had been stolen from them.

The 1996 Olympics were a chance for Atlanta to demonstrate itself as a major international city. However, Atlanta had problems as the city was inundated with vendors and salespeople selling Olympic-related merchandise and attempting to make a fast buck off the Olympics. The atmosphere was unsavory and commercialized and not appreciated by many foreign visitors. The major problem that occurred at the 1996 Olympics came on Saturday, 27 July, shortly after midnight, when a bomb exploded in the Centennial Olympic Park, where many spectators and fans congregated and partied throughout the night. The bomb killed two people and injured several more. As of April 2001, the perpetrator, or perpetrators, of the blast has, or have, not been found.

The biggest medal winner at Atlanta was American swimmer Amy Van Dyken, who won four gold medals. She was challenged in the pool by the Irish swimmer Michelle Smith, who won three gold medals. But Smith was dogged by doping rumors because her times had improved so dramatically. In track & field athletics, Michael Johnson was expected to be the most publicized athlete, and he did win the 200 meters in world record time, and added a second gold medal in the 400 meters. But he was overshadowed by Carl Lewis, competing in his fourth Olympics, who came through as had done so often, winning a fourth long jump gold medal in his last Olympics.

The 18th Olympic Winter Games (1998)   The 18th Olympic Winter Games were held in Nagano, Japan, from 7 through 22 February 1998. At the 97th IOC Session in Birmingham, England on 15 June 1991, Nagano won the nomination in the fourth round (46 votes) over Salt

Lake City, Utah, USA (42 votes, fourth round); Östersund, Sweden (third round); Aosta, Italy (second round); and Jaca, Spain (first round). Nagano had been an "upset" choice over the more favored selections of Salt Lake City and Östersund.

A number of new events made their Olympic début in Nagano, probably foremost among these being women's ice hockey, which was won by the United States team in a mild upset over the favored Canadians. Snowboarding and curling also were new to the program. Snowboarding had four events—men's and women's halfpipe and giant slalom. There were 72 nations present at Nagano, a record for the Olympic Winter Games, with 2,175 athletes competing (1,389 men and 786 women).

In men's ice hockey, the big story was the presence of the top professional players in the world for the first time ever. The National Hockey League (NHL) closed down its mid-season schedule for two weeks to allow all the pros to represent their countries, reminiscent of the "Dream Team" of NBA players at Barcelona. The difference in ice hockey, however, was that the top players were not solely from one nation, but were spread among several hockey powers—Canada, United States, Russia, Sweden, Finland, and the Czech Republic. The two favorites, the United States and Canada, went out early, and neither won a medal. The final came down to Russia against the Czech Republic, and the Czechs won in a slight upset, aided by the superb goaltending of Dominik Hašek of the Buffalo Sabres of the NHL. The Czech team defeated successively the three greatest hockey nations in Olympic history—Canada, Russia, and the United States.

Norway's Bjørn Dæhlie added to his list of Olympic records by winning four medals and three golds, to bring his overall Olympic total to 12 medals and eight gold medals, all Olympic Winter Games' records. Russia's Larisa Lazutina won the most medals at Nagano, with five in women's Nordic skiing. She and Dæhlie were the only athletes to win three gold medals at Nagano.

Also dominant at Nagano were the Dutch speed skaters, whose men won nine of 15 Olympic medals, and four of five events. Marianne Timmer also added two golds in the women's 1,000 and 1,500. Germany's Gunda Niemann won three medals in speed skating, bringing her Olympic career total to eight, equalling the Olympic speed-skating record.

The Games of the XXVIIth Olympiad (2000) The Games of the XXVIIth Olympiad were held in Sydney, New South Wales, Australia, from 16 September to 1 October 2000, with preliminary football (soccer) matches actually opening the Games on 14 September. In a closely fought contest, Sydney was awarded the 2000 Olympics during the 101st IOC Session in Monte Carlo on 23 September 1993 over Beijing, China, by only two votes (45–43) in the fourth round. Other candidate cities participating in the voting were Manchester, England (third round); Berlin, Germany (second round); and Istanbul, Turkey (first round). Brasilia, Brazil; Milan, Italy; and Tashkent, Uzbekistan, also made bids to the IOC but withdrew before the final vote. At Sydney, 199 nations competed, along with East Timor, not yet an IOC member, but whose athletes (four men and one woman) competed at the invitation of the IOC as Independent Olympic Athletes (IOA). There were 10,651 competitors—6,582 men and 4,069 women.

The 2000 Olympic Games began on a Sydney evening in which the Olympic Torch was lit by Australian 400-meter runner, Cathy Freeman. Freeman was a decidedly political choice, as she was of aboriginal origin, and the country had effectively adopted her in keeping with their recent policy of making amends to the aboriginal peoples, for years of mistreatment. If Freeman, who went on to win the 400 meters, could be considered a perfect choice for the final torch bearer, as many felt she was, it was only the beginning of many perfect choices made by the Australian hosts.

The venues were centered around Sydney Olympic Park, built on the site of an old cattleyard. This one relatively small region contained virtually all the major venues for the Olympic events. The park served as an international collegial meeting place, while providing easy access for all spectators to the venues. And the venues met with uniform raves from the athletes, fans, and media alike.

Strangely, no single athlete dominated the 2000 Olympic Games, though several tried. Marion Jones (USA) tried to win five gold medals in track & field. She won three, and added two bronzes but it seemed almost anti-climactic. Australia's Ian Thorpe was predicted to dominate the pool, but he won only one individual event, and added another gold in a relay. In cycling, the Dutchwoman, Leontien Zijlaard-van Moorsel won three gold medals and four medals in all. But no athlete seemed bigger than the host city itself. Sydney was the star of the 2000 Olympic Games.

Were the Sydney Olympic Games a perfect Olympics? No, because nothing of that sort could ever exist. But they were close, and at the Closing Ceremony, there were few who had attended who would not be willing to cede all future Olympic Games to the New South Wales capital. As he has done several times before, IOC President Samaranch declared the Sydney Olympics "the best ever." This time, there were no dissenters.

The 19th Olympic Winter Games (2002) The 19th Olympic Winter Games will be held in Salt Lake City, Utah, United States, from 8 to 24 February 2002. At the 104th IOC Session in Budapest, Hungary on 16 June 1995, Salt Lake City was chosen as the host city in round one over three other finalist cities with 55 votes. The other finalist cities were Östersund, Sweden (14 votes); Sion, Switzerland (14 votes); and Quebec City, Quebec, Canada (7 votes). Ten cities made preliminary bids; the other six candidate cities were as follows: Almaty, Kazakstan; Graz, Austria; Jaca, Spain; Poprad-Tatry, Slovakia; Sochi, Russia; and Tarvisio, Italy. On 24 January 1995, the IOC Evaluation Commission eliminated all but four bidding cities in a new effort to decrease time, effort, and costs by so many bid candidates.

In late 1998–early 1999, the Salt Lake City bid was rocked by rumors of rampant bribery given to IOC Members in an attempt to secure the bid. This led to the Olympic Bribery Scandal, and multiple investigations of the IOC, the Salt Lake City Bid Committee, and the Olympic Movement in general. Full details of this can be found in the article discussing the Olympic Bribery Scandal.

The Games of the XXVIIIth Olympiad (2004) The Games of the XXVIIIth Olympiad are scheduled to be held in Athens, Greece, from 13 to 29 August 2004. Athens was awarded the 2004 Olympics during the 106th IOC Session in Lausanne on 5 September 1997 over Rome, Italy (fourth round); Cape Town, South Africa (third round); Stockholm, Sweden (second round); and Buenos Aires, Argentina (first round). There were originally 11 candidate cities. Because of the number of candidate cities, the IOC Evaluation Commission eliminated all but the above five cities prior to the voting. The other candidate cities, which did not advance to the voting round, were: Istanbul, Turkey; Lille, France; Rio de Janeiro, Brazil; San Juan, Puerto Rico; Seville, Spain; and St. Petersburg, Russia.

The 20th Olympic Winter Games (2006)   The 20th Olympic Winter Games are scheduled to be held in Turin (Torino), Italy, from 11 to 26 February 2006. At the 109th IOC Session in Seoul, Korea, on 19 June 1999, Turin was chosen as the host city in round one with 53 votes, against 36 votes for Sion, Switzerland, the only other city that advanced to the voting round. There were other candidate cities, but the IOC Evaluation Commission eliminated all but Turin and Sion prior to the vote. The other candidate cities were Helsinki, Finland (with Lillehammer, Norway); Klagenfurt, Austria (with Cortina d'Ampezzo, Italy, and Ješnice, Slovenia); Poprad-Tatry, Slovakia; Zakopane, Poland.

The Games of the XXIXth Olympiad (2008)   The host city for the Games of the XXIXth Olympiad will be chosen at the 111th IOC Session in Moscow, Russia in July 2001. As of February 2000, 10 cities have made application to the IOC to host the 2008 Olympic Games, as follows: Bangkok, Thailand; Beijing, China; Cairo, Egypt; Havana, Cuba; Istanbul, Turkey; Kuala Lumpur, Malaysia; Osaka, Japan; Paris, France; Seville, Spain; and Toronto, Ontario, Canada.

Introduction to the Olympic Movement

The Olympic Movement began with the Ancient Olympic Games that were held in Greece on the Peloponnesus peninsula at Olympia, Greece. The recorded history of the Ancient Olympic Games begins in 776 B.C., although it is suspected that the Games had been held for several centuries by that time. The Games were conducted as religious celebrations in honor of the god Zeus. The Ancient Olympic Games were contested through 393 A.D., when they were stopped by imperial decree of the Roman Emperor Theodosius I.

For almost 15 centuries, the world did not have Olympic Games, although they were not forgotten and were often mentioned in literature. In the 19th century, a series of attempted revivals of the Olympic Games were held in various parts of the world. The most prominent of these were the Much Wenlock Olympian Games, held in Shropshire, England, and beginning in 1850, and the Zappas Olympic Games, held in Athens, Greece, which were first conducted in 1859. The Zappas Olympic Games were held four times and were strictly Greek national sporting festivals. The Much Wenlock Olympian Games were the brainchild of Dr. William Penny Brookes. Modern scholars of the Olympic Movement give much credit to Brookes as one of the men who originated the idea of reviving the Ancient Olympic Games.

However, full credit for the renovation of the Olympic Games is usually given to the Frenchman Baron Pierre de Coubertin. To Coubertin, in particular, should be given credit for instituting the Modern Olympic Movement, and for his efforts, Coubertin has been termed *le rénovateur.* Pierre de Coubertin was a French aristocrat born in 1863, who in the 1880s became interested in education and the French educational system and sought ways to improve it. He traveled to Great Britain, the United States, and Canada to study their educational systems, and became fascinated with the fact that their educational systems emphasized physical education as being an important part of their overall development. In

England, he was especially entranced by the teachings of Thomas Arnold, the former headmaster at Rugby School, who developed the philosophy of "muscular Christianity," a concept by which athletic endeavors supposedly made one a better person spiritually.

Coubertin's studies led him to the study of the Ancient Greeks and the Ancient Olympic Games. The Ancient Greeks also believed in a philosophy similar to muscular Christianity, epitomized by the well-known saying "*Mens sana in corpore sano,*" or in English, "A sound mind in a sound body." The Greek philosophy was actually called *kalokagathia*, or the harmonic combination of beauty and goodness. In concert with his study of the Ancient Greek philosophy of *kalokagathia*, Coubertin became entranced by the idea of the Ancient Olympic Games.

In Coubertin's mind, all of this seemed to fit together into one coherent goal. He would develop a Movement that would emphasize international sports and athletics as a way of furthering the education of young men (but not women, as we will learn later). This Movement would have as its finest hour an international gathering of these young men in a great sporting festival reminiscent of the Ancient Olympics, the Modern Olympic Games. What could be more perfect?

Coubertin first publicly suggested the idea of modern Olympic Games at a meeting of sports dignitaries at the Sorbonne in 1892, but nothing came of this. In 1894, he was in charge of the Paris International Athletic Congress, which was held ostensibly to discuss amateurism. However, Coubertin had different ideas and suggested the resurrection of the Olympic Games. His idea met with favor among the candidates and the Modern Olympic Games began two years later in Athens, Greece.

The early years of the Olympic Movement were difficult. In 1896, the Greeks actually resisted Coubertin's efforts and were not necessarily enthralled with the idea of holding Modern Olympic Games. They were a poor country and the effort was a difficult one for them. But Coubertin and the Greeks persisted and worked together and the 1896 Olympic Games were successful, although they looked nothing like the more modern festivals. In both 1900 and 1904 the Olympic Games were held in conjunction with World Fairs, virtually as sideshows to the fairs. In 1900, the French were holding the Exposition Universelle in Paris and the 1900 Olympic Games suffered for the lack of attention. A similar fate awaited the 1904 Olympic Games, held in concert with the Louisiana Purchase International Exposition.

Although the Greeks had not been keen on holding the 1896 Olympics, they quickly warmed to the idea. In 1906, the Greeks held another Olympics, outside of the normal quadrennial cycle. Usually termed Intercalated or Interim Olympics, the IOC still does not recognize these Games, which is unfortunate, as, after the debacles of 1900 and 1904, the 1906 Olympic Games were the best held to date, and probably saved the nascent Olympic Movement. The Greeks actually planned to hold "Greek Olympic Games" every four years, spaced in between the "International" Olympic Games, but because of Greek political and financial troubles, it never came to be.

In 1908, the Olympic Games were held in London and all that could be heard was bickering between the British hosts and the American officials, who protested multiple events and acted every bit like the "ugly American." But the Games were actually the most international to date and were well run—even if the United States' officials thought otherwise. In addition, the 1908 Olympics forced many sports to form International Federations to govern their sports on a worldwide basis, and set up standard sets of rules, in order to prevent future repeats of the many rules controversies from 1908.

After 1908, the Olympic Games simply took off as the most successful sporting event in the world. Since 1896, the Olympic Games have been held every four years, with the exception of 1916, 1940, and 1944, when they were not held because of the World Wars. In 1924, the first Olympic Winter Games were held in Chamonix, France. These Winter Olympics have since been contested every four years, save 1940 and 1944 (see above), until 1992. In that year, the cycle for Olympic Winter Games changed and the next ones were contested in 1994, with a new four-year cycle to ensue such that the next Winter Olympics will be held in 2002. This ensures that the Olympic Games and the Olympic Winter Games are not held in the same calendar year.

In 1894, Coubertin was responsible not simply for suggesting the revival of the Olympic Games, but also for the formation of the International Olympic Committee (IOC). The IOC has existed since 1894 as an international nongovernmental organization (NGO) whose responsibilities include the planning and staging of the Olympic Games, overseeing the Olympic Movement, and spreading its philosophy, termed *Olympism*.

The IOC, and its responsibilities and philosophy, have evolved greatly over its first century of existence. Originally, the IOC basically consisted of a group run by Coubertin. Although there were other members, he was in charge and the ideas and plans he espoused were usually accepted without argument by the other members of the IOC. Coubertin initially ran the IOC out of his home in Paris at 20, rue Oudinot. In April 1915, he moved to Lausanne, Switzerland, and established the IOC headquarters in that city, where it has remained since that time.

Through World War II, and even until the early 1960s, the IOC, the Olympic Games, and the Olympic Movement did not change a great deal, although they all became a bit larger and better known. However, the IOC was still run basically by its president and a small headquarters staff, and with relatively small financial backing.

In the 1960s, television began to realize the importance of televising the Olympic Games and, since that time, things have changed greatly. With network telecasts of the Olympic Games came huge fees paid by the networks for that right. The money generated has given the IOC and the Olympic Movement significant financial freedom. This has enabled the IOC to expand its horizons in an effort to spread its philosophy of Olympism, and also to lend financial support to various structures within the Olympic Movement via Olympic Solidarity.

In the 1980s, the IOC began to seek other sources of financing its operations, via a commission of the IOC, originally termed the Commission for New Sources of Financing, and now called simply the *Finance Commission*. This has only served to strengthen the financial situation of the IOC and allow it to pursue its purpose even more aggressively.

The increasing economic independence, however, has also engendered great problems. The Olympic Games became so publicized that they became subject to great political manipulation, ending in several boycotts. In 1968, political activists in Mexico City protested the Mexican government's staging of the Olympic Games, The Mexican army and police intervened and killed several hundred protesters. In 1972, Arab terrorists kidnapped most of the Israeli Olympic team in the Olympic Village and, eventually, after hours of negotiations, savagely murdered 11 of the Israelis. Between 1968 and 1988, all the Olympic Games saw some form of protest or boycott.

Coubertin hated politics, stating, "We have not worked, my friends and I, to restore the Olympic Games to have them made a museum piece or a movie, nor for commercial or political interests to take over."[1] And so, the IOC has attempted to remain nonpolitical. However, this is changing.

The IOC, and current IOC President Juan Antonio Samaranch, have more recently been quoted as saying that the mere act of declaring the group nonpolitical is, in itself, a political statement. The IOC realizes it cannot operate in a vacuum, attempting to divorce itself from all the political problems of a world that, superficially at least, appears to have no desire to pursue freedom for all people and more internationalism. Samaranch's philosophy of not allowing the IOC to be politically isolated is best exemplified by his negotiations with respect to the 1988 Seoul Olympics, in which he attempted to negotiate with DPR Korea (North) in an effort to allow it to host several Olympic events.

The purpose of the IOC may seem to the rest of the world to be to stage Olympic Games. But the IOC would state that its primary reason for existence is to spread the philosophy of Olympism via the Olympic Movement. It is not easy to define either Olympism or the Olympic Movement. Both are defined in the *Olympic Charter*, basically the constitution of the IOC, and full definitions are given within this dictionary.

The *Olympic Charter* states simply that "The Olympic Movement, led by the IOC, stems from modern Olympism." The IOC has, however, defined the concept more fully in some of its press releases. It has stated that the Olympic Movement encompasses the International Olympic Committee (IOC), the International Federations (IFs), and the National Olympic Committees (NOCs) and that the IOC is the supreme authority of the Olympic Movement. The Olympic Movement should also include the Organizing Committees of the Olympic Games (OCOGs or COJOs), which are groups formed in the host cities, whose only purpose is the staging of the Olympic Games.

The International Federations are the international governing bodies of the individual sports on the Olympic Program, and also of the IOC affiliated sports. The IOC gives the IFs almost complete autonomy in designing, organizing, and regulating the Olympic competitions under their aegis. The IFs define amateurism for each sport and thus Olympic eligibility. The IFs provide the international officials who conduct the Olympic events. The IFs also set qualifying regulations for the Olympic sports, as it would not be possible for all athletes who wish to compete at the Olympic Games to do so.

National Olympic Committees are the governing bodies of Olympic sports in their respective countries or areas. (This is an important distinction as not all NOCs represent autonomous nations.) The NOCs are responsible for fielding Olympic teams to represent their nation or NOC. The NOCs also work closely with groups termed National Governing Bodies (NGBs). NGBs are the national governing organizations for individual sports. They come under the umbrella both of their own NOC and their own IF. Thus, for example, U.S.A. Track & Field (US-ATF), which governs track & field in the United States, is a subset of both its NOC, the U.S. Olympic Committee, and its IF, the International Amateur Athletic Federation.

The philosophy of Olympism is even more difficult to define with precision, but certainly stems from the writings and philosophy of Coubertin. The IOC defines Olympism in the *Olympic Charter* as follows: "Olympism is a philosophy of life, exalting and combining in a balanced whole the qualities of body, will and mind. Blending sport with culture and education, Olympism seeks to create a way of life based on the joy found in effort, the educational value of good example, and respect for universal fundamental ethical principles. The goal of Olympism is to place everywhere sport at the service of the harmonious development of man, with a view to encouraging the establishment of a peaceful society concerned with the preservation of human dignity."[2]

However, most scholars of the Olympic Movement would tell you that Olympism is even more encompassing than the above rather broad definition. Coubertin considered sport a method of education, and stated that, "sport is not a luxury activity, or an activity for the idle, or even a physical compensation for cerebral work. It is, on the contrary, a possible source of inner improvement for everyone. Sport is part of every man and woman's heritage and its absence can never be compensated for."[3]

This basically outlines Coubertin's philosophy of "sport for all," a concept which is a cornerstone of the modern Olympic Movement. In 1919, Coubertin defined this philosophy thusly: "All sports for all people. This motto will no doubt be criticized as utopian lunacy, but that doesn't worry me. I have given it considerable thought and I believe its realization is just and possible."[4] He also noted, "Class distinctions should have no place in sport."[5]

On Olympism, Coubertin defined it as, " . . . not a system but a state of mind. It may be applied to the most diverse situations and is not the exclusive monopoly of any one race or time. The Olympic spirit is a state of mind created by the cultivation of both effort and eurhythmy . . . which in a paradoxical sense are the basis of all absolute virility."[6]

Coubertin was not a great classics scholar, but he understood a great deal about the religious and philosophical aspects of the Ancient Olympic Games. His philosophy of Olympism was based on the ancient Greek ideal of *kalokagathia,* or the harmonic combination of beauty and goodness. Certainly, his philosophy of sport for all is also based somewhat on the Greek motto of *Mens sana in corpore sano,* or "a sound mind in a sound body."

To the bulk of the world, the Olympic Movement is the Olympic Games, and nothing else. Certainly they are the best-publicized aspect of the Olympic Movement, and the Olympic Games themselves now see politicians, philosophers, and the IOC itself wrestling with several controversial issues pertaining to the Games.

One is the commercialization of the Olympic Games. Although the IOC has become financially independent, this is not always considered a good thing. Many sports historians and philosophers of sport yearn for the days when Avery Brundage was IOC President and the IOC was run on a financial shoestring. Though it was less glamorous, Brundage simply did not allow commercialism and fought its encroachment into the Olympic Games to his dying day.

Commercialism has become a much bigger problem for the IOC now that financial riches have befallen the Olympic Movement. In the 1980s, the IOC President, Juan Antonio Samaranch, stated that one of his goals was to bring the IOC financial freedom. In the 1970s, although television rights fees for the Olympic Games were increasing dramatically, bringing significant dollars to the IOC, the IOC was fully dependent on the largesse of the television networks, notably the American network hosting the Olympic Games. Samaranch was assisted by IOC Member Dick Pound, a Canadian tax lawyer, and together they devised The Olympic Programme, known as *TOP.* TOP enlists major international corporations to support the Olympic Movement during each millennium. Membership in TOP is very expensive, with fees now reaching toward $50 million/quadrennium, but it is also very exclusive. Pound and the IOC made the exclusivity important, but demanded that the corporations pay dearly for it. Via TOP, and television rights fees, which continued to increase dramatically through the 1980s, the IOC was awash with riches by the 1990s.

And at Atlanta in 1996, many people thought that these riches had gone overboard in an orgiastic display of commercialism. Downtown

Atlanta was a city plastered with marketing and merchants, with every corporation, and seemingly everybody, trying to sell something related to the Olympic Games. Even the IOC was taken aback, stating that something would have to be done in the future to control this, and prevent such gross spectacles at future Olympic Games.

Another debate that has enveloped the Olympic Movement has been the concept of amateurism, a concept that has engendered multiple philosophical imbroglios since its inception in 19th century England. Coubertin actually tired of debating the concepts of amateurism, finally declaring, "All I ask of the athlete . . . is loyalty to sport."[7] The Ancient Olympic Games are considered by many journalists and the lay public to have been contested by "amateur" athletes, but that is almost certainly false. In fact, the Ancient Greeks did not even have a word for the modern term "amateur," and all of the greatest Greek athletes were paid, and paid well, for their efforts.

Amateurism with respect to the Olympic Games is also dying out. Each International Federation is now responsible for providing its own definition of amateurism. The IOC leaves Olympic eligibility requirements to the International Federations and this situation has allowed professionals to compete in the Olympic Games in many sports: track & field athletics, basketball, cycling, football (soccer), figure skating, and volleyball, among them.

Some sporting purists would demur, stating that the Olympics should remain an amateur festival, but they usually have only a neophyte's understanding of the original meaning of the Olympic Games and the Olympic Movement. In today's world, many of the top international athletes are highly paid for their performances, and to exclude them would prevent the world's greatest athletes from competing in the world's greatest sporting event—the Olympic Games. It is very unlikely, however, that prize money will be given at the Olympic Games. It is offered at many of the International Federation's World Championships, but Samaranch has noted, "I think the Olympic Games are different."[8]

"Gigantism" is a term that deals with the increasing size of the Olympic Games and the commensurate increase in costs. This concept is interwoven with the commercialism of the Olympic Games, because as the Games increase in size and thus become more expensive, increased financial resources must be generated via commercialism to conduct the Olympic Games and run the Olympic Movement.

Gigantism of the Olympic Games is a very difficult problem to solve. To make the Olympic Games smaller, only two real solutions exist: 1) decrease the number of sports and events; or 2) decrease the number of competitors in each sport. Decreasing the number of competitors also raises difficult philosophical questions. The simple solution would be to limit each event only to the top-rated athletes in the world in that event. But this would virtually eliminate many of the world's sporting nations. Of the 199 National Olympic Committees (NOCs) currently recognized by the IOC, only a few can be considered sporting powers. Sports facilities and training techniques are simply not available to many of the world's athletes. To limit events to only the top competitors would prevent many of the world's NOCs from competing in the Olympic Games. This completely violates the IOC's ideals of sport for all and of promoting internationalism and international goodwill by bringing together the youth of all nations in a great sporting festival.

Further, the IOC has now mandated that any sport wishing to be represented on the Olympic Program must present an equal program for men and women. While this is certainly desirable, it adds twice the number of athletes in the Olympic Games every time a sport is added. But in a few cases, women may not be fully qualified according to the *Olympic Charter*. To be eligible for a spot in the Olympic Games, a sport is supposed to be practiced in 75 nations and four continents. At the Olympic Winter Games, the rule is 40 nations and three continents. Recently, women's bobsled and skeleton racing has been added to the program of the 2002 Winter Olympics in Salt Lake City. But a few critics noted that there are not close to 40 nations in the world in which women compete in these two sports. Further, the same critics in the media have also questioned whether or not there are actually 40 nations that compete in skeleton racing for men.

But the IOC is fully committed to equalizing the Olympic Program for men and women. To this end, it has sponsored conferences on Women and Sport, at which all aspects of women's sports participation has been discussed. More recent societal questions have arisen, however. When South Africa banned blacks from their Olympic teams, the IOC took action, banning the South African Olympic Committee, effectively kicking South Africa out of the Olympics until that ban was lifted, and apartheid became only a memory. Many nations, notably the Muslim nations, and especially Afghanistan, have prohibitions against women in sport, in part because the standard athletic uniforms are often far too revealing for the religious strictures mandated in those nations. A prohibition against women in sport is as wrong as was apartheid in South African sports. The IOC has been mostly silent on this issue, but women's groups are mobilizing against these restrictions and the problem may become more prominent in the near future.

In addition to bringing in more women to the Olympic Program, the IOC has other problems concerning gigantism at the Olympic Games. Mainly, there are multiple sports that want to be in the Olympics. In addition to the Olympic Sport Federations, whose sports are on the Olympic Program, the IOC recognizes 26 other International Sporting Federations, including dance sport (ballroom dancing), sumo wrestling, rugby football, water skiing, bowling, and netball. All of them want to be in the Olympic Games. Further, the General Association of International Sports Federations (GAISF) currently (2000) recognizes 74 sporting federations (and 16 other federations ancillary to sport). Seventeen members of the GAISF are not even recognized by the IOC, but all of them would like to be. And if recognized, you can be certain that all of these sports will try to get on the Olympics Program.

At the December 1999 IOC Session in Lausanne, at which multiple changes to the *Olympic Charter*, and other rules, were made, one of these concerned the Olympic Program. The IOC mandated a maximum of 280 events in future Olympic Games, even though the Sydney Olympic Program for 2000 had 300 scheduled events. Further, 14 IFs are already applying for admission to the Olympic Program. Many close observers of the Olympic Movement feel this rule has minimal chance of actually being implemented.

The IOC also has an unwritten rule limiting the number of athletes at the Olympic Games to 10,000. There were 10,310 in Atlanta in 1996, and there were "only" 271 events, as opposed to the 300 held in Sydney. So by adding more events, or more sports, the IOC will need to decrease the number of athletes per event and sport. But there is another problem. The IOC is fully committed to having all member nations compete in the Olympics. In fact, the IOC 2000 Commission passed another change to the *Olympic Charter*, stating basically that all NOCs are expected to compete in the Olympic Games—an anti-boycott clause. So if there will be fewer athletes permitted per event, but all members NOCs are expected to compete, there may be less room for elite athletes in the Olympic Games. But the IOC does not want this either. Each year the IOC opens up the Olympic Program to more and more true professionals, and there are currently very few federations that limit who may compete in the Olympic Games in their sport.

None of these are easy problems concerning the Olympic Program, and it is not certain how they will be resolved. In an ideal world, all the best athletes from all the nations would compete in all the world's sports. But that would probably allow 20,000 athletes to compete and take gigantism up another level, and significantly increase the costs of the Olympic Games. Paying for these huge Games would be difficult, and the payment would likely be earned only by "selling the Olympic soul to the devil," or the television networks and marketing groups.

Many other problems are currently plaguing the IOC. Drug use in sports has become even more rampant in the past decade. Testing has seemed to have minimal effect. In 1998, the Tour de France was rocked by revelations of drug use among professional cyclists (who are now eligible to compete in the Olympic Games). It was not unexpected but it received major play in the media, both written and spoken, and it again cast international professional sport in a very bad light. The IOC has responded by forming the World Anti-Doping Agency (WADA). Announced in 1999, WADA will initially be headed by IOC Vice President Dick Pound. In early 1999, the IOC held a conference on the problems of doping in sport, which included setting up the structure of WADA. The IOC has passed several rules to help, including adding an anti-doping statement to the Olympic Oath, and perhaps most important, requiring that Olympic Sport Federations follow the rules of WADA and the IOC on doping in sport.

In addition to WADA, another international entity helps combat drugs in sports, the Court of Arbitration for Sport (CAS). The CAS was formed in the early 1980s and is based in Lausanne, Switzerland. However, in the late 1990s, the IOC increased its importance by requiring Olympic athletes to allow any disputes during the Olympic Games to be settled by the CAS, rather than going to the judicial system.

Of the many problems that have beset the Olympic Movement, it was rocked by its greatest scandal ever in late 1998, and one that threatened its very existence. In November 1998, a Salt Lake City television station revealed that the Salt Lake Bid Committee had paid the tuition for the daughter of an IOC member. It was not an isolated event. The ensuing scandal eventually saw 10 members of the IOC resign and the scandal spread beyond the Salt Lake City bid committee, with bid and organizing committees in Atlanta, Nagano, and Sydney being implicated. Further, the Toronto bid committee for the 1996 Olympics had released a report in 1991 that told of IOC members requesting and being given gifts in exchange for votes to become the Olympic host city.

The Olympic bribery scandal forced the IOC to confront its problems. It was investigated on several fronts, and several investigative reports were issued concerning the scandal. The IOC formed a committee, headed by IOC Vice President Dick Pound, and they released a report on the scandal in March 1999. Salt Lake City requested and received a similar report from its Board of Ethics. The United States Olympic Committee formed a commission, headed by former U.S. Senator George Mitchell, and their report was released in early March 1999. The United States Federal Bureau of Investigation (FBI) has also been investigating the Olympic Movement and the IOC, and that investigation continues through 2000.

In response to these reports, the IOC formed two important new commissions—the IOC Ethics Commission and the IOC 2000 Commission. The Ethics Commission set up guidelines for conduct by IOC Members and Bid Committees. The IOC 2000 Commission made 50 recommendations to the IOC, several of them based on the earlier reports, and in December 1999, at the IOC session, the IOC enacted all 50 of the recommendations, in an effort to overcome the effects of the scandal.

It is sad that the public, especially the American public, via the media, often hears about the Olympic Movement only during times of controversies. For there is much good in the Olympic Movement, and the IOC truly attempts to accomplish many admirable things. The Olympic Movement is first and foremost a movement of internationalism. The IOC wants to be known as a peace organization. To that end, it has recently reinstituted the Olympic Truce, reminiscent of the truce of Ancient Greece, with the Olympic Truce receiving the imprimatur of the United Nations.

Also, the drugs and doping problems in sport are often taken as a negative of the Olympic Games and international sport, but in reality, the IOC was the first sporting organization to begin testing for drugs, and it still institutes stricter penalties, and enforces the penalties more often, than the four North American professional sports (baseball, football, basketball, and ice hockey), and the major European professional sports of cycling and soccer football. Unfortunately, this is never mentioned by the press, who instead prefer to dote on the marketing powerhouses of the professional sports, and emphasize every drug penalty handed out to an Olympic athlete.

During the 1990s, the IOC also began a closer alliance with the United Nations, and specifically UNESCO. Together, these two organizations promoted the passage of a modern version of the Olympic Truce, calling for the cessation of international hostilities during the celebration of the Olympic Games and Olympic Winter Games.

Finally, the IOC has also become more concerned with the environment of late. It now promotes, and virtually demands, the concept of "green" Olympic Games. This concept really began with the Lillehammer Winter Olympics of 1994. The Lillehammer Organizing Committee designed all of their sports stadia and settings with the concept of doing minimal harm to the environment. The IOC has seized upon this idea as a good one, and is now requiring that future candidate cities give primary consideration to this concept.

Thus, there are many good things that the IOC does under the umbrella of the Olympic Movement, even if many of them are transparent to the public. In fact, a few critics of the IOC have recently said that they actually try to do too much. These critics have noted that the IOC should return to what is its primary mission—to hold international sporting events in the form of the Olympic Games and the Olympic Winter Games. Although it is difficult to criticize an organization for trying to do too many good things, people who continually criticize the IOC add even that to their myriad polemics. The IOC has been the recipient of a great deal of money since the early 1980s and it is trying to use this money to accomplish what it considers necessary to promote international sport as a means to a more peaceful world.

Thus, we have come full circle, from a small, simple religious festival in Ancient Greece, to a huge festival seen on television by billions of people that American sportscaster Jim McKay has termed, "The largest peacetime gathering of humanity in the history of the world."[9] To the athletes, the Olympic Games are the supreme test of their abilities. But even to the athletes, the Olympic Games are more than that, witnessed by the statement of Al Oerter, an Olympic legend and four-time discus gold medalist: "There is no job, no amount of power, no money to approach the Olympic experience."[10]

Though "just" a big sporting event, even the politicians have realized that the Olympics are more than that. Former California Governor Jerry

Brown once commented, "These are just games and people should see them for fun; there shouldn't be any ulterior motives to the Olympics. They're just games, frivolous things. They're not really necessary. But don't forget some of the least necessary things in life are the most important. Art, religion, friendship, leisure time, games—they make life worth living."[11]

And the Olympic Movement itself, as discussed, encompasses much more than the Olympic Games. Via its philosophy of Olympism, it attempts to bring together people of all nationalities in peaceful competition, creating an air of internationalism rarely seen in today's divisive world. This has perhaps been best summed up by the emotional speech of Lord Killanin, outgoing IOC President, at the closing ceremonies of the 1980 Lake Placid Winter Olympics. Referring specifically to the planned U.S.-driven boycott of the Moscow Olympics, Killanin stated, "Ladies and gentlemen, I feel these Games have proved that we do have something to contribute to the mutual understanding of the world, what we have in common and not what our differences are. If we can all come together it will be for a better world and we shall avoid the holocaust, which may well be upon us if we are not careful."[12]

NOTES

1. Speech to the sports youth of all nations at Olympia, Greece, 17 April 1927; quoted in *The International Pierre de Coubertin Committee*, p. 15. (Lausanne: International Pierre de Coubertin, 1983.)

2. *Olympic Charter*, p. 10. Lausanne: International Olympic Committee, 1995.

3. Durántez Corral, Conrado. *Pierre de Coubertin: The Olympic Humanist*, p. 27. Lausanne: International Olympic Committee and International Pierre de Coubertin Committee, 1994.

4. *Ibid*, p. 29.

5. *Ibid*, p. 29.

6. *Ibid*, p. 36.

7. *Ibid*, p. 33.

8. *USA Today*, March 1995.

9. Mallon, Bill. *The Olympics: A Bibliography*, p. ix. New York: Garland, 1984.

10. *Ibid*, p. v.

11. *Los Angeles Times*, 1982.

12. Lord Killanin. *My Olympic Years*, p. 187. London: Secker & Wartburg, 1983.

The Dictionary

– A –

Aamodt, Kjetil André [NOR–ASK]. B. 2 September 1971. Kjetil André Aamodt's record of five Olympic medals (one gold, two silver, two bronze) in Alpine skiing has only been matched by Vreni Schneider (SUI), Alberto Tomba (ITA), and Katja Seizinger (GER) (qq.v.). Aamodt's only gold medal came in the super giant slalom in 1992 when he also took bronze in the giant slalom. In 1994, he won a silver in the downhill and Alpine combined and a bronze in the super giant slalom.

Acrobatics. Acrobatics has never been contested at the Olympic Games, even as a demonstration sport. However, the International Federation of Sports Acrobatics (IFSA) has previously been recognized by the IOC, although it is not currently recognized as of 2000.

Aeronautics. Aeronautics is governed internationally by the Fédération Aéronautique Internationale (FAI), which was created in 1905 and is recognized by the IOC. There are 95 affiliated nations as of late 2000. At the 1936 Olympic Games a gold medal for Merit for Aeronautics was presented to Hermann Schreiber.

Afghanistan [AFG]. Afghanistan first competed at the 1936 Olympics in Berlin, the same year in which its National Olympic Committee was recognized by the IOC. Since then the country has failed to be represented only at the Olympic Games of 1952, 1976, 1984, 1992, and 2000. Afghanistan's National Olympic Committee was suspended by the IOC in 1999, and it was not eligible to compete at Sydney. Afghanistan has never competed at the Olympic Winter Games.

No Afghan athlete has won a medal while representing Afghanistan, their best finish being fifth by Mohammed Ebrahimi in 1964 featherweight freestyle wrestling. The most successful Afghani at the Olympic games was Sayid M. Yusuf, who won a gold medal in 1928 as a member of the Indian hockey (field) team.

Albania [ALB]. Albania's Olympic Committee was founded in 1958, and recognized by the IOC in 1959, but Albania did not compete at the Olympics until 1972. Albania then did not compete again at the Olympics for 20 years, returning in 1992, 1996, and 2000. Albania has not won any medals, and has never competed at the Olympic Winter Games.

Alekseyev, Vasiliy Ivanovich [URS–WLT]. B. 7 January 1942, Pokrovo-Shishkino, Ryazan Oblast. Unbeaten from 1970 to 1978, Vasiliy Alekseyev is the greatest super-heavyweight lifter in history. His feat of winning eight successive gold medals at the Olympic Games and World Championships (1970–1977) equaled the record of Americans John Davis and Tommy Kono (qq.v.). Alekseyev won the gold medal in the unlimited class at the 1972 and 1976 Olympics. He competed in 1980 at Moscow, although injured, but did not finish. Alekseyev also won eight European titles and set 79 world records. He was finally defeated at the 1978 World Championships when suffering from a damaged hip tendon.

Algeria [ALG]. Algeria formed a National Olympic Committee in 1963 that was recognized by the IOC in 1964, and Algeria first competed officially at the 1964 Olympic Games. It has since competed at the Olympic Games of 1968, 1972, and all Olympics since 1980. Algeria competed at the Winter Olympics for the only time to date in 1992. Through 2000, Algerians have won seven medals, five in boxing and two in track & field athletics. Prior to Algeria's independence in July 1962, several Algerian athletes competed for France at the Olympics. The first were four gymnasts from Oran who took part in the 1900 Olympic Games and they had the distinction of being the first African Olympians. Two Olympic marathon winners, Mohammed Bouguerra El Ouafi (1928), and Alain Mimoun O'Kacha (1956), were both Algerians representing France.

Ali, Muhammad (né Cassius Marcellus Clay) [USA–BOX]. B. 17 January 1942, Louisville, Kentucky. Muhammad Ali first gained international prominence as Cassius Clay by winning the light-heavyweight gold medal at the 1960 Rome Olympics. In February 1964, he upset Sonny Liston to win the world heavyweight championship. Shortly after the fight, he embraced the Muslim faith and took the name Muhammad Ali. No fighter defeated him for the rest of the 1960s. But Ali was defeated by the U.S. draft board when he refused induction to military service based on a conscientious objection, and he was subsequently stripped of his heavyweight title. Eventually, Ali won his battle against the draft board in the Supreme Court, but the best years of his career were lost. He returned to fighting in 1970 and the next year lost a much ballyhooed fight against Joe Frazier (q.v.). In 1974, Ali regained the heavyweight championship against George Foreman (q.v.) and, after losing to Leon Spinks in 1978, he would become the only man to hold the title three times by defeating Spinks in a rematch. Ali's career professional record was 56 wins (37 by knockout) and 5 losses. At the 1996 Olympic Games, Ali was given the honor of lighting the Olympic Flame (q.v.) at the Opening Ceremony. Sadly, he now suffers from a relatively advanced case of Parkinson's Disease.

Alpine Skiing. Alpine ski racing is the newer form of ski racing, as Nordic (q.v.), or cross-country, competitions were held in the Scandinavian countries for many years before Alpine racing was developed. The first known Alpine skiing race was in 1911 at Montana, Switzerland, when the British organized a downhill race for a challenge cup given by Lord Roberts of Kandahar. The first slalom-style race was held in 1922 at Mürren, Switzerland.

Alpine skiing was first placed on the Olympic program in 1936 at Garmisch-Partenkirchen. The only event that year was a combined competition of both downhill and slalom. In 1948, this was held again along with separate downhill and slalom races. In 1952, the giant slalom was added as an event, and in 1988, the super giant slalom became a fourth separate event. Alpine combination, a point-scored mix of downhill and slalom, returned to the Olympic Winter Program in 1988, after not being contested from 1952 to 1984.

Events for both sexes were held in 1936, and have been at all Olympics since. Men and women contest Alpine skiing separately.

Interestingly, the program for men and women has been identical at all Olympics. The sport is governed by the Fédération Internationale de Ski (FIS) which had 100 member nations as of April 2000.

The two greatest Alpine skiers among the men have been Toni Sailer of Austria and Jean-Claude Killy of France (qq.v.), both of whom won all three gold medals available, in 1956 and 1968, respectively. Kjetil André Aamodt of Norway, Alberto Tomba of Italy, Vreni Schneider of Switzerland, and Katja Seizinger of Germany (qq.v.) have won the most Olympic medals with five each. Austria, Switzerland, and France have been the top nations in Olympic Alpine skiing, with Italy and the United States not far behind.

Alpinism. Alpinism is governed internationally by the Union Internationale des Associations d'Alpinisme (UIAA), also known by the name of The International Mountaineering and Climbing Federation. It was created in 1932 and is recognized by the IOC, with 82 affiliated nations as of 2000. Gold medals for Merit for Alpinism were presented at the 1924, 1932, and 1936 Olympic Games. In addition, Coubertin had plans for medals to be awarded for alpinism at the Olympic Games.

American Football. *See* FOOTBALL, AMERICAN.

American Samoa [ASA]. American Samoa has competed at the 1988, 1992, 1996, and 2000 Olympics and the 1994 Olympic Winter Games. In 1992, Robert Peden won two matches in flyweight boxing to finish equal fifth of 30 in his class, the top finish to date from this small island country.

Ancient Olympic Games. The Ancient Olympic Games were one of the four great Panhellenic sporting festivals of Ancient Greece, along with the Isthmian, Nemean, and Pythian Games (qq.v.). The Olympic Games were considered to be the greatest of the Panhellenic contests. The first recorded Olympics are known to have been held in 776 B.C., although it is probable that they began several centuries earlier. The Games lasted until 393 A.D. when they were banned by imperial decree of the Roman Emperor Theodosius I. The Ancient Olympic Games were held in Olympia, which was near the city-state of Elis on the Greek Peloponnesus. (They were *not* held on or near Mt. Olympus, as is often incorrectly written.) The Ancient Olympic Games were held quadrennially. Winners at the Ancient Olympic Games received crowns of wild olive.

The origins of the Ancient Olympic Games are uncertain, but several traditional explanations exist. One connects the Games to Pelops, after whom the Peloponnesus was named. Pelops was a Phrygian who made his way to the peninsula which would later take his name. There he defeated Oenomaus, King of Pisa, in a chariot race, which Oenomaus had ordered as a race in which Pelops could win the hand of his daughter, Hippodameia. Oenomaus was thrown from his chariot and killed and Pelops was worshipped as a hero. He took over the kingdom and the Games were supposedly held at his tomb and in his honor. Later beliefs, popularized by Pindar (q.v.), state that the Games originated to honor Hercules and he founded them after his victory over Augeas. Hercules declared the Games to be in honor of his father, Zeus.

Originally, the Ancient Olympic Games consisted of only a single footrace, one length of the Ancient Olympic stadium of about 192 meters, and now termed the *stadion* (q.v.) race. Champions are recorded in this event from 776 B.C. (Coroebus of Elis) until 269 A.D. A second race of two laps of the stadium, termed the *diaulos* (q.v.), was added in 724 B.C., followed in 720 B.C. by the *dolichos* (q.v.), which was a long distance race of about 20–25 laps of the stadium. Wrestling champions are recorded from 708 B.C., while boxing (q.v.) was added to the list of victors in 688 B.C. The pentathlon (q.v.), an all-around championship of five events, was added at the Olympics of 708 B.C. The pankration (q.v.), which was a brutal combination of wrestling and boxing, was known to have been contested at the Ancient Olympics from 648 B.C.

In addition to these, a number of horse races and chariot races were contested at the Olympic Games. There were events at Olympia for boys, which was defined as being older than 12 but less than 18 years old. Competitions for heralds and lyre playing were also contested at the Ancient Olympics.

Athletes from the Peloponnesus dominated the earliest Olympics, winning the first 13 *stadion* events, but Greeks from other city-states later produced many Olympic champions. Elis produced the most known Ancient Olympic champions with 110 recorded victories, followed by Sparta with 76 known victories. In the later years of the Ancient Olympics, athletes from the Roman Empire began to compete at Olympia, winning many titles. The Ancient Olympic Games reached their zenith in the Golden Age of Greece, dimming once the Roman Empire took over the celebrations.

Andersen, Hjalmar Johan "Hjallis" [NOR–SSK]. B. 12 March 1923, Rødoy. Hjallis Andersen was the winner of three gold medals at the 1952 Winter Games (1,500 meters, 5,000 meters, 10,000 meters). His winning margin in the 5,000 meters was an astounding 11 seconds and he also won the 10,000 meters by a substantial margin. Andersen retired after the 1952 Games but returned to competition in 1954 to win his fourth Norwegian title, having earlier won the World, European, and Norwegian all-around titles in 1950–1952. He set one world record at 5,000 meters and three at 10,000 meters.

Anderson, Paul Edward [USA–WLT]. B. 17 October 1932, Toccao, Georgia. D. 15 August 1994, Vidalia, Georgia. After winning the world heavyweight title by a record margin in 1955, Paul Anderson won the Olympic gold medal in Melbourne the following year. He was quite possibly the strongest man who ever lived. Anderson set hundreds of records as a powerlifter, including a bench press of 625 lbs. (284 kg.), a squat with 1,200 lbs. (545 kg.), a dead-lift of 820 lbs. (373 kg.), and three repetitions in the squat with 900 lbs. (409 kg.). In addition he performed a back-lift off trestles, supporting 6,270 lbs. (2,850 kg.)—the greatest weight ever lifted by a human.

Andersson, Agneta [SWE–CAN]. B. 25 April 1961, Karlskoga. With seven Olympic medals and three gold medals, Sweden's Agneta Andersson trails only Birgit Schmidt-Fischer among female canoeists at the Olympics. Andersson began her Olympic career in 1984, winning gold in both the K1 and K2 events and a silver in the K4. She competed at the 1988 Olympics but failed to medal. In 1992, she won silver at K2 and bronze at K4. She ended her career in 1996 with gold in K2 and bronze in the K4 event. Andersson was less successful at the World Championships in terms of titles, claiming only the 1993 K2 gold, but she won 11 medals at the Worlds in an international career that began in 1979.

Andorra [AND]. At the end of 1967, an Andorran committee that had been set up to form an NOC, approached the IOC with a view to obtaining recognition in time to send a team of Alpine skiers to the 1968 Olympic Winter Games in Grenoble. Because the draft constitution submitted did not comply with the Olympic rules on many points, the application was rejected and it was not until 1975 that the IOC approved a revised set of rules. This enabled Andorra to take part in the 1976 Olympic Winter Games in Innsbruck. Since then, they have competed in every Olympics, both Winter and Summer. Andorra has not yet won a medal at the Olympics.

Andrianov, Nikolay Yefimovich [URS–GYM]. B. 14 October 1952, Vladimir. Nikolay Andrianov was the most successful Olympic male gymnast of all time. Between 1972 and 1980, he won seven gold medals (six individual, one team), five silver, and three bronze for a total of 15 medals, an Olympic record for men in any sport. At the World Championships, he won gold on the rings in 1974, the all-around and rings in 1978, and the team event in 1979. He also won seven silver medals at the World Championships. Andrianov's international career started at the 1971 European Championships, where he was a late substitute but he won six medals that year, including a bronze in the all-around. In individual European Championships, he eventually won eight gold, six silver, and two bronze medals.

Angola [ANG]. Angola's first application for Olympic recognition was rejected at the 1975 IOC session in Lausanne but after the formation of a National Olympic Committee in 1979, recognition was granted in 1980. After first competing at the Olympics that year, Angola has also competed at the Olympic Games of 1988, 1992, 1996, and 2000, but has not yet competed at the Olympic Winter Games. The top Angolan Olympic performance likely occurred in 1992 at Barcelona when its basketball team qualified for the Olympics, but drew the United States "Dream Team" (q.v.) as a first-round opponent. It eventually finished 10th of 12 teams. In 1996, Angola's women handball team did qualify for the Olympic tournament, finishing 8th of eight teams. In 1996, their women's handball team also qualified for the Olympics, also finishing in 8th, albeit last, place.

Antigua and Barbuda [ANT]. Antigua and Barbuda formed an NOC in 1965 with the object of participating in the 1966 British Commonwealth Games that year. After being refused recognition in 1975, because its statutes did not conform with IOC requirements, recognition was granted in 1976, and Antigua and Barbuda competed at the 1976 Olympic Games. It has participated at all subsequent Summer Games except for 1980, but has not yet competed at the Olympic Winter Games. Antigua and Barbuda has not yet won a medal at the Olympics.

Antilles (West Indies). *See* WEST INDIES FEDERATION.

Apene—Ancient Olympic Sport. The apene race was a chariot race in which two mules pulled the chariot. The first known winner was Thersias of Thessaly in 500 B.C. The event was discontinued after 444 B.C.

Aquatics. The International Olympic Committee recognizes a sport termed *aquatics*, which consists of four disciplines (q.v.)—swimming, diving, synchronized swimming, and water polo (qq.v.). Aquatics is governed by the Fédration Internationale de Natation Amateur (FINA), which was formed in 1908 and currently has 176 members.

Archery. Though only recently returned to the Olympic program, archery is one of the oldest known sports. Use of the bow and arrow for hunting can be traced back to the Aurignacians, a race of people existing 15,000 years ago. By the 14th century, archers were found to be valuable as soldiers and the English kings made archery practice mandatory for the British soldiers. Archery as a sport became popular in the 16th and 17th centuries. In 1676, the first organized group, the Royal Company of Archers, was formed in England for the purpose of advancing the sport. This was followed in 1781 by the Royal Toxophilite Society. The first British championships were conducted in 1844.

Archery is governed worldwide by the Fédération Internationale de Tir à l'Arc (FITA), which was founded in 1931. Through 2000, 128 nations were members of FITA. Archery was first held as a sport in the 1900 Paris Olympics and again in 1904, 1908, and 1920, but then left the Olympic Program. In those years, it was possible for an athlete to compete in multiple events and win several medals. The top Olympic medal winner is Hubert Van Innis of Belgium, who competed in the 1900 and 1920 Olympics, winning 10 medals, 6 of them gold.

When the sport was returned to the Olympics in 1972, there was only one event for men and one for women. In 1988, team events for men and women were added to the program. Also, in 1988, the individual formats were changed. Previously (1972–1984), men and women shot a Double FITA Round (288 arrow at various distances). Now, qualifying is contested over 72 arrows, and the archers and teams then engage in single-elimination matches until a champion is crowned.

Argentina [ARG]. Argentina first competed officially at the 1924 Olympics in Paris. Prior to that, three Argentine athletes had competed at the Olympics—Eduardo Camet as a fencer in 1900, Henri Torromé in 1908 figure skating, and a boxer, Angel Rodriguez, in 1920. Since 1924, Argentina has competed at every Olympic Games with the exception of 1980. Argentina has competed at the Olympic Winter Games of 1928, 1948, 1952, and all Winter Games since 1960. Through 1998, Argentine athletes have won 54 medals, 13 of them gold. Argentina has won more Olympic gold medals than any other South American country.

Armenia [ARM]. Armenia's first connection with the Modern Olympics can be traced to the 1912 Olympics when two Armenian track & field athletes represented Turkey. These two athletes, Mığır Mığıryan and Haret Papazyan, comprised the entire Turkish team in 1912, but they had, in fact, been sent to Stockholm by the Armenian General Sports Union. From 1918, Armenia enjoyed a brief period of independence and planned to take part in the 1920 Olympics, but their hopes were thwarted when the country was occupied by Russian forces in 1920. For many years, the Russian IOC Member, Prince Urosov, championed the cause of a group of émigrés known as the *Young Armenian Emigrants Union*, but he failed to gain Olympic recognition for them. In his *Olympic Memoirs*, Coubertin aptly wrote, "Armenia existed only as a hope and a memory in the hearts of its loyal subjects."

As part of the Soviet Union, Armenian athletes competed for the USSR Olympic team from 1952 to 1988 and in 1992 they formed part of the Unified Team (q.v.). Having eventually obtained independence, an NOC was established in 1990 and IOC recognition was sought the following year. This was provisionally granted in 1992 and full IOC recognition was given in 1993, thereby enabling Armenia to compete as an independent nation at the Olympics. Armenia competed for the first time at the 1994 Olympic Winter Games in Lillehammer. At the Lillehammer opening ceremony, the Armenians wore replicas of the uniform that they had hoped to wear at the 1920 Olympics. Armenia first competed at the Summer Olympics in 1996. Armenia has won three Olympic medals, one of each color.

Art Contests. Art contests were held at the Olympics of 1912, 1920, 1924, 1928, 1932, 1936, and 1948. The winners of the competitions were awarded gold, silver, and bronze medals, similar to the winners of the athletic competitions. The events were inspired by Pierre de Coubertin (q.v.), who wished to combine the competitions in sports with competitions in the arts. The art competitions were dropped from the Olympic program because of the difficulty of determining the amateur status of the artists. Competitions were held in Architectural Designs, Designs for Town Planning, Sculpture—Medals, Sculpture—Reliefs, Sculpture—Any Kind, Applied Graphics, Drawings and Water-Colors, Other Graphic Arts, Paintings, Dramatic Works, Epic Works, Literature—All Kinds, Lyrics, Musical Compositions for One Instrument, Musical Compositions for Orchestra of All Kinds, Musical Compositions of Songs for Soloist or Choir, With or Without Instrumental Accompaniment, Music—All Kinds, Merit for Aeronautics, and Merit for Alpinism. Two artists won three medals—Alex Walter Diggelmann of Switzerland (all in applied graphics) and Joseph Petersen of Denmark (one in epic works and two in literature—all kinds). Jean Jacoby of Luxembourg was the only artist to win two gold medals in the art competitions; one in drawings and water colors and one in paintings. In 1912, de Coubertin won a gold medal in the literature category. Coubertin's gold medal was for his work entitled "Ode to Sport," which he entered under the dual pseudonym of Georg Hohrod and Martin Eschbach. Two arts medalists also won medals in sports at the Olympic Games. Alfred Hajós of Hungary won two swimming gold medals in 1896 and a medal for designs for town planning in 1924. Walter Winans, who won running deer shooting medals in 1908 and 1912 also won an arts gold medal in sculpture in 1912.

Aruba [ARU]. Aruba's Olympic Committee was formed in 1985 and recognized by the IOC in 1986. Aruba competed in the Olympic Games for the first time in 1988 at Seoul and also competed in 1992, 1996, and 2000, but has not yet competed at the Olympic Winter Games.

Association des Comités Nationaux Olympiques [ACNO]. The Association des Comités Nationaux Olympiques was formed in 1968 by Giulio Onesti, then the president of the Italian Olympic Committee, as a method of uniting the various National Olympic Committees. Originally entitled the *PGA (Permanent General Assembly of National Olympic Committees)*, this would allow them a more unified voice to present their concerns to the International Olympic Committee. This union of NOCs greatly displeased then IOC president Avery Brundage. The group was later renamed the *Association of National Olympic Committees (ANOC)*, but is better known by the French name given. ACNO is currently based in Paris and its president, as of 2000, is Mexico's Mario Vázquez Raña. Formation of the ACNO has been responsible for the foundation of various continental and regional associations of National Olympic Committees. *See also* ASSOCIATION DES COMITÉS NATIONAUX OLYMPIQUES D'AFRIQUE [ACNOA]; EUROPEAN OLYMPIC COMMITTEES [EOC]; OCEANIA NATIONAL OLYMPIC COMMITTEES [ONOC]; OLYMPIC COUNCIL OF ASIA [OCA]; ORGANIZACIÓN DEPORTIVA CENTROAMERICANA Y DEL CARIBE [ODECABE]; and PAN AMERICAN SPORTS ORGANIZATION [PASO].

Association des Comités Nationaux Olympiques d'Afrique [ACNOA]. This group consists of the National Olympic Committees from the African nations. The association has its headquarters in Yaoundé, Cameroon. The president of ACNOA is major-general Francis Nywangweso of Uganda and the secretary-general is Tomas Sithole of Zimbabwe (both as of December 2000).

Association des Comités Nationaux Olympiques d'Europe [AC-NOE]. *See* EUROPEAN OLYMPIC COMMITTEES (EOC).

Association Générale des Fédérations Internationales de Sports [AGFIS]. *See* GENERAL ASSOCIATION OF INTERNATIONAL SPORTS FEDERATIONS (GAISF).

Association of the International Olympic Winter Sports Federations [AIOWF]. In 1982, led by Marc Hodler of Switzerland and the International Ski Federation, the Winter Sports Federations formed their own group, the Association of the International Winter Sports Federations. The AIOWF deals with specific questions concerning winter sports in general, and the Olympic Winter Games, in particular. It is also responsible for choosing the delegations and appointments of the winter sports representative to IOC Commissions (q.v.). The group is based in Oberhofen, Switzerland. Hodler has been the president since the group's inception.

Association of Summer Olympic International Federations [ASOIF]. On 20 May 1983, 21 International Federations governing sports on the program of the Olympic Games met in Lausanne and established the Association of Summer Olympic International Federations (ASOIF). The ASOIF constitution defines its purpose as "to coordinate and defend the common interests of its members to ensure close cooperation between them, the members of the Olympic Movement and those of other organizations, with the aim of preserving the unity of the Olympic Movement while maintaining the authority, independence and autonomy of the member International Federations." The ASOIF is currently based in Rome, Italy, and its president, as of late 2000, is Denis Oswald of Switzerland and the Fédération Internationale des Sociétés d'Aviron (FISA).

Association of the IOC-Recognized International Sports Federations [ARISF]. The IOC recognizes a number of international sports federations whose sports are not yet on the Olympic program. This recognition is important, for it is a first step toward getting a sport admitted to the Olympic program. As of April 2000, the IOC has recognized the international federations for the following sports (in addition to those on the Olympic program): aeronautics, alpinism, automobile racing, billiards, body building, bowling, bowls, bridge, chess, dance sport, golf, karate, korfball, life saving, motorboating, motorcycling, netball, orienteering, pelota basque, polo, racquetball, roller skating, rugby football, squash, sumo wrestling, surfing, tug-of-war, underwater swimming, water skiing, and wushu (qq.v.). These IOC Recognized International Sports Federations have grouped together to form the Association of the IOC Recognized International Sports Federations. They are headquartered in Leidschendan, The Netherlands, and the ARISF currently has 30 member federations, as noted. The current (2000) president is Ralf Froehling of the Union Internationale Motonautique. The statutes of the ARISF state that its aims are "to determine the consensus of the member federations on questions relating to the Olympic Movement . . . and to coordinate and defend the common interest of its members in [that] context."

Astakhova, Polina Grigoryevna [URS/UKR–GYM]. B. 30 October 1936, Donetsk, The Ukraine. Polina Astakhova won team gold medals at the 1956, 1960, and 1964 Olympic Games, a feat that she shares with Larisa Latynina, making them the only gymnasts to be members of three gold-medal winning teams. Astakhova also won a gold on the uneven parallel bars and placed third in the individual all-around in both 1960 and 1964. She added silver medals in both 1960 and 1964 in the floor exercises, and her final Olympic tally included 10 medals: five gold, three silver, and two bronze. At the world championships, she was less successful, but was a member of the Soviet Union team that won the team title in both 1958 and 1962.

Athletes Commission. The Athletes Commission was formed in 1981 as a solution to the complaint at the 1981 Olympic Congress that Olympic athletes had very little say in the workings of the International Olympic Committee (IOC) (q.v.) and the Olympic Movement. It was felt that the IOC had too few former Olympic athletes among its members, that those athletes had competed many years previously, and that they were far removed from their competitive days. The only Chairman of the Athletes Commission has been Peter Tallberg of Finland, an IOC Member and a former yachtsman who competed in the Olympic Games in 1960, 1964, 1968, 1972, and 1980. The remainder of the Athletes Commission is made up of former Olympic athletes, most of whom are not IOC Members. The current vice chairman is Prince Albert of Monaco, an IOC Member but also a competitor in the bobsled events at three Olympic Winter Games. The Athletes Commission has been charged with three responsibilities: 1) discuss its views biannually with the IOC Executive Board and report to the IOC session, 2) delegate athlete representatives to other IOC commissions, and 3) establish working groups to act as liaison to the OCOGs.

Athletics (Track & Field). Athletics, or track & field, is the original Olympic sport. The first event contested in the Ancient Olympics (q.v.) was the *stadion* (q.v.), a sprint of about 190 meters. Recorded victors in this event are known as far back as 776 B.C. Other athletics events in the Ancient Olympics included longer races, races in armor, and a pentathlon consisting of the *stadion*, long jump, discus throw, javelin throw, and wrestling.

Throughout recorded sports history, athletics has always been practiced. Many of the attempted revivals of the Olympics in the 19th century consisted mostly of athletics events. Since the revival of the Olympics in 1896, athletics has been the most publicized sport on the Olympic program. Today, athletics is rivaled only by football (soccer) and volleyball as the sport practiced in the most countries in the world. The sport is governed internationally by the International Amateur Athletic Federation (IAAF), which was formed in 1912 and had 210 member nations as of 2000.

Athletics has been held at every Olympics. Women's athletics began at the 1928 Olympics and has been contested continually since. The program has varied but has been fairly standard since 1932. The current program includes sprint races (100, 200, and 400 meters), middle-distance races (800, 1,500, and 5,000 meters), distance races (10,000 meters and marathon [26+ miles]) (q.v.), hurdle races (110 meters for men, 100 meters for women, and 400 meters for both), steeplechase (3,000 meters for men only), walking events (20 km. for men and women, and 50 km. for men), flat jumping events (long jump and triple jump), vertical jumping events (high jump and pole vault), throwing events (shot put, discus throw, hammer throw, and javelin throw), and multi-events (decathlon for men [q.v.] and heptathlon for women).

Although women (q.v.) were first allowed to compete in only a few events, today they have a program with almost as many events as the men. The only current differences in the women's program is that they do not compete in a steeplechase event, they have only one walking event (20 km.), and they compete in the heptathlon, as opposed to the decathlon for men.

The United States' men have always been the top performers in the world in track & field athletics. Among the women, the USSR and the GDR were the top powers since their admission to the Olympics, and prior to their dissolution by the political events at the end of the 1980s.

Attempts at Revival. Prior to the 1896 Olympic Games in Athens, multiple efforts had been made at attempting to resurrect the Ancient Olympic Games (q.v.) and stage them with a program mainly containing contemporary events. These include Robert Dover's Cotswold Olimpick Games, the Much Wenlock Olympian Games, and the Zappas Olympic Games in Athens (qq.v.). Other attempts at Olympian-type festivals are known to have been held in Ramlösa, Sweden (near Helsingborg) in 1834 and 1836 under the initiative of Professor Gustav Johann Schartau of the University of Lund; in Montreal, Québec, Canada, in the early 1830s and 1840s; in England held by the National Olympian Association from 1866 to 1883, which was an offshoot of the Much Wenlock Olympian Games, as well as the Olympic Festivals of Liverpool (1862–1867); the Morpeth Olympic Games in Morpeth, England (1873–1958); and the Olympic Games at Lake Palič, held from 1880 to 1914 in Palič, a spa eight kilometers east of Subotica, then in Hungary and now in the Vojvodina province of Serbia. In addition, various Highland and Caledonian Games were held in the 19th century, which brought together various Celtic peoples in athletic competition. See Appendix XVIII for listing of all known attempts at revival prior to 1896. However, none of these events had the international flavor of Pierre de Coubertin's (q.v.) revived Olympic Games.

Much of the impetus for revival in the 19th century was due to recent archaeological finds at Ancient Olympia and other classical sites in Greece. These digs were initiated by A. Blouet, a Frenchman, and continued by the Germans, notably Ernst Curtius. They were begun in 1875 by Curtius and his reports on his finds were issued between

1890 and 1897. However, the German government published yearly reports between 1875 and 1881.

The idea of revival was also in the air for at least a century prior to Coubertin. The terms *Olympic* and *Olympian* was apparently used frequently to refer to any athletic contest. Note Shakespeare's phrases from the late 1500s: " . . . such rewards as victors weare at the Olympian Games" *(Henry VI,* Act 2) and " . . . Olympic wrestling" *(Troilus and Cressida,* Act 4). Milton discussed "As at th' Olympian Games or Pythian fields" in *Paradise Lost* in 1667.

Professor John Lucas of Penn State University discovered a letter from T. B. Hollis written in 1788 to Josiah Willard, president of Harvard University, in which Hollis states, "Our documents carry mention of an eventual rebirth of the Olympic Games in America. The friends of this latter [idea] want and pretend to be capable of it: after having acted according to Greek Principles, they must practice Greek exercises."

In 1793, Johannes C. F. Guts-Muths discussed the Ancient Olympics in his *Gymnastik für Jugend,* and by the second edition in 1804, he was considering a revival. In 1813, the philologist and historian Bartold Georg Niebuhr wrote of " . . . a vast hall [in Rome] which, once properly decorated, could serve for the resumption of the Olympic Games."

Thus, Pierre de Coubertin did not come to his Olympic idea without help. However, a great deal of credit is due him as he was the visionary who, apart from William Penny Brookes (q.v.), really envisioned the possibility of a great international festival, bringing together the youth of all nations in peaceful competition. Without Coubertin's vision, it is almost certain that the Olympic Games would have been revived. But it is not as certain that they would be anything like the Olympic Games we know today.

Aussie Rules. *See* FOOTBALL, AUSTRALIAN RULES.

Australia [AUS]. Australia, whose Olympic Committee was formed and recognized by the IOC in 1895, has competed at every Summer Olympic Games. In 1908 and 1912, it competed as *Australasia* in a combined team with New Zealand. Australia has also competed at the Olympic Winter Games—those of 1936 and continuously since 1952. Australia has been successful in many sports, but particularly so in swimming and track & field (qq.v.). Through 2000, Australia has won 350 medals, including one at the Olympic Winter Games, of which 102 were gold medals. Australia has also hosted the Games of the XVIth Olympiad in 1956 in Melbourne, and recently hosted the sublime Games of the XXVIIth Olympiad in 2000 in Sydney.

Australian Rules Football. *See* FOOTBALL, AUSTRALIAN RULES.

Austria [AUT]. Austria competed at the first Olympics in 1896 and has missed only one Games since—those of 1920 when it was not invited as an aggressor nation in World War I. Austria has also competed at every Olympic Winter Games, where it has often been the dominant nation in Alpine skiing (q.v.). It is one of only three countries (with Norway and Liechtenstein) to have won more medals at the Winter Olympics than at the Summer Olympics. Through 2000, Austrian athletes have won 146 medals (39 gold medals) at the Olympic Winter Games and 87 medals (20 gold medals) at the Summer Olympics. Austria has also twice hosted the Olympic Winter Games, those of 1964 and 1976, both times in Innsbruck.

Automobile Racing. Automobile racing has never been contested at the Olympic Games, even as a demonstration sport. But in 1900 at Paris, auto racing was contested during the sporting events held in conjunction with the Exposition Universelle. As it is difficult to know which events were Olympic in that year, some historians list the auto racing events in their records. In 1908 at London, automobile racing was on the preliminary program but the sport was not contested and there have been no moves to include the sport in the Olympic Games since. Internationally, automobile racing is governed by the Fédération Internationale de l'Automobile (FIA), which was founded in 1904 and currently has 117 affiliated member nations. Automobile racing is actually precluded by the *Olympic Charter,* in which Rule 52.4.2 states, "Sports, disciplines or events in which performance depends essentially on mechanical propulsion are not acceptable."

Averof, Georgios [GRE]. B. 15 August 1818, Metsovo, Greece. D. 15 July 1899, Alexandria, Egypt. Georgios Averof was a Greek merchant, resident in Egypt, who acquired enormous wealth as a trader in Alexandria. Averof's donation of almost one million drachma for the excavation and rebuilding of the ancient Panathenaic stadium for the 1896 Games ensured that the first Modern Olympics were staged in an appropriate setting. A dedicated patriot, he had already given several schools and a military academy to the nation but as a man of a shy, retiring nature, he declined an invitation to be a guest at the Olympic Games that he had personally financed. His generosity was marked by the erection of a life-size statue that was unveiled shortly before the Games opened. His nephew was a member of the IOC from 1926 to 1930.

Azerbaijan [AZE]. From 1952 to 1988 athletes from Azerbaijan formed part of the Soviet Union Olympic team and at Barcelona in 1992, four Azerbaijani athletes were chosen for the Unified Team. After independence and formation of an NOC, Azerbaijan was granted recognition by the IOC in 1992, and first competed as an independent nation at the 1996 Olympic Games and the 1998 Olympic Winter Games. Azerbaijan athletes have won four Olympic medals, including two gold medals.

– B –

Babashoff, Shirley Frances [USA–SWI]. B. 31 January 1957, Whittier, California. Shirley Babashoff was the winner of a record eight Olympic medals, a total matched at the time among Olympic women swimmers by Kornelia Ender and Dawn Fraser. Her two gold medals both came in the 4 x 100-meter freestyle relay (1972, 1976), to which she added two silver medals in 1972 and four in 1976. Babashoff was the world champion at 200 meters and 400 meters in 1975 and set many world records in individual and relay events between 1974 and 1976.

Badminton. Badminton was invented in India. It was adopted by English soldiers there in the 19th century, who brought the game to Britain and eventually to many other countries. The game was originally called *Poona*. The new sport took hold in England when it was exhibited there in 1873 at a party given by the Duke of Beaufort at his country estate, *Badminton*, in Gloucestershire.

Badminton was contested as a demonstration sport at the 1972 Olympic Games in Munich. It made its début as a full medal sport in 1992 at Barcelona. After 1972, it was not again a demonstration sport until its appearance at Barcelona on the medal program. This is an unusual mode of entry into the Olympics. Men and women compete in singles and doubles and there is a mixed doubles event at the Olympics. Badminton is governed by The International Badminton Federation (IBF), which was formed in 1934 and which had 145 members as of December 2000.

Bahamas, The [BAH]. Because the Bahamas did not have an NOC at the time of the 1948 Olympic Games, their two leading yachtsmen chose to represent Great Britain, which was permitted under Olympic rules as the Bahamas was a British colony. In 1952 an NOC was established and recognized by the IOC and the Bahamas competed at the Olympic Games under their own name for the first time that year. Since then they have failed to be represented only at the Moscow Games in 1980, and have not yet competed in the Olympic Winter Games. Bahamian athletes have won six medals.

Bahrain [BRN]. The Bahrain Olympic Committee was organized in 1978 and recognized by the IOC in 1979. Bahrain has competed at the Olympic Games of 1984, 1988, 1992, 1996, and 2000. The top finish by a Bahraini athlete was 14th in the 1992 men's hammer throw by Reyadh Rasheed Saad Al-Ameeri. Bahrain has not yet competed at the Olympic Winter Games.

Baillet-Latour, Count Henri de [BEL]. B. 1 March 1876, Antwerp. D. 6 January 1942, Brussels. Henri de Baillet-Latour was a Belgian aristocrat who proved himself to be an able sports administrator at an early age. Elected to the IOC in 1903 at the age of 27, he organized the Olympic Congress (q.v.) in Brussels two years later and, after playing a major role in securing the 1920 Games for Antwerp, he became president of the Belgian Olympic Committee in 1923, serving until 1942. He was named to the IOC Executive Board in 1921 and remained in that capacity until he took over as IOC president in 1925, following Coubertin's (q.v.) resignation. During his presidency, the IOC was concerned with the problems of the definition of an amateur and the program of the Olympic Games. Baillet-Latour remained president until his death in 1942.

Balczó, András [HUN–MOP]. B. 16 August 1938, Kondoros. András Balczó was the winner of a record six individual and seven team titles in the modern pentathlon (q.v.) at the World Championships. After placing fourth at the 1960 Olympics he won team gold and individual silver medals in 1968 and then, in 1972, he won the individual title and a silver medal in the team event for a total of six Olympic medals (three gold, three silver). Although the reigning world champion, Balczó did not compete in the 1964 Games, but his overall record is the greatest of any modern pentathlete.

Ballangrud, Ivar (né Ivar Eriksen) [NOR–SSK]. B. 7 March 1904, Lunner, Hadeland. D. 1 June 1969, Trondheim. Ivar Ballangrud's record of seven Olympic medals has only been matched by Clas Thunberg (FIN) among male speed skaters. In 1928, he won the 5,000 meters and, in 1936, he was the winner at 500 meters, 5,000 meters, and 10,000 meters. He also won two silver medals (1932, 1936) and a bronze (1928). Ballangrud's record at the World Championships has never been approached; he won the 5,000 meters seven times, the 1,500 meters and 10,000 meters four times each, and was a four-time winner of the overall title. He also set a total of five world records at 3,000 meters, 5,000 meters, and 10,000 meters.

Ballroom Dancing. *See* DANCE SPORT.

Bandy. Bandy was contested as a demonstration sport at the 1952 Olympic Winter Games. It is an outdoor form of ice hockey (q.v.) played on a large rink with 11 players to a side. The International Bandy Federation (IBF) is a provisional member of the General Association of International Sports Federations (GAISF) (q.v.), but it is not currently recognized by the IOC.

Bangladesh [BAN]. The Bangladesh Olympic Association was formed in 1979 and recognized by the IOC in 1980. Bangladesh did not compete in Moscow in 1980, but has been represented at all the Olympic Games since 1984. Bangladesh athletes have never competed at the Olympic Winter Games and the country has yet to win an Olympic medal.

Barbados [BAR]. The Barbados Olympic Association was formed in 1955, but, as an independent country, Barbados did not compete in the Olympics until 1964. Barbados has since competed at every Olympic Games except for 1980. It has not won a medal in those years. Barbados has not yet competed at the Olympic Winter Games. In 1960, Barbados competed with Jamaica and Trinidad representing the West Indies Federation. One of the Barbadan runners, James Wedderburn, ran with three Jamaicans as a member of the 4 x 400-meter relay team and helped win a bronze medal.

Baseball. Baseball is an American sport, the game having been invented in the early 19th century. Popular lore attributes its discovery to Abner Doubleday in Cooperstown, New York, but research indicates that it is unlikely that he actually discovered the game. Its exact origins are unclear, although it is probably based somewhat on the British games of cricket and rounders.

American baseball has been contested at the Olympics as a demonstration sport (q.v.) in 1912, 1936, 1956, 1964, 1984, and 1988. In 1952, Finnish baseball was demonstrated at the Helsinki Olympics. American baseball became a full medal sport at Barcelona in 1992. The Americans do not dominate the sport in international play because the Cubans and several Central American countries produce excellent teams, although the United States upset the Cubans and won the gold medal at Sydney in 2000. Internationally, baseball is governed by the International Baseball Association (IBA), which was founded in 1938 and has 109 members at the end of 2000.

Basketball. Basketball is one of the few sports for which the precise origin is known. The game was invented in 1891 by James W. Naismith, an instructor at the International YMCA Training School in Springfield, Massachusetts, now Springfield College. The game was originally played with peach baskets and an attendant on a ladder retrieved the ball after a made basket. Naismith formulated 13 rules of the game, of which 12 still form the basics of the modern game.

In 1936, basketball made its first appearance as a medal sport at the Olympics. In 1976, women's basketball was added to the program. The United States has dominated international basketball until recently. The U.S. won all the Olympic titles until 1972 when it was upset by the Soviet Union in a very controversial game. The Soviet women were originally the top team on the female side, but the U.S. women now have surpassed them.

Today, basketball has become one of the most popular sports in the world. U.S. college basketball is wildly popular in the United States and the National Basketball Association (NBA) has engendered international interest. In addition, multiple international leagues have added to the growth of the sport. In 1992, for the first time, the United States was allowed to use professional players from the NBA. This NBA All-Star Team, dubbed "The Dream Team" (q.v.) by the world's media, is certainly the greatest basketball team ever assembled and dominated the 1992 Olympic tournament. An NBA All-Star team also represented the United States in 1996 and 2000, winning those gold medals as well, though the margin between the NBA and the rest of the world is shrinking. The sport is governed worldwide by the Fédération Internationale de Basketball Amateur (FIBA). As a measure of its popularity, FIBA currently (2000) has 210 member nations. *See also* DREAM TEAM, THE—1992 USA BASKETBALL; UNITED STATES BASKETBALL TEAM—1960; and UNITED STATES BASKETBALL TEAM—1984.

Baszanowski, Waldemar [POL–WLT]. B. 15 August 1935, Grudziadz. Never weighing more than 70 kg., Waldemar Baszanowski was one of the greatest lifters ever pound-for-pound. He won gold medals in both 1964 and 1968 at the Olympics in the lightweight class and was also World Champion in 1961 and 1965. Baszanowski was a great technician who did very well in the quick lifts of snatch and clean & jerk, and was the first man to clean & jerk two-and-one-half times his bodyweight. He set 24 world records, capped by his greatest day, 26 June 1964, when he broke the world overall record three times in the same competition.

Baumgartner, Bruce Robert [USA–WRE]. B. 2 November 1960, Haledon, NJ. Bruce Baumgartner is the greatest heavy wrestler ever produced in the United States. A freestyler, he competed four times at the Olympic Games (1984–1996) and won a medal at each Olympics, one of only four Olympic wrestlers to win medals at four Games. Baumgartner won the unlimited class freestyle gold medal in 1984 and 1992, won silver in 1988, and finished his career in Atlanta with a bronze. He was also World Champion in 1987, 1991, and 1995, and runner-up at the worlds in 1989–1990, and 1994. He won the Pan-American Games gold medal three times consecutively: 1987, 1991, and 1995. His record in the World Cup was particularly impressive, with seven titles: 1984–1986, 1989–1991, and 1994.

Beach Volleyball. *See* VOLLEYBALL.

Beamon, Robert "Bob" [USA–ATH]. B. 29 August 1936, Jamaica, New York. With a single performance, lasting no more than a few seconds, Bob Beamon achieved sporting immortality at Mexico City in October 1968. His long jump of 8.90 meters (29'2½") gave him the Olympic gold medal and a new world record by a massive margin. Rated by many as the greatest performance in track & field history, his record was thought to be unbeatable. But like all records, it was inevitably surpassed and, in 1991, the record fell to Mike Powell (USA). Beamon never again approached the form he showed at the 1968 Olympics and he turned professional in 1972.

Bechuanaland. *See* BOTSWANA.

Behrendt, Jan [GDR/GER–LUG]. B. 29 November 1967, Ilmenau; and **Krausse, Stefan [GDR–LUG].** B. 17 September 1967, Ilmenau. Jan Behrendt and Stefan Krausse have formed a redoubtable doubles luge team, competing first for the German Democratic Republic and since 1992 for Germany. At the Olympics, they won gold medals in 1992 and 1998, silver in 1988, and bronze in 1994. Behrendt and Krausse began to compete together internationally at the 1985 European Junior championships. Together, they won four World Championships: 1989, 1991, 1993, and 1995; and were runners-up in 1996–1997. They were also World Cup champions in 1994–96 and European champions in 1996. They announced their retirement after the 1998 Winter Olympics.

Belarus [BLR]. The National Olympic Committee of the Republic of Belarus was formed in 1991 after the break-up of the Soviet Union. Many Belarus (formerly Belorussia, or Byelorussia [White Russia]) athletes competed from 1952 to 1988 for the Soviet Union, and Belarus athletes were present at both Albertville and Barcelona in 1992 as members of the Unified Team (q.v.). Belarus competed as an independent nation for the first time at the 1994 Olympic Winter Games in Lillehammer, with 33 athletes who won two medals. They first competed independently at the Summer Olympics in 1996, and through 2000, they have won four gold medals and 36 medals. Belarus has never hosted an Olympic Games, but in 1980, several preliminary football (soccer) matches were held in Minsk, the capital of Belarus.

Belgium [BEL]. Belgium has competed at every Olympic Games, with the exception of 1896 and 1904. Belgium began competing at the Olympic Winter Games in 1924, and also competed in figure skating and ice hockey (qq.v.) in 1920, but the country missed the 1960 and 1968 Olympic Winter Games. Belgium has won 141 medals (37 gold medals) in the Olympic Games, four medals in the Olympic Winter Games, and eight medals in the now defunct Art Contests (q.v.). Belgium also hosted the Games of the VIIth Olympiad at Antwerp in 1920.

Belize [BIZ]. As *British Honduras*, this country formed a National Olympic Committee in 1967 and made three Olympic appearances in 1968, 1972, and 1976. As *Belize*, it has been represented at the Olympics of 1984, 1988, 1992, 1996, and 2000. Belize has never competed at the Olympic Winter Games and has never won an Olympic medal.

Belousova, Lyudmila (later Protopopov) [URS–FSK] B. 22 November 1935, Ulyanovsk; and **Protopopov, Oleg. Alekseyevich [URS–FSK].** B. 16 July 1932, Moscow. The husband and wife team of Lyudmila Belousova and Oleg Protopopov won the Olympic pair skating title in 1964 and 1968. As the first Russian pair skaters to achieve international acclaim, they provided the stimulus that ultimately led to many successes by future generations. They began skating as a pair shortly before 1957 and were married that year. In addition to their two Olympic gold medals, they were World Champions four times (1965–1968). After losing their world title in 1969, they turned professional and later settled in Switzerland.

Belov, Sergey Aleksandrovich [URS–BAS]. B. 23 January 1944, Nashchekova, Tomsk Oblast. Sergey Belov played guard for the Soviet national basketball team from 1967 until 1980. He won four Olympic medals, bronzes in 1968, 1976, and 1980, and a gold medal in 1972. In addition, Belov played on teams that won the World Championships in 1967 and 1974 and European Championships in 1967, 1969, 1971, and 1979.

Benin [BEN]. Benin was originally part of French West Africa, but became independent from France under the name of *Dahomey* in 1960. Dahomey competed in the 1972 Olympics at Munich. The name was changed to *Benin* in 1975 and, after missing the 1976 Games, it has competed at every Olympics since 1980. Benin has never competed in the Olympic Winter Games and has not yet won an Olympic medal. Benin's best Olympic performance came in 1980 when featherweight boxer Barthelemy Adoukonou received a first-round bye, won one match, and then lost in the third round to place equal ninth of 35 boxers.

Beresford, Jack, Jr. [GBR–ROW]. B. 1 January 1899, Chiswick, Middlesex. D. 3 December 1977, Shiplake-on-Thames, Oxfordshire. With five medals Jack Beresford was the most successful Olympic oarsman of the pre-World War II era. To his gold medals in the single sculls (1924), coxless fours (1932) and double sculls (1936), he added silver in the single sculls (1920) and the eights (1928). Beresford's remarkable career spanned five Olympic Games and it was almost certainly only the cancellation of the 1940 Games that prevented a sixth Olympic appearance. He was awarded the Olympic Diploma of Merit in 1949. At Henley, he won the Diamond Sculls four times (1920 and 1924–1926), the Nickalls Challenge Cup in 1928 and 1929 (coxless pairs with Gordon Killick), and the Double Sculls Challenge Cup in 1939 with Dick Southwood. He also won the Wingfield Sculls for seven consecutive years from 1920. His father, Julius Beresford (né Wisniewski), won an Olympic silver medal in the eights in 1912.

Bermuda [BER]. Bermuda first entered international competition in 1930 at the British Empire Games in Canada. Following this, an NOC was formed in 1935 and IOC recognition was granted in 1936. Bermuda has competed at the Olympics since 1936, failing to appear only in 1980. It has competed at the Olympic Winter Games of 1992, 1994, and 1998. Bermuda's athletes have won one medal, a bronze medal in boxing in 1976 by Clarence Hill.

Bhutan [BHU]. Bhutan established an NOC in February 1983. This was noted by the IOC Executive Board later that year and provisional IOC recognition was granted in April 1984. Bhutan took part in the 1984 Olympics, since which time they have been represented in their national sport by a total of 16 archers at five Olympics (1984–2000). Bhutan has not been represented in any other sport. It has won no medals and has not yet competed at the Olympic Winter Games. In 1984, Doriji Thieley finished 53rd of 62 archers in the men's individual event, the best finish by a Bhutanese athlete.

Biathlon. Attempts to introduce a winter multi-event, patterned after the modern pentathlon (q.v.), began in 1948, when the winter pentathlon (q.v.) was contested at the St. Moritz Olympics as a demonstration sport. It consisted of cross-country and downhill skiing, and also shooting, fencing, and horse riding. Biathlon, which consists of cross-country skiing in which the runner stops at intervals to shoot a rifle at a target, was known in the 1920s but was not popular until the 1950s. The first World Championships were held in 1958 at Saalfelden, Austria. The sport quickly was placed on the Olympic program, showing up at Squaw Valley in 1960. Women's biathlon made its Olympic début in 1992 as a full medal sport at Albertville. In 1924, a military patrol race was a medal sport on the Olympic Winter program. Military ski patrol was similar to a team biathlon event, with team members skiing together.

Biathlon is currently governed by the International Biathlon Union (IBU), which had 60 member nations as of December 2000. Beginning in 1948, biathlon was governed by the Union Internationale de Pentathlon Moderne et Biathlon, which oversaw both sports, but the organization split into two governing bodies in 1993.

Biathlon events have consisted of a single men's race and a men's relay until 1980 when a second individual event was contested. The event is scored by time. In the longer individual race, a one-minute penalty is assessed for a missed shooting bulls-eye, and a two-minute penalty is assessed for missing a target. In the shorter individual race and the relay, missing a target is penalized by requiring the skier to ski a 150-meter penalty loop. Women (q.v.) currently also compete in the Olympics in both a short (7.5 km.) and a long (15 km.) individual race, and a relay race. In 2002, a new individual pursuit event for men (12 km.) and women (10 km.) will be added to the Olympic Winter program.

Bicycle Polo. First played in Ireland in 1891, the game's growing popularity led to a demonstration match between Ireland and Germany being included in the program at the 1908 Olympic Games. Although the sport has been included in the Asian Games, the chances of it becoming an Olympic sport appear to be very remote.

Bikila, Abebe [ETH–ATH]. B. 7 August 1932, Mout. D. 25 October 1973, Addis Ababa. Though his life came to a tragic early end, Abebe Bikila is usually considered the greatest marathoner ever. He was the first person to win the Olympic marathon consecutively, doing so in 1960 and 1964. His marathon career began only a few months before the Rome Olympics in 1960, when he won a trial race in the altitude of Addis Ababa. Between that race and a marathon he won in Seoul in October 1966, Bikila ran 15 marathons, winning 14, losing at the 1963 Boston Marathon, in which he finished fifth. He sustained an injury in 1967 and never fully recovered, which caused him to withdraw after starting the 1968 Olympic marathon in Mexico City. Late in 1969, Bikila was in a car accident, and the injuries he sustained rendered him a permanent quadriplegic. He lived only a few more years, dying in October 1973. His funeral in Addis Ababa was attended by thousands who came to mourn their nation's first great, and still greatest, runner.

Billiards. Billiards, and the many pool variants, have never been on the Olympic program. But the World Confederation of Billiards Sports (WCBS) is currently recognized by the IOC. Founded in 1992, the federation currently has 97 affiliated member nations.

Biondi, Matthew Nicholas [USA–SWI]. B. 8 October 1965, Moraga, California. Matt Biondi won 11 swimming medals at the 1984, 1988, and 1992 Olympics, matching the record of Mark Spitz (q.v.). He was at his best at the 1988 Games, winning seven medals (five gold, one silver, one bronze) and, although essentially a freestyle swimmer, he won his silver medal in the 100-meter butterfly. Biondi set seven individual world records and won six gold medals at the World Championships (1986, 1991). In 1986, he won seven medals at the World Championships and added four more in 1991.

Blair, Bonnie Kathleen [USA–SSK]. B. 18 March 1964, Cornwall, New York. With victories in the 500 meters in 1988, 1992, and 1994, Bonnie Blair is the only woman to have won an Olympic speed skating event at three successive Games. She also won the 1,000 meters in 1992 and 1994 after taking the bronze in 1988, and her total of five gold medals has only been bettered by the Russian Lidiya Skoblikova (q.v.). Blair won four World Championships, those being the World Short-Track Championships in 1986, and the World Sprints in 1989 (at which meet she set a longstanding world record of 159.435 points for the sprint all-around), 1994, and 1995. During her career, she set four world records in the 500 meters.

Blankers-Koen, Francina Elsje "Fanny" (née Koen) [NED–ATH]. B. 26 April 1918, Baarn. Fanny Blankers-Koen was an outstanding all-around athlete who made her Olympic début as a high jumper in 1936. World War II deprived her of the opportunity of making further Olympic appearances until 1948 when, at the age of 30 and the mother of two, she was the star of the London Games. Blankers-Koen won the 100-meters, 200-meters, 80-meters hurdles and ran the anchor leg on the winning relay team. She set world records at eight different events, won five European titles (1946–1950) and a statue was erected in her honor in her native Amsterdam. She married her coach, Jan Blankers, a Dutch Olympic triple jumper in 1928.

Bleibtrey, Ethelda (later MacRobert, then Schlafke) [USA–SWI]. B. 27 February 1902, Waterford, New York. D. 6 May 1978, Atlantis, Florida. Ethelda Bleibtrey was the first American female swimmer of international renown and the first female star of the Olympic pool. At the 1920 Games, she won a gold medal in each of the three swimming events for women: 100-meters and 300-meters freestyle and relay. She would almost certainly have won a fourth had a backstroke event been included as she was, at the time, a world record holder in this style. Bleibtrey set seven world records before turning professional in 1922, after which she became a swimming instructor.

Blonay, Baron Godefroy de [SUI]. B. 25 July 1869, Wiederschöfal. D. 14 February 1937, Biskra, Algeria. Baron Godefory de Blonay was appointed as the first Swiss IOC Member in 1899 and remained a member until his death in 1937. He was a founder of the Swiss Olympic Committee in 1912 and was its first president (1912–1915). During the latter part of World War I, he served as provisional IOC president (1916–1919) when Pierre de Coubertin (q.v.), who had enlisted in the French army, felt that it would not be appropriate for a military man to serve as head of the IOC. After Coubertin was discharged from the military because of his age, Blonay relinquished his presidential duties and Coubertin again took over the presidency. Blonay was a member of the IOC Executive Board (q.v.) from 1921 to 1937, and was president of the Executive Board from 1921 to 1925. He then was Vice-President of the IOC from 1925 until his death in 1937. Although Blonay was a close friend of Coubertin, when he attempted, as president of the Executive Board, to obtain certain administrative functions for this group, severe tensions developed between them. A distinguished Egyptologist, Blonay lived in Paris for many years but eventually settled in Switzerland, where he taught at the University of Neuchâtel.

Bobsledding. Bobsledding as a sport originated in Switzerland in 1888 when an Englishman, Wilson Smith, connected two sleighs with a board to travel from St. Moritz to Celerina. Bobsledding was first practiced on the Cresta Run at St. Moritz, but the run was not suitable for the faster bobsleds so a separate bob run was constructed there in 1904, the world's first.

Bobsledding was on the program of the first Olympic Winter Games in 1924 with a single four-man event. In 1928, the event was one for sleds with either four or five men. In 1932, the present program of two events, one for two-man sleds, and one for four-man sleds, began. In 2002 at Salt Lake City, women (q.v.) will compete in

Olympic bobsledding for the first time, in a two-person event. The bobsledding federation currently also governs the sled sport of skeleton (q.v.). Skeleton appeared on the Olympic program at the Cresta Run in St. Moritz in both 1928 and 1948. Skeleton has recently been placed back on the Olympic program and a skeleton event for men and women will be held in 2002 at Salt Lake City.

Bobsledding has been contested at all Olympic Winter Games, except in 1960 at Squaw Valley. Because of the distance to travel to California, only nine countries indicated that they would enter bobsled teams. The Squaw Valley organizers thus decided not to build a bob run and the sport was not held that year.

Bobsledding has been dominated by the Swiss, the Italians, and, until 1992, the German Democratic Republic. The sport is governed by the Fédération Internationale de Bobsleigh et de Tobogganing (FIBT), which was founded in 1923 and had 54 members at the beginning of the new millennium. *See also* SKELETON.

Body Building. Body building has never been on the Olympic program, but the sport is governed by the International Federation of Body Builders (IFBB), which has achieved provisional recognition by the IOC. Founded in 1946, the IFBB currently has 145 affiliated member nations.

Bohemia [BOH]. Prior to becoming the largest province of Czechoslovakia in 1918, Bohemia appeared at the Olympics of 1900, 1906, 1908, and 1912. In those Olympics, Bohemian athletes won six Olympic medals.

Bolivia [BOL]. Bolivia formed a National Olympic Committee in 1932 and had a single swimmer at the 1936 Olympics in Berlin, but the nation did not compete at the Olympics again until 1964. It has since competed continuously with the exception of Moscow in 1980. Bolivian athletes have not yet won an Olympic medal. Bolivia has also competed five times at the Olympic Winter Games, sending Alpine skiers in 1956, 1980, 1984, 1988, and 1992. Bolivia did not compete at the 1994 nor the 1998 Olympic Winter Games.

Bosnia-Herzegovina [BIH, formerly BSH]. Until 1992, Bosnia-Herzegovina was a republic in the state of Yugoslavia. In that year, Bosnia-

Herzegovina, along with several other Yugoslav republics, declared independence, but unfortunately, the Serbians declared war on the republic. Still, Bosnia-Herzegovina quickly formed a National Olympic Committee and, on the eve of the 1992 Olympics, was granted provisional recognition by the IOC and competed at Barcelona. Despite the civil war in the country, Bosnia-Herzegovina valiantly sent competitors to the 1994 Olympic Winter Games in Lillehammer. Bosnia-Herzegovina also competed at the 1996 and 2000 Olympic Games and the 1998 Olympic Winter Games. The 14th Olympic Winter Games were held in Sarajevo in 1984 in what was then part of Yugoslavia, but Sarajevo is presently the capital city of Bosnia-Herzegovina. With the conflicts in the Balkans there have been nationalistic uprisings that may cause Bosnia and Herzegovina to split into two nations. In early 2000, the IOC announced that they had brokered an agreement with Bosnia and Herzegovina so that they competed as one nation, with athletes from both ethnic groups, at the 2000 Olympic Games.

Botswana [BOT]. Botswana formed an Olympic Committee in 1978 and has competed at every Olympics since 1980. Formerly called *Bechuanaland*, the country never made an Olympic appearance under that name. Botswanan athletes have yet to win an Olympic medal and the country has not yet competed at the Olympic Winter Games.

Bowling. Ten-pin bowling (as opposed to lawn bowling or bowls) was a demonstration sport (q.v.) in Seoul at the 1988 Olympic Games. Its governing body, the Fédération Internationale de Quilleurs (FIQ), was founded in 1952 and is currently one of the IOC Recognized International Federations, with 120 national members.

Bowls. Bowls has never been contested at the Olympic Games, even as a demonstration sport, but the Confédération Mondiale des Sports de Boules (CMSB) is currently one of the IOC Recognized International Federations. There are 73 affiliated nations in the CMSB as of 2000.

Boxing. Boxing was contested at the Ancient Olympic Games (q.v.) and many other sporting festivals in Ancient Greece. Boxing was then even a more brutal sport. The combatants wore leather thongs on their hands. Originally, the thongs were simple straps of leather but later they were reinforced with sharp pieces of metal, and the glove was called a *cestus*. The first known Ancient Olympic boxing champion was Onomastos of Smyrna, who won in 688 B.C. The last known was Varasdates of Armenia, in 369 A.D., who is also the last known champion of the Ancient Olympic Games. Professional boxing has been around since the early 18th century, with a recognized list of professional champions dating from the late 1700s.

Boxing made its first Olympic appearance in 1904 at St. Louis. All the entrants were Americans and the event doubled as the AAU Championships for that year. Boxing was again contested at the 1908 Olympics in London. In 1912, boxing could not be on the Olympic program because boxing was illegal in Sweden at that time. Since 1920, boxing has been on the program of every Olympic Games.

The United States has traditionally been the premier nation in Olympic boxing. However, it has been surpassed in the last 20 years by first the Soviet Union and, more recently, by Cuba. Three boxers have won three Olympic gold medals, László Papp of Hungary, Teófilo Stevenson of Cuba, and Félix Savón Fabré of Cuba. A number of Olympic boxers have gone on to become professional World Champions, notably Cassius Clay (Muhammad Ali), George Foreman, Joe Frazier, Sugar Ray Leonard (qq.v.), Oscar De La Hoya, and Lennox Lewis.

Olympic boxing is contested in 12 weight classes. Amateur matches are three rounds of three minutes each with a one-minute rest between rounds. There are five judges who score the match. Scoring is now done by a complicated system in which the judges register successful punches. If three of the five judges register a punch within one second, that scores one point for the boxer who lands the punch. Decisions are made only by the punches landed for a point score. At the Olympics, all weight classes are conducted by single-elimination tournaments. There is currently no match for third place, with both losing semi-finalists receiving bronze medals.

Amateur boxing is governed by the Association Internationale de Boxe Amateur (AIBA), which currently has 190 member nations and was founded in 1946.

Boyarskikh, Klavdiya [URS–NSK]. B. 11 November 1939, Verkhnyaya Pyshma, Sverdlovsk. To three gold medals (5 km., 10 km., and relay) at the 1964 Olympics, Klavdiya Boyarskikh added two further golds at the 1966 World Championships to establish herself as the world's leading female cross-country skier of the 1960s.

Boycotts and Politics. The Olympic Games have rarely been able to escape the influence of politics since they became a major international event. The first significant intrusion of politics occurred in 1936 (*see* THE GAMES OF THE XITH OLYMPIAD) when several nations considered boycotting the Berlin Olympics to protest the policies of Germany's Adolf Hitler.

Minimal political intrusions occurred in 1948 and 1952. In 1956, however, a small boycott ensued because of the recent incursion of Soviet troops into Hungary, and because of an Egyptian-Israeli dispute over the Sinai peninsula. *See* THE GAMES OF THE XVITH OLYMPIAD.

The Rome Olympics in 1960 were once again free of significant political conflicts. In 1964, a dispute arose concerning the eligibility of certain nations that had competed at the Games of the New Emerging Forces (GANEFO) in 1963. *See* THE GAMES OF THE XVIIITH OLYMPIAD.

In 1968, the Mexican government faced numerous student protests over the presence of the Olympic Games in the Mexican capital despite the poverty and hunger of many of its citizens. As the protest movement gathered momentum leading up to the Games, the Mexican Army took charge on the night of 2 October. As 10,000 people demonstrated in the Square of the Three Cultures in Mexico City, the army surrounded the crowd and opened fire. More than 250 people were killed and thousands were injured or imprisoned. *See* THE GAMES OF THE XIXTH OLYMPIAD.

The worst intrusion of politics into the Olympics occurred in 1972 when Arab terrorists representing the Black September movement entered the Olympic village and took as hostage 11 Israeli competitors and coaches. The hostages were all eventually murdered. *See* THE GAMES OF THE XXTH OLYMPIAD.

Shortly before the 1976 Olympics were due to start, they were marred by a boycott of 22 African countries, Guyana, and Chinese Taipei (then Taiwan). This was in protest of a recent tour of South Africa by the New Zealand national rugby team. Because South Africa was ostracized from international sporting competition, the African nations demanded that New Zealand not be allowed to compete at Montreal. However, as the IOC had no control of international rugby (q.v.), New Zealand was properly allowed to start in the Olympics.

The Taiwan boycott occurred when the Canadian government did not allow the Taiwanese team to enter the country, as it did not recognize the island nation, in violation of its agreement as host country to admit all eligible nations in honoring the *Olympic Charter*. The Canadians eventually acquiesced and gave permission for the Taiwanese to compete, but refused to allow them to do so as the Republic of China, its official national name and the name by which it was then recognized by the IOC. Several other countries protested and threatened withdrawal, notably the United States. However, these protests were short-lived and the IOC finally gave in to the Canadian government. Taiwan withdrew and did not compete. *See* THE GAMES OF THE XXIST OLYMPIAD.

The largest-scale Olympic boycott occurred in 1980. The Games were held in Moscow in July 1980. In December 1979, Soviet troops entered Afghanistan. The United States led a vocal protest and eventually boycotted the 1980 Olympic Games. It was joined by approximately 63 other nations who also boycotted. *See* THE GAMES OF THE XXIIND OLYMPIAD.

In 1984, the Soviet Union exacted its revenge on the United States when it boycotted the Los Angeles Olympic Games. This was officially because of concerns over security and the safety of its athletes, but there was little doubt as to the reason, which was revenge for the 1980 U.S.-led boycott. The Soviet Union boycott was joined, quite naturally, by other members of the Soviet bloc, including Eastern Europe and Cuba. Only Romania, among Soviet-bloc nations, defied the Soviet-led boycott. *See* GAMES OF THE XXIIIRD OLYMPIAD.

The IOC awarded the 1988 Olympics to Seoul. This was a highly controversial decision as many prominent nations in the Olympic Movement did not have diplomatic relations with the Seoul government. The problem became more complicated in 1985 when North Korea demanded that it be allowed to co-host the Games with the Republic of Korea. Over the next three years the IOC negotiated with North Korea and offered to allow it to stage several events. When the IOC would not concede further to the North's demands, North Korea announced that it would definitely boycott the Seoul Olympics.

By then, however, most of the Soviet-bloc countries had agreed to compete in Seoul, making 1988 the first Summer Olympic competition in 12 years between the United States, the Soviet Union, and the German Democratic Republic. After North Korea's official boycott announcement, Cuba and Ethiopia also announced that they would boycott the Olympics. Nicaragua, Albania, and the Seychelles also did not attend the Olympics, although their reasons may not have been directly related to any boycott. *See* THE GAMES OF THE XXIVTH OLYMPIAD.

In 1992, the Olympics were held in Barcelona. These Games were remarkably free of political protest and intrusions. They were the first Olympic Games since 1968 that saw no form of boycott.

In addition to boycotts of the Olympic Games, political problems have haunted the IOC since the end of World War II. This has mostly been in terms of the official recognition of certain nations. In many cases, the nations have not been on good political terms with other IOC members, and these IOC members have protested their official recognition.

In particular, the IOC has dealt with the problems of the "two" Germanys (*see* GERMANY and the GERMAN DEMOCRATIC REPUBLIC); the "two" Chinas (*see* CHINA and CHINESE TAIPEI); the "two" Koreas (*see* KOREA, DEMOCRATIC PEOPLE'S REPUBLIC OF and KOREA, REPUBLIC OF); and the question of recognition of South Africa (*see* SOUTH AFRICA) despite its apartheid policies. Similar problems existed in the later 1960s and early 1970s concerning Rhodesia (*see* ZIMBABWE).

Brazil [BRA]. Brazil has competed at every Olympics since 1920, with the sole exception of 1928. It has competed at the Olympic Winter Games in 1992, 1994, and 1998. Brazil's successes have come in a variety of sports. It has won medals in several different sports, and has always had one of the top basketball and football (soccer) teams. Brazilian athletes have won 66 Olympic medals, 12 of them gold medals, the most medals by any South American country.

Bridge. Bridge has never been contested at the Olympics but the World Bridge Federation (WBF) was recognized by the International

Olympic Committee (IOC) in 2000. Founded in 1958, the WBF currently has 115 national members.

British Virgin Islands [IVB]. The British Virgin Islands formed an NOC in 1980 that was recognized in 1982. The nation has competed at every Olympic Games since 1984, but they have not yet been represented at the Olympic Winter Games. No athlete from this island has won an Olympic medal.

Brookes, William Penny [GBR]. B. 1809, Much Wenlock, England. D. 10 December 1895, Much Wenlock, England. William Penny Brookes was the founder of the Much Wenlock Olympian Games (q.v.), an early influence on the thinking of Pierre de Coubertin (q.v.) toward the revival of the Olympics. Brookes was a doctor who was educated at various schools in Shropshire. He began his study of medicine at Guy's and St. Thomas's Hospitals in London in about 1827. He finished his studies in Paris and Padua, returning to Much Wenlock in 1831 to carry on the general practice of medicine, which his father had started. He founded the National Olympian Association in 1865, the forerunner of the British Olympic Association. He was active in public affairs, serving as Justice of the Peace and Commissioner for Roads for the borough of Wenlock, and in 1841 formed the Wenlock Agricultural Reading Society. He eventually became a Licentiate of the Society of Apothecaries and, in 1881, a Fellow of the Royal College of Surgeons.

Brookes was an invited dignitary to Coubertin's Sorbonne Congress of 1894 that founded the Modern Olympic Games, but he was unable to attend because of illness. He and Coubertin corresponded frequently and Brookes had Coubertin visit the Much Wenlock Olympian Games in October 1890. In 1881, Brookes was the first person who proposed that international Olympian Games be staged again, to be held in Athens. See also MUCH WENLOCK OLYMPIAN GAMES.

Brundage, Avery [USA]. B. 28 September 1887, Detroit, Michigan. D. 7 May 1975, Garmisch-Partenkirchen, Germany. Avery Brundage was an American who served as president of the IOC from 1952 to 1972, the longest reign ever aside from Pierre de Coubertin (q.v.), and Juan Antonio Samaranch (q.v.). As a participant in the track & field events in 1912 (decathlon and pentathlon), he is the only IOC president to have actually competed in the Olympics (through 2001). Having made a fortune in the construction business, he enjoyed the financial freedom to devote his time to the administrative side of sport. Brundage served seven terms as president of the Amateur Athletic Union (AAU), was president of the U.S. Olympic Committee for 25 years, and, after becoming a member of the IOC in 1936, he was elected to the IOC Executive Board (q.v.) in 1937, and as IOC vice president in 1946, before becoming president six years later. His dedication to amateurism bordered on the fanatical and anachronistic, but he gradually lost his lifelong battle to the rising tide of commercialism in sport. Although never terribly popular, and undoubtedly the most controversial IOC president ever, Brundage traveled constantly in the cause of Olympism and did much to widen the international scope of the Olympic Movement.

Brunei [BRU]. The Brunei National Olympic Council was formed in 1984 and recognized by the IOC in that year. After sending an official as an observer to both Seoul (1988) and Barcelona (1992), Brunei first competed at the 1996 Olympic Games where they were represented by a single competitor in the skeet shooting event. In 2000 at Sydney, Brunei was represented by one male runner and one male shooter.

Budo. *Budo* is a general term referring to the many different forms of Japanese martial arts. In 1964, the Japanese gave exhibitions of Japanese archery *(kyudo),* fencing *(kendo),* and wrestling *(sumo)* (qq.v.) at the Tokyo Olympics, all of which are examples of *budo*.

Bulgaria [BUL]. Five Bulgarian athletes went to Athens for the 1896 Olympic Games, but due to a misunderstanding over the use of the Gregorian and the Julian Calendars, they arrived too late to compete. It was not until 1923 that an NOC was formed and IOC recognition followed in the next year. Bulgaria first competed at the Olympic Games in 1924, and it has since missed only the Olympic Games of 1932, 1948, and 1984. Its first appearance in the Olympic Winter Games was in 1936 and it has competed at all celebrations since. Bulgaria has had its greatest successes in strength sports, mainly weightlifting and wrestling. In the 1980s, it was the premier nation in the world in weightlifting. Bulgarian athletes have won 197 Olympic medals, 49 of them gold.

Burghley, Lord; David George Brownlow Cecil, later the Sixth Marquess of Exeter [GBR]. B. 9 February 1905, Stamford, Lincolnshire. D. 22 October 1981, Stamford, Lincolnshire. Lord Burghley was the Olympic 400-meter hurdles champion in 1928 and later a distinguished sports administrator. In 1933, at the age of 28, he was elected a member of the IOC. Three years later, he became Chairman of the British Olympic Association and president of the British Amateur Athletic Association. In 1946, Lord Burghley took over from J. Sigfrid Edström as president of the International Amateur Athletic Federation (IAAF) and was Chairman of the Organizing Committee for the 1948 Olympic Games. He failed in a bid for the IOC presidency in 1952 and 1964, but from 1952 to 1966 he served as vice president of the IOC.

Burkina Faso [BUR]. Taka Gangua and Taki N'Dio competed in the javelin throw in 1924 for France, but were nationals of what was then called *Upper Volta*. The country sent a single competitor to the 1972 Olympics, representing *Upper Volta*. The country changed its name to *Burkina Faso* in 1984, and as *Burkina Faso,* its first Olympic participation occurred in 1988 at Seoul. It has also competed in 1992 and 1996. No athlete from this nation has won an Olympic medal.

Burma [BIR]. *See* MYANMAR.

Burundi [BDI]. Burundi's National Olympic Committee was founded in 1990 and given official recognition by the IOC in September 1993. Burundi first competed at the 1996 Olympic Games, but has not yet competed at the Olympic Winter Games. In 1996, Burundi won one medal, a gold by Venuste Niyangabo in the men's 5,000 meters of track & field athletics. Burundi also competed at the 2000 Olympic Games.

Button, Richard Totten "Dick" [USA–FSK]. B. 18 July 1929, Englewood, New Jersey. Dick Button was noted for bringing a new dimension of athleticism to figure skating. Between 1943 and 1952, he was only defeated twice and his many victories included the Olympics of 1948 and 1952. He was the World Champion for five consecutive years (1948–1952). Button was U.S. champion for seven consecutive years (1946–52), won the North American title in 1947, 1949, and 1951, and in 1948, became the only American to win the European championships in 1948. After his European title, the event was closed to non-Europeans. Known for his innovative, dynamic free skating, Button was undefeated to the end of his career in 1952, after having finished second at the 1947 World Championships. A Harvard-educated lawyer, Button later became an award-winning television commentator and sports-event producer.

– C –

Cambodia [CAM]. Cambodia made its first Olympic appearance at the Equestrian Olympic Games of 1956 in Stockholm, although it did not compete at the Melbourne Olympics that year. It again participated in 1964 and 1972. It has yet to win a medal. Briefly known as *Kampuchea*, the country has retaken the name *Cambodia*. With the frequent changes in government, the status and even the existence of an NOC has often been in doubt, but the latest body was recognized by the IOC in 1994, and Cambodia competed at Sydney in 2000, represented by four athletes, two men and two women.

Cameroon [CMR]. In 1959, Cameroon approached the IOC for advice concerning the establishment of an NOC. It took four years for plans to reach fruition, with the NOC being formed in 1963 and receiving IOC recognition in the same year. Cameroon made its Olympic début in 1964 at Tokyo and has appeared at all Games since. It has not yet attended the Olympic Winter Games. Cameroon athletes have won three Olympic medals, two in boxing. But the highlight of their Olympic performances was the gold medal won at Sydney in 2000 by their men's football (soccer) team.

Canada [CAN]. Canada first appeared officially at the 1904 Olympic Games in St. Louis. However, in 1900, two Canadian citizens competed, both under U.S. colors (George Orton in steeplechase and

Ronald MacDonald in the marathon). Since 1900, Canada has failed to be represented only at the 1980 Moscow Olympic Games. It has appeared at every Olympic Winter Games since their inception in 1924, and, in addition, its ice hockey team (q.v.) competed in the 1920 hockey tournament, winning decisively. This began a trend that continued until the Soviet Union entered the Olympic ice hockey tournaments, starting in 1956. Canada has won 309 Olympic medals (77 gold), 230 of them at the Olympic Games and 79 at the Olympic Winter Games. Canada has also hosted the Games of the XXIst Olympiad at Montreal in 1976, and the 15th Olympic Winter Games at Calgary in 1988.

Canadian Ice Hockey Teams [1920–1952]. Canada (q.v.) dominated ice hockey (q.v.) at the Olympics from 1920 through 1952, winning all the Olympic tournaments during that time with the exception of the 1936 Olympic Winter Games, when it was upset by a British team that contained a number of Canadians who held dual British citizenship. Canada was always represented by a club team during their ice hockey reign. The teams were as follows: 1920—Winnipeg Falcons; 1924—Toronto Granites (with the addition of two players from the Winnipeg Falcons and Montreal Victorias); 1928—Toronto Varsity Graduate Team; 1932—The Winnipegs (with the addition of two players from the Selkirk Fisherman); 1936—Port Arthur Bearcats (with the addition of several players from the Montreal Victorias); 1948—Royal Canadian Air Force Flyers; and 1952—Edmonton Mercurys. During this era of dominance, the Canadians posted a record of 35 wins, one loss, and three ties in Olympic competition. The loss was to Great Britain, 2–1, in 1936. The ties were in 1932 to the United States (2–2), in 1948 to Czechoslovakia (0–0), and in 1952 to the United States (3–3). In 1956, the Soviet Union entered the ice hockey tournament at the Olympic Winter Games and began its own period of dominance. *See also* SOVIET UNION ICE HOCKEY TEAMS [1956–1992].

Canoe & Kayaking. Many years ago, canoeing began as a means of transportation. Competition in canoes began in the mid-19th century. The Royal Canoe Club of London was formed in 1866 and was the first organization interested in developing the sport. In 1871, the New York Canoe Club was founded.

In 1924, canoeing was on the Olympic program as a demonstration sport (q.v.). Canoeing became a full medal sport in 1936 with both canoe and kayak events. The program has varied a great deal over the years with many events now discontinued and several new ones added. Women (q.v.) began Olympic canoeing in 1948, competing only in kayaks, which is still the case. Whitewater canoeing, or slalom canoeing, was held at the 1972 Olympics in Munich and returned to the Olympic Program in 1992 at Barcelona, and has also been on the Olympic Program in both 1996 and 2000. The two types of canoe events are often called *flatwater* and *whitewater*, or *sprint* and *slalom*. The two types of canoes used are the kayak, in which the paddler sits inside a covered shell, and the Canadian, in which the paddler kneels with the top of the canoe open. The events are usually designated by codes, such as K1-500. The code indicates the type of canoe (K = kayak, C = Canadian), the number of canoeists (1, 2, or 4), followed by the distance (500 or 1,000 meters).

Canoeing is governed worldwide by the Fédération Internationale de Canoë (FIC), which was founded in 1924 and currently has 108 member nations. The top medal winners in Olympic canoeing history have been Sweden's Gert Fredriksson and Romania's Ivan Patzaichin (qq.v.). Among women, Germany's Birgit Schmidt-Fischer and Sweden's Agneta Andersson (qq.v.) have won the most canoeing medals.

Cape Verde [CPV]. Cape Verde's Olympic Committee was formed in 1989 and given official recognition by the IOC in September 1993. Cape Verde made its Olympic début in 1996, and also competed in 2000, but it has not yet competed at the Olympic Winter Games.

Čáslavská, Věra [TCH–GYM]. B. 3 May 1942, Prague. Attractive, vivacious, and talented, Věra Čáslavská was the outstanding gymnast at the 1964 and 1968 Games. In Tokyo, she won three gold medals and a silver, and in Mexico she won four golds (one shared) and two silvers. Having earlier won a silver medal in 1960, Čáslavská 's total of 11 Olympic medals has only ever been bettered by Larisa Latynina (URS) (q.v.) among female gymnasts. After winning her final gold medal in 1968, she married Czech Olympic silver medalist (1,500 meters in 1964) Josef Odložil (1938–1993), in Mexico. In 1989, she was appointed president of the Czech Olympic Committee, and in 1995 Věra Čáslavská was elected as a member of the International Olympic Committee.

Cayman Islands [CAY]. The Cayman Islands Olympic Committee was formed in 1973 and was recognized by the IOC in 1976. The Cayman Islands first competed at the 1976 Olympic Games and has been represented at every Olympics since, with the exception of 1980. It has not yet competed at the Olympic Winter Games nor has it won an Olympic medal.

Central African Republic [CAF]. A Central African Republic NOC was formed in 1961 and, after lengthy negotiations over the suitability of the statutes of the NOC, the IOC granted full recognition in 1965. Since first competing at the 1968 Olympic Games, the Central African Republic has participated in all subsequent Olympics. The Central African Republic has not yet competed at the Olympic Winter Games and it has not yet won a medal at the Olympics.

Central America. Central America is a region and, as such, has never had full recognition by the IOC. But from 1918 to 1940, Pedro Jaime de Matheu was an IOC Member to the Central American region. De Matheu was from the area that later became El Salvador.

Ceylon [CEY]. *See* SRI LANKA.

Chad [CHA]. Chad's NOC was formed in 1963 and recognized by the IOC in 1964. Chad first competed at the Olympic Games in that year. With the exception of the Olympics of 1976 and 1980, Chad has taken part in every Games since making its début in 1964. Chad has not yet competed at the Olympic Winter Games and has never won an Olympic medal. The first Chadian athlete to compete at the Olympics was high jumper Mahamat Idriss, who represented France in 1960. When Chad competed as an independent nation in 1964, Idriss finished ninth in the high jump, which remains Chad's best performance at the Olympics. Chad has not yet competed at the Olympic Winter Games.

Chand, Dhyan [IND–HOK]. *See* DHYAN CHAND.

Chariot Races—Ancient Olympic Sport. Multiple chariot races were contested at the Ancient Olympic Games (q.v.). These include the apene, the synoris, a foals' synoris race, the tethrippon, a foals' tethrippon, a chariot race for foals, a chariot race for 10 horses, and an event listed simply as chariot race. The last three were contested only in 65 A.D.

Charpentier, Robert [FRA–CYC]. B. 4 April 1916, Paris. D. 28 October 1966. Robert Charpentier was the winner of the individual road race at the 1936 Games when he also won gold medals in the team road race event and the 4,000-meter team pursuit. Charpentier got started in cycling when he was an apprentice to a butcher and made his deliveries on his bicycle. He was runner-up at the 1935 amateur world championship road race. World War II prevented him from having any success after the 1936 Olympics as a professional.

Chess. Chess has never been on the Olympic Program, even as a demonstration sport (q.v.). However, in 1999, the International Olympic Committee recognized the world governing body of chess, the Fédération Internationale des Échecs (FIDE). Founded in 1924, the FIDE had 159 members at the end of 2000.

Chile [CHI]. Chile's intial Olympic appearance came in 1912. Since that time, however, it has missed only the Games of 1932 and 1980. Chile first competed at the Olympic Winter Games of 1948 and has competed 12 times in the winter celebrations, missing only 1972 and 1980. Chilean athletes have won nine Olympic medals, six silver and three bronze. Chile formed its National Olympic Committee in 1934 and was recognized by the IOC in the same year.

China, People's Republic of [CHN]. Although the current NOC was recognized by the IOC in 1979, the first Chinese Olympic Committee was formed in 1910 and recognized in 1922. China competed at the Olympic Games of 1932, 1936, and 1948. In September 1949, Chinese Communists assumed control of the government, and many of the former rulers escaped to the island province of Taiwan, including many former members of the Chinese Olympic Committee (possibly as many as 19 of 26). Athletes from the Chinese mainland did compete at the 1952 Olympic Games in Helsinki. Thus began a 40-year political problem for the IOC: the question of the "two Chinas."

In May 1954, at the 50th IOC session in Athens, the IOC voted by 23–21 to recognize both the Chinese Olympic Committee in Beijing (then Peking) (as *the Olympic Committee of the Chinese Republic*, later [in 1957] as *the Olympic Committee of the People's Democratic Republic of China*) and in Taipei (as the *Chinese Olympic Committee*).

Both Chinas were invited to the 1956 Olympics in Melbourne. Beijing accepted the invitation on 20 November, which led Taipei to reject the invitation. However, Taipei changed its decision and elected to compete, which caused Beijing to withdraw in protest. At Melbourne, no athletes from mainland China competed, while 21 athletes from the island nation competed under the banner of the Republic of China. The Beijing committee withdrew from the IOC on 19 August 1958, in protest of the International Olympic Committee's continued recognition of Taiwan.

A request to be recognized again was submitted in 1975. The IOC requested the All-China Sports Federation to send its rules for inspection, a standard procedure. The All-China Sports Federation took two years to comply, but its application was eventually approved on 25 November 1979.

In the interim, the IOC sent a three-member contingent, led by New Zealander Lance Cross, to inspect sporting facilities in China. Cross reported to the IOC at its 81st session in Montevideo in April 1979. The IOC made the following recommendations at this session: "In the Olympic spirit, and in accordance with the Olympic Charter, the IOC resolves: 1) to recognize the Chinese Olympic Committee located in Peking [Beijing], and 2) to maintain recognition of the Chinese Olympic Committee located in Taipei. All matters pertaining to names, anthems, flags and constitutions will be the subject of studies and agreements which will have to be completed as soon as possible." The full session approved this motion by 36–30. The IOC Executive Board modified this slightly, changing part two to read "to maintain recognition of the Olympic Committee located in Taipei . . ."

China returned to the Olympic fold in 1980 at Lake Placid. It did not compete in 1980 at Moscow, but China has competed at all other Olympic Games and Olympic Winter Games since 1984. Chinese athletes have won 237 Olympic medals, 80 of them gold, all since 1984. Chinese women have won more medals (133, 44 gold) than Chinese men (101, 34 gold) (*n.b.*, three in mixed events). Chinese athletes excel in gymnastics, table tennis, diving, and swimming.

Chinese Taipei (aka Taiwan, Formosa, Republic of China) [TPE]. The Chinese Taipei Olympic Committee was first formed in 1949 by members of the mainland Chinese committee who had fled to the island. The IOC official policy at this time was that the mainland Chinese Olympic Committee had simply changed its address and was now located on the island of Taiwan. For many years thereafter, the country was embroiled in a dispute with mainland China over recognition by the IOC. *See also* CHINA, PEOPLE'S REPUBLIC OF.

In October 1959, the IOC Executive Board recommended that the Olympic Committee in Taiwan be recognized as the "Olympic Committee of the Republic of China," but it also insisted that, at the 1960 Olympic Opening Ceremonies, this team should march behind a banner reading "Formosa." The banner eventually read "Taiwan/ Formosa" but the placard bearer also posted a sign of his own, reading "Under Protest."

The greatest controversy concerning the participation of the athletes from Chinese Taipei occurred in 1976 at Montreal. In 1970, Canada had given political recognition to mainland China. Only a few weeks before the Montreal Olympics, Canada's government announced that it would not allow Chinese Taipei athletes to compete under the name of the "Republic of China." This was in complete violation of the *Olympic Charter* and the contract Montreal had signed as host of the Olympic Games, in which it agreed to allow all eligible athletes to enter the nation with the use of the Olympic Identity Card. The United States Government protested vociferously, even threatening a boycott. Eventually, however, the U.S. athletes competed, although Chinese Taipei refused to compete under any name other than the Republic of China. On 11 July, only six days before the start of the Olympics, the IOC Executive Board gave in and proposed to the full IOC that the island nation should compete at Montreal as Taiwan. The IOC approved this recommendation by 58–2, with six abstentions. Chinese Taipei/Taiwan/Republic of China withdrew in protest and did not compete at the 1976 Olympics.

After competing for several years under the banner "China" or "Republic of China," the IOC eventually banned the country from competing under this name. The current NOC was recognized in its present form on 26 November 1979, and on 23 March 1981 it signed an agreement with the IOC in which the NOC agreed to change its name to the Chinese Taipei Olympic Committee and compete under a new flag and emblem.

Taiwan/Chinese Taipei first competed at the Olympic Games in 1956, and since then has taken part at every Olympics with the exception of 1976 and 1980. It has competed in nine Olympic Games under various names—the Republic of China (1956), Taiwan (1960–1972), and Chinese Taipei (1984–1996). The nation has competed at eight Olympic Winter Games: as Taiwan from 1972 to 1976, and as Chinese Taipei from 1984 to 1998. The nation has won 10 Olympic medals, but has yet to win a gold medal.

Chukarin, Viktor Ivanovich [URS/UKR–GYM]. B. 9 November 1921, Mariupol (now Zdhanov). D. 26 August 1984, Lvov. A former World War II prisoner of war, Viktor Chukarin was 30 years old when the USSR first competed at the Olympic Games in 1952. Despite these handicaps, he dominated the gymnastics competition in Helsinki, winning the all-around title in addition to taking gold in the team event and two gold and two silver medals on the individual apparatus events. In 1956, Chukarin successfully defended his all-around title and added two more gold, a silver, and a bronze medal to bring his tally of Olympic medals to a then record total of 11. He was also World All-Around Champion in 1954 and, after retiring, he became head of gymnastics at the Lvov Institute of Physical Culture.

Chun Lee-Kyung [KOR–STK]. B. 6 January 1976. In the relatively new Olympic sport of short-track speed skating, Chun Lee-Kyung has been the most successful Olympian to date. She competed in both 1994 and 1998, winning the 1,000 meters at both Olympics, and skating on the winning relay team both times, to earn her four gold medals. To that, she added a bronze in the 500 meters in 1998. Chun was also a three-time World Champion, in 1995–1997.

Citius, Altius, Fortius. *See* OLYMPIC MOTTO.

Claudius, Leslie Walter [IND–HOK]. B. 25 March 1927. Leslie Claudius shares with Udham Singh the distinction of being one of only two players to win four Olympic medals for hockey (field). To his gold medals in 1948, 1952, and 1956, he added a silver in 1960 when he captained the team.

Clay, Cassius Marcellus [USA–BOX]. *See* ALI, MUHAMMAD.

Cochelea-Cogeanu, Veronica [ROM–ROW]. B. 15 November 1965. Among women, only her countrywoman, Elisabeta Lipa-Oleniuc (q.v.), has won more Olympic rowing medals than the six won by Veronica Cochelea-Cogeanu. Lipa-Oleniuc and Cochelea-Cogeanu combined for five of these medals—1988 double sculls silver medal, 1988 quadruple sculls bronze medal, 1992 double sculls silver medal, and 1996 and 2000 coxed eights gold medals. Cochelea-Cogeanu also won a silver medal with the quad in 1992. She was less success-ful at the World Championships, winning only one gold, that in the 1993 eight. Her 1988 Olympic appearance was as *Miss Cogeanu*, but she competed as *Veronica Cochelea* after marrying.

Coe, Sebastian Newbold [GBR–ATH]. B. 29 September 1956, Chiswick, London. Sebastian Coe is considered by many track ex-perts as the greatest 800-meter runner in history. His world record (1:41.73) for the distance, set in 1981, remained unbeaten for 16 years. Coe never won an Olympic title at this distance and had to set-tle for a silver medal in 1980 and 1984, but he won a gold medal in the 1,500 meters at both Games. A controversial omission from the 1988 British Olympic team denied him the opportunity of further honors. A prolific record breaker, he set nine outdoor and three indoor world records. After retirement, Coe continued to serve the sport as an administrator and, in 1992, was elected a Member of the British Parliament, at which he served through 1997.

Colombia [COL]. Colombia first competed at the 1932 Olympic Games, represented by a lone athlete, marathon runner Jorgé Perry Villate. The country first formed a National Olympic Committee, however, only in 1936 and this NOC was recognized by the IOC in 1939. Colombia has since competed at every Olympics with the exception of 1952. It has yet to compete in the Olympic Winter Games. Colombian athletes have won seven Olympic medals through 2000.

Comăneci, Nadia [ROM–GYM]. B. 12 November 1961, Onesti, Moldavia. Nadia Comăneci was the first gymnast in Olympic history to be awarded a perfect score of 10.0. She first achieved this landmark as a 14-year-old on the uneven parallel bars in 1976 and the judges awarded her maximum marks a further six times during the Games. In the 1976 and 1980 Games, Comăneci won a total of nine Olympic medals (five gold, three silver, one bronze). Following the 1980 Games, natural physical development began to inhibit her performance and after a victory at the 1981 World Student Games she retired. In 1989, she defected from Romania and settled in North America. She has since married American Olympic gymnastic medalist Bart Conner.

Comité International Pierre de Coubertin. *See* INTERNATIONAL PIERRE DE COUBERTIN COMMITTEE.

Commission for Culture and Olympic Education. The Commission for the International Olympic Academy (IOA) (q.v.) and Olympic Education was first formed in 1967, with Danish IOC Member Ivar Emil Vind as the first chairman. The current chairman is the Greek IOC Member Nikos Filaretos. This Commission oversees the IOA in Olympia, Greece, and the Commission has as its mission following the activities of the IOA, contributing to the success of the IOA, receiving the periodical reports of IOA sessions, and keeping the IOC informed of the progress of the IOA. This Commission also helps promote Olympic Education by spreading the message of Olympism (q.v.). In addition to IOC members, the IOA/Education Commission has representatives from the NOCs, IFs, and former Olympic athletes, as well as several academic scholars, usually sports historians or sociologists. The original name of this commission was the Commission for the International Olympic Academy, but the name was enlarged in 1993, reflecting the increased emphasis on Olympic Education. Upon the recommendations of the IOC 2000 Commission (q.v.), the Commission for the International Olympic Academy and Olympic Education was merged with the Cultural Commission (q.v.) in early 2000.

Commission for the Olympic Movement. The Commission for the Olympic Movement (q.v.) was formed in 1982, but its forerunner was the Tripartite Commission, which existed from 1975 to 1981. The Tripartite Commission was formed in response to complaints from the NOCs and IFs, who felt that they had little say in the Olympic Movement, and no process through which to voice their opinions officially. The Tripartite Commission consisted of members of the IOC, the NOCs, and the IFs. The Commission for the Olympic Movement has a similar composition. The chairman of this commission has always been the IOC president, originally Lord Killanin (q.v.) (Tripartite Commission), and since 1980, Juan Antonio Samaranch (q.v.). The makeup of the Olympic Movement Commission is currently as follows: all members of the Executive Board (q.v.) (15 IOC members) are joined by 11 representatives of the NOCs and 11 IF representatives, and one representative of the IOC-recognized international federations.

Commissions of the IOC. The International Olympic Committee has created a number of commissions that deal with specific issues related to the Olympic Movement (q.v.). The currently recognized commissions (at the end of 2000) are as follows: Athletes Commission; Commission for Olympic Education and Culture; IOC 2000 Commission (dissolved); Eligibility Commission; Ethics Commission; Finance Commission; Juridical Commission; Marketing Commission; Medical Commission; Press Commission; Radio and Television Commission; Olympic Solidarity Commission; Sport and Law Commission; Sport and Environment Commission; Sport for All Commission; Coordination Commission for the Olympic Games; IOC Evaluation Commission for the Olympic Games and Olympic Winter Games; the Pierre de Coubertin Commission; and Olympic Collectors Commission. Several of the IOC commissions have subcommissions, notably: Medical Commission—Subcommission on Doping and Biochemistry of Sport, Subcommission on Biomechanics and Physiology of Sport, Subcommission on Sports Medicine and Coordination with the NOCs, Subcommission on Out of Competition Testing; Coordination Commission for the Olympic Games—Summer 2000 Subcommission, Winter 2002 Subcommission, Summer 2004 Subcommission, and Winter 2006 Subcommission; Commission for the Olympic Program—Summer Subcommission, and Winter Subcommission. In addition, the IOC also recognizes several working groups that often have the status of a commission, at least briefly. Currently, these include: Philatelic Working Group, Council of the Olympic Order, Women and Sport Working Group, Olympic Movement Commission Working Group, Olympic Programme Working Group, and the Bureau for the Olympic Movement. *See* the various entries for each of the commissions.

Commonwealth of Independent States [CIS]. In 1992, former republics of the Union of Soviet Socialist Republics (Soviet Union) competed at the Olympic Games in Barcelona and the Olympic Winter Games in Albertville. By then, the former republics had formed the Commonwealth of Independent States. Because of the short time after the break-up of the Soviet Union, it was agreed that the former republics would compete as one team, which was called the *Unified Team* (q.v.), *L'Équipe Unifiée*, which, loosely, represented the Commonwealth of Independent States. *See also* UNIFIED TEAM and UNION OF SOVIET SOCIALIST REPUBLICS.

Comoros Islands [COM]. The Comoros Islands NOC was founded in 1979, but was not recognized by the IOC until September 1993. The nation first competed at the Olympic Games in 1996, but it has not yet competed at the Olympic Winter Games. At Atlanta in 1996, the Comoros Islands were represented by three male and one female athletes. At Sydney in 2000, two athletes—one male and one female—competed for the Comoros Islands.

Competition for Heralds—Ancient Olympic Sport. This event was held at the Ancient Olympic Games (q.v.) from at least 396 B.C. to 261 A.D. The last four known championships were won by Valerius Eclectus of Sinope.

Competition for Trumpeters—Ancient Olympic Sport. The competition for trumpeters was held from at least 396 B.C. to 217 A.D. at the Ancient Olympic Games (q.v.). The event was won consecutively from 328 B.C. through 292 B.C. by Herodoros of Megara.

Congo, Democratic Republic of the [COD]. This nation was formerly known as the *Belgian Congo*, but changed its name to the *Democratic*

Republic of the Congo in June 1960. In October 1971, the name was changed to Zaire, but in May 1997, the nation took back the name the *Democratic Republic of the Congo*. As the *Democratic Republic of the Congo*, Zaire was represented by five cyclists at the Mexico City Olympics in 1968. The nation's second Olympic appearance came 16 years later in Los Angeles as *Zaire*, where it was represented by three track & field athletes—two men and a woman—and six boxers. Zaire also competed in 1988, 1992, and 1996. The country never competed in the Olympics as *the Belgian Congo*, and competed as the *Democratic Republic of the Congo* again in 2000. No athlete from this variantly named nation has yet won an Olympic medal.

Congo, People's Republic of the [CGO]. Since making its Olympic début in 1964, the Congo has competed at every Olympic Games with the exception of 1968 and 1976. It has never competed at the Olympic Winter Games. Its best finish in the Olympics was sixth, albeit last, in women's handball in 1980.

Connolly, James Brendan Bennett [USA–ATH]. B. 28 November 1865, South Boston, Massachusetts. D. 20 January 1957, Boston, Massachusetts. James Connolly was the first champion at the Modern Olympic Games and the first known Olympic champion since Varasdates in the fourth century A.D. Connolly achieved this distinction by winning the hop, step, & jump (now known as *the triple jump*) on 6 April 1896. He also tied for second place in the high jump and placed third in the long jump in Athens and in 1900, he narrowly failed to retain his hop, step, & jump title. Connolly did not take part in the 1904 Games and made his final Olympic appearance in 1906 when he failed to record a valid jump in either of the horizontal jumps. Unable to obtain a leave of absence from Harvard to travel to Greece for the first Modern Games, he quit college, but his place in Olympic history no doubt provided ample compensation. James Connolly later became well known as a writer of seafaring novels.

Cook Islands [COK]. The Cook Islands Sports and Olympic Association was first organized and recognized by the IOC in 1986. The Cook Islands first competed at the 1988 Olympics in Seoul, and also competed in 1992 at Barcelona, 1996 in Atlanta, and 2000 in Sydney.

The nation has not yet competed at the Olympic Winter Games and has not won an Olympic medal.

Coordination Commissions for the Olympic Games. In 1985, the International Olympic Committee (IOC) (q.v.) formed the Study and Evaluation Commission for the Preparation of the Olympic Games. The name was changed to the Coordination Commission for the Olympic Games in 1986. The Coordination Commission consists of several subcommissions at any one time, as each Olympic Games in the planning stage has a subcommission of the Coordination Commission. For instance, there are current subcommissions for the 19th Olympic Winter Games (Salt Lake City 2002), the Games of the XXVIIIth Olympiad (Athens 2004), and the 20th Olympic Winter Games (Turin 2006). Each subcommission has a separate chairman, and multiple members serving various purposes—media, athletes, television, environment, as well as IOC members. The subcommissions work closely with their associated Organizing Committee of the Olympic Games (OCOG) (q.v.) to help them plan and organize the Olympic Games, and act as liaisons between the IOC, the OCOG, the International Federations (IFs) (q.v.), and the National Olympic Committees (NOCs) (q.v.).

Coroebus of Elis [GRE–ATH]. *fl. ca.* 800–750 B.C. Coroebus was a cook in the city-state of Elis in Ancient Greece. His Olympic fame rests on the fact that he is the first recorded champion in Olympic history, as in 776 B.C. he won the *stadion* (q.v.) race. His feat was inscribed on his tomb.

Costa Rica [CRC]. Costa Rica has competed at 11 Olympic Games: 1936, and continuously since 1964. Costa Rican athletes have won four medals, by the swimming sisters, Silvia and Claudia Poll Ahrens. The nation has competed at four Olympic Winter Games: 1980, 1984, 1988, and 1992.

Côte d'Ivoire [CIV]. Formerly known as the *Ivory Coast*, Côte d'Ivoire formed an NOC in 1962, which was recognized by the IOC in 1963. Côte d'Ivoire has competed in the Olympic Games since 1964, missing only the 1980 Games. The country has not yet appeared at the Olympic Winter Games. Côte d'Ivoire can claim one Olympic medal, a silver won by Gabriel Tiacoh in the 400 meters (track & field athletics) in 1984.

Cotswold Olimpick Games. *See* ROBERT DOVER'S GAMES.

Coubertin, Baron Pierre de (né Pierre Frédy) [FRA]. B. 1 January 1863, Paris. D. 2 September 1937, Geneva. Pierre de Coubertin is the founder of the Olympic Movement (q.v.). His inspirational idea to revive the ancient Greek festivals grew out of his general interest in physical education and, at the early age of 24, he began a campaign to restructure educational methods in France along the lines of the British Public School system, of which he was a great admirer. His idea of reviving the Olympic Games grew more from his interest in sociology, history, and education than from any particular enthusiasm for competitive sports, but it was these sports that were to provide his lasting monument. In view of his aesthetic inclination, it must have been a source of satisfaction that he won the prize for literature in the Art Contests in 1912 (q.v.). His entry, "Ode to Sport," was submitted under a pseudonym. Taking over as president of the IOC from Demetrios Vikelas in 1896, Coubertin faced many problems in the turbulent early years of the Modern Olympic Movement and the current strength of the movement is a tribute to his dedication and diplomacy in the difficult pioneering days. From 1896 to 1924, he attended every celebration of the Games, except those of 1904 and 1906, but at the Paris Games of 1924, he resigned the presidency of the IOC at the age of 61 on the grounds that he was too old to continue in office. Surprisingly, his interest in Olympic matters seemed to have declined rapidly, but he recorded a message that was replayed at the opening ceremony of the 1936 Olympic Games in Berlin. The following year Coubertin collapsed and died from a heart attack while walking in Lagrange Park in Geneva and, although he is buried in Geneva, his heart is preserved in a marble stele at Ancient Olympia. Many other aspects of Coubertin's involvement with the Olympic Movement are covered in the separate entries on various subjects in this volume. *See also* the BIBLIOGRAPHY for a list of some of his published works on the Olympic Movement.

Court of Arbitration for Sport [CAS]. At the end of the 20th century and the dawn of the new millennium, sport, like many other facets of society, has become beset by many legal challenges. Many of these deal with drug use in sport, or doping. When athletes are accused of doping, they usually challenge the legality of the testing system, ensuring a long, and often expensive, legal battle. In the mid-1980s, the International Olympic Committee (IOC) (q.v.) attempted to solve some of these legal problems by forming the Court of Arbitration for Sport, based in Lausanne, Switzerland. The CAS was formed in 1983 by the IOC, but was restructured in 1994 as an independent body. At major international sporting events, athletes must sign an agreement that any legal problems that may ensue from their participation, including a doping disqualification, will be adjudicated by submitting the problem for arbitration to the CAS. Of minor importance in the first few years of its existence, the CAS has now assumed a prominent role at major international sporting events. Many of the IFs and other sport governing bodies have agreed to give the CAS binding authority to rule on disputes involving sports law. When a dispute arises, the parties may choose one arbitrator from CAS's pool of 150 internationally recognized arbitration experts, or each party may choose one arbitrator with the CAS choosing a third arbitrator to serve as the president of the panel for that dispute. Costs of the arbitration process are paid by the loser in the dispute, as is common in European courts of law. During the Olympic Games a panel of CAS arbitrators is available for emergency decisions to be adjudicated within 24 hours.

Cricket. Cricket was contested only at the 1900 Olympics, when a British squad beat a French team that actually consisted of British residents of France.

Croatia [CRO]. Until the Yugoslavian civil war of 1991, Croatia had never competed at the Olympics as an independent nation. However, prior to 1991, many top Yugoslavian athletes were from Croatia, including several of the top Yugoslavian basketball players. Croatia made its Olympic début at the 1992 Olympic Winter Games in Albertville and has since competed in the 1994 and 1998 Winter Olympics. Croatia competed at Barcelona in 1992, where its best finish was a silver medal in basketball. They lost only to the "Dream Team" (q.v.). Croatia also competed at the 1996 Olympic Games in Atlanta. Through 2000, Croatian athletes have won seven Olympic medals.

Croquet (Roque). Croquet was contested at the 1900 Olympics in Paris, with three events. Two of the competitors were women (q.v.), among the first women to compete in the Modern Olympic Games. In 1904, roque, an American variant of croquet, was on the Olympic program as well. The sport has not been held at the Olympics since 1904. The name *roque* is derived by dropping the first and last letters from the name of its parent game of croquet.

Cross-Country Skiing. *See* NORDIC SKIING.

Cuba [CUB]. In 1900, the fencer Ramón Fonst competed at the Olympic Games and actually won the first gold medal for the small Caribbean country. Fonst also competed in the 1904 Olympics along with a few other Cuban athletes. In 1924, Cuba was represented by nine competitors, while in 1928, the country had one competitor. In 1948, Cuba sent a full team to the London Olympic Games and its participation was continuous until it elected to boycott the 1984 Olympic Games in Los Angeles. In support of the North Korean government, Cuba also elected not to compete in 1988 in Seoul. Cuba returned to the Olympics in 1992. Cuban athletes have not yet competed in the Olympic Winter Games. Cuba has been successful in several sports, winning 137 Olympic medals (55 gold), but by far its greatest success has come in boxing. Since the mid-1970s, Cuba has probably had the best amateur boxers in the world. Cuba is also the dominant nation internationally in baseball and won the gold medal in both 1992 and 1996 at the Olympics.

Cultural Commission. The Cultural Commission of the IOC was created in 1969 with Polish IOC Member Włodzimierz Reczek serving as the first chairman of the commission. The Cultural Commission consisted of six IOC members, two representatives of the IFs and NOCs, one athlete representative, and several independent members. Based on recommendations of the IOC 2000 Commission and approved at the 108th IOC session in December 1999, the Cultural Commission and the Education/IOA Commissions were recently merged into a single

Commission for Culture and Olympic Education (q.v.). In 2000, the IOC also created a new Department of Culture and Education.

Curling. Curling was a demonstration sport (q.v.) at the 1932, 1988, and 1992 Olympic Winter Games. In 1924, it also appeared on the Olympic Winter program, and recent evidence indicates that curling was a full medal sport that year. Previously, it has been considered a demonstration sport in 1924. In addition, in 1936 and 1964, German curling *(Eisschießen)* was contested as a demonstration sport. Curling returned to the Olympic Winter Program as a full medal sport at the 1998 Olympic Winter Games in Nagano. The sport is governed by the World Curling Federation (WCF), founded in 1966, and with 35 member federations as of 2000.

Cuthbert, Elizabeth "Betty" [AUS–ATH]. B. 20 April 1938, Merrylands, Sydney. Betty Cuthbert won two gold medals in the individual track sprints and a third gold in the relay at the 1956 Olympics. The 18-year-old Australian was instantly acclaimed as a national heroine by the Australian crowd. Injury spoiled her chances at the 1960 Games, but she came back to win the 400 meters in 1964 and claim her fourth Olympic gold medal. Including relays, Cuthbert set 18 world records. Sadly for such a fine athlete, she now suffers from multiple sclerosis, although at the Opening Ceremony in 2000, she carried the Olympic Torch into the stadium while in her wheelchair.

Cycling. Bicycles were first developed in the late 18th century and have since been used as a form of transportation. Originally, the front wheel was much larger than the rear wheel and the rider was elevated a great deal, making them difficult to control and very dangerous. In 1885, J. K. Starley of England devised the more modern bike with a chain and gearing to allow the wheels to be of equal size. Although bike races had been held on the old "penny farthings," the new bikes stimulated the growth of bicycle racing as a sport.

From 1880 to 1900, cycling became immensely popular both in Europe and the United States. The sport was primarily a professional one at that time. The sport continues its grip on the European continent to this day, but bike racing ceased to be a popular sport in the United States at about the time of the Depression. Only the American

Olympic victories at Los Angeles in 1984 and the recent exploits of Greg LeMond and Lance Armstrong have again stimulated interest in bicycle racing in the United States.

Cycling is one of the few sports that has been on the program of every Olympic Games. The program has varied, but now consists of an individual pack-style road race, individual time trial road race, track races, and cross-country mountain biking. In 1984, women (q.v.) were admitted to Olympic cycling with a single road race. In 1988, a sprint race on the track for women was also held and, in 1992, the women contested an individual pursuit track race. In 2000 at Sydney, three new track events for men were added—the Olympic sprint, a three-man sprint contest; the Madison, a two-man sprint-type event; and the keirin, a paced, pack-style race. A track time trial over 500 meters was also added to the Olympic program for women.

The Europeans have dominated Olympic cycling, notably the French, Italians, and Germans. However, the East Europeans have also won many medals, especially on the track. Mountain biking has recently become a very popular sport. In 1993, the IOC approved mountain biking as an Olympic event that appeared on the Olympic program for the first time at the 1996 Atlanta Olympics. Cycling is governed by the Union Cycliste Internationale (UCI), which was founded in 1900, and had 169 members as of December 2000.

Cyprus [CYP]. The Cyprus National Olympic Committee was formed in 1974 and recognized by the IOC in 1978. Since making its official Olympic début in 1980, Cyprus has competed at the Olympics of 1984–1996. Its first Olympic participation, however, occurred at the Olympic Winter Games of 1980 in Lake Placid, and it has sent competitors to every Winter Olympics since. However, already in 1896, several athletes of Cypriot nationality competed, representing Greece. Cyprus has not yet won an Olympic medal.

Czech Republic [CZE]. Formerly a part of Czechoslovakia (q.v.), the Czech Republic has been represented at the Olympics by many athletes. However, the Czech Republic did not compete officially at the Olympics as an independent nation until its appearance at Lillehammer for the 1994 Olympic Winter Games. The Czech Republic has since competed at the 1996 and 2000 Olympic Games and the 1998

Olympic Winter Games. As an independent nation, the Czech Republic has won 22 medals, including seven gold medals.

Czechoslovakia [TCH]. Athletes from what later became Czechoslovakia first competed at the 1900 Olympics, representing Bohemia (q.v.). In 1920, Czechoslovakia sent its first true Olympic team to Antwerp. From 1920 to 1992, the only Olympic Games not attended by Czechoslovakia, including the Olympic Winter Games, was the 1984 Los Angeles Olympics. Czechoslovakia excelled in many different sports at the Olympics. The country's most noteworthy athletes were distance runner Emil Zátopek and female gymnast Věra Čáslavská (qq.v.). Czechoslovakia split peacefully into the Czech Republic and Slovakia (qq.v.) on 1 January 1993.

– D –

Dæhlie, Bjørn [NOR–NSK]. B. 19 June 1967, Råholt. With 12 medals and eight gold medals, Bjørn Dæhlie is the most successful male Nordic skier in Olympic history, and is now considered the greatest cross-country skiier of all-time. In 1992, he won the combined pursuit, the 50-km. classical, and was a member of the winning relay team, while in 1994, he was the winner of the 10-km. classical and the combined pursuit. To these gold medals, he added silver in the 30 km. in 1992 and 1994, and a third silver in the relay in 1994. In 1998 at Nagano, Dæhlie won four more medals—three gold in the 10 km., 50 km., and the relay, and a silver in the pursuit race. His records of 12 medals and eight gold are absolute records for the Olympic Winter Games in any sport. Dæhlie has won a further nine titles at the World Championships and was World Cup champion for cross-country in 1992–1993, and 1995–1997.

Dahomey. *See* BENIN.

Dance Sport. The International Dance Sport Federation (IDSF), which governs ballroom-type dancing competitions, was founded in 1957 and currently has 71 affiliated member nations. The IDSF was given IOC recognition in 1997.

Daniels, Charles Meldrum [USA–SWI]. B. 24 March 1885, Dayton, Ohio. D. 9 August 1973, Carmel Valley, California. Charles Daniels' three Olympic gold medals for swimming in 1904 and one in 1906 were won against rather limited opposition, but he proved his true worth in 1908 by winning the 100-meter freestyle against a truly international field. Despite the increased number of swimming events on the Olympic Program, Daniels' total of four individual gold medals in swimming has not yet been beaten by a man, although Hungary's Krisztina Egerszegi (q.v.) has won five individual gold medals. Daniels set seven world records over various distances between 1907 and 1911 but his most significant legacy to the sport was his development of the American crawl stroke. He was a fine all-round sportsman, excelling at golf, squash, and bridge.

Davis, John Henry, Jr. [USA–WLT]. B. 12 January 1921, Smithtown, New York. D. 13 July 1984, New York. John Davis was six times a world weightlifting champion and twice an Olympic gold medalist. His Olympic gold medals came in the unlimited class in 1948 and 1952, and he would undoubtedly have been a medal contender in 1940 and 1944. Davis set 18 world records between 1946 and 1951. Never defeated between 1938 and 1953, his only defeat prior to his retirement was a second place at the 1954 World Championships to Doug Hepburn of Canada.

Dean, Christopher [GBR–FSK]. *See* JAYNE TORVILL.

Decathlon. The decathlon is considered the truest test of all-around athletic ability. A portion of the track & field athletics program, it consists of 10 events conducted over two days: Day One—100 meters, long jump, shot put, high jump, and 400 meters; Day Two—110-meter hurdles, discus throw, pole vault, javelin throw, and 1,500 meters. The winner of the Olympic decathlon is usually given the nickname of the "World's Greatest Athlete." Two decathletes have won the Olympic decathlon twice: Bob Mathias (USA) and Daley Thompson (GBR) (qq.v.).

Decugis, Maxime Omer "Max" [FRA–TEN]. B. 24 September 1882, Paris. D. 6 September 1978, Biot. Max Decugis was the winner of a record six Olympic medals (four gold, one silver, one bronze) for lawn tennis between 1900 and 1920. His victories included the mixed doubles in 1906 when he was partnered by his wife. Although the Olympic tournaments during that era attracted many of the world's top players, Decugis's greatest non-Olympic achievement was to win the Wimbledon doubles with his countryman André Gobert in 1911, when they defeated the previously unbeaten holders, Tony Wilding (NZL) and Major Josiah Ritchie (GBR). He was also an eight-time French singles champion (1903–1904, 1907–1909, and 1912–1914), although the event was then closed to French players only.

Demonstration Sports. Numerous sports have been contested at the Olympic Games and Olympic Winter Games as demonstration sports. These have usually been sports that were being considered for the Olympic Program, or a sport indigenous to the country hosting the Olympic Games. In 1992, the IOC announced that demonstration sports would no longer officially be contested at the Olympic Games. *See also* AMERICAN FOOTBALL; AUSSIE RULES FOOTBALL; BADMINTON; BANDY; BASKETBALL; BICYCLE POLO; BOWLING; BUDO; CANOE & KAYAKING; CURLING; DOGSLED RACING; FREESTYLE SKIING; GLIDING; ICE DANCING (in Figure Skating); JEU DE PAUME; JUDO (Women); KORFBALL; LACROSSE; MILITARY PATROL; PELOTA BASQUE; ROLLER HOCKEY; SHORT-TRACK SPEED SKATING; SKIJÖRING; SPEED SKATING (Women); SPEED SKIING; TAEKWONDO; TENNIS; WATER SKIING; and WINTER PENTATHLON.

Denmark [DEN]. Denmark's connection with the Olympic Movement (q.v.) began in 1894 when Frederik Bajer, a member of the Danish Parliament, was an honorary member of the International Congress in Paris at which the Olympic Games were revived. After Denmark had participated in the 1896 Olympics, the first Danish IOC Member, Niels Holbeck, was co-opted in 1899, but it was not until 1905 that a Danish NOC was formed. Denmark has competed at every summer Olympic Games except 1904, but their attendance at the Olympic Winter Games has been less consistent. Since making their winter début in 1948, they have missed the Winter Olympics of 1956, 1972,

1976, 1980, and 1984. In their nine appearances at the Olympic Winter Games, they have been represented by a total of only 25 athletes. Danish athletes have won 162 Olympic medals, 40 of them gold. Denmark has won one medal in the Olympic Winter Games, a silver in curling in 1998.

Dhyan Chand [IND–HOK]. B. 28 August 1905, Allahabad. D. 3 December 1979. Dhyan Chand won three gold medals as a center-forward and is considered the greatest hockey (field) player ever. He learned the game from British army officers and had his first international competition in 1926 on a tour of Australia and New Zealand. He led India to gold medals in 1928, 1932, and 1936. In 1947–1948, Dhyan Chand was still the star of the Indian team but declined selection to the 1948 team, which prevented him from being the only hockey player to have won four gold medals. His younger brother, Roop Singh, played on the 1932 and 1936 Olympic teams and his son, Ashok Kumar, won an Olympic bronze medal in 1972.

Diaulos Race—Ancient Olympic Sport. The *diaulos* race was one of the major running events of the Ancient Olympic Games (q.v.). It consisted of a race of two laps of the stadium or about 385 meters. Champions are known from 724 B.C. (Hypenos of Pisa) through 153 A.D. (Demetrios of Chios). The greatest champions of the *diaulos* were Leonidas of Rhodes ([4 titles] 164–152 B.C.), Chionis of Sparta ([3 titles] 664–656 B.C.), Hermogenes of Xanthos ([3 titles] 81–89 A.D.), and Astylos of Kroton and Syracuse ([3 titles] 488–480 B.C.). An athlete from Argos also won the event four times, but his name is not known.

Dibiasi, Klaus [ITA–DIV]. B. 6 October 1947, Solbad Hall, Austria. After winning a silver medal in the platform diving at the 1964 Olympics, Klaus Dibiasi went on to win the gold on the platform at the next three Games (1968, 1972, 1976) and remains the only Olympic diver to have won three successive gold medals in the same event. A silver in the springboard in 1964 gave him what was then a record total of five Olympic medals. He also won the world platform title (1973, 1975), the European platform (1966, 1974), and the European springboard championship (1974). Dibiasi was born in Austria of Italian parents, who returned to Italy when he was a child. He was coached by his father, a former Italian champion and a 1936 Olympian.

Di Centa, Manuela [ITA–NSK]. B. 31 January 1963. In her first three Olympic appearances, Manuela Di Centa failed to win a single medal but at Lillehammer in 1994 she uniquely won a medal in all five cross-country skiing (q.v.) events. To her gold medals in the 15 km. and 30 km., she added silver in the 5 km. and combined pursuit, and a bronze in the relay. Di Centa also claimed relay medals at the 1992 and 1998 Olympic Winter Games, giving her seven Olympic medals in all, a total surpassed among women only by Raisa Smetanina, Galina Kulakova, and Lyubov Yegorova (all Soviets). In late 1999, Di Centa was named one of the new athlete members to the IOC.

Didrikson, Mildred Ella "Babe" (née Didrikson, later Mrs. Zaharias) [USA–ATH]. B. 26 June 1911, Port Arthur, Texas. D. 27 September 1956, Galveston, Texas. Babe Didrikson is considered by many authorities to be the greatest all-round sportswoman in history. At the 1932 Olympics, she won gold medals in the 80-meter hurdles and the javelin, and a silver in the high jump. She set new world records in each of these three disparate events. Didrikson was an All-American basketball player and held the world record for throwing a baseball, but she excelled as a golfer after giving up track & field athletics. She won the U.S. Amateur title in 1946 and the U.S. Open in 1948, 1950, and 1954, her third victory being by a record margin of 12 strokes, and coming after surgery for colon cancer.

Diem, Carl [GER]. B. 24 June 1882, Wurzburg. D. 17 December 1962, Cologne. Carl Diem is one of the co-founders of the International Olympic Academy (q.v.) and is one of the most important writers and historians of the Olympic Movement (q.v.), authoring dozens of books and articles on Olympism and the Olympic Movement. He studied at the University of Berlin, after which, from 1917 to 1933, he was secretary-general of the German Committee for Physical Education. He was secretary-general of the Organizing Committee of the 1936 Olympic Games and conceived the idea of the Olympic Torch Relay (*see* OLYMPIC FLAME). From 1938 to 1944, at Coubertin's (q.v.) request, he served as Director of the International

Olympic Institute in Berlin. After World War II, Diem was a sports consultant to the German government. A sports university was founded in his honor, the Carl-Diem-Sporthöchscule in Cologne.

Dietrich, Wilfried [FRG–WRE]. B. 14 October 1933. D. 3 June 1992. A competitor at five Olympic Games (1956–1972), Wilfried Dietrich competed in seven Olympic tournaments (four freestyle and three Græco-Roman) and won five medals (one gold, two silver, two bronze), a record for an Olympic wrestler. All his medals came in the unlimited class and unusually included a gold in the freestyle and a silver in the Græco-Roman style in 1960. Dietrich was the World Champion in 1961 and he was unbeaten in the unlimited freestyle from 1955 to 1962. At the World Championships, he also won two silver and two bronze medals between 1957 and 1969.

Dimas, Pyrros (né Pirro Dhima) [GRE-WLT]. B. 13 October 1971, Tirane, Albania. Although born in Albania, Pyrros Dimas has always competed internationally for Greece. Though the weight classes changed several times in the 1990s, Dimas was world champion between 80–85 kg. in 1993, 1995, and 1998. To those titles he added three consecutive Olympic gold medals in 1992, 1996, and 2000, one of only three weightlifters to have accomplished that feat.

D'Inzeo, Piero B. 4 March 1923, Rome; and **D'Inzeo, Raimondo** B. 2 February 1925, Poggio Mirteto, Rietil, **[ITA–EQU].** Piero and Raimondo D'Inzeo were Italian brothers who both competed in the equestrian events at eight Olympic Games (1948–1976), a record bettered only by Austrian yachtsman Hubert Raudauschl, who competed at nine Olympics. They each won six Olympic medals (Raimondo—one gold, two silver, three bronze; Piero—two silver, four bronze), with their best collective performance coming in 1960, when they took the first two places in the individual show jumping. Raimondo was also the World Individual Champion in 1956 and 1960. Both brothers followed their father in making their career in the Italian cavalry.

Disciplines. The International Olympic Committee recognizes three levels of competition—sports, disciplines, and events. *Sports* are well known and relatively self-explanatory. *Events* are any competition at which final results occur and medals are awarded at the Olympic Games. *Disciplines* are considered a subcategory of sports. Rule 52.2 defines a discipline, which is essentially a branch of a sport. The standards of admission to the Olympic Program are the same for a discipline as they are for a sport. Most sports, such as track & field athletics, or shooting, do not have disciplines, but consider all events part of one sport. There are seven summer Olympic sports that recognize disciplines, as follows: Aquatics—diving, swimming, synchronized swimming, and water polo; Canoe & Kayaking—sprint (flatwater) and slalom (whitewater); Cycling—track, road, and mountain biking; Equestrian—three-day event, dressage, jumping; Gymnastics—artistic, rhythmic, and trampoline; Volleyball—indoor volleyball and beach volleyball; and Wrestling—freestyle and Græco-Roman. Three winter Olympic sports recognize disciplines, as follows: Bobsledding—bobsled and skeleton; Skating—figure skating, speed skating, and short-track speed skating; and Skiing—Alpine skiing, cross-country skiing, freestyle skiing, Nordic combined, ski jumping, and snowboarding.

Dityatin, Aleksandr [URS/RUS–GYM]. B. 7 August 1957, Leningrad. By winning a medal in all eight gymnastics events at Moscow in 1980, Aleksandr Dityatin established a record that remains unique in Olympic history. His three gold medals came in the team and individual all-around, and on the rings, to which he added four silver medals and one bronze medal. His finest performance was in the horse vault, when he received the first perfect score (10) ever awarded to a male gymnast at the Olympics. Dityatin was equally dominant at the World Championships, winning 12 medals (seven gold, two silver, three bronze).

Diving. Diving is not considered to be a separate sport by the organizing body of world aquatics, Fédération Internationale de Natation Amateur (FINA). FINA contests four disciplines of aquatic competition—swimming, diving, synchronized swimming, and water polo. Usually, the diving results are listed with the swimming. FINA was formed in 1908 and currently has 171 affiliated nations.

Diving contests are known to have been held in the 19th century, although the sport is relatively modern. It was held at the 1904 Olympics in St. Louis, and its appearance on the Olympic program has been continuous since 1904. Diving has been contested in two basic events at the Olympics: 3-meter springboard and 10-meter platform, with both men and women contesting both events. Four new diving events were added to the Olympic program for 2000, the first change to the diving program since 1924. These were two-person synchronized diving competitions for men and women on both platform and springboard.

The United States has absolutely dominated the sport of diving, perhaps more than any sport has been dominated in the Olympics. In the late 1980s, the Chinese entered diving competition and posed the first serious threat to this dominance. While the United States' Greg Louganis (q.v.), considered the greatest diver ever, was still competing, the Chinese men posted few victories, but the Chinese women have been almost unbeatable of late.

Djibouti [DJI]. The Djibouti NOC was founded in 1983 and recognition by the IOC in 1984 enabled them to make their Olympic début at the Los Angeles Games that year. Since then, they have competed at every Summer Olympics but have not yet participated in the Olympic Winter Games. Their appearances have been highlighted by their excellent marathon runners, one of whom (Ahmed Salah) won a bronze medal in 1988 at Seoul.

Dmitriyev, Artur [EUN/RUS–FSK]. B. 21 January 1968. Artur Dmitriyev began his pairs figure skating career with Nataliya Mishkutyenok, and after placing third in 1990, they were World Champions in 1991–1992, and won the Olympic gold medal in 1992. At the 1994 Lillehammer Olympics, they placed second behind Sergey Grinkov and Ekaterina Gordeeva, who had been gold medallists in 1988, but Dmitriyev and Mishkutyenok recovered to win the 1994 World Championships. Dmitriyev then began competing with Oksana Kazakova and together they won the gold medal at Nagano in 1998, after placing third at the 1997 World Championships. Dmitriyev competed for the Soviet Union early in his career, for the Unified Team at Albertville in 1992, and later competed for Russia.

Dogsled Racing. A dogsled race with seven dogs per team was held at the 1932 Olympic Winter Games as a demonstration sport (q.v.). The race was run over 40.5 km. (25.1 miles), lasting two days. Twelve sleddog teams from Canada and the United States took part, with Émile St. Goddard of Canada winning the event.

Doherty, Reginald Frank [GBR–TEN]. B. 14 October 1872, Wimbledon, Surrey. D. 29 December 1910, Kensington, London. Reggie Doherty and his younger brother, Laurie, dominated world tennis at the turn of the century. As a doubles pairing, they were virtually unbeatable, winning the Wimbledon title eight times, the U.S. title twice, and all five of their Davis Cup rubbers. Together, they won the 1900 Olympic doubles title. In 1908, Reggie won a second gold medal in doubles when he was partnered by George Hillyard. Reggie Doherty confirmed his status as the world's leading player of the era by winning the Wimbledon singles title four years in succession (1897–1900).

Dolichos Race—Ancient Olympic Sport. The *dolichos* race was the long-distance running race of the Ancient Olympic Games (q.v.), consisting of a running event of 20–25 laps (circa 4,000–5,000 meters). Champions are known from 720 B.C. (Akanthos of Sparta) through 221 A.D. The last known champion, Graos of Bithynia, is the only runner known to have won the race three times at Olympia.

Dominica [DMA]. Founded in 1987, the Dominica NOC was not recognized by the IOC until 1993 and the country made its Olympic début in 1996 when five track & field athletes and one swimmer competed at the Atlanta Olympics. Dominica competed at Sydney represented by 13 athletes, 11 men and two women. Dominica has not yet competed at the Olympic Winter Games.

Dominican Republic [DOM]. The first Dominican Republic NOC was established in 1946 as a prerequisite to allow the Dominican Republic to participate in the Central American and Caribbean Games to be held that year. In 1953, the Olympic Sports Commission took control of participation in Olympic and Regional Games and in 1962 the NOC was re-established in its present form. This body was recognized by the IOC in 1962. Albert Torres was the first Dominican Republic athlete to make an Olympic appearance, competing in the

1964 100-meter dash. The Dominican Republic has competed eight times since, never failing to appear since its début. It has not yet competed in the Olympic Winter Games. Through 2000, the Dominican Republic has won one Olympic medal, a bronze by Pedro Nolasco in 1984 bantamweight boxing.

Doping. *Doping* refers to the illegal use of drugs to enhance performance in sport and is considered illegal by the International Olympic Committee (IOC) and the International Federations (IFs). The IOC rules against doping are contained in Rule 48 of the *Olympic Charter* (q.v.). Basically, the IOC has a proscribed list of medications which are considered to be illegal for use by athletes taking part in its competitions. After each Olympic Games, all medalists, and certain other randomly selected athletes, are chosen to submit a urine sample that is then tested for these drugs. If any of the proscribed drugs are present in the athlete's urine in sufficient quantities, he or she may be disqualified from competition, pending further urine studies and, usually, legal hearings. In the 1980s and 1990s, when these penalties have been handed out, they have virtually always been contested by the athletes and their lawyers.

In addition, it is considered unlikely that previous IOC methods of testing for illegal drugs were sufficient to prevent athletes from using drugs. This is because athletes, coaches, and their doctors were able to learn enough about the drugs in order to know how long they had to be withdrawn from the athlete before a competition. This would enable the athlete to pass frequent drug tests despite being habitual users of the drugs. This is now being circumvented by IFs, NOCs, and National Governing Bodies performing random, out-of-competition tests of athletes at all times of the year.

Doping is not new. In the ancient Olympics, trainers gave athletes various concoctions that they felt would improve their performance. The first physician to be considered a specialist in sports medicine was Galen, who prescribed as follows: "The rear hooves of an Abyssinian ass, ground up, boiled in oil, and flavored with rose hips and rose petals, was the prescription favored to improve performance." The name *doping* itself comes from the 19th century, when the term *dop* was used to describe a South African drink that was an extract of cola nuts to which was added xanthines (found in caffeine) and alcohol. The drink was intended to improve endurance and the term *doping* was derived from it.

Numerous doping scandals have existed in sports. The most famous occurred at the 1988 Seoul Olympics when the original 100-meter champion Ben Johnson tested positive for stanazolol, an anabolic steroid, and was disqualified. At the 1960 Rome Olympics, Danish cyclist Knut Enemark Jensen collapsed and died during the cycling road race. He was later found to have been given amphetamines (Ronital) and nicotinyl tartrate (a nicotine-type of stimulant). In the 1967 Tour de France, the great British cyclist, Tommy Simpson, collapsed and died while ascending Mont Ventoux. He was found to have been heavily dosed with stimulants. In 1998, a major doping scandal enveloped the Tour de France, and many of the professional cyclists and their team trainers were charged with legal action by the French authorities.

The deaths of Jensen and Simpson alerted the sporting authorities to the dangers inherent in drug use in sports. At the 1968 Olympic Winter Games, the IOC tested for drugs for the first time. The first athlete to be disqualified in the Olympics for drug use was Sweden's Hans-Gunnar Liljenvall at the 1968 Olympic Games. Liljenvall was a modern pentathlete who had helped his team win a bronze medal. Prior to the shooting event, he drank a few beers to help steady his nerves. This was commonplace among modern pentathletes in those days, but it cost him and his teammates a bronze medal.

In the 1970s and 1980s, the athletes of the German Democratic Republic (GDR—East Germany) were suspected of doping violations that were never detected. No GDR athlete ever failed a doping test at the Olympics. After the fall of the Berlin Wall and the reunification of the two Germanys, former German athletes and coaches revealed that much of the success of the great GDR athletic machine was due to the systematic use of illegal drugs. In the 1990s, the Chinese women swimmers and runners have been suspected of using similar practices to make great strides in their sports. Adding to this suspicion is that several of the former GDR coaches now coach in China.

In 1999, the International Olympic Committee was instrumental in pushing the fight against drugs to a new level, by forming the World Anti-Doping Agency (WADA [q.v.]). Headed intially by Canadian IOC Member Dick Pound (q.v.), WADA's task is to oversee and monitor the use of drugs in international sport and find better methods of prevention and detection, as well as educating athletes to the danger and impropriety of drug use in sports. *See* Appendix XVII for a complete list of all positive doping tests that have occurred at the Olympic Games.

Dream Team, The—1992 USA Basketball. The Dream Team was the basketball team that represented the United States at the 1992 Olympics. For the first time, all basketball professionals were declared eligible to compete at the Olympics, including members of the National Basketball Association (NBA), the United States' major professional league. This allowed the U.S. to field a team of multiple professional all-stars, which was certainly the greatest basketball team ever assembled. The team gained incredible attention from the media and fans, both in the United States and Spain, as well as throughout the world, and easily won the gold medal. The team members were Charles Barkley, Larry Bird, Clyde Drexler, Patrick Ewing, Earvin "Magic" Johnson, Michael Jordan, Christian Laettner, Karl Malone, Chris Mullin, Scottie Pippen, David Robinson, and John Stockton. Subsequent U.S. teams, made up of NBA players, have been labelled *Dream Team II* and *Dream Team III*, but the 1992 team is considered by far the most outstanding.

Dresden Four, The—GDR Coxless Four Rowing Team [1968–72]. Also known as *the Einheit Dresden Four*, this coxless four rowing team won Olympic gold medals in 1968 and 1972 and was never beaten in international competition. Representing the GDR, they were World Champions in 1966 and 1970, and European Champions in 1967 and 1971. The team members were Frank Forberger, Dieter Grahn, Frank Rühle, and Dieter Schubert.

– E –

Eagan, Edward Patrick Francis "Eddie" [USA–BOX/BOB]. B. 26 April 1898, Denver, Colorado. D. 14 June 1967, New York. Eddie Eagan was the Olympic light-heavyweight boxing champion in 1920 and a member of the winning four-man bobsled crew in 1932. He is the only man to have won an Olympic gold medal at both the Winter and Summer Games. While a Rhodes Scholar at Oxford University, Eagan made a second appearance at the Summer Games in 1924 when he was eliminated in the semi-finals of the heavyweight boxing.

Ecuador [ECU]. Ecuador sent three track & field competitors to the 1924 Olympic Games—Alberto Jurado Gonzales, Luis Jarrin, and Belisario Villacis—prior to the Ecuadorean NOC being formed in 1925. A gap of 44 years then occurred before it returned to the Olympics at Mexico City and it has competed continuously since. It has never appeared at the Olympic Winter Games. Ecuador has won one medal at the Olympics, a gold in 20-km. race walking at the 1996 Olympics by Jefferson Perez.

Edström, Johannes Sigfrid [SWE]. B. 21 November 1870, Morlanda, 65 km. D. 18 March 1964, Stockholm. As president of the International Olympic Committee (IOC) and the International Amateur Athletic Federation (IAAF), Sigfrid Edström was a man of immense sporting influence. Born in Sweden and educated partly there and in the United States and Switzerland (1891–1893), he was one of the organizers of the 1912 Olympic Games in Stockholm. During those Olympic Games, he took the initiative of founding the IAAF, for which he served as the first president, remaining in that office from 1913 until 1946. Edström founded the International Chamber of Commerce in 1918 (president, 1939–1945), the Federation of Swedish Industries in 1910 (Chairman, 1928–1929), and was Chairman of the Swedish Employers' Confederation from 1931 to 1942. His main business career was as Managing Director (1903–1933) and Chairman of the Board (1934–1949) for Allmåna Svenska Elektriska Aktiebolagel (ASEA), a world leader in the high-tension current industry. Edström was elected an IOC member in 1921 and became a member of the IOC Executive Board (q.v.), when it was created in the same year. He chaired the Olympic Congresses (q.v.) in 1921 and 1925 and was appointed vice president of the IOC in 1937. Following the death of IOC president Henri de Baillet-Latour (q.v.) in 1942, Edström was, as a neutral, well placed to keep the Olympic Movement (q.v.) alive during the war years as a de facto president. In 1946, in the first post-war IOC session in Lausanne, he was elected president by acclamation. On his retirement in 1952, at the age of 81, he was given the title of Honorary President of the IOC. In 1947, he was awarded the Olympic Cup (q.v.) for his contributions to the Olympic Movement.

Edwards, Teresa [USA–BAS]. B. 19 July 1964, Cairo, Georgia. One of the greatest female guards to ever play basketball, Teresa Edwards played collegiately at the University of Georgia, where she was a consensus All-American in 1984 and 1985. Her record is unmatched by women in international competition. She won gold medals at the 1984, 1988, 1996, and 2000 Olympics, and a bronze medal at the 1992 Olympics, and her five Olympic medals, and four golds, are both Olympic basketball records. She also was the playmaking leader of championship teams at the 1986 and 1990 World Championships, the 1986 and 1990 Goodwill Games, and the 1987 Pan-American Games. In 1991, she played on the U.S. team that won a bronze at the Pan-American Games. She was the USA basketball player of the year in both 1987 and 1991.

Egerszegi, Krisztina [HUN–SWI]. B. 16 August 1974, Budapest, Hungary. Krisztina Egerszegi established herself as one of the greatest backstrokers in swimming history. When only 14 years old, she won a gold and silver in the two backstroke events at the 1988 Olympics. In 1992, she returned to win three individual gold medals, in the 100-meter backstroke, the 200-meter backstroke, and the 400-meter individual medley. In 1996 at Atlanta, Egerszegi won her third consecutive gold medal in the 200 backstroke, making her only the second swimmer, after Dawn Fraser in the 100 free, to win the same event at three straight Olympics. She is the only Olympic swimmer to have won five individual gold medals. At the European Championships, she won three silver medals in 1989 and three gold medals in 1991 and 1993. At the 1991 World Championships, she won both backstroke events. She set two world records during her career, one each in the 100-meter and 200-meter backstroke.

Egypt [EGY]. Egypt first competed at the 1896 Olympic Games and after missing the Olympics of 1900 and 1904, they were again represented at the Intercalated Games of 1906. They were not present at the

1908 Olympics, but after forming an NOC in 1910, they were more formally represented at the 1912 Stockholm Olympics. Since then, they have been absent only from the Olympics of 1932, 1956 (missing Melbourne, but not Stockholm), and 1980. Egypt's absence from the 1932 Olympics was the result of political turmoil that resulted in the NOC being disbanded in 1929, but it was re-established in time for a large team (53 athletes) to be sent to the Berlin Olympics in 1936. From 1960 through 1968, Egypt competed as the United Arab Republic (UAR), joining in a union in 1960 with Syria, although all but three of the 74 UAR athletes were Egyptian. Egypt's greatest Olympic successes have come in the strength sports of weightlifting and wrestling. Egypt competed at the Olympic Winter Games only in 1984 at Sarajevo.

Ehrig-Schöne-Mitscherlich, Andrea [GDR–SSK]. B. 1 December 1960, Dresden. Andrea Ehrig won seven Olympic speed skating medals: one gold, five silver, and one bronze. After starting with a silver in 1976, she failed to win a medal in 1980, but won her only gold in 1984 at her favorite distance of 3,000 meters. She ended her Olympic career in 1988 with silvers in the 3,000 and 5,000 meters and a bronze in the 1,500 meters. Primarily a distance skater, Ehrig set world records over the three distances at which she won Olympic medals. Her first Olympic appearance, when only 15 years old, was under her maiden name of Mitscherlich. She later competed under her married name of Schöne. Following her second marriage in 1985 to fellow Olympic speed skater Andreas Ehrig, she made her final Olympic appearance under that name.

El Salvador [ESA]. El Salvador's National Olympic Committee was formed in 1949, but it was not recognized by the IOC until 1962. Six years then passed before El Salvador competed at the Olympic Games in 1968. Since then, it has been absent only from the Olympics of 1976 and 1980. It has won no Olympic medals to date and has not yet competed at the Olympic Winter Games. Their best Olympic performance was a fifth-place finish by Maureen Kaila Vergana in the 1996 women's points race cycling.

Elvstrøm, Paul Bert [DEN–YAC]. B. 25 February 1928, Gentofte (Hellerup), Copenhagen. Paul Elvstrøm competed as a yachtsman in eight Games over a 40-year period. Although three other competitors have had similarly lengthy Olympic careers, none of them could match Elvstrøm's record of successes. He won the Firefly class in 1948 and the Finn class in 1952, 1956, and 1960, and was the first competitor in any sport to win individual gold medals at four successive Games. After being a reserve on the Danish team in 1964, Elvstrøm then competed in 1968 and 1972 without winning a medal. He also competed in 1984 and 1988 when his daughter, Trine, crewed for him.

Ender, Kornelia (later Matthes, then Grummt) [GDR–SWI]. B. 25 October 1958, Plauen. Kornelia Ender is one of only three women swimmers to have won a total of eight Olympic medals, a record she shares with Shirley Babashoff and Dawn Fraser. She won four gold medals in 1976 in the 100- and 200-meter freestyle, the 100-meter butterfly, and the 400-meter medley relay. The most prolific record breaker of modern times, she set 23 world records (1973–1976) in currently recognized events and her total of 10 medals (eight gold, two silver) at the World Championships is also a record. She married first Roland Matthes and then Olympic decathlete Steffen Grummt.

Endo, Yukio [JPN–GYM]. B. 18 January 1937, Akita. Yukio Endo won seven Olympic medals and five gold medals in gymnastics. He helped Japan to the all-around team championship in 1960, 1964, and 1968. In 1964 he was the individual all-around champion and added a gold medal on the parallel bars. His other two individal medals were silver in the 1964 floor exercises and the 1968 horse vault. Endo won only one individual title at the World Championships, that being the 1962 floor exercise title. In 1962, he won seven medals at the Worlds, and followed that with three more in 1966. In both years, he won golds with the Japanese team.

Engel-(Gulbin-)Krämer, Ingrid [GDR–DIV]. B. 29 July 1943, Dresden. Ingrid Krämer won gold in both platform and springboard diving in 1960, making her the first non-American female to achieve this feat. After repeating this double at the 1963 European Championships, Engel-Krämer was a strong favorite to retain both titles in 1964, but she was successful only in the springboard, narrowly losing her platform crown. At her third Olympics in Mexico in 1968, she competed only in the springboard where she finished fifth. She competed under three different names at the Olympics. She appeared under her maiden name of Krämer in 1960, while in 1964 she used the name of her first husband (Engel) and in 1968 that of her second husband (Gulbin).

Equatorial Guinea [GEQ]. Equatorial Guinea's NOC was formed in 1980 and recognized by the IOC in 1984, which enabled the nation to make its Olympic début at the Los Angeles Games that year. Since then, it has been represented at every Olympic Games, but only had athletes in the track & field events until 2000 at Sydney, when two swimmers (one male and one female) and two track & field athletes represented the nation at the Olympics.

Equestrian Events. Equestrian events have been on the Olympic program since 1900 when jumping events were held at the Olympics in Paris. However, equestrian events were not held again until 1912 in Stockholm. Since that year, the sport has always been on the Olympic program.

There are three equestrian disciplines contested, with an individual and team event in each, making six events on the Olympic program. These are jumping (or show jumping, or Grand Prix de Nations as a team event), dressage, and the three-day event. *Jumping* consists of jumping over a series of obstacles in an attempt to not disturb the fences. *Dressage* is a sort of ballet on horseback in which the rider has the horse perform certain intricate maneuvers of stepping. The scoring is done by judges who evaluate how well the horse executes the moves. The three-day event combines the above two disciplines, and adds a third competition of riding a cross-country course. Scoring is by a series of tables evaluating each day's performance. It actually occurs now over four days at the Olympics as two days are devoted to the dressage.

Equestrian sports are governed by the Fédération Équestre Internationale (FEI), which was formed in 1921 and had 125 member nations at the end of 2000. The top nations at the Olympics in equestrian events have been Germany, Sweden, the United States, and France.

Eritrea [ERI]. The IOC granted provisional recognition to the NOC for Eritrea in 1998 and full recognition followed in 1999. Eritrea was the northernmost province of Ethiopia until it became independent in May 1993. Prior to Eritrean independence, several of their athletes competed for Ethiopia at the Olympics. Eritrea first competed at the Olympics in 2000 at Sydney, represented by two male and one female runners in track & field athletics.

Estonia [EST]. Three Estonian athletes were members of the Russian team at the 1912 Olympic Games and, as a separate nation, Estonia competed at the Olympic Games continuously from 1920 to 1936. At the 1924 Olympic Winter Games, speed skater Christfried Burmeister participated in the Opening Ceremony but he did not take part in the competitions that followed, and Estonia first competed at the Olympic Winter Games of 1928 and also competed in 1932 and 1936. From 1952 to 1988, Estonia was a republic of the USSR and thus did not compete as an independent nation, but many Estonian athletes competed for the Soviet Union. After the Soviet Revolution of 1991, Estonia declared and was granted its independence. The nation returned to the Olympic fold by competing in 1992 in both Albertville and Barcelona, and has competed at every Olympic Games and Olympic Winter Games since. Estonia has won 26 Olympic medals, 21 from 1920 to 1936, 2 in Barcelona, and 3 in Sydney. Eight of these were gold medals, including an emotional victory for Erika Salumäe (q.v.) in women's match sprint cycling in 1992. Estonia has never hosted an Olympic Games, but in 1980, all of the sailing events of the Moscow Olympics were actually held in the Gulf of Finland off Tallinn, the capital of Estonia.

Ethiopia [ETH]. Ethiopia made its first Olympic appearance in 1956. It has since missed the 1976, 1984, and 1988 Olympics, all due to political boycotts, making Ethiopia one of only three nations—with Egypt and the DPR Korea (North)—to have boycotted three Olympic Games. The country has made no appearances at the Olympic Winter Games. Ethiopia's top athletes have been distance runners. Heading this list is Abebe Bikila (q.v.), Olympic marathon champion in 1960 and 1964, and generally considered the greatest marathoner of all time. Ethiopia has won 24 Olympic medals, 12 of them gold, all in track & field athletics.

European Olympic Committees [EOC]. The National Olympic Committees from Europe have formed this group to further their interests with the International Olympic Committee. The EOC is headquartered in Rome, Italy. The president as of 2000 is Dr. Jacques Rogge of Belgium. The group's name was changed to *European Olympic Committees (EOC)* in November 1994 at its meeting in Atlanta. Prior to that time it was known as the *Association des Comités Nationaux Olympiques d'Europe (ACNOE).*

Evans, Janet Elizabeth [USA–SWI]. B. 28 August 1971, Fullerton, California. Janet Evans is considered by most swimming experts as the greatest female long distance swimmer of all time. She entered the 1988 Olympics as the world record holder in the 400 meters, 800 meters, and 1,500 meters and improved her own world record in winning the 400 meters, in addition to taking gold medals in the 800 meters and the 400-meter individual medley. At her second Olympic appearance in 1992, Evans successfully defended her 800-meters title, but suffered her first defeat in the 400 meters since 1986 when she placed second to Dagmar Hase (GER). She won a host of medals at the World Championships, the Goodwill Games, and other major championships and brought a new dimension to long-distance swimming for women. Evans finished her career at the 1996 Olympics Games where, then past her prime, she finished sixth in the 800-meter freestyle.

Ewry, Raymond Clarence "R.C." [USA–ATH]. B. 14 October 1873, Lafayette, Indiana. D. 29 September 1937, Queens, New York. R. C. Ewry was a victim of polio as a child, but remedial leg-strengthening exercises resulted in his becoming the greatest exponent of the now-defunct standing jumps. He was unbeaten in 10 Olympic competitions, winning the standing high jump and standing long jump four times each (1900, 1904, 1906, 1908) and the standing triple jump twice (1900, 1904). His 10 individual gold medals remain an Olympic record for any sport. Ewry retired shortly after the 1908 Games having won 15 AAU (Amateur Athletic Union [USA]) titles and setting world records in each of his three specialty events.

Executive Board of the IOC. The Executive Board of the International Olympic Committee manages the affairs of the IOC. It functions by making its recommendations to the IOC sessions. These recommendations are rarely overturned, thus the Executive Board effectively runs the IOC. It consists of the president of the IOC, four vice presidents, and, beginning in 2000, 10 additional members, for a total of 15 members. Prior to 2000, the Executive Board consisted of 11 members, the president, vice president, and six other members, but the size of the Board was increased based on the recommendations of the IOC 2000 Commission (q.v.). The commission also mandated that future Executive Boards should have representative members from the various classes of IOC Members: independent members, National Olympic Committee members, International Federation members, and athletes. Executive Board members are elected by the IOC sessions. The vice presidents and Board Members are elected for four-year periods. Founded in 1921, it was known as the *Executive Committee* until 1955.

– F –

Federal Republic of Germany [FRG]. *See* GERMANY.

Fencing. Fencing began as a form of combat and is known to have been practiced well before the birth of Christ. As a sport, fencing began in either the 14th or 15th century and both Italy and Germany lay claims to the origins of the sport. In 1570, Henri Saint-Didier of France gave names to fencing's major movements and most of that nomenclature remains.

Until the 17th century, the fencing weapons were large and unwieldy, like the combat weapons. However, the combat sword evolved into the épée and, somewhat, into the sabre. The foil was originally a practice weapon for combat and became popular as a sporting event in the late 19th century.

The foil is a light, quadrangular tapering blade in which only hits made with the blade point on the opponent's torso count. The épée, developed from the dueling weapons of European noblemen, is the same length as the foil, but is heavier and has a larger handguard. Hits must also be made with the tip of the blade, but can be scored over the opponent's entire body. The sabre owes its origins to the Middle

Eastern scimitar and the 18th century cavalry sabre. Hits may be scored with the tip of the blade, with its front edge, or with the last one-third of its back edge. The target area is from the bend of the hips up, including the head and arms.

Fencing was first contested at the 1896 Olympics and is one of the few sports to have been contested at every Olympic Games. Women's fencing first appeared in the Olympics in 1924. Today, men compete in the Olympics with three types of swords—the foil, the épée, and the sabre—in both team and individual events, thus six events in all. Women have competed in the Olympics in the foil and épée, with both a team and an individual event, épée having been added to the Olympic Program at the 1996 Olympics in Atlanta. Electronic scoring has been used for the foil and épée for decades now, while electronic scoring for the sabre made its Olympic début at Barcelona.

Fencing is governed worldwide by the Fédération Internationale d'Éscrime (FIE), which was formed in 1913 and had 99 member nations affiliated as of 1999. Fencing has been dominated at the Olympics by France and Italy in the foil and épée, and Hungary in the sabre.

Ferguson, Ian Gordon [NZL–CAN]. B. 20 July 1952. After an undistinguished Olympic début in 1980, Ian Ferguson retired from canoeing and went into business. After a two-year hiatus, Ferguson came back in 1983 and won a silver medal at the 500 meters at the World Championships. Then in 1984, at the age of 32, he won three gold medals at the Los Angeles Olympics in the K1-500, K2-500, and the K4 event. Paul McDonald joined Ferguson in the last two events. At the 1988 Olympics, they retained the Olympic K2-500 title and won a silver in the K2-1,000.

Figure Skating. Figure skating began in the mid- to late-19th century almost concurrently in Europe and North America, but two Americans are responsible for major developments in its history. In 1850, Edward Bushnell of Philadelphia revolutionized skating technology when he refined the use of steel-bladed skates. This allowed the creation of fancy twists and turns on the ice. Another American, Jackson Haines, a ballet master, visited Vienna in the 1860s and added the elements of music and dance to figure skating. Originally, free skating was subordinate to school figures, or the tracing of pretty patterns on the ice.

International figure skating competitions were held in Europe in the 1880s and the International Skating Union (ISU) was formed in 1892, the first true international governing body of any winter sport (now with 72 members, but representing only 55 nations). Originally, men and women competed together, with the first world championship being held in what was then and is now St. Petersburg, Russia (formerly Leningrad) in 1896. The first women's championship was held in 1906.

Figure skating is the oldest sport on the Winter program. It was contested at the London Olympics of 1908 and again in 1920 at Antwerp. Events for men, women, and pairs were contested through 1972. In 1976, ice dancing, long a popular event, was added to the program as a fourth event, although it had been held as a demonstration event (q.v.) in 1968.

Scoring has evolved during the century also, as the former predominance of compulsory figures in the scoring gave way in the early 1970s. A short program of free skating was added, primarily to equalize results among skaters who were excellent at compulsories, but lesser free skaters, to those who were poor compulsory skaters but top-notch free skaters. This was exemplified in that era by Beatrix "Trixi" Schuba (AUT), who was an excellent skater in compulsories, but was a relatively poor free skater, and Janet Lynn (USA), who was a superb free skater but usually was beaten by Schuba because of her difficulty with the compulsories. This gave impetus to the movement to decrease the importance of compulsory figures. At the end of the 1980s, the International Skating Union ruled that compulsory figures would no longer be held at international competitions. They last were contested at the 1990 World Championships and they have not been a part of the Olympic figure skating program since 1988.

Since World War II, figure skating has been dominated in the men's and women's singles by the United States, which has won six men's gold medals and six women's gold medals. In pairs and ice dancing, by far the dominant nation has been the Soviet Union and its former republics. Since 1964, the Soviet Union (or its former republics) has won every pairs and dance gold medal available, with the exception of the 1984 ice dancing gold medal that went to Great Britain's Jayne Torvill and Christopher Dean.

Fiji [FIJ]. Fiji formed a National Olympic Committee in 1949 and first competed at the Olympics in 1956. Fiji has since competed at all the Olympics with the exception of 1964 and 1980. It has competed at the Olympic Winter Games in both 1988 and 1994, their sole representative on each occasion being Nordic skiier, Ruscale Rogoyawa. It has won no medals. Its best Olympic performance to date occurred in 1992, Anthony Philip finished 10th of 44 sailors in the Lechner boardsailing class.

Finance Commission. The Finance Commission is one of the most important commissions as the Olympic Movement, like all organizations, depends on finances to remain solvent. The Finance Commission was formed in 1967 at a time when the IOC was almost bankrupt. The original chairman was Lord Luke of Great Britain. Currently, the Finance Commission is chaired by Marc Hodler of Switzerland, who in late 1998 spoke to the media after the IOC session and discussed the problems in the bidding process, which led to the Olympic Scandal of 1999. With the exception of a financial advisor, all members of the Finance Commission are IOC Members.

Finland [FIN]. Finland first competed at the 1906 Intercalated Games in Athens and also appeared two years later at the 1908 London Olympics. Its first Olympic Winter appearance was in 1924 at Chamonix, although it had two skaters entered in the figure skating events in 1920. Since those dates, Finland's participation has been continuous, never missing an Olympic Games nor an Olympic Winter Games. Finland's greatest successes have come in the distance running events in the Summer Games. In those events, led by Hannes Kolehmainen, Paavo Nurmi, and Lasse Virén (qq.v.), Finland has been the preeminent nation, until the recent advent of the African distance runners. Prior to World War II, Finland was also the dominant nation in wrestling. In the Winter Games, Finland has excelled at Nordic skiing and, in the early Games, at speed skating. Finland hosted the Games of the XVth Olympiad in Helsinki in 1952. Through 2000, Finland has won 432 Olympic medals, 139 of them gold. Of these, 136 medals, and 38 gold, were won at the Olympic Winter Games.

Flanagan, John Jesus [USA/IRL–ATH]. B. 9 January 1873, Kilbreedy, County Limerick, Ireland. D. 4 June 1938, Kilmallack, County Limerick, Ireland. John Flanagan's three successive victories in the hammer throw (1900, 1904, 1908) remained an Olympic record for any track & field event until Al Oerter won his fourth consecutive gold medal in the discus in 1968. Flanagan would almost certainly have won four Olympic titles had the hammer been included in the program at the 1896 Games, and had he competed. Between 1896 and 1909, he improved the world best for the hammer no less than 18 times, his first record coming when he won the British title in 1896 shortly before he emigrated to the United States.

Football, American. American football was a demonstration sport at the 1932 Olympics.

Football, Association (Soccer). Football (soccer) is the world's most popular sport, played in more countries than any other. The World Cup of football, the quadrennial competition played in the even year between Olympics (last in 1998), is considered the most watched single sporting event on the planet. The sport is governed internationally by the Fédération Internationale de Football Association (FIFA), which was formed in 1904 and had 204 members as of December 2000.

The origins of football are vague. The Greeks played a game that loosely resembled its modern counterpart, as did the Romans. By the 14th century, it was so popular in England that King Edward II issued a proclamation on 13 April 1314, forbidding the game "forasmuch as there is great noise in the city caused by hustling over large balls from which many evils might arise which God forbid; we commend and forbid, on behalf of the King, on pain of imprisonment, such game to be used in the city of the future." In 1349, Edward III objected to the game because it prevented the practice of archery, necessary for the military strength of the country. Banning the game had little effect, however, as similar edicts had to be issued in 1389 (Richard II), 1401 (Henry IV), 1436 (Henry VIII), 1457 (James II), and again in 1491.

Gradually, despite attempts to ban it, football spread throughout the world, becoming popular almost everywhere, with the United States being a notable exception. Football was first contested at the 1900 and 1904 Olympics. The sport has been played at every Olympics since, with the exception of 1932 in Los Angeles.

The World Cup began in 1930 and brings together the world's top professional players. In recent years, Olympic eligibility has become a problem. Eastern European countries stated that they had no true professionals, although their players were state supported. Thus, they often entered similar teams in both the World Cup and the Olympics, and the Eastern Europeans have been dominant in Olympic football since the 1950s. Recently, however, eligibility rules have changed as other countries may be allowed to use some of their professional players who have competed in the World Cup. The problem is not yet fully resolved. Currently, professional players may compete at the Olympics providing they are not more than 23 years old, although each team is allowed three exceptions to the age rule. There is some sentiment among IOC officials to change this and allow all professionals to compete.

Football (soccer) for women is now becoming more popular, with the first women's World Cup being contested in 1991. Women's football appeared on the Olympic program for the first time in 1996. *See also* URUGUAY FOOTBALL TEAMS [1924 and 1928].

Football, Australian Rules (Aussie Rules). Australian Rules Football was a demonstration sport at the 1956 Olympics in Melbourne.

Foreman, George [USA–BOX]. B. 22 January 1948, Marshall, Texas. George Foreman won the 1968 Olympic heavyweight boxing championship. After the Olympics, Foreman quickly turned professional and began knocking out fighters left and right with his powerful punching ability. In 1973, he fought Joe Frazier (q.v.) for the heavyweight title, winning easily. Foreman defended the title twice but, on 30 October 1974 in Zaire, Muhammad Ali (q.v.) stopped him in eight rounds in "The Rumble in the Jungle." Foreman was never a championship factor again in his "first" career. However, in 1987, George Foreman, by then weighing close to 300 pounds, began a comeback. Through 1990, he was not defeated in that comeback. In April 1991, he fought for the heavyweight title again and lost a 12-round decision to Evander Holyfield. In 1994, however, he defeated Michael Moorer to claim the World Boxing Association (WBA) and International Boxing Federation (IBF) world heavyweight championships at the age of 46 years. Foreman lost those titles in 1995 when he refused to fight certain opponents, as mandated by those governing bodies, and has since retired.

Formosa. *See* CHINESE TAIPEI.

France [FRA]. France can be said to be the home of the Modern Olympic Games, being the home of Pierre de Coubertin (q.v.), their founder. Not unexpectedly, it has competed at every celebration of the Olympic Games and at every Olympic Winter Games. In addition to appearing at all the Olympic Games, France has hosted five Olympic Games, second only to the United States. These were the Games of the IInd Olympiad in Paris in 1900, the Games of the VIIIth Olympiad in Paris in 1924, the 1st Olympic Winter Games in Chamonix in 1924, the 10th Olympic Winter Games in Grenoble in 1968, and the 16th Olympic Winter Games in Albertville in 1992. France's greatest athletic successes have come in the sports of cycling and fencing, sports at which it has often been the dominant nation. France has won 675 Olympic medals (208 gold) with 63 having been won at the Olympic Winter Games, of which 18 have been gold medals.

Fraser, Dawn Lorraine [AUS–SWI]. B. 4 September 1937, Balmain, Sydney. The greatest female sprint swimmer ever, Dawn Fraser was the first woman swimmer to win eight Olympic medals, a record since surpassed. She won four gold and four silver medals at the Games of 1956, 1960, and 1964, including three successive golds in the 100-meter freestyle, a record for any Olympic swimming event equalled only by Krisztina Egerszegi (HUN) (q.v.) in the 200 backstroke in 1988–1996. Fraser was denied the opportunity of adding to her medal total when she received a lengthy suspension following misbehavior at the 1964 Games. Dawn Fraser set 27 individual and 12 relay world records. During her career, she won 30 Australian championships (23 individual and 7 team) and at the British Empire and Commonwealth Games, she won eight medals: six gold and two silver. She represented Balmain in the New South Wales Parliament from 1988 to 1991.

Frazier, Joseph "Joe" [USA–BOX]. B. 12 January 1944, Beaufort, South Carolina. Joe Frazier won a gold medal as a heavyweight boxer at the 1964 Olympics. Frazier first won the heavyweight World Championship in 1970 by stopping Jimmy Ellis in five rounds. He defended the title four times before being knocked out by George Foreman (q.v.). Frazier later fought three tremendous battles with Muhammad Ali (q.v.). The first, in 1971, was the fight of the century, a battle of undefeated heavyweight champions, and Frazier won by a decision in 15 rounds. Frazier was on the losing end in the next two fights, but all three were great spectacles. After losing his heavyweight title, he continued to fight for a few years before retiring in the mid-1970s. Despite the acclaim accorded Muhammad Ali, which somewhat diminished Frazier's appeal, his opponent knew of his greatness, describing him as follows, "Fighting Joe Frazier is the closest thing to death that I know of. Of all the men I fought in boxing, including Sonny Liston and George Foreman, the roughest and toughest was Joe Frazier . . . If God ever calls me to a Holy War, I want Joe Frazier fighting beside me."

Fredriksson, Gert Fridolf [SWE–CAN]. B. 21 November 1919, Nyköping. With eight medals (six gold, one silver, one bronze) between 1948 and 1960 Gert Fredriksson is the most successful male canoeist in Olympic history. He was at his best in the K1–1,000 meters, winning a gold medal at three successive Games (1948–1956) and in the K1–10,000 meters, in which he won two gold medals (1948, 1956) and a silver (1952). He is one of only 12 Olympians to have won gold medals at four or more consecutive Olympic Games. At the World Championships, he won four individual titles and a further three in the relay. In 1956, Fredriksson was awarded the Mohammed Taher Trophy by the IOC. *See* Appendix V.

Frédy, Pierre. *See* COUBERTIN, BARON PIERRE DE.

Freestyle Skiing. Freestyle skiing was held at the 1988 Winter Olympics as a demonstration sport. In 1992, moguls was contested as a full-medal sport in Albertville. In Lillehammer in 1994, both moguls and aerials were full-medal events. Moguls consists of a timed race down a short course made up entirely of small hills termed *moguls*. The skiier receives a point score for style which is added to a point score for the time, to derive an overall score. *Aeriels* is a jumping event in which skiiers take off from an elevated platform after a short run, and then execute intricate gymnastics-like maneuvers in the air. The contest is decided by point scores awarded by judges. The third event of freestyle skiing is ballet, but that event has not yet appeared on the Olympic program. Freestyle is considered a discipline (q.v.) of the sport of skiing by the IOC and, as such, it is governed by the Fédération Internationale de Ski (FIS).

Fu Mingxia [CHN–DIV]. B. 16 August 1978. China's Fu Mingxia was the top female diver of the 1990s. She has been at her best on the platform, winning the Olympic gold medal in that event in 1992 and 1996, and was World Champion in 1991 and 1994. In 1996, Fu won both the springboard and platform at the Olympics, duplicating the feats of Vicky Draves (1948), Pat McCormick (1952–1956), and Ingrid Krämer (1960), who also won both events at the same Olympics. Fu retired briefly after the 1996 Olympics, but returned to compete in the 2000 Olympics, defending her springboard gold medal and winning a silver medal in the new synchronized springboard event.

– G –

Gabon [GAB]. Gabon formed a National Olympic Committee in 1965, but did not compete at the Olympics until 1972. Gabon has competed at six Olympic Games, those of 1972, 1984, 1988, 1992, 1996, and 2000. It has never had an athlete compete at the Olympic Winter Games and no athlete from Gabon has won an Olympic medal.

Gambia, The [GAM]. The Gambia's National Olympic Committee was formed in 1972 and recognized by the IOC in 1976. The Gambia has competed at the Olympic Games of 1984, 1988, 1992, 1996, and 2000, but has never competed at the Olympic Winter Games. The Gambia has yet to win an Olympic medal.

Games of the New Emerging Forces [GANEFO]. These were very controversial Games. In the summer of 1962, Jakarta hosted the Asian Games, but it refused to issue visas to athletes from Taiwan and Israel. For this, the IOC suspended the Indonesian NOC. Unfortunately for the IOC, similar rulings had recently been made by France and the United States, which refused to issue visas to East German athletes competing in those countries. Those nations were not suspended. In response to the IOC actions, Indonesian President Sukarno proposed the Games of the New Emerging Forces in early 1963 to "promote the development of sports in new emerging nations so as to cement friendly relations among them." The original conference on these games occurred in April 1963, with the following nations present: Cambodia, China, Guinea, Indonesia, Iraq, Mali, North Vietnam, Pakistan, the United Arab Republic, and the Soviet Union. But Sukarno denounced the IOC in his opening speech and also noted, "Let us frankly declare that sport has something to do with politics. And Indonesia now proposes to mix sport with politics." GANEFO was an obvious attempt to compete against the Olympic Games. GANEFO I was held in November 1963 in Jakarta, Indonesia, with 50 nations present. The problem was that China, DPR Korea (North), and North Vietnam were present, none of which were recognized by several of the IFs organizing sports at GANEFO, notably the IAAF (track & field athletics) and FINA (swimming). Indonesia athletes also competed, quite naturally, since they hosted the Games. In response, the IOC banned the athletes from Indonesia and DPR Korea who had competed at GANEFO from participating at the 1964 Tokyo Olympics. (China and North Vietnam could not compete at Tokyo because they did not have recognized NOCs.) Indonesia and DPR Korea responded by demanding that their athletes be reinstated or their entire teams would boycott the Tokyo Olympics. The athletes were not reinstated, and the two nations did not compete at Tokyo. One athlete, North Korean runner Sin Kim-Dan, was sorely missed because she was the world record holder in the 800 meters for women, and would have been favored at Tokyo. Sukarno was ousted from power in 1965, and the IOC rescinded its suspension of Indonesia. GANEFO II went on, however, in Phnom Penh, Cambodia, in 1966, and again North Korea competed. For this, North Korea was also suspended from the 1968 Olympic Games at

Mexico City. By then, however, the idea of the Games of the New Emerging Forces had lost favor. They were not held again.

Games of the Olympiad. *See* the sections entitled "The Olympic Games" and "Olympic Winter Games."

Geesink, Antonius Johannes "Anton" [NED–JUD]. B. 6 April 1934, Utrecht. With the introduction of judo to the Olympic program in 1964, Anton Geesink provided one of the surprises of the Games by winning the open class. He had, however, earlier destroyed the myth of Japanese invincibility by becoming the first non-Japanese *judoka* to win a world title in 1961. Between 1953 and 1967, Geesink won 13 European titles in the open and unlimited classes. He later became a member of the IOC.

Gender Verification. Men and women compete in most Olympic events separately. The exceptions are few, but they have competed against each other in certain shooting events, equestrian events, and sailing and also compete concurrently in figure skating [pair and dance]. They have previously competed concurrently in mixed doubles in tennis and currently do so in mixed doubles badminton.

The two sexes compete separately in most events because of the physical advantage claimed by men. Men posing as women would have a significant competitive advantage over natural women. At the 1936 Olympics, Dora Ratjen of Germany finished fourth in the women's high jump, but was later found (1938) to be a hermaphrodite. There were several other similar examples in the 1930s, notably Czechoslovakia's Ždenka Koubková, who competed in track & field events internationally, but never competed at the Olympics. The 1932 women's 100-meter Olympic champion was Stanisława Walasiewiczówna of Poland. At her death in 1980, her autopsy revealed she had mixed sexual characteristics. Her original birth certificate was later examined and "she" was found to have been christened Stefania Walasiewiczówna.

In the 1960s, concern about this problem of men posing as women to gain a competitive advantage led to the introduction of gender verification, at the time called *sex testing*. Then, several of the women track & field athletes were suspected of being genetically male. Sex testing began at the 1966 European Athletics Championships, and began at the

Olympics in 1968. At the 1966 European Athletics Championships, Ewa Kłobukowska of Poland was disqualified from further international competition. Kłobukowska had won a gold and bronze medal at the 1964 Olympic Games. Because of the obvious emotional and psychological trauma entailed in such an announcement, all subsequent sex testing results have not been released publicly.

From 1968 to 1988, all women wishing to compete in the Olympics were required to undergo sex testing. (With one exception, that being Princess Anne of Great Britain, who competed in the 1976 Olympics in the equestrian events.) Testing was initially done by obtaining a buccal smear, or a scraping of the cells of the inner wall of the mouth. The cells were examined for the presence of a Barr body, which occurs almost exclusively in females. Females are genetically labeled as *XX*, while men are labeled as *XY*, those being the classifications of the respective sex chromosomes. The second X chromosome possessed by women contains a structure termed the *Barr body*.

Though some men did attempt to breach the rules and compete as women, the entire subject of mixed sexual characteristics is a highly complex and emotional one. A number of people with mixed sexual identity may have elected to compete as women for psychological reasons. In addition, doctors typically label babies with indeterminate genitalia as women. And in certain cases of mixed sex classification, some people who would be considered women lack a Barr body, and would thus have been disqualified. Because of these problems, the test has now been changed and the buccal smear is no longer used. Women are now cleared for international competition by doctors after simply undergoing a physical examination. In the late 1980s, this method was replaced by a polymerase chain reaction evaluation, looking for the Y-linked SRY gene (sex-determining region Y), and this method was used at both the 1992 and 1996 Olympics.

But problems still existed. It has been noted that the tests fail to exclude all potential impostors, are discriminatory against women with disorders of sexual development, and can be psychologically devastating for a female athlete failing such a test. Thus, during the 1996 IOC World Conference on Women and Health, the IOC passed a resolution "to discontinue the current process of gender verification during the Olympic Games." The IOC Athletes' Commission (q.v.) recommended to the IOC Executive Board in January 1999 that gender identification should be eliminated, and this decision was ratified by the IOC Executive Board in June 1999.

General Association of International Sports Federations [GAISF]. In the early 1960s, many sports federations were unhappy that they had so little influence with the International Olympic Committee. Led by the Frenchman Roger Coulon, President of the Fédération Internationale des Luttes Amateurs (FILA [wrestling]), the federations banded together in 1967 to form the General Assembly of International Federations (GAIF), later the General Association of International Sports Federations (GAISF), or Association Générale des Fédérations Internationales de Sports (AGFIS). The headquarters is currently in Monte Carlo and the President as of 2000 is Dr. Kim Un-Yong (KOR). As of 2000, there are 75 sports member federations, and 16 affiliated federations. Many of these federations govern Olympic sports (35), several are IOC-recognized federations (30), but as of 2000, 10 of them are not directly affiliated with the IOC and the GAISF gives them a small voice within the Olympic Movement. The aims of the GAISF are "to act as a forum for the exchange of ideas and for discussion on common problems in sport; to collect, collate, and circulate information; to provide members with secretarial and translating services, the organization of meetings, technical documentation and consultancy; to collect news bulletins, technical rules and regulations from members; to assemble and coordinate the dates of main international competitions; and to publish a half-yearly calendar."

Georgia [GEO]. Many Georgian athletes competed from 1952 to 1988 for the Soviet Union. Its top sports were judo and wrestling. In fact, Georgian *judoka* won more medals for the Soviet Union than any other republic, including Russia. The most famous Georgian Olympic athletes were wrestlers David Gobedzhishvili and Levan Tediashvili, and track & field athletes Viktor Saneyev and Robert Shavlakadze. Georgian athletes were present at Barcelona in 1992 as members of the Unified Team (q.v.). Georgia's first Olympic appearance as an independent nation occurred in 1994 at Lillehammer, where it was represented by five athletes who competed in luge, Alpine skiing, and ski jumping. Georgia also competed at the 1996 Olympic Games in Atlanta, the 1998 Olympic Winter Games in Nagano, and the 2000

Olympic Games in Sydney. Georgia has won eight Olympic medals, all bronze medals, and all at the Summer Olympics.

Gerevich, Aladár [HUN–FEN]. B. 16 May 1910, Jászbéreny. D. 14 May 1991, Budapest. Aladár Gerevich was one of the greatest of Olympic fencers. His six successive gold medals in the sabre team event at every Games from 1932 to 1960 stands as a record for any Olympic sport. In the sabre, he also won individual gold in 1948, silver in 1952, and bronze in 1936, and a further bronze in the foil team event in 1952. Gerevich confirmed his reputation as the world's greatest sabreur with three individual titles at the World Championships (1935, 1951, 1955). His wife, son, and father-in-law were also Olympic medalists.

German Democratic Republic [GDR]. The German Democratic Republic (frequently termed *East Germany*) was formed on 7 October 1949 after the division of Germany into two countries after World War II. The problem of the "Two Germanys" perplexed the International Olympic Committee (IOC) for two decades. (*See also* GERMANY.) From 1956 until 1964, the two nations purportedly competed at the Olympics as a single combined team. However, it should be noted that in 1952, a combined German team was planned and envisioned by the IOC, but the GDR refused to start in an all-German team and no East German athletes competed on the 1952 "combined" team. In 1968 at Mexico City and Grenoble, the two Germanys competed as separate teams, but under the same banner, and using the same anthem and flag. The German Democratic Republic, however, was forced to use the name *East Germany* in 1968, a name that it detested. At the IOC session in 1968, full recognition came to the German Democratic Republic when it was allowed to compete at the Olympics, beginning in 1972, using its correct name, with its own anthem, emblems, and uniforms.

Between 1956 and 1988, the GDR developed into a true Olympic powerhouse. Since the 1968 Olympics, with the United States and the Soviet Union, it was one of the three most powerful sporting nations in the world. The German Democratic Republic, competing as an independent nation, won 563 Olympic medals, 445 at the Olympic Games and 118 at the Olympic Winter Games. Of these, 202 were gold medals, 43 of which were won at the Olympic Winter Games.

The sporting leviathan was fully state-supported, with the help of a highly advanced sports medicine program, and the athletes were treated royally in their country. After the reunification of Germany, it was revealed that the GDR's sports medical program had helped develop many of its athletes by the use of drugs. *See also* DOPING.

German Federal Republic [FRG]. *See* GERMANY.

Germany [GER/FRG]. Prior to World War II, Germany appeared at all Olympics (Winter and Summer) with the exception of 1920 and 1924, when, as an aggressor nation in World War I, it was not invited. Because of its actions in World War II, and because no true German state existed at the time, Germany was again not allowed to compete in 1948. After World War II, Germany split into two nations. The Federal Republic of Germany (FRG) (West) was proclaimed in Bonn on 23 May 1949 from the former United States, British, and French Zones of occupation. The occupying powers restored civil status on 21 September 1949. The German Democratic Republic (GDR) (East) (q.v.) was formed on 7 October 1949 from the former Soviet Zone of Occupation. As well, the province of The Saar formed an independent country until 1956. The Saar (q.v.) competed independently in 1952, its only Olympic appearance.

From 1952 to 1968, the problem of the "two Germanys" was a major political problem for the International Olympic Committee (IOC). The FRG Olympic Committee was formed on 24 September 1949 and requested IOC recognition immediately. On 29 August 1950, the IOC Executive Board gave provisional recognition to the FRG Olympic Committee. Full recognition came in May 1951 at the 46th IOC session in Vienna. The GDR formed an Olympic Committee on 22 April 1951 and also asked for recognition. In 1952, a German team was entered at Oslo and Helsinki. Although titularly a combined German team, it was made up entirely of athletes from the Federal Republic of Germany.

At the 51st IOC session in Paris in 1955, the GDR was granted recognition by the IOC by a vote of 27–7. However, the proviso to this recognition was that both Germanys would compete at the Olympics with a combined team. IOC President Avery Brundage (q.v.) boasted, "We have obtained in the field of sports what politicians have failed to achieve so far."

In 1956, 1960, and 1964, a combined East and West German team competed under one flag. On 6 October 1965, at the 64th IOC session in Madrid, the IOC gave the GDR the right to enter a separate team at the 1968 Olympic Games. However, the decision mandated that both Germanys compete with the same uniforms, using the same flag adorned with the Olympic Symbol, and using the same anthem, the choral theme from Beethoven's Ninth Symphony. In addition, the GDR agreed to compete as *East Germany*, a name it did not recognize.

At the 68th IOC session at Mexico City in 1968, the IOC voted 44–4 that, beginning in 1972, both the FRG and the GDR could compete separately at the Olympic Games, wearing their own uniforms, and using their own flag and anthem, and with the correct names of their nations.

On 3 October 1990, the GDR and the FRG dissolved their separate governments to once again form a single united German state. Competing in Albertville and Barcelona in 1992 was a single team representing a unified Germany.

Germany, wholly or separately, has always been one of the most powerful nations at the Olympics. Germany has also hosted three Olympic Games: the Games of the XIth Olympiad in Berlin in 1936, the 4th Olympic Winter Games in Garmisch-Partenkirchen, also in 1936, and the Games of the XXth Olympiad in Munich in 1972. In addition, the 1916 Olympic Games were originally planned for Berlin, and the 1940 Olympic Winter Games were rescheduled for Garmisch-Partenkirchen after Sapporo and then St. Moritz withdrew as hosts.

Germeshausen, Bernhard [GDR–BOB]. B. 28 August 1951, Heiligenstadt. Bernhard Germeshausen won the two-man bob in 1976 with his compatriot Meinhard Nehmer (q.v.), and they were both members of the winning four-man crew in 1976 and 1980. The three Olympic gold medals they each won stand as the current Olympic record for bobsledding. Germeshausen also won silver in the two-man event at the 1980 Olympics (partnering Hans-Jürgen Gerhardt), and he was the winner at the World Championships in the two-man in 1981 (with Gerhardt) and in the four-man in 1977 and 1981.

Ghana [GHA]. Ghana first appeared at the Olympics in 1952, as the *Gold Coast*. It did not attend the 1956 Olympics, but competed from 1960 through 1972. After boycotting the 1976 and 1980 Olympics,

Ghana has attended the Olympic Games from 1984 through 2000, but has never competed at the Olympic Winter Games. Ghanian athletes have won four medals at the Olympic Games.

Gibraltar. The application of the Gibraltarian Olympic Committee for IOC recognition was on the agenda for discussion at the San Francisco IOC session in 1960, and on numerous subsequent occasions. Each time Gibraltar's application was denied and it became increasingly apparent that Spain was making territorial claims on the British Colony, and was actively opposing Gibraltar's recognition. Although the *Olympic Charter* (q.v.) prohibits any political interference, the Spanish Ministry of Foreign Affairs chose to blatantly ignore these provisions and issued a directive on 5 September 1985 banning Gibraltarians from competing in championships held on Spanish soil even though Gibraltar was a member of several International Federations. After 40 years, Gibraltar remains excluded from the Olympic Movement (q.v.) and has never been permitted to compete at the Olympics. Yet, as of December 2000, Gibraltar is a member of 10 International Federations (IFs).

Gliding. A gliding exhibition was held at the 1936 Olympics in Berlin. The sport is not recognized by the IOC, nor by the General Association of International Sports Federations (GAISF).

Gold Coast. *See* GHANA.

Golf. Golf was on the program of the 1900 and 1904 Olympics. In 1900, men and women competed in separate individual events. In 1904, a men's individual match-play event and a team stroke-play event were contested. Golf was on the Olympic schedule in both 1908 and 1920, but was not contested in either year. The World Amateur Golf Council is recognized by the IOC, headed by the Executive Directors of the United States Golf Association and the Royal & Ancient Golf Club of St. Andrews (Scotland). There has been recent discussion of golf becoming an Olympic sport again in the near future.

Goodwill Games. The Goodwill Games were held for the first time in 1986 in Moscow. They were the brainchild of Ted Turner of Atlanta,

Georgia, the head of Turner Broadcasting and the Cable News Network. Turner was upset about the boycotts of the Olympics in both 1980 and 1984 and saw the need to hold a "peaceful" sporting festival outside of the Olympic Movement (q.v.). They have been held in 1990 in Seattle, Washington, 1994 in St. Petersburg, Russia (the former Leningrad and Petrograd), and in 1998 in New York City. The 2001 Goodwill Games are planned for Brisbane, Australia. With the breakup of the Soviet Union, the need for a Goodwill Games is now far from clear. In addition, the Games have lost significant amounts of money at each celebration and although it would seem that their future would be in doubt, Turner has insisted on continuing these Games, which have no direct Olympic affiliation. In 2000, the 1st Winter Goodwill Games were contested in Lake Placid, New York, USA.

Gould, Shane Elizabeth [AUS–SWI]. B. 23 November 1956, Brisbane. Shane Gould was a swimmer of phenomenal talent who became the first woman to hold the world freestyle record at every distance from 100 meters to 1,500 meters. She achieved this remarkable feat in December 1971, just three weeks after her 15th birthday. At the Olympic Games the following year, she won the 200- and 400-meter freestyles and 200-meter individual medley, each in a new world record time, and, in addition to her three gold medals, she took the silver in the 800 meters and the bronze in the 100-meter freestyle. In 1973, still aged only 16, she retired, but during her brief career, she had become one of the legends of the sport.

Grafström, Gillis Emanuel [SWE–FSK]. B. 7 June 1893, Stockholm. D. 14 April 1938, Potsdam, Germany. Gillis Grafström was the supreme figure skater in the years following World War I. He won a record three Olympic gold medals (1920, 1924, 1928) and, in 1932, earned a silver medal in Lake Placid. He was also a three-time World Champion (1922, 1924, 1929). A noted amateur painter and sculptor, he skated more for aesthetic pleasure than for the competitive challenge. Grafström was a professional architect, who worked mainly in Germany and spent little time in his native Sweden.

Great Britain [GBR]. Great Britain is the only nation that has never failed to be represented at the Olympic Games, including all the usual exceptions. It competed at the 1906 Intercalated Games in Athens, the 1908 figure skating events in London, the 1920 figure skating events in Antwerp, and at the 1956 Equestrian Olympics in Stockholm. Through 1920, Great Britain competed as a combined team with Ireland (q.v.), which was still not an independent nation, and its 1904 participation is due only to three Irish athletes. Great Britain has won 656 Olympic medals, 188 of them gold, most of them at the Summer Olympics. Great Britain has twice hosted the Olympic Games, the Games of the IVth Olympiad in London in 1908, and the Games of the XIVth Olympiad in London in 1948.

Greece [GRE]. Greece is the home of the Olympics, the Ancient Olympic Games (q.v.) having been held there from at least 776 B.C. through 393 A.D. The Modern Olympic Games were revived and first held in Athens in 1896. Prior to 1896, several attempts at revival of the Olympics were contested in Greece, notably the Zappas Olympics of 1859, 1870, 1875, and 1889 (q.v.). Since 1896, Greek participation has been continuous at all Games of the Olympiad. Greece has also competed at the Olympic Winter Games, first appearing in 1936 and missing only the 1960 Squaw Valley Olympics. Greece hosted the Games of the Ist Olympiad in Athens in 1896, and the Intercalated Olympic Games of 1906, and Athens will host the Games of the XXVIIIth Olympiad in 2004. Greek athletes have won 120 medals in the Olympics (32 gold), with 83 of those occurring in 1896 and 1906.

Greenland. Traditionally, Greenland's Olympic affairs have been overseen by Denmark (q.v.), but in 1996, they started to make efforts to establish their own Olympic identity. So far, they have not been successful although, at the 1998 Olympic Winter Games, three Greenlandic Nordic skiers competed as part of the Danish team. As of 2000, Greenland is a member of four Internatonal Federations.

Grenada [GRN]. The Grenada Olympic Association was founded in 1982 and, after provisional IOC recognition was granted that year, full recognition was accorded in 1984. This enabled Grenada to make their Olympic début at the 1984 Olympic Games and they have competed at each of the Olympics since. They have not yet competed at the Olympic Winter Games.

Griffith Joyner, Delorez Florence (née Griffith) [USA–ATH]. B. 21 December 1959, Los Angeles, California. D. 21 September 1998, Los Angeles, California. Florence Griffith Joyner was a superb sprinter who completely dominated the women's track season in 1988. After setting a world record for 100 meters at the 1988 U.S. Olympic Trials, she won three gold and one silver medal at the Seoul Games. Victories in the 100 meters and 200 meters, in which she twice broke the world record, were followed by a third gold in the sprint relay and a silver in the 4 x 400-meters relay. She had previously won a silver medal in the 200 meters in 1984. The flamboyant outfits she wore on the track made her a darling of the media who gave her the name "Flo-Jo" after her marriage in 1987 to the 1984 Olympic triple jump gold medalist, Al Joyner. She tragically died very young from a seizure disorder.

Grishin, Yevgeny Romanovich [URS–SSK]. B. 23 March 1931, Tula. Yevgeny Grishin was the winner of gold medals for speed skating in the 500 meters and 1,500 meters at both the 1956 and 1960 Winter Games. He set world records at both distances, but was at his best at 500 meters, winning six world titles and achieving the distinction of being the first skater to break the 40-second barrier. Grishin became a coach with the national speed skating squad after he retired from competition.

Groß, Michael [FRG–SWI]. B. 17 June 1964, Frankfurt. Michael Groß won six Olympic medals, three gold, mostly in the butterfly and sprint freestyle swimming events. He was known as "The Albatross" because of his enormous arm span of over seven feet (2.14 meters). At the World Championships, he won a record 13 medals (five gold, five silver, three bronze), and he also won a record 18 medals at four European Championships (13 gold, four silver, one bronze). During his career, Groß set 10 world records in individual events. His top Olympics was 1984 when he won the 200-meter freestyle and the 100-meter butterfly, and took silver at the 200-meter butterfly and in anchoring the 4 x 200-meter freestyle relay.

Grøttumsbråten, Johan [NOR–NSK]. B. 24 February 1899, Sørkedalen, Oslo. D. 21 January 1983. Together with fellow Norwegian, Thorleif Haug, Johan Grøttumsbråten dominated the Nordic skiing events at the early editions of the Winter Games. In 1924, he won silver at 18 km., bronze in the 50 km. and the Nordic combined event, and then in 1928 he won the 18 km. and the Nordic combined. Grøttumsbråten won his third gold and sixth medal overall in 1932 when he successfully defended his title in the Nordic combined event.

Guam [GUM]. Guam formed an NOC in 1976, but it was not recognized by the IOC until 1986. Guam's initial Olympic appearance came at the 1988 Olympic Winter Games, but they have not taken part in the Olympic Winter Games since. Guam has participated in the Olympic Games of 1988, 1992, 1996, and 2000.

Guatemala [GUA]. Guatemala first competed in the 1952 Olympics. It did not appear again until 1968, but has not missed an Olympic Games since. Guatemala appeared at its only Olympic Winter Games in 1988 at Calgary. Its top performances have been a tie for fifth (quarter finals) by Carlos Mo Ha-Taracena in 1984 light-flyweight boxing, and a sixth-place finish by Edgardo Zachrisson in skeet shooting at Montreal in 1976.

Guiana, British. *See* GUYANA.

Guinea [GUI]. Guinea formed an NOC in 1964, which was recognized by the IOC in 1965. Since making its Olympic début in 1968, Guinea has competed at seven Olympic Games, missing only 1972 and 1976. It has never competed at the Olympic Winter Games, nor has any Guinean athlete won a medal.

Guinea-Bissau [GBS]. The Olympic Committee of Guinea-Bissau was given official recognition by the IOC in June 1995 at the 104th IOC session in Budapest. The nation made its Olympic début at the 1996 Olympic Games in Atlanta, and also competed in 2000 at Sydney. Guinea-Bissau did not compete at the 1998 Olympic Winter Games.

Guyana [GUY]. Guyana has competed at 12 Olympic Games since 1948, missing only 1976. It competed from 1948 to 1964 as *British Guiana*, competing first as *Guyana* in 1968. Guyana has never competed at the

Olympic Winter Games. Guyana has won one Olympic medal, a bronze medal in 1980 bantamweight boxing by Michael Anthony.

Gyarmati, Dezső [HUN–WAP]. B. 23 October 1927, Miskolc. Dezső Gyarmati is considered the greatest of all Olympic water polo players. His feat of winning medals at five successive Games (gold 1952, 1956, 1964; silver 1948; bronze 1960) has never been matched. A national hero, he coached the Hungarian team that won the Olympic title in 1976 and later became a member of Parliament. Gyarmati married the 1952 Olympic 200-meter breaststroke champion Eva Székely. Their daughter, Andrea, was an Olympic silver medalist in the 100-meter backstroke in 1972 and she later married Mihály Hesz, a 1968 Olympic canoeing champion.

Gymnastics. Gymnastics is an ancient sport, having been practiced in various forms in Ancient Greece and Rome. However, gymnastics competitions are relatively modern. The modern development of gymnastics began in the mid-19th century in Europe. Gymnastics societies were formed in Germany (Turnvereins) and Bohemia of the Austro-Hungarian Empire (Sokols). Similar societies were formed in France and Switzerland and then spread generally throughout Europe. The sport is governed worldwide by the Fédération Internationale de Gymnastique (FIG), which was founded in 1881 and currently has 125 member federations.

Modern competitive gymnastics has developed from two systems—the German Turnverein system emphasizing apparatus work of a formal nature and stressing muscular development, and the Swedish system of free exercises concerned with developing rhythmic movements.

Gymnastics has been contested at every Olympic Games. The program has varied widely, but since World War II, it has been fairly constant. Men compete in teams on six apparatuses—still rings, floor exercises, horizontal bar, parallel bars, pommelled horse, and horse vault. The top competitors in the team event are eligible for the individual all-around event (maximum of three per nation). This is conducted again on all six apparatuses. The top performers in each apparatus are then advanced to the individual apparatus finals, now with a maximum of two performers from any nation per event. Individuals must be all-around performers; it is not possible to specialize on a single apparatus and enter in that.

Women's competition is similar, except that they compete in only four events—uneven parallel bars, floor exercises, horse vault, and balance beam. In 1984, rhythmic gymnastics for women was added to the Olympic program. Trampoline (q.v.) events for men and women were added to the gymnastics program at Sydney in 2000.

At the Olympics, the Soviet Union and its republics have been dominant in the women's events. Romania has also had superb female gymnasts, notably the remarkable Nadia Comăneci. Men's gymnastics has been divided almost evenly since World War II by the Japanese and Soviet Union. The Chinese men are also now of top caliber.

– H –

Hackl, Georg [FRG/GER–LUG]. B. 9 September 1966, Berchtesgarden. Georg Hackl is the only lugist to have won medals at four consecutive Olympics in singles. After a silver medal in 1988 at Calgary, Hackl also became the first man to defend the Olympic luge singles title, winning in both 1992 and 1994. In 1998, Hackl won the Olympic singles luge for the third consecutive time. In addition to his Olympic successes, Hackl was singles world champion in 1989 and 1990, and also won the luge World Cup in those years. In 1993, he was second in the World Championships and the World Cup, after having placed third in the World Cup in the Olympic year of 1992.

Haiti [HAI]. Haiti formed an NOC in 1956 that was recognized by the IOC in the same year. Haiti has a curious Olympic history. A fencer named Léon Thiercelin represented it at the 1900 Olympics in Paris. Its next appearances were in 1924, 1928, and 1932, followed by a long gap before its return to the Olympic fold in 1960. Haiti did not attend the 1964 or 1968 Olympics. Despite having appeared in five Olympics through 1960, it had a total Olympic representation of only 12 men to that date. Haiti has since appeared at each Olympics since 1972, except for 1980. It has not yet competed in the Olympic Winter Games. Haiti has won two medals in the Olympic Games through 2000.

Hakulinen, Veikko Johannes [FIN–NSK]. B. 4 January 1925, Kurkijoki. Veikko Hakulinen won seven medals (three gold, three silver, one bronze) in cross-country skiing at four Olympic Winter Games. His first gold came in the 1952 50-kilometer event, the second in the 1956 30 kilometers, and the last in the 1960 cross-country relay. His last gold medal, at the age of 35 years, 51 days, makes him the oldest gold medallist in cross-country skiing at the Olympics. Hakulinen competed at the Olympics for a fourth time in 1964 in the biathlon, having previously won a world team silver at his new sport in 1963. He was also world cross-country skiing champion in 1954 and 1958 over 15 kilometers and in the relay in 1954 and 1968. Hakulinen was the outstanding Nordic skier of his generation, and he continued competing well into his sixties, by which time he had also become proficient at ski orienteering.

Hall, Lars [SWE–MOP]. B. 30 April 1927, Karlskrona. D. 26 April 1991, Täby. After winning the Modern Pentathlon World Championships in 1950 and 1951, Lars Hall won individual gold medals at the 1952 and 1956 Olympic Games. He is the only modern pentathlete in history to win two Olympic titles. In 1952, he became the first non-military winner of the event. Hall also won an Olympic team silver in 1952 and was a member of the winning team at the World Championships four times (1949–1951 and 1953).

Hämäläinen-Kirvesniemi, Marja-Liisa (née Hämäläinen) [FIN–NSK]. B. 10 September 1955, Simpele, Finnish South Karelia. After competing without distinction in the 1976 and 1980 Winter Games, Marja-Liisa Hämäläinen achieved unprecedented success at the 1984 Games. With victories in the 5 km., 10 km., and 20 km., she became the first woman to win three individual gold medals for Nordic skiing at one Games. She also won a bronze medal in the relay and won a second relay bronze in 1988, but illness prevented her from adding to her medal tally at her fifth Olympics in 1992. At the 1994 Olympic Winter Games, she finished her Olympic career with bronze medals in the 5-km. and 30-km. races, giving her a total of seven Olympic medals. After her triple victory in 1984, she married Harri Kirvesniemi, himself an Olympic Nordic skiing bronze medalist. Hämäläinen-Kirvesniemi is the only woman, and one of three athletes, to compete in six Olympic Winter Games.

Handball (Team Handball). Handball is a team sport that combines aspects of basketball, soccer, and water polo (qq.v.). It is played on a basketball-sized court by teams of seven players who attempt to score goals by throwing a ball slightly smaller than a volleyball into a goal on the ground which is about the size of a lacrosse goal.

The game was invented in Germany in the early 20th century and became very popular in Europe. At the 1936 Olympics, the Germans added it to the program, but it was contested outdoors on a large field with 11 men to a side. It was not again on the Olympic program until 1972, when it was added to the Olympics at Munich. This time the sport was contested as described above with seven men to a side and indoors. In 1976, women's handball became an Olympic sport.

Handball is immensely popular in Europe, surpassed by only football (soccer), cycling, athletics (track & field), and, perhaps recently, basketball and volleyball. The same popularity has not extended to other areas of the world, notably the United States; thus the sport has been dominated by the Europeans. The sport is governed worldwide by the International Handball Federation (IHF), which was founded in 1946 and currently has 146 members.

Haug, Thorleif [NOR–NSK]. B. 28 September 1894, Lier. D. 12 December 1934, Drammen. Thorleif Haug was the winner of all three Nordic skiing events (18 km., 50 km., and Nordic combination) at the 1st Olympic Winter Games in 1924, and the 29-year-old Norwegian was considered the star of the Games. Although his feat has been equaled on many occasions, no Nordic skier has yet succeeded in winning more than three gold medals at one Games. In 1924, he was also awarded the bronze medal in the ski jump, but 50 years later, it was discovered that the scores had been incorrectly calculated and that Anders Haugen (USA) had finished third, with Haug in fourth place. Haug's daughter later presented her father's bronze medal to the rightful owner.

Heiden, Eric Arthur [USA–SSK]. B. 14 June 1958, Madison, Wisconsin. Eric Heiden is recognized as the greatest speed skater of all time. He completely dominated the 1980 Olympic Winter Games speed skating, winning the gold medal at all five distances. He set new Olympic records in every event, adding a world record in the 10,000 meters. At the World Championships following the 1980 Olympics, he suffered his first defeat since 1977, after which he retired. Heiden then turned to cycling and, after coming close to making the U.S. Olympic team in a second sport, he had a brief career as a professional cyclist, once winning the United States' professional championship, and competing in one Tour de France. His sister, Beth, was also an outstanding speed skater and cyclist, winning world championships in both sports. Eric Heiden later attended medical school and now practices as an orthopaedic surgeon, specializing in sports medicine.

Henie, Sonja (later Topping, Gardiner, and Onstad) [NOR–FSK]. B. 8 April 1912, Oslo. D. 12 October 1969, in flight, Paris-Oslo. Sonja Henie was a triple Olympic gold medalist (1928, 1932, 1936), who did more to popularize figure skating than any other individual. After winning 10 world and three Olympic titles, she turned professional in 1936 and soon amassed a fortune. Her flair for showmanship ensured the success of the 10 feature films she made in Hollywood and accelerated the public awareness of ice skating as a sport. Henie toured the world with spectacular ice reviews, achieving great popularity, particularly in the USA. She was initially idolized in her native Norway, but had some image problems after World War II when she was perceived to be a Nazi sympathizer who failed to support war-relief efforts in Norway. Henie later suffered from leukemia and died during a flight from Paris to Oslo, where she was to visit a medical specialist.

Hildgartner, Paul [ITA–LUG]. B. 8 June 1952, Kienz. One of the few lugers to win three Olympic medals and two gold medals, Paul Hildgartner uniquely won his gold medals 12 years apart. In 1972, Hildgartner joined Walter Plaikner to win the Olympic doubles luge gold medal. He then turned to singles luge exclusively, earning a silver medal in 1980 and winning the Olympic title in 1984 at Sarajevo. Hildgartner was also World Champion in singles in 1978 and in doubles in 1971 (with Plaikner). Hildgartner was the singles World Cup leader in both 1981 and 1983.

Hockey (Field). Hockey is the oldest known ball and stick game. Records exist of it having been played in Persia in 2000 B.C. It became so popular by the Middle Ages that it was banned in England for a time because it interfered with the practice of archery, which was the basis for national defense.

The modern game of hockey, however, was developed in England in the late 19th century. It spread throughout the British Empire, as a result, and most of the dominant nations in the sport have been nations that are, or were, members of that Empire. This includes India, Pakistan, Australia, New Zealand, and the United Kingdom. India's dominance in this team sport is matched only by the United States' dominance of basketball, Hungary's dominance of water polo, and Canadian and Soviet dominance of ice hockey (qq.v.). Between 1928 and 1956, India won six gold medals and 30 consecutive games.

Hockey appeared on the Olympic program in 1908 and 1920. In 1928, it was held at Amsterdam and it has been an Olympic sport since. In 1980, hockey for women was first introduced as an Olympic sport. Hockey is governed internationally by the Fédération Internationale de Hockey (FIH), which was formed in 1924 and had 118 member nations at the end of 2000. *See also* INDIA FIELD HOCKEY TEAMS [1928–1964].

Honduras [HON]. Honduras has competed at the Olympics Games of 1968, 1976, 1984, 1988, 1992, 1996, and 2000. In 1992, Honduras competed at Albertville in its only appearance at the Olympic Winter Games to date.

Hong Kong, China [HKG]. Hong Kong first competed at the 1952 Olympic Games and has since missed only the 1980 Moscow Olympics. Hong Kong has never competed at the Olympic Winter Games. Despite this long Olympic history, prior to 1992, no Hong Kong athlete had ever finished in the top 10. In 1996, Lee Lai-Shan won Hong Kong's first, and to date, only, Olympic medal, a gold in boardsailing. On 1 July 1997, China regained sovereignty over Hong Kong, but it was agreed that the territory would retain a separate Olympic identity as *Hong Kong, China*.

Honorary IOC Members. The matter of Honorary IOC Membership was first raised in 1948. Following a proposal by Lord Arthur Porritt (NZL), it was agreed that those IOC Members who has passed the age limit of 70 would be eligible to become Honorary Members and would be entitled to attend future IOC sessions. They would be permitted to take part in the discussions but would not be accorded a vote. The first Honorary Member to be appointed was the 86-year-old Riccardo Aldão (ARG).

Hoplite Race. *See* RACE IN ARMOR.

Hoppe, Wolfgang [GDR/GER–BOB]. B. 14 November 1957, Apolda. Wolfgang Hoppe started his sports career in track & field athletics and won the GDR junior decathlon championship in 1976. He later turned his talents to bobsledding and became the world's top driver in the 1980s. In the two-man event, Hoppe won Olympic gold in 1984 and a silver in 1988 and was three times the world champion. He was equally accomplished in the four-man event, winning an Olympic gold in 1984, a silver in 1988 and 1992, and ending his Olympic career with a four-man bronze in 1994. Hoppe won the World Championship in the four-man event in 1991 and at the European Championships he won the two-man title in 1986–1987 and the four-man event in 1987.

Hungary [HUN]. Hungary was one of the countries that attended the first Olympic Games in 1896 in Athens. A National Olympic Committee was formed in Hungary in 1895 by Dr. Ferenc Kémény, who was one of the founding members of the IOC. Hungary has missed only two Olympics, including the Winter Games, at which it has appeared at all celebrations.

Hungary was not invited to the 1920 Olympics in Antwerp, having been an aggressor nation in World War I, and Hungary chose not to attend the 1984 Los Angeles Olympics. Hungary has been very successful in a variety of sports, but by far its greatest honors have come in fencing. In one fencing discipline, the sabre, it has been the dominant nation, and in fact, between 1908 and 1960 Hungary won 9 of 11 team titles and 10 of 11 individual titles in this event. Through 2000, Hungary has won 447 Olympic medals, including 150 gold. All but six of these came at the Summer Olympics.

Hurley, Marcus Latimer [USA–CYC]. B. 22 December 1883, New York, NY. D. 28 March 1941, New York, NY. With four gold medals in the 1904 Olympic cycling events, Marcus Hurley tied a record for individual golds at one Games that stood until Eric Heiden's domination of the 1980 speed-skating events. Hurley was the greatest American amateur cyclist of his era. He won the U.S. amateur sprint championship from 1901 until 1904 and was world amateur sprint champion in 1904, as well. Hurley was also an excellent basketball player at Columbia University, captaining that team in 1908, and earning All-American honors from 1905 to 1908. He also captained the New York AC basketball team that won the Metropolitan championship in 1905. Hurley was later enshrined in the College Basketball Hall of Fame.

– I –

Ice Dancing. *See* DEMONSTRATION SPORTS and FIGURE SKATING.

Ice Hockey. Ice hockey is a Canadian sport that began in the early 19th century. Around 1860, a puck was substituted for a ball, and in 1879, two McGill University students, W. F. Robertson and R. F. Smith, devised the first rules, combining field hockey and rugby regulations. Originally, the game was played nine to a side. The sport became the Canadian national sport with leagues everywhere. In 1894, Lord Stanley of Preston, Governor-General of Canada, donated the Stanley Cup that was first won in 1894 by a team representing the Montreal Amateur Athletic Association.

Ice hockey was contested at the 1920 Summer Olympics at Antwerp, held in early April. These were also the first World Championships and were played by seven-man sides, the only time seven-man teams played in the Olympics. In 1924, the Olympics began using the current standard of six men on the ice at a time.

Ice hockey has been held at every Olympic Winter Games. Canada dominated early Olympic ice hockey tournaments as might be expected. In 1956, the Soviet Union first entered the Olympic Winter Games and won the ice hockey tournament quite handily. It was the pre-eminent country until its political division, its dominance interrupted only by major upset victories by the United States in 1960 and 1980.

Women's ice hockey appeared for the first time on the Olympic program in 1998 at Nagano. The sport is governed by the International Ice Hockey Federation (IIHF), which was founded in 1908, and had 55 affiliated nations at the end of 1999. (*See also* CANADIAN ICE HOCKEY TEAMS [1920–1952] and SOVIET UNION ICE HOCKEY TEAMS [1956–1992])

Ice Skating. *See* FIGURE SKATING, ICE HOCKEY, and SPEED SKATING.

Iceland [ISL]. Iceland sent one athlete to the 1908 Olympics, Johannes Jósepsson, a wrestler. The country also sent two athletes to the 1912 Olympics, but did not again appear until 1936. Since that time, it has never failed to be present at an Olympic Games. It has competed at all the Olympic Winter Games since 1948, except for 1972. Iceland has won three medals in the Olympic Games, a silver in triple jump (track & field athletics) by Vilhjálmur Einarsson in 1956, a bronze in half-heavyweight judo by Bjarni Fridriksson in 1984, and a bronze by Vala Flosadóttir in women's pole vault in 2000. It could be argued that Icelanders have won a gold medal. In 1920, Canada won a gold medal in ice hockey at Antwerp, represented by the club team, the Winnipeg Falcons. Of the eight Canadians on that team, seven were of Icelandic origin and had dual citizenship.

Independent Olympic Athletes [IOA]. At Sydney in 2000, the IOC allowed athletes from the disputed nation of East Timor (q.v.) to compete under the designation of Independent Olympic Athletes (IOA). This was despite the fact that the nation did not yet have a National Olympic Committee recognized by the IOC. East Timor was represente by four athletes—three men and one women, who competed in track & field athletics, boxing, and weightlifting.

Independent Olympic Participants [IOP]. In 1992, at Barcelona, 58 athletes (39 men and 19 women) from Yugoslavia were allowed to compete as Independent Olympic Participants. The United Nations Security Council Resolution No. 757 had placed a ban on Yugoslav teams competing internationally because of the war in Bosnia-Herzegovina. However, the IOC made arrangements allowing individual athletes to compete, provided that they did not officially represent Yugoslavia.

India [IND]. India's first Olympic appearance can be traced to 1900 when Norman Pritchard, a British resident of Calcutta, competed in the sprints at Paris, representing the London Athletic Club and Great Britain. India's next Olympic appearance, and first real one, occurred in 1920, although India's NOC was not formed until 1927. India has competed at all the Olympic Games since 1920. In 1928, India entered its first field hockey team and won the gold medal. This was the first of six consecutive gold medals won by India in men's field hockey. Twelve of India's 16 medals in the Olympics have been won by its field hockey team. India has competed at the 1964, 1968, 1988, 1992, and 1998 Olympic Winter Games.

India Field Hockey Teams [1928–1964]. India (q.v.) dominated Olympic hockey (field hockey) from its first appearance in 1928 through 1964. During that time, India won 30 consecutive games (1928–1960), the streak being broken, 1–0, in the 1960 finals by Pakistan. India won the gold medal in seven of the eight Olympics between 1928 and 1964, inclusive, losing only in 1960 to Pakistan, but still taking a silver medal. India continued to be one of the top nations in Olympic hockey through the 1970s, winning a bronze medal in 1968 and 1972, and another gold medal in 1980. Since that time, India's best finish has been fifth in 1984. Overall, India has an Olympic hockey record of 71 wins, 19 losses, and 10 ties. It has outscored its opponents 386 goals to 102 goals. India's women have competed in Olympic hockey since 1980, but with less success, not having won any medals to date.

Indonesia [INA]. Indonesia formed a National Olympic Committee in 1946, but did not compete at the Olympics until 1952. Indonesia missed the 1964 Olympic Games when it withdrew after several of its athletes were banned for their participation at the 1963 Games of the New Emerging Forces (GANEFO, *See* KOREA, DEMOCRATIC PEOPLE'S REPUBLIC OF and THE GAMES OF THE XVIIITH OLYMPIAD). Indonesia also boycotted the 1980 Olympics. The country has never competed at the Olympic Winter

Games. Indonesia's national sport is badminton, at which it is one of the dominant countries in the world and in the Olympics. Through 2000, Indonesia has won 16 Olympics medals, 12 of them in badminton, three in weightlifting, and one in archery.

International Federations [IFs]. International Federations are nongovernmental organizations that administer sports on an international level. The IFs' role is to establish and enforce the rules governing the practice of their sport, promote development of their sport internationally, and assume responsibility for the technical control of their sport at the Olympic Games. The sports governed by the IFs may be admitted to the Olympic program if they satisfy the following requirements: Games of the Olympiad—the sports must be widely practiced by men in at least 75 countries and four continents and by women in at least 40 countries and three continents; Olympic Winter Games—the sports must be widely practiced in at least 25 countries and three continents. There are two categories of International Federations affiliated with the IOC. One is the International Olympic Federations, which govern sports currently on the Olympic Program. There are 35 such IFs. A second category relates to IOC-Recognized International Federations, of which there are currently 30. These federations are not yet on the Olympic Program, but IOC recognition is a necessary first step to that end. *See* the individual sports of the Olympics, which give the names, dates of foundation, and number of member nations for the various International Federations.

International Olympic Academy [IOA]. The idea of an International Olympic Academy was first conceived in the 1930s by Ioannis Ketseas (q.v.), an IOC Member in Greece, and Carl Diem (q.v.). The idea never died, but it took many years of informal discussions before the foundation of an academy, to be located at Olympia, Greece, was unanimously approved by the IOC during a session in Rome in 1949. Of the 80 invitations sent to NOCs for the first preliminary session, only four replies were received and all of these were in the negative. Ketseas, who was now working closely with Diem, a German professor with a passionate interest in Olympic matters, persisted with his goal and with the assistance of Olympic and archaeological bodies from Germany and Greece, the Academy eventually came into being and has subsequently prospered. The first session was held from 16–23 June 1961. A plot of some 150 acres of land bordering the Ancient Olympic stadium was acquired by the IOA, buildings were erected, and the complex, which now provides accommodations, a library, and several sports facilities, is a popular center for students of the Olympic Movement (q.v.). The IOA holds an annual session each summer during which students of the Olympic Movement gather for several days to hear speeches and discussions on Olympic subjects. In addition, many other international symposia are held at the IOA each year. The idea of Olympic Academies has now spread and, as of 1995, there were also 72 National Olympic Academies, helping to spread the message of Olympism and the Olympic Movement.

International Olympic Committee [IOC]. The International Olympic Committee is the international governing organization of the Olympic Movement (q.v.) and the Olympic Games. It is a nongovernmental, nonprofit organization of unlimited duration, in the form of an association with the status of a legal person, recognized by decree of the Swiss Federal Council of 17 September 1981. The International Olympic Committee was founded by Pierre de Coubertin (q.v.) in 1894, at the Olympic Congress (q.v.) that re-established the Olympic Games. The IOC is currently based in Lausanne, Switzerland, and has been since Coubertin moved there during World War I. The mission of the IOC is to lead the Olympic Movement in accordance with the *Olympic Charter* (q.v.).

The IOC consists of members who are chosen and co-opted to membership. IOC member nations may have one member on the IOC, although not all do. However, until recently any nation that had hosted the Olympic Games or Olympic Winter Games was entitled to a second member on the IOC. IOC members are not considered to be members from their respective nations. Rather, they are considered to be IOC ambassadors to, or in, their respective nations. The IOC 2000 Commission (q.v.) helped change the structure of the IOC in late 1999. In the future, there will be four classes of IOC Members: independent members, co-opted as they have always been; athlete members, who have competed in the most recent Olympic Games; International Federation (q.v.) president members; and National Olympic Committee president members. The eventual size of the IOC was also restricted to

115 members, as follows: 70 independent members, 15 athlete members, 15 IF president members, and 15 NOC president members. Previously, IOC members were elected for life, but the new changes to the *Olympic Charter* call for re-election every eight years, with athlete members restricted to one term.

The IOC is led by a president, four vice presidents, and an Executive Board (q.v.). The president is elected initially for a term of eight years, but may be re-elected for one further term of four years. Prior to 1999, presidents could be re-elected with no term limits, but this was changed based on the recommendations of the IOC 2000 Commission. Vice presidents and Executive Board members are elected for a term of four years. They may not be re-elected to the same position for consecutive terms, although they may return to that position on the Executive Board after a period of four more years.

IOC sessions consist of meetings of the entire membership and are required to be held at least once a year. The IOC session is considered to be the supreme organ of the IOC, but may delegate its powers to the Executive Board. The Executive Board meets more frequently and works by making recommendations to the IOC sessions, which is then responsible for enacting or denying its recommendations. Day-to-day decisions are delegated to the IOC president.

The *Olympic Charter* is the document that specifies the principles, rules, and by-laws of the IOC. Only IOC sessions have the power to modify and interpret the *Olympic Charter*. *See* Appendix I for list of IOC Presidents, Appendix IV for list of all IOC Members, and the separate biographies of IOC presidents: DEMETRIOS VIKELAS, BARON PIERRE DE COUBERTIN, COUNT HENRI DE BAILLET-LATOUR, J. SIGFRID EDSTRÖM, AVERY BRUNDAGE, LORD KILLANIN, and JUAN ANTONIO SAMARANCH.

International Pierre de Coubertin Committee. The International Pierre de Coubertin Committee was founded in 1976. It is committed to the dissemination and study of Coubertin's (q.v.) works and his humanitarianism. The first president of the International Pierre de Coubertin Committee was Dr. Paul Martin (SUI), followed in 1977 by Geoffroy de Navacelle (FRA), Coubertin's grand-nephew. The current president is Conrado Durántez Corral (ESP). Navacelle and IOC President Juan Antonio Samaranch are currently honorary presidents of the International Pierre de Coubertin Committee. This committee is independent of the IOC Commission, the Pierre de Coubertin Commission, although several executives serve on both boards.

International Society of Olympic Historians [ISOH]. The International Society of Olympic Historians was founded in 1991 to promote and study the history of the Olympic Movement (q.v.) and the Olympic Games. The immediate worldwide response from Olympic historians provided a clear indication of the need for such an organization, with over 300 members from 50 nations at the end of 2000. A journal of the group, *Journal of Olympic History*, is published three times per year, and the Web site is accessible via **http://www.olykamp.org/isoh**. The first president was Ian Buchanan (GBR), who served two terms (1991–2000). The officers elected at the Sydney Olympics in 2000 were: president Bill Mallon (USA); vice president Karl Lennartz (GER); secretary-general Tony Bijkerk (NED); and treasurer David Wallechinsky (USA).

IOC Ethics Commission. The IOC Ethics Commission was formed in 1999 in response to the Olympic bribery scandal (q.v.). The Ethics Commission's primary focus was to address the responsibilities of the International Olympic Committee (IOC), oversee the selection process of host cities, and investigate any allegations of breaches of conduct by IOC members or Olympic candidate or host cities. The original Ethics Commission consisted of eight members—three IOC members (chairman Judge Kéba Mbaye, R. Kevan Gosper, and Chiharu Igaya), and five independent members, as follows: Javier Perez de Cuellar—former United Nations secretary-general, Robert Badinter—former president of the French Constitutional Court, Kurt Fürgler—former president of the Swiss Confederation, Charmaine Crooks—five-time Olympic runner from Canada, and Howard Baker—former White House Chief of Staff, former majority leader of the United States Senate. The current committee (April 2000) consists of seven members, as Gosper has dropped off. In the summer of 1999, the Ethics Commission produced an IOC Code of Ethics.

IOC 2000 Commission. The IOC 2000 Commission was another commission formed in response to the Olympic bribery scandal (q.v.). The purpose of the IOC 2000 Commission was to study the structure of the International Olympic Committee (IOC) (q.v.), and the Candidate City bidding process, and make recommendations to update these entities to prevent many of the problems that were occurring. The IOC 2000 Commission was made up of 82 members, with less than half of them IOC Members, and with an Executive Board of 26 members, of whom 13 were IOC Members. The commission produced an intermediary report in June 1999 and its final report was released in November 1999. The IOC 2000 Commission made 50 recommendations to the IOC in its Final Report, with recommendations made by each of the working groups. At the IOC session in December 1999, the IOC approved all 50 of the recommendations, which has led to a major re-writing of the *Olympic Charter* (q.v.). A summary of the recommendations is as follows:

1. Members: The maximum IOC membership should be 115, with 15 active athletes (defined as having taken part in the Olympic Games or Olympic Winter Games within four years of their membership), 15 International Federation (IFs [q.v.]) presidents, 15 presidents of National Olympic Committees (NOCs [q.v.]) or Continental Associations, and 70 members elected on an individual basis.
2. Procedure for Selecting Candidates and Electing Members: Proposed forming a Nomination Committee. Each of these four classes of IOC members can propose candidate members. The Nomination Committee will consist of seven members, including at least one athlete, elected for a four-year period. The Nomination Committee will consist of three members elected by the IOC, three by the IOC Ethics Commission (q.v.), and one by the Athletes Commission. The Nomination Committee will evaluate prospective members who will be voted upon by the full IOC session.
3. Nationality: One member per nation for members chosen on an individual basis; one member per nation among the athletes; one member per nation among NOC Presidents; no restrictions on nationality among IF presidents.
4. Terms of Office: Term limit of eight years, renewable, with re-election to follow the same procedure as election.
5. Age Limit: 70 years of age for all members and all functions. However, current members will be "grandfathered" to follow the limit of 80, which existed prior to this vote.

6. Rights and Responsibilities of Members: When a vote concerns a country of a member, the member may not take part in the vote.

7. Honorary Members: Awarded to members of 10 years' standing and for exceptional services. The current rule to remain in force through 31 December 2001.

8. Executive Board (q.v.): Increase number of members to 15, with four vice presidents. Four-year term limits on the Board.

9. President: Elected for an eight-year term; may be re-elected one time for a four-year second term of office.

10. Current Members: Current members will be "grandfathered" in place for eight years, at which time they will be subject to re-election, as will all new members.

11. Transition Period: During the transition period, to conclude 1 January 2001, the number of IOC members may be greater than the recommended 115.

12. Entry into Force: The new rules will come into force on 1 January 2000, with an implementation period of one year allowed.

13. Program and Participation: 13.1 The obligation of each NOC to participate in the games of the Olympiad will be added to the *Olympic Charter*—somewhat of an "antiboycott" clause. All NOCs will be allowed to enter six athletes in the Games of the Olympiad—even if they do not meet the minimum qualification standards. 13.2 Sports Program: A maximum of 280 events is recommended for future Games of the Olympiad. Events included in World Championships programs do not necessarily need to be included in the Olympic Games. Significant discussion followed this vote, as there will be 300 events at Sydney in 2000 and 14 sports are currently applying for admission to the Olympic Program. President Juan Antonio Samaranch (q.v.) suggested that the IOC Sports Commission study this proposal and make recommendations to the next IOC session.

14. Finance: The IOC will transfer knowledge concerning licensing programs to future Organizing Committees of the Olympic Games (OCOGs). The IOC will also provide guidelines and recommendations concerning ticketing and pricing to the OCOGs.

15. Paralympics: The Paralympics must be held in the same city as the Olympics, following the Games. The IOC will formalize its relationship with the International Paralympic Committee.

16. Management of the Olympic Games: The IOC will establish an operational structure to transfer knowledge and expertise from one edition of Olympic Games and Olympic Winter Games to the next.

17. Athletes (1): Defined an active Olympic athlete as one who is still competing or has participated in the most recent edition of the Olympic Games.

18. Athletes (2): Athletes should be represented at all levels of the Olympic Movement.

19. Athletes (3): The Athletes Commission should be represented on the IOC Executive Board, and recommends the same for IFs, NOCs, and National Governing Bodies (NGBs) (q.v.).

20. Athletes (4): Organizing Committees of the Olympic Games (OCOGs) must include an athlete on their boards.

21. Athletes (5): The IOC Athletes Commission must be allocated a budget for its operation.

22. Athletes (6): During the Closing Ceremony of the Olympic Games and Olympic Winter games, the elected athletes will be recognized by their peers and the Olympic Family.

23. Role of Olympic Solidarity (q.v.): Olympic Solidarity should act as the coordinator of development programs for all members of the Olympic Movement.

24. Decentralized Programs: Olympic Solidarity must provide support to continental/regional games under IOC patronage and will also help develop regional and subregional sports training centers.

25. Humanitarian Projects: These will be pursued and reinforced if they relate to members of the Olympic Movement and the development and practice of sport.

26. Information Transfer: Olympic Solidarity will ensure that all NOCs have access to the technology necessary for information transfer between sectors of the Olympic Movement.

27. Education: Proposed that NOCs include a session in all Olympic Solidarity–funded programs to educate the participants concerning the Olympic Movement.

28. Regional Information Centers: Proposed that Olympic Solidarity set up regional and subregional sports information centers to help disseminate information on the Olympic Movement and sports administration.
29. Evaluation/Accountability: Better coordination between the IOC departments and an improved auditing procedure of Olympic Solidarity will be implemented.
30. Education and Culture (1): Merge the Cultural and IOA/Education Commissions into a single Commission on Education and Culture. Create a new department of Education and Culture within the IOC. Hire additional professional staff for the Olympic Studies Centre at the Olympic Museum.
31. Education and Culture (2): Multiple recommendations to spread the message of Olympism to appropriate regional structures, including publishing the *Olympic Review* (q.v.) and the Official Reports of the Olympic Games on the Internet.
32. Education and Culture (3): Creation of a traveling exhibit of the Olympic Movement and Olympic History to be set up in host cities, with a clause added to the host city contract.
33. Education and Culture (4): Greater recognition of the IOC on the educational importance of the Olympic Flame (q.v.) relay and participation by the IOC Executive Board in the flame-lighting ceremonies at Olympia.
34. Doping (q.v.) (1): The Athletes' Oath (q.v.) will be amended to include a statement concerning drug-free sport.
35. Doping (2): Implementation by the World Anti-Doping Agency (WADA) (q.v.) of an athletic passport concerning the athlete's health, allowing doping controls to be carried out and to monitor the participant's health.
36. Doping (3): The IOC will conduct out-of-competition drug tests beginning at the time of accreditation of athletes at the Olympic Games and Olympic Winter Games.
37. Doping (4): In the event of an appeal against sanctions, the "B" sample should be tested by a different laboratory than the one that tested the "A" sample.
38. Doping (5): Sports not conforming to the Olympic Movement Anti-Doping Code and that do not perform out-of-competition drug testing will be dropped from the Olympic

Program. IOC-recognized sports not conforming to this code will lose their recognition.

39. Relations with Governments and Nongovernmental Organizations (NGO) (1): The IOC will provide more assistance to the NOCs to develop closer relationships with their respective local governments.

40. Relations . . . (2): The passage of the United Nations' Olympic Truce (q.v.) could be supplemented by similar declarations from world leaders and other NGOs to support the Olympic Truce.

41. Relations . . . (3): The Olympic Truce will be given greater prominence. Six months prior to the Olympic Games or Olympic Winter Games, the IOC president will contact the protagonist nations in major internal and international conflicts and ask them to observe the Olympic Truce for the duration of the Games. During the Opening Ceremony, the IOC president will refer to the Olympic Truce and will note that it is a first step toward lasting peace.

42. Internal Communications: Internal communications within the Olympic Movement must be open, substantive, two-way, and timely.

43. External Communications: An IOC spokesperson will be appointed to support the IOC president and other IOC executives. The Communications Department of the IOC will develop a pro-active approach to media relations. IOC sessions will be open to the media on closed-circuit television.

44. Transparency (1): The flow of IOC funds for each Olympiad will be disclosed beginning with the current Olympiad, via independent, external auditors.

45. Transparency (2): The IOC will disclose the allocation of funds to each NOC and IF and each entity of the Olympic Movement will submit to the IOC an accounting of its expenditure of funds provided by the IOC.

46. Transparency (3): The IOC will seek a more transparent disclosure of fund distribution to be phased in over future Olympiads.

47. Transparency (4): Each bid city must disclose the source of funding for bid expenditures, which will be audited at the conclusion of the bid process.

48. Transparency (5): The IOC will encourage NOCs and IFs to disclose their sources and uses of funds.

49. Role of the NOCs in the Bid Process: The NOC should be involved in any Olympic candidature as a full partner with the bid committee and should take responsibility for the Olympic bid to the IOC.

50. New Candidature Procedure: A new bid acceptance phase will be instituted, with multiple recommendations, as follows:

50.1 Strict minimum technical requirements will be applied to the selection of a bid city.

50.2 A new bid acceptance process in which representatives of the IOC, IFs, NOCs, athletes, and external experts will examine the proposed bids and recommend to the IOC Executive Board (q.v.), which cities should be accepted as candidate cities.

50.3 The IOC will enter into a contractual agreement with the NOC and the Bid Committee.

50.4 The IOC will issue candidate city manuals and prepare candidature files.

50.5 An Evaluation Commission will be formed to visit each of the candidate cities.

50.6 Selection of final candidate cities, if necessary. The Executive Board may reduce the number of candidates by selecting a limited number of cities.

50.7 It is not considered necessary for IOC Members to visit the candidate cities nor for the representatives or candidate cities, or third parties acting on their behalf ("agents"), to visit IOC Members.

In the end, all 50 recommendations of the IOC 2000 Commission were approved, most of them unanimously. The main points of contention were the age limit, which had eight dissenting votes, and Recommendation 50.7, which eliminated IOC Members' visits to candidate cities, but even those passed with over 90 percent of the vote.

Iran [IRI, formerly IRN]. Although Iran was represented in 1900 by a fencer, Prince Freydoun Malkom, it was only in 1947 that Iran formed an NOC. Iran was granted IOC recognition in the same year. Apart from boycotting the Olympics of 1980 and 1984, Iran has competed at every Olympic games since it made its Olympic début as a team in 1948. It has competed at the Olympic Winter Games of 1956, 1964, 1968, 1972, 1976, and 1998. All of Iran's success has come in the strength or combative sports of weightlifting, wrestling, and taekwondo. Through 2000, it has won 40 Olympic medals (eight gold medals) with 28 medals won in wrestling, 11 won in weightlifting, and 1 in taekwondo.

Iraq [IRQ]. Iraq formed its National Olympic Committee in 1948 and made its first Olympic appearance in that year. Iraq then did not compete until the Rome Olympics of 1960. Iraq missed the 1972 and 1976 Olympics but has competed continuously since, including the 1984 Olympic Games. Iraq has never competed at the Olympic Winter Games. One Iraqi athlete has won an Olympic medal, that being a bronze medal by Abdul Wahid Aziz in lightweight weightlifting in 1960.

Ireland [IRL]. Ireland formed a National Olympic Committee in 1922, shortly after it became independent of Great Britain (q.v.) in December 1921. Ireland first competed as a separate state in the 1924 Olympic Games at Paris. Prior to that time, however, many Irish athletes had competed—mostly for Great Britain. In addition, many of the great American weight-throwers had been recent Irish emigrants. Ireland also entered separate teams in 1908 field hockey and the 1912 cycling road race, although the 1912 cycling team technically was a second team representing Great Britain. Since 1924, Ireland has competed at every Olympic Games, except those of 1936. Ireland has competed at the Olympic Winter Games in 1992 and 1998. Through 2000, Ireland has won 20 Olympic medals: eight gold, six silver, and six bronze.

Israel [ISR]. The formation of the state of Israel as an independent Jewish state occurred on 15 May 1948. Israel dates its National Olympic Committee to 1933, but that was a Palestinean organization, and not truly a precursor of the current NOC. The original Palestine Olympic Committee was recognized by the IOC in 1934, and was to represent

Jews, Muslims, and Christians from the Palestine region. However, the rules of the original Palestine NOC stated, "Palestine is the National Home of the Jews, and so the Palestine NOC represents the Jewish National Home." Given that manifesto, the Palestine NOC refused to compete at the 1936 Olympic Games in Berlin, in protest of Adolf Hitler's policies. After World War II, the 1948 London Organizing Committee originally invited the Palestine NOC but later withdrew the invitation. The problem of the status of the Palestine Olympic Committee was solved in 1951 when the Israel Olympic Committee was formed.

Israel competed at its first Olympics in 1952 at Helsinki, the same year that its National Olympic Committee was formally recognized by the IOC. Israel has missed only the 1980 Moscow Olympics since 1952. Israel made its first Olympic Winter Games appearance in 1994 at Lillehammer and also participated in 1998 at Nagano. The zenith of Israel participation came in 1992 when two Israeli *judoka* won the nation's first medals. The nadir occurred at Munich on 5 September 1972 when Arab terrorists savagely and cowardly murdered 11 Israeli athletes and officials. Through 2000, Israel has won four Olympic medals—the two afore mentioned in judo, one in canoeing, and one in sailing.

Isthmian Games. The Isthmian Games were ancient sporting festivals that were held biennially. With the Olympic Games, Nemean Games, and Pythian Games, they were one of the four great sporting festivals of ancient Greece. The Isthmian Games were contested at the sanctuary of Poseidon at the Isthmus of Corinth. They are first known to have been held in 582 B.C. and lasted through the fourth century A.D. Their origin is attributed to Sisyphus, King of Corinth. Champions at the Isthmian Games originally received crowns of dry wild celery, which was later changed to a crown of pine wreath during Roman times. One report suggests that the Isthmian Games were highly commercialized.

Italy [ITA]. Italy has never missed an Olympic Winter Games and has missed only the Olympic Games of 1904. Although it is usually considered not to have competed in 1896, recent research has discovered that an Italian shooter named Rivabella did compete in

1896. But Italy did not form a National Olympic Committee until 1908, and it was not until 1915 that this committee was recognized by the IOC. Italy has had success in many different sports. Italy has often been the dominant country in cycling and fencing. Italy has won 558 Olympic medals, 207 of them gold. Of these, 77 medals and 27 gold have been won at the Olympic Winter Games. Italy also hosted the Games of the XVIIth Olympiad at Rome in 1960, and the 7th Olympic Winter Games at Cortina d'Ampezzo in 1956. Italy is also scheduled to host the 20th Olympic Winter Games in Torino (Turin) in 2006.

Ivory Coast [CIV]. *See* CÔTE D'IVOIRE.

– J –

Jager, Thomas Michael [USA–SWI]. B. 6 October 1964, East St. Louis, Illinois. Tom Jager won seven Olympic swimming medals and five gold medals. All of his golds came in relays. His individual medals were a silver in the 1988 50-meter freestyle and bronze in the 1992 50-meter freestyle. Jager was a pure sprinter, specializing in the 50 free, at which he set six world records. He won the first two world championships at that event in 1986 and 1991. His other major international titles came in the 50 free at the 1989 and 1991 Pan-Pacific Championships. His great sprint rivals were Matt Biondi (q.v.), who beat him at the Olympics in 1988, and Aleksandr Popov (RUS), who won the 50 freestyle in 1992 and 1996.

Jamaica [JAM]. Jamaica has sent athletes to all the Olympic Games since 1948. In 1960, Jamaica, Barbados, and Trinidad combined to form the West Indies Federation (q.v.) team. That team won two medals, one of which was won by George Kerr, a Jamaican, in the 800 meters, while the other was a bronze in the 4 x 400-meter relay. Three members of that team were Jamaican while one was from Barbados. In 1988, Jamaica competed at its first Olympic Winter Games, represented by the now-famous Jamaican Bobsled Team, which also represented the nation at Albertville in 1992 and Lillehammer in 1994. Two members of the bobsled team, the brothers Dudley and

Christian Stokes, also competed in 1998, their fourth appearance. A movie, *Cool Runnings*, was later made about the Jamaican bobsled team. Jamaica has won 30 Olympic medals through 1998, 29 of them in track & field athletics, led by its outstanding sprinters. The other medal was a bronze in cycling won by David Weller in the 1,000-meter time trial.

Japan [JPN]. Japan first competed at the 1912 Olympic Games, its delegation and Olympic Committee led by Dr. Jigoro Kano, the founder of judo. Japan has since failed to compete only at the Games of 1948, when, as an aggressor nation in World War II, it was not invited, and 1980, when it chose to boycott (q.v.) the Moscow Olympics. At the Olympic Winter Games, Japan first competed in 1928 and has since missed only 1948 when it also was not invited. Japan was the dominant country in men's gymnastics from 1956 until the mid-1980s. In addition, at times it has been the top country in swimming and one of the top in wrestling and weightlifting. Japan has won 325 Olympic medals (105 gold medals), of which 29 (eight gold) have come at the Olympic Winter Games. Japan hosted the Games of the XVIIIth Olympiad in Tokyo in 1964, the 11th Olympic Winter Games in Sapporo in 1972, and the 18th Olympic Winter Games in Nagano in 1998. Prior to the outbreak of hostilities, Japan was also scheduled to host both editions of the 1940 Olympics; the Olympic Winter Games were scheduled for Sapporo, and the Games of the XIIth Olympiad were scheduled for Tokyo.

Jernberg, Sixten [SWE–NSK]. B. 6 February 1929, Lima, Dalarria (Dalecarlia). Sixten Jernberg is one of the most successful male Olympic Nordic skiers, who set records that have only been broken recently by Bjørn Dæhlie (NOR) (q.v.). Between 1956 and 1964, Jernberg won four gold, three silver, and two bronze for a record total (at the time) of nine Winter Olympic medals. He added three gold and two bronze medals at the 1954, 1958, and 1962 World Championships, including four medals in the 50 km. Between 1952 and 1964, he took part in 363 ski races, winning 134. In his prime years of 1955–1960, Jernberg won 86 of 161 races. Initially a blacksmith and then a lumberjack, his daily work provided the essential stamina for the rigors of long-distance cross-country skiing.

In 1965, the IOC awarded him the Mohammed Taher Trophy. *See* Appendix V.

Jeu de Paume (Court Tennis or Real Tennis). *Jeu de paume,* or game of the hand, the original version of tennis, has been contested in the Olympics only in 1908, when the gold medal was won by American Jay Gould. In 1928, the sport was a demonstration event in Amsterdam. The sport is variously also called *court tennis, real tennis,* and *royal tennis.*

Johansson, Ivar [SWE–WRE]. B. 31 January 1903, Kuddby, Ostergötland. D. 4 August 1979. Ivar Johansson is one of only three men to have won Olympic gold medals in both styles of wrestling and also one of four wrestlers to have won a total of three Olympic gold medals. In 1932, he won the freestyle middleweight and the Græco-Roman welterweight titles and, in 1936, he won the Græco-Roman middleweight. Johansson won nine European Championships between 1931 and 1939, six at Græco and three at freestyle. He was a 22–time Swedish champion, winning 13 at Græco and 9 at freestyle. His last Swedish title came in 1943 at the age of 40.

Johnson, Michael Duane [USA-ATH]. B. 13 September 1967, Dallas, Texas. Michael Johnson is acknowledged as the greatest long sprinter in the history of track & field, specializing in the 200 and 400 meters. Johnson made his Olympic début in 1992, but was ill at the time, and his only medal, a gold, came in the 4 x 400-meter relay. At Atlanta in 1996, he won both the 200 and 400 meters, the first man to accomplish that feat at the Olympics, with his 200-meter victory achieved in the stunning world record time of 19.32. Johnson's Olympic career ended at Sydney, where he defended his 400-meter title, and added a third gold in the 4 x 400 relay, giving him six gold medals in all. At the World Championships, Johnson was even more dominant, winning the 200 meters in 1991 and 1995, and the 400 meters in 1993, 1995, 1997, and 1999. He added the 400-meter world record in August 1999, when he ran 43.18 in Seville, Spain. With his upright style and short, rapid strides, he was an unmistakable figure on the track and is universally recognized as being the greatest one-lap runner ever.

Jones, Marion Lois [USA-ATH]. B. 12 October 1975, Los Angeles, California. Marion Jones first came to prominence as a high school sprint star in the early '90s. She narrowly missed making the 1992 U.S. Olympic team in the individual sprints as a high school senior, and she declined a place on the relay team. She then attended the University of North Carolina, where she starred as a point guard on the basketball team, and led the team to the NCAA Women's Championship in 1994. She ran no international track while in college, but returned to star at the 1997 World Championships when she won gold medals in the 100 meters and 4 x 100-meter relay. In 1998, she won 34 individual events, losing only a late-season long-jump competition. At the 1999 World Championships, she defended her title at 100 meters, but was injured in attempting to win the 200. Jones set herself the goal of winning five gold medals at the 2000 Olympic Games. She succeeded in winning five medals, three of them gold. The golds came in the 100, 200, and 4 x 400-meter relay, while she earned bronze medals in the long jump and 4 x 100 relay. She is married to C. J. Hunter, who was 1999 World Champion in the shot put.

Jordan [JOR]. Jordan formed a National Olympic Committee in 1957 that was recognized by the IOC in 1963. However, it was not until 1980 that Jordan's athletes competed on Olympian fields, since which time they have participated at every Olympic Games. Jordan has not yet appeared in the Olympic Winter Games. In 2000, Mohammad Al-Fararjeh finished seventh in light-heavyweight taekwondo, the best ever finish by a Jordanian Olympian.

Jordan, Michael Jeffrey [USA–BAS]. B. 17 February 1963, Brooklyn, New York. Michael Jordan is considered by most experts to be the greatest basketball player of all time. He played collegiately at the University of North Carolina, where he helped it win an NCAA (National Collegiate Athletic Association) championship in 1983. In 1984, Jordan led the United States to an Olympic gold medal (*See* UNITED STATES BASKETBALL TEAM—1984.) Turning to professional basketball after his junior year in college, he became the greatest scorer in the National Basketball Association (NBA), leading the league in scoring every year, except one in which he sat out most of the season with an injury. In 1991, Jordan finally achieved his greatest thrill, leading the Chicago Bulls to an NBA Championship, and completing his Triple Crown of titles. Jordan eventually led the Bulls to six NBA titles (1991–1993, 1996–1998). In 1992, Jordan also played on the Dream Team (q.v.) that won the basketball gold medal at Barcelona. Jordan did not play in the NBA in 1994 and for most of the 1995 season, as he attempted a career in professional baseball, playing in the minor leagues. Since his retirement from the NBA after the 1998 season, Jordan has become an owner of the NBA's Washington Wizards.

Judo. The founder of judo, Dr. Jigaro Kano, was a long-time member of the International Olympic Committee. Judo is a form of wrestling that was developed by Dr. Kano from the ancient Japanese schools of *yawara* and *jujitsu*. He founded his first *dojo* (judo school) in 1882, termed the *Kodokan*. The contestants are termed *judoka* and are classified into grades consisting of pupils (*Kyu*) and degrees *(Dan)*. There are five classes of *Kyu*, advancing to first *Kyu*, and wearing a brown belt. Thereafter, the *judoka* achieve a *Dan,* beginning with first *Dan* (black belt) and advancing theoretically to 12th *Dan* (white belt). Fighting ability and technical knowledge advance a *judoka* to fifth *Dan,* after which advancement depends on service to the sport. Leading international *judoka* are usually fourth or fifth *Dan.* The 11th and 12th *Dan* have never been awarded.

Judo made its first Olympic appearance in 1964, but was not included on the program of the 1968 Olympic Games. Judo returned to the Olympic fold in 1972 and the 1992 Olympics included judo events for women (q.v.) for the first time. The sport, not surprisingly, has been dominated by the Japanese, followed by the Soviet Union, with Korea also winning many medals. The sport is governed internationally by the International Judo Federation (IJF), which was formed in 1951 and had 183 members as of December 2000.

Juridical Commission. Originally called the *Legal Commission*, the Juridical Commission was formed in 1974 with Marc Hodler as the original chairman. The current chairman is the Senegalese Judge Kéba Mbaye. There are five other members of the commission, all IOC Members, and all either lawyers in their day job or who are legally trained.

– K –

Kakhiashvili, Akakios (né Kakhi Kakhiashvili) [GRE/EUN-WLT].
B. 13 July 1969, Tbilisi, Georgia. Akakios Kakhiashvili was born in
Soviet Georgia and first competed at the Olympic Games in 1992,
representing the Unified Team (Équipe Unifié), and earning a gold
medal in the 90-kg. class. Kakhiasvili then emigrated to Greece, for
whom he has competed internationally since 1995. Representing
Greece, he was World Champion in 1995 and 1998, and won further
Olympic gold medals in both 1996 and 2000, one of only three
weightlifters to win three gold medals.

Kalpe–Ancient Olympic Sport. The *kalpe,* or race for mares, was a
truly curious event. It is not known how many laps of the hippodrome
were contested but, on the last lap, the rider dismounted and ran
alongside the mare to the finish. The race was first contested in 496
B.C. and was dropped in 444 B.C. although only one winner is
known, that being Pataikos of Dymai in 496 B.C.

Kampuchea. *See* CAMBODIA.

Kania-Busch-Enke, Karin [GDR–SSK]. B. 20 June 1961, Dresden.
Initially a leading figure skater, Karin Kania later became a champion
speed skater and is one of the very few athletes to have reached world
class in both disciplines. Because she felt that chances for improvement on her ninth place in the 1977 European Figure Skating Championships were limited, she turned to speed skating with considerable
success. Her total of eight medals (three gold, four silver, one bronze)
between 1980 and 1988 remains an Olympic record for speed skating
and her record at the World Championships was even more impressive. She won the sprint title a record six times (1980, 1981, 1983,
1984, 1986, 1987) and her five victories in the overall event were
also a record for the Championships—even though she missed the
1985 Championships because of pregnancy.

Karate. Karate has never been on the Olympic program. But the Fédération Mondiale de Karaté (FMK) is recognized by the IOC. Founded
in 1992, the FMK had 150 affiliated member nations as of 2000.

Karelin, Aleksandr [URS/EUN/RUS-WRE]. B. 19 September 1967. Aleksandr Karelin is one of only four men to have won three Olympic gold medals in wrestling (the others being Ivar Johansson [SWE], Aleksandr Medved [URS/UKR], Carl Westergren [SWE]) (qq.v.). Known for his strength, Karelin won his first gold medal in 1988 in the super-heavyweight Græco-Roman event, competing for the Soviet Union. He defended that title in 1992, competing for the Unified Team, and in 1996, competing for Russia. He was also World Champion in the same class nine times (1989–1991, 1993–1995, and 1998–1999) being undefeated in international competition between 1988 and 1996. Karelin's 12 World and Olympic championships is an all-time best. Karelin competed at Sydney in 2000, attempting to win his fourth consecutive Olympic gold medal, for which he was the heavy favorite. In perhaps the biggest upset of the Olympics, he lost, 1–0, in the final to the unheralded American, Rulon Gardner.

Kárpáti, György [HUN–WAP]. B. 23 June 1935, Budapest. György Kárpáti played at outside forward and used his great swimming speed to great effect. In his prime, he was considered the fastest water poloist in the world. When only 17 years old, he won his first Olympic gold medal in 1952. This was followed by another gold in 1956, a bronze in 1960, and a third gold in 1964. Kárpáti was a member of the Hungarian water polo team that won the European Championships in 1954 and 1962.

Kárpáti, Rudolf [HUN–FEN]. B. 17 July 1920, Budapest. D. 1 February 1999. Rudolf Kárpáti was a member of the noted Hungarian fencing teams that dominated sabre competition for more than three decades. In team sabre, he won Olympic gold medals at four successive Olympics (1948–1960) and he was a member of the winning team at five World Championships (1953–1955, 1957–1958). Individually, Kárpáti was twice Olympic sabre champion (1956 and 1960) and twice World sabre champion (1954 and 1959). After his retirement, Rudolf Kárpáti became President of the Hungarian Fencing Federation and an administrator with the Fédération International d'Éscrime (FIE). He was also a talented musician and was the leader of the People's Army Central Artistic Ensemble.

Kato, Sawao [JPN–GYM]. B. 11 October 1946, Sugadaira, Niigata Prefecture. Sawao Kato was the winner of a record (for men) eight gold medals for gymnastics. He was a member of the winning all-around team in 1968, 1972, and 1976, and also took the individual title on the first two occasions, but had to settle for a silver medal in 1976. Kato's other gold medals came in the individual floor exercises (1968) and the individual parallel bars (1972, 1976).

Kayaking. *See* CANOE & KAYAKING.

Kazakstan (formerly Kazakhstan) [KAZ, formerly KZK]. Kazakstan's National Olympic Committee was recognized by the IOC in 1992, shortly after the break-up of the Soviet Union (USSR) (q.v.). Many Kazakstani athletes competed from 1952 to 1988 for the Soviet Union, and Kazakstani athletes were present at Barcelona and Albertville in 1992 as members of the Unified Team (q.v.). Kazakstan first competed at the Olympics as an independent nation in 1994 at Lillehammer, where its great cross-country skier Vladimir Smirnov won three medals, one gold and two silver. Kazakstan made its summer début at the 1996 Olympic Games in Atlanta, and also competed in 1998 at Nagano. Through 2000, Kazakstani athletes have won 23 medals, seven gold (five of the medals at the Olympic Winter Games).

Keles, Ancient Olympic Sport. In the *keles*, or horse race, the horse with a rider covered six full laps of the hippodrome. The first known champion was in 648 B.C. (Krauxidas of Krannon), with champions known through 193 A.D. (Theopropos of Rhodes). Hieron, Tyrant of Syracuse, is the only known two-time champion (476 and 472 B.C.).

Keleti, Ágnes [HUN–GYM]. B. 9 January 1921, Budapest. Ágnes Keleti won 10 Olympic gymnastic medals (five gold, three silver, two bronze) in 1952 and 1956, making her Hungary's most successful female Olympian. Keleti won her first gold in 1952 and then dominated the gymnastics competition at the 1956 Olympics, winning four gold medals. She was originally a fur worker and later a professional cellist. After the 1956 Melbourne Olympics, she defected to Australia, but she eventually settled in Israel, where she became the national women's gymnastics coach.

Kelly, John Brenden "Jack" [USA–ROW]. B. 4 October 1889, Philadelphia, Pennsylvania. D. 26 June 1960, Philadelphia, Pennsylvania. Jack Kelly is the greatest sculler the United States has ever produced. Kelly joined the Vesper Boat Club in 1909. Between 1909 and his competitive retirement after the 1924 Olympics, Kelly won every sculling title available to him, including the World Championship in both singles and doubles, the Olympics in singles and doubles, and many national titles in both boats. Kelly never won the Diamond Sculls at the Henley Regatta because he was denied entry as the Vesper Boat Club was banned for, in the view of the British rowing officials, earlier professional activities. Kelly fathered two very famous children—John Kelly, Jr., another Olympic rower who was later U.S. Olympic Committee President, and the late Grace Kelly, the American movie star who later became Princess Grace of Monaco.

Kendo (Japanese fencing). *See* BUDO.

Kenya [KEN]. The Kenyan NOC was founded in 1955 and recognized by the IOC in the same year. In 1956, it made its Olympic début. Since then, it has been absent only from the Olympics of 1976 and 1980, both of which it boycotted. Kenya has won 54 Olympic medals through 2000, with 16 gold. Kenya has won seven medals in boxing, but all of its other medals have been won by its excellent runners, the most outstanding of these having been Kipchoge Keino. Kenya first competed at the Olympic Winter Games in 1998, when their sole representative, Paul Boit, finished in 92nd and last place in the 10-km. cross-country skiing event. Boit is the nephew of former Kenyan middle-distance Olympian, Mike Boit.

Ketseas, Ioannis [GRE]. B. 16 September 1887, Athens. D. 6 April 1965, Athens. Ioannis Ketseas was the co-founder of the International Olympic Academy (IOA) with Carl Diem (q.v.). His lifelong interest in sports led to his becoming President of the Hellenic AAU (SEGAS) in 1929, and president of the Greek Federation of Lawn Tennis in 1939. From 1946 to his death in 1965, he was an IOC member in Greece. His business was as general director of the National Bank of Greece from 1906–1928, and he also served the Greek government as Minister of Foreign Affairs from 1921 to 1922. He and Diem founded the IOA officially in 1961, although they had promulgated the idea for almost 30 years. Ketseas served as the first Chairman of the Ephoria of the IOA, its ruling council, from 1961 to 1965.

Killanin, Michael Morris, 3rd Baron of Dublin and Spiddal [IRL]. B. 30 July 1914, London, England. D. 25 April 1999, Dublin. Lord Killanin was elected as president of the Olympic Council of Ireland in 1950. He became an IOC member two years later. In 1967, he was elected to the Executive Board (q.v.). In 1968, he ascended to third vice president of the IOC and in 1970, he was named first vice president. Lord Killanin was elected as president of the IOC in 1972 and held that office until his retirement in 1980, when he was awarded the Olympic Order (q.v.) in Gold. He was also elected honorary president for life of the IOC. A noted journalist, author, and film producer, Lord Killanin also served as a director of many leading Irish business companies.

Killy, Jean-Claude [FRA–ASK]. B. 30 August 1943, Saint-Cloud, Seine-et-Oise. At his Olympic début in 1964, Jean-Claude Killy placed fifth in the giant slalom. Four years later, he matched Toni Sailer's (q.v.) 1956 record by winning Olympic gold in all three Alpine skiing events. Unlike Sailer, who won his events by substantial margins, all Killy's victories were narrow ones and he only won the slalom after the controversial disqualification of the Austrian, Karl Schranz. Killy was also World Champion in the Alpine combination (1966, 1968) and downhill (1966), and was a convincing winner of the first two World Cup competitions (1967, 1968). Following his retirement at the end of the 1968 season, he amassed a fortune from endorsements and he also became involved in motor racing, films, and professional ski racing. Killy was co-president of the Organizing Committee for the 1992 Olympic Winter Games in Albertville. He then became president of the Amaury Group, which controls the Tour de France, the Paris-Dakar auto rally, and *L'Équipe* (the French sporting daily newspaper). Killy is the only person to have won an Olympic gold medal and been awarded the Olympic Order in Gold. In addition, in 1995, Killy was elected as a member of the International Olympic Committee.

Kim, Nelli Vladimirovna [URS–GYM]. B. 29 July 1957, Surab, Lenin-abad. Nelli Kim was born of a Korean father and a Russian mother. Blessed with striking good looks, she was the darling of the media who also recognized her exceptional talent as a gymnast. She débuted at the World Championships in 1974 as a 17-year-old, finishing third on the balance beam. At the 1976 Montreal Olympics, Kim won three gold medals, but is best remembered for scoring a perfect 10.0 in the vault and floor exercise. At the 1980 Olympics, she helped the Soviet Union retain the team championship, and shared first place in the floor exercises. Kim was also impressive at the World Championships, at which she won 11 medals between 1974 and 1979. She married international gymnast Vladimir Akhasov.

Kim Soo-Nyung [KOR–ARC]. B. 5 April 1971, Choong Chung Book Province. In only a few short years, Kim Soo-Nyung established herself as the greatest woman archer of the modern era. In 1988, Kim won an individual and team gold medal in archery at the Olympics. Nicknamed "Viper," she was women's individual and team world champion in both 1989 and 1991. Through 1990, she held every women's world record at all distances, and overall as well. At the Barcelona Olympics, she again helped Korea to the team gold, but finished second in the individual event. Kim also competed at Sydney in 2000, winning a bronze medal in the individual event, and helping Korea win another team gold medal.

Kiraly, Charles Frederick, "Karch" [USA–VOL]. B. 3 November 1960, Jackson, Michigan. Karch Kiraly is regarded by many as the greatest volleyballer ever. In 1986, the Fédération Internationale de Volleyball (FIVB) declared him the top player in the world, the first time that distinction had been given. He won gold medals at the 1984 and 1988 Olympics, 1985 World Cup, 1986 World Championships, 1987 Pan-American Games, and in beach volleyball at the 1996 Olympics. Kiraly played at UCLA (University of California at Los Angeles) in college, where he led them to three NCAA (National Collegiate Athletic Association) championships and was twice named most valuable player of the NCAA Tournament. Playing professionally in Italy, he helped Il Messaggero win the 1991 World Club Championship. Later, a star at beach volleyball, he was the leading professional money winner at that sport from 1991 to 1994, and when that sport débuted at the 1996 Olympic Games, Kiraly won the gold medal, partnered with Kent Steffes.

Klimke, Reiner [FRG/GER–EQU]. B. 14 January 1936, Münster. Reiner Klimke's six gold and two bronze medals in dressage events stand as the Olympic record for any of the equestrian disciplines. He won team gold in 1964, 1968, 1976, 1984, and 1988 and the individual gold in 1984. Kleimke's two bronze medals came in the individual event in 1968 and 1976. He also had a fine record at the World Championships, winning six gold medals (two individual [1974, 1982] and four team [1966, 1974, 1982, 1986]).

Kolehmainen, Johan Pietari "Hannes" [FIN–ATH]. B. 9 December 1889, Kuopio. D. 11 January 1966, Helsinki. Hannes Kolehmainen was the first of the great Finnish distance runners. At the 1912 Olympics, he won the 5,000 meters with a new world record, the 10,000 meters, and the individual cross-country race, in which he also won a silver medal in the team event. Kolehmainen also set a world record for 3,000 meters in a heat of the team event. The cancellation of the 1916 Games undoubtedly prevented him from winning further Olympic honors, but he returned in 1920 and won the gold medal in the marathon. Kolehmainen set eight world records or bests, at distances varying from 3,000 meters to the marathon.

Kono, Tommy Tamio [USA–WLT]. B. 27 June 1930, Sacramento, California. Between 1953 and 1959 Tommy Kono was undefeated as a weightlifter in world and Olympic competition, adding six straight world titles to his two Olympic gold medals in the 1952 lightweight class and 1956 light-heavyweight class. He also won three straight gold medals in the Pan-American Games, in 1955, 1959, and 1963. Kono is the only man to ever set world records in four distinct classes, and he won 11 Amateur Athletic Union (AAU) championships—in three different weight classes.

Korbut, Olga Valentinovna [URS/BLR–GYM]. B. 16 May 1955, Grodno, Belarus, USSR. Olga Korbut burst onto the world's gymnastics scene at the 1972 Olympics in Munich, amazing experts with her flexibility and daring moves. A fall on the uneven parallel bars dropped her to seventh overall in the all-around individual. However, she won three gold medals: two individual in the apparatus finals (balance beam and floor exercises), and one with the Soviet all-around team. Korbut never defeated her teammate, Lyudmila Turishcheva (q.v.), but she was the darling of the fans and the media for her courage to try new moves, and her willing smile. She later won the 1973 World University Games all-around title, and was second at the 1973 Europeans and 1974 World Championships in all-around. She competed at the 1976 Olympics, winning a gold medal in the team event and a silver on the balance beam. Korbut retired from competition in 1977 and has now settled in Atlanta, Georgia.

Korea, Democratic People's Republic of (North) [PRK]. The Democratic People's Republic (DPR) of Korea (often termed *North Korea*) proclaimed its establishment on 9 September 1948. DPR Korea applied to the IOC for recognition in June 1956 and received provisional IOC recognition in 1957, on the understanding that it would only be allowed to compete at Rome in 1960 as a combined team with the Republic of Korea.

Originally, the IOC policy was for both Koreas to form a combined team, similar to Germany (q.v.) in 1956–1964. DPR Korea agreed to this, but Korea (South) said it was impossible. DPR Korea received full IOC recognition for its Olympic Committee in March 1962. DPR Korea then competed at the Innsbruck Olympic Winter Games in 1964, but with a flag that did not conform to the IOC decision made at the 1963 session in Baden-Baden.

DPR Korea was to make its début at the Olympic Games in 1964 in Tokyo but withdrew. This was because, in November 1963, DPR Korea had competed at the Games of the New Emerging Forces (GANEFO) (q.v.). These highly controversial games (*see* THE GAMES OF THE XVIIITH OLYMPIAD) were not recognized by the IOC because GANEFO organizers refused admission to Israel and Taiwan. All athletes competing in shooting, swimming, and athletics at GANEFO were banned by their international federations from competing at Tokyo in 1964. This included several athletes from DPR Korea, including its greatest athlete, 800-meter world-record holding runner Dan Sin-Kim. When these athletes were not allowed to compete, DPR Korea withdrew in protest.

GANEFO II was held from 25 November to 6 December 1966 and DPR Korea again competed at these games. Because of this, the track & field athletes from DPR Korea who had competed at GANEFO II were subsequently barred from the 1968 Mexico City Olympics, and the nation withdrew again, choosing not to send any athletes.

The 1968 withdrawal was also partly motivated by anger over a recent IOC decision. At the 68th session in Mexico City shortly before the Olympics, the IOC decided that, after 1 November 1968, the nation would be referred to as the *Democratic People's Republic of Korea*, but that at Mexico City, the nation would compete under its geographic name of North Korea. Precisely similar decisions were made with respect to East Germany and Taiwan, who were forced by the IOC to compete at Mexico City under names they did not recognize, rather than their proper names of the *German Democratic Republic* and *Republic of China*.

DPR Korea made its first Olympic appearance at the Olympic Winter Games in Innsbruck in 1964. The nation has also competed at the Winter Games of 1972, 1984, 1988, 1992, and 1998. DPR Korea has competed at the Olympic Games of 1972, 1976, 1980, 1992, 1996, and 2000, also skipping the 1984 Los Angeles Olympics and the 1988 Seoul Olympics. DPR Korea has won 32 Olympic medals through 2000, including eight gold medals, which includes one silver and one bronze medal won at the Winter Games.

DPR Korea withdrew from the 1984 Olympics in obvious sympathy with the Soviet boycott (q.v.) of the Los Angeles Olympics. DPR Korea withdrew from the 1988 Olympics in protest of the hosting of the Games by the rival government of the Republic of (South) Korea. Long political discussions were held from 1985 to 1988 between representatives of the NOCs of the two countries. These dealt with demands by the North Koreans to co-host the 1988 Olympics or at least host several of the events. The Korean Olympic Organizing Committee and the IOC were never able to satisfy the demands of the North Koreans and talks eventually broke off, resulting in the North Korean boycott. *See* THE GAMES OF THE XXIVTH OLYMPIAD.

At the 2000 Opening Ceremony in Sydney, a historic event occurred when the teams from the Democratic People's Republic of Korea and the Republic of Korea marched into the stadium together, led by one flagbearer from each nation at the head of the combined contingent. This "athletic peace" was brokered by the IOC, and occurred at a time when the two Koreas were also beginning to have some political exchanges for the first time in decades. The flagbearer for DPR Korea at Sydney was the official, Pak Jang-Chul, while the Republic of Korea was led by basketball player Chung Eun-Song. *See also* KOREA, REPUBLIC OF.

Korea, Republic of (South) [KOR]. The Republic of Korea, as we know it today, was created on 15 August 1948, after the end of World War II. Korea first officially competed at the 1948 Olympic Games in London. However, in both 1932 and 1936, during the occupation of the country by the Japanese (1910–1945), several Korean athletes competed at the Olympic Games wearing the colors of Japan. Korea has competed at all Olympics since 1948 with the exception of 1980, when it boycotted (q.v.) the Moscow Olympics. Korea also made its first Olympic Winter Games appearance in 1948 and has since missed only the Winter celebration of 1952.

Since 1948, Korea has done well in combative sports, winning virtually all of its medals in boxing, wrestling, judo, and weightlifting. The women have also medaled in volleyball, basketball, field hockey, table tennis, and archery. Korea has won 170 medals through 2000, 55 of them gold. Sixteen of these were won at the Olympic Winter Games. Korea ably hosted the Games of the XXIVth Olympiad in Seoul in 1988. *See also* KOREA, DEMOCRATIC PEOPLE'S REPUBLIC OF [NORTH].

Korfball. Korfball was contested as a demonstration sport (q.v.) at the Olympics of 1920 and 1928. The International Korfball Federation (IKF) is a recognized federation by the IOC. Founded in 1933, the IKF has 34 affiliated member nations as of December 2000.

Koss, Johann Olav [NOR–SSK]. B. 29 October 1968, Drammen. Johann Olav Koss was the winner of the 1,500 meters, 5,000 meters, and 10,000 meters speed skating events at the 1994 Winter Games, setting a world record in each event. He had earlier won Olympic gold in the 1,500 meters and silver in the 10,000 meters in 1992. In 1994, he donated his first gold medal cash bonus to Olympic Aid for Sarejevo and retired shortly after the Lillehammer Games to pursue a career in medicine. Koss was world all-around champion in 1990, 1991, and 1994, and was also World Cup champion at the distance events in 1991. In 1999, he was named one of the new athlete members to the IOC.

Kovács, Pál [HUN–FEN]. B. 17 July 1912. D. 8 July 1995, Debrecen. Pál Kovács began his sports career as a promising hurdler, but he later turned to fencing and was a member of the winning Hungarian sabre team at five successive Olympics (1936–1960). In the individual sabre, he was Olympic champion in 1953 after winning a bronze in 1948. Kovács was also world sabre champion in 1937 and 1953. In 1980, he became vice president of the Fédération International d'Éscrime (FIE).

Kraenzlein, Alvin Christian [USA–ATH]. B. 12 December 1876, Milwaukee, Wisconsin. D. 6 January 1928, Wilkes Barre, Pennsylvania. At the 1900 Games, Alvin Kraenzlein won the 60 meters, the 110 and 200-meter hurdles, and the long jump, and his four individual gold medals remain the unmatched record for a track & field athlete at one Games. His pioneering technique of straight-leg hurdling brought him two world hurdle records in addition to his five world records in the long jump. Although a qualified dentist, Kraenzlein never practiced, preferring to become a track coach, notably of the German and Cuban national teams and at the University of Michigan.

Krausse, Stefan. *See* BEHRENDT, JAN.

Kulakova, Galina Alekseyevna [URS–NSK]. B. 29 April 1942, Logachi, Udmurtya. Galina Kulakova was the greatest cross-country skier of the 1970s, setting records for Olympic medals that would stand until the program was expanded for women (q.v.) in late 1980s. Her finest Olympics came in 1972 at Sapporo when she won both individual events for women (5 and 10 km.) and helped the Soviet Union to a relay gold medal. She repeated this triple at the 1974 World Championships. In all, she won eight Olympic medals and four gold at four Olympics, those of 1968 through 1980. She earned five golds at the World Championships, with a 5-km. individual and relay gold in 1970 added to her feats of 1974. Her career was marred somewhat by a doping positive for ephedrine at the 1976 Olympics.

In an unusual ruling, the IOC gave her a warning, but no suspension and allowed her to enter the remaining races.

Kurland, Robert Albert [USA–BAS]. B. 23 December 1924, St. Louis, Missouri. Bob "Foothills" Kurland was the first dominating seven-footer to play college basketball; so dominant, in fact, that he caused the rules makers to outlaw goaltending, because he could block almost every shot from going into the basket. In 1945 and 1946, he led his Oklahoma A&M team to the NCAA (National Collegiate Athletic Association) championship and then went on to play for six years with the Phillips 66ers, being named Amateur Athletic Union (AAU) All-America every year he played. While playing with Phillips, Kurland became the first man to play on two Olympic championship teams.

Kuwait [KUW]. Kuwait's National Olympic Committee was formed in 1957 and recognized by the IOC in 1966. Kuwait has competed continuously at the Olympic Games since 1968. It has yet to win a medal and it has never competed at the Olympic Winter Games. Kuwait's best Olympic finish was equal fifth in 1980 football (soccer).

Kyrgyzstan [KGZ]. Kyrgyzstan's National Olympic Committee was recognized by the IOC in 1992 shortly after the break-up of the Soviet Union. Several Kyrgyzstani athletes competed from 1952 to 1988 for the Soviet Union, and Kyrgyzstani athletes were present at Barcelona in 1992 as members of the Unified Team (q.v.). Kyrgyzstan's first Olympic appearance as an independent nation occurred in 1994 at Lillehammer, represented by Yevgeniya Roppel. They were also represented by a lone biathlete at the 1998 Nagano Winter Olympics. Kyrgyzstan made its Olympic Games début in 1996 at Atlanta.

Kyudo (Japanese archery). *See* BUDO.

– L –

Lacrosse. Lacrosse was twice on the Olympic program as a full medal sport, in 1904 and 1908. Lacrosse has also been contested as a demonstration sport at the Olympics, in 1928, 1932, and 1948. Strangely, lacrosse does not have an IF that is a member of the General Association of International Sports Federations.

Lagutin, Boris Nikolayevich [URS/RUS–BOX]. B. 24 June 1938, Moscow. Boris Lagutin began his boxing career in 1955. He won his first international title in 1960 and won a bronze medal in the light-middleweight class at the Rome Olympics that year. In 1964 and 1968, Lagutin won the gold medal in the light-middleweight class, making him the second Olympic boxer to win three Olympic medals (after Lázsló Papp [HUN] [q.v.]), and only the second to defend his Olympic title in the same class—after Great Britain's Harry Mallin (q.v.). Lagutin was also European champion in 1961 and 1963.

Laos [LAO]. Laos formed an NOC in 1975 and saw it recognized by the IOC in 1979. Laos's first Olympic appearance was in 1980 at Moscow. The country competed again in 1988, 1992, 1996, and 2000. It has not competed at the Olympic Winter Games and has never won a medal.

Latvia [LAT]. Prior to its annexation by the Soviet Union in 1940, Latvia competed at the Olympics of 1924, 1928, 1932, and 1936, winning three medals. Latvia also competed at the Olympic Winter Games of 1924, 1928, and 1936. From 1952 to 1988, many Letts (preferred to Latvians) competed for the USSR. After the Soviet revolution of 1991, Latvia declared and was granted its independence, and its NOC was recognized by the IOC in 1991. Latvia returned to the Olympic fold in 1992 by competing at both Albertville and Barcelona in 1992, and has also competed at Lillehammer in 1994, Atlanta in 1996, Nagano in 1998, and Sydney in 2000. Through 2000, Latvia has won 10 medals, one gold, six silver, and three bronze.

Latynina, Larisa Semyonova (née Diriy) [URS–GYM]. B. 27 December 1934, Kherson. Larisa Latynina was a Russian gymnast whose total of 18 Olympic medals is an absolute Olympic record. Between 1956 and 1964, she won nine gold, five silver, and four bronze medals with individual gold coming in the floor exercises (1956, 1960, 1964). She dominated other major championships to a similar extent and at the Olympic, World, and European Championships, Latynina won 24 gold, 15 silver, and five bronze for a total of 44 medals. This phenomenal record was achieved despite the fact that her career was interrupted when she gave birth to two children.

Lazutina, Larisa [EUN/RUS–NSK]. B. 1 July 1965. Larisa Lazutina followed in the skisteps of Galina Kulakova, Yelena Välbe, and Raisa Smetanina (qq.v.) as the greatest Russian female cross-country skier. She won 11 championships at the Olympics and World Championships, trailing only the 16 won by Välbe. These include six relay titles—Olympics in 1992, 1994, and 1998, and Worlds in 1993, 1995, and 1997. In 1998 at Nagano, she put on her greatest performance, winning medals in all five events open to women, with three gold (5 km., pursuit, relay), a silver in the 15 km., and a bronze in the 30 km. Her individual world championships have come in the 1993 and 1995 5 km., the 1995 15 km., and the 1995 pursuit.

Lebanon [LIB]. After the establishment of an NOC in 1947, Lebanon was awarded IOC recognition in 1948, and made its Olympic début that year. Since then, Lebanon has competed at every Olympic Games, with the exception of 1956 when they boycotted (q.v.) in protest against the Israeli occupation of the Sinai Peninsula. Lebanon competed at every Olympic Winter Games from 1948 to 1992, but was not present at the Winter Olympics of 1994 or 1998. Through 2000, Lebanon has won four Olympic medals.

Lednev, Pavel Serafimovich [URS/UKR–MOP]. B. 25 March 1943, Gorky. Although Pavel Lednev never won the Olympic individual modern pentathlon title, he won a record seven Olympic medals. In the team event, he took gold in 1972 and 1980 and silver in 1976. In the individual event, he won silver in 1976 and bronze in 1968, 1972, and 1980. In contrast to his Olympic record, Lednev was the individual winner at the World Championships four times (1973, 1974, 1975, 1978) and was twice a member of the winning team at the World Championships (1973, 1974).

Lee, Willis Augustus, Jr. [USA–SHO]. B. 11 May 1888, Natlee, Kentucky. D. 25 August 1945, Portland, Maine. Willis Lee is the only man to win five gold medals for shooting at one Games. He achieved this feat in 1920 when he also won a silver and a bronze and all seven medals were won in team events. A U.S. Naval Academy graduate, he enjoyed a highly successful naval career and commanded the U.S. Pacific fleet during World War II, eventually rising to the rank of Vice-Admiral. Lee was a member of champion Navy rifle teams in 1908, 1909, 1913, 1919, and 1930. He was a distant relative of Robert E. Lee.

Leino, Eino Aukusti [FIN–WRE]. B. 7 April 1891, Kuopio. D. 30 November 1986, Tampere. Eino Leino had a very unusual wrestling career. He won medals in freestyle at four consecutive Olympics, making him one of only four wrestlers to win medals at four Games. In 1920, he won the gold medal in the middleweight division, his only Olympic title. He followed this with a welterweight silver in 1924, a lightweight bronze in 1928, and a welterweight bronze in 1932. Strangely, Leino never competed at the European or World Championships. From 1920, he lived in the United States, competing mostly there, and winning Amateur Athletic Union (AAU) Championships in 1920 and 1923.

Lemming, Eric Otto Valdeinar [SWE–ATH]. B. 22 February 1880, Göteborg. D. 5 June 1930, Göteborg. Eric Lemming was the first of the great modern javelin throwers. He was Olympic javelin champion in 1906, 1908, and 1912, winning both the orthodox and freestyle event in 1908. He would almost certainly have been the champion in 1900 had the javelin been on the program, but, in the absence of his specialty event, he competed in six other field events, placing fourth in the pole vault and the hammer. In 1906, he also won bronze medals in the shot, pentathlon, and tug-of-war. As a 19-year-old, Lemming set a world javelin best of 49.32 meters (161'10") in 1899 and made 13 further improvements to the record, culminating with a mark of 62.32 meters (204'5") in 1912, which was later accepted as the first official International Amateur Athletic Foundation (IAAF) record.

Leonard, Ray Charles, "Sugar Ray" [USA–BOX]. B. 17 May 1956, Wilmington, North Carolina. Sugar Ray Leonard won a gold medal at the 1976 Olympics in Montréal rather easily. After the Olympics, Leonard immediately became one of the top professional welterweight boxers. In 1979, he won his first world title by defeating Wilfred Benitez for the WBC version of the welterweight championship. Leonard eventually won world titles in five different weight classes, from welterweight to light-heavyweight. One of the fastest boxers ever, his skills were virtually unmatched and he deserves comparison as a fighter to his namesake, Sugar Ray Robinson. His popularity also enabled him to command ring fees that made him one of the wealthiest athletes of his time.

Leonidas of Rhodes [GRE–ATH]. *fl. ca.* 180–130 B.C. Leonidas of Rhodes was the greatest runner and sprinter of the Ancient Olympic Games. He won 12 Olympic titles, the most by any athlete, ancient or modern. In 164, 160, 156, and 152 B.C., he was proclaimed *triastes* or Olympic champion in three events, the *stadion*, *diaulos*, and race in armor (*hoplite*) (qq.v.).

Lesotho [LES]. Lesotho formed an NOC in 1971, which was recognized by the IOC in 1972. Lesotho made its Olympic début that year, and has since competed at every Olympic Games, except for those of 1976, when it joined the African boycott (q.v.). Lesotho has never competed at the Olympic Winter Games and has never won an Olympic medal.

Lewis, Frederick Carlton "Carl" [USA–ATH]. B. 1 July 1961, Birmingham, Alabama. Carl Lewis is considered by many to be the greatest track & field athlete of all time and, with 9 Olympic gold medals, 11 Olympic medals, and seven golds at the World Championships, it is a justifiable claim. His Olympic gold medals came in 1984 (100 meters, 200 meters, 4 x 100-meters relay, long jump), 1988 (100 meters, long jump), 1992 (4 x 100-meters relay, long jump), and 1996 (long jump). His four victories in 1984 matched the record set by Jesse Owens at the 1936 Games. He twice set individual world records at 100 meters (1988, 1991) and in the relays he was a member of teams that posted world records at 4 x 100 meters six times and 4 x 200 meters three times. In 1996 at Atlanta, Lewis ended his Olympic career by equalling Al Oerter's (q.v.) record of winning the same Olympic event four times consecutively, with Lewis's feat occurring in the long jump.

Liberia [LBR]. Liberia first competed at the Olympics in Melbourne in 1956. It has since missed the Olympic Games of 1968, 1976, 1980, and 1992. Liberia has not competed at the Olympic Winter Games and has not won an Olympic medal.

Libya [LBA]. Libya formed an NOC in 1962. Although it was recognized by the IOC in 1963, Libya did not take part in the 1964 Olympic Games. Libya's first appearance was in 1968, since which time they have competed in the 1980, 1988, 1992, 1996, and 2000 Olympics. Libya has not competed at the Olympic Winter Games and has not won an Olympic medal.

Liechtenstein [LIE]. Liechtenstein made its first Olympic appearances at the Games of 1936, both Winter and Summer. Since that time, it has failed to appear only at the 1952 Oslo Winter Olympics, the 1956 Melbourne Olympics, and the 1980 Moscow Olympics. Liechtenstein has the rare distinction of having won medals at the Olympic Winter Games (nine, two gold) but not at the Games of the Olympiad. This is because of the country's outstanding Alpine skiers, and especially two families, the Frommelts and the Wenzels.

Lipa-Oleniuc, Elisabeta (née Oleniuc) [ROM–ROW]. B. 26 October 1964. Elisabeta Lipa-Oleniuc is the only rower to have won seven Olympic medals, and the only women rower to win four gold medals. In 1984, as *Miss Oleniuc*, she won the double sculls (with Marioara Popescu). After her marriage, she took the silver medal in this event in 1988 (with Veronica Cogeanu [*see* COCHELEA-COGEANU]) and 1992 (with Veronica Cochelea-Cogeanu [q.v.]). She also won a second gold in the single sculls in 1992 and a bronze in the quadruple sculls in 1988. Lipa-Oleniuc was also World Champion in 1989 in single sculls. Her Olympic career continued with golds in the Romanian eight in both 1996 and 2000.

Lithuania [LTU, formerly LIT]. Prior to its annexation by the Soviet Union in 1940, Lithuania competed at the Olympic Games of 1924 and 1928, but failed to win any medals. Lithuania also competed at the 1928 Olympic Winter Games. From 1952 to 1988, many Lithuanians competed for the USSR. After the Soviet revolution of 1991,

Lithuania declared and was granted its independence, and its National Olympic Committee was recognized by the IOC in 1991. Lithuania returned to the Olympic fold in 1992 by competing at both Albertville and Barcelona. Subsequently, the nation has competed at the Olympics in Atlanta in 1996 and Sydney in 2000, and the Olympic Winter Games of 1992, 1994, and 1998. Through 2000, Lithuanians have won eight Olympic medals, three of them gold.

Louganis, Gregory Efthimios [USA–DIV]. B. 29 January 1960, San Diego, California. Greg Louganis is considered the greatest diver of all time. After winning Olympic silver on the platform in 1976, he missed the 1980 Games because of the boycott (q.v.), when he would have been favored to win both diving events. But Louganis returned to win the springboard-platform double in both 1984 and 1988. His 1988 springboard gold was the stuff of high drama when he struck his head on the board during qualifying. He required stitches to continue competing but managed to qualify and won the gold medal the next day. Louganis also took both titles at the World Championships of 1982 and 1986, having earlier won the platform in 1978. Of Samoan and European descent, he studied classical dance for many years and this training provided the basis for the elegance and artistry of his performances. Louganis's superiority over his contemporaries was considerable and he held many records for the highest marks ever achieved in competition. After his career ended, it was revealed that he had been HIV-positive at the time of the 1988 Olympics when he sustained his head wound during qualifying.

Louis, Spyridon [GRE–ATH]. B. 12 January 1873, Amarousi. D. 26 March 1940. As the winner of the first Olympic marathon at Athens in 1896, Spyridon Louis's place in sporting history is assured. Having placed only fifth in one of the Greek trial races, he was not favored to win the Olympic title, but his unexpected triumph gave Greece its only victory in a track & field athletics event at the 1896 Olympics Games and Louis was accorded the status of a national hero. Despite the acclaim, Louis returned to his village of Amarousi, where he worked as a shepherd, and he never raced again. He remained an Olympic legend and was a guest of the Organizing Committee at the 1936 Games in Berlin.

Luding-Rothenburger, Christa (née Rothenburger) [GDR–SSK/CYC]. B. 4 December 1959, Weißwasser. Christa Luding-Rothenburger is the only woman to win medals at both the Winter and Summer Games. A speed skating gold medalist at 500 meters (1984) and 1,000 meters (1988), she also won a silver in the cycling match sprint in 1988. Luding-Rothenburger also earned a speed skating silver medal in 1988 and bronze medal in 1992 in the 500 meters. She was a World Champion at both sports, winning the speed skating sprint title in 1985 and 1988 and the cycling sprint championship in 1986. Although many athletes have demonstrated the affinity between cycling and speed skating, few have competed at the top level in both sports at the same time and only Sheila Young (USA) and Beth Heiden (USA) have approached Luding-Rothenburger's success at both.

Luge. Tobogganing is one of the oldest winter sports. Descriptions of it in the 16th century are found in literature. As a racing sport, it can be traced to the mid-19th century when British tourists started sledding on the snowbound roads of the Alps. The original form of the sport was the skeleton sleds that were used on the Cresta Run at St. Moritz. Twice this sport was contested in the Olympics, in 1928 and 1948, both times when the Winter Games were held at St. Moritz. *See* SKELETON and BOBSLEDDING.

Luge spread to Switzerland in the 1890s as a variant of the skeleton race. The first recorded competitions took place in 1890 at the Innsbruck-based Academic Alpine Club. An International Tobogganing Association was formed in 1913 and the first European Championships were held in 1914 at Reichenfeld, Austria.

At the IOC meeting in Athens in 1954, luge tobogganing was recognized as an official Olympic sport, but luge events were not contested in the Olympics until 1964. The first world luge championships were contested in Oslo in 1955. It was planned to introduce the sport at the 1960 Olympic Winter Games but the Squaw Valley organizers had decided not to build a bob run and not to hold bobsled events, and they likewise opposed building a luge run for the participation of only a few countries. Thus, luge's Olympic début was delayed until 1964. Since that time, luge has been contested at all Olympic Winter Games, with a singles and doubles event for men, and a singles event for women.

The sport has been dominated by the Germans, Austrians, and Italians. Luge is now governed by the Fédération Internationale de Luge de Course (FIL), which was formed in 1957 and currently has 45 members.

Luxembourg [LUX]. Luxembourg is usually considered to have first competed at the 1912 Olympic Games, the same year that it formed its National Olympic Committee. However, it was recently discovered by French athletics historian, Alain Bouillé, that Michel Theato, the winner of the 1900 marathon, was from Luxembourg, not France, as previously believed. Thus, Luxembourg has competed at a total of 19 celebrations of the Olympiad since 1912, missing only the 1932 Los Angeles Games. It has also competed at the Olympic Winter Games of 1928, 1936, 1988, 1992, 1994, and 1998. Luxembourg has won five Olympic medals (two gold) in sporting events (two at the Olympic Winter Games), and three Olympic medals in the now-defunct Art Contests (q.v.).

– M –

Macedonia, Former Yugoslav Republic of (FYROM) [MKD, formerly MCD]. This former Yugoslav republic declared its independence from Yugoslavia on 8 September 1991. The Olympic Committee of the Former Yugoslav Republic of Macedonia was formed in 1992 and recognized by the IOC in 1993. The republic first competed at the Olympics as an independent nation in 1996 and at the Olympic Winter Games in 1998. The name of the nation, since its independence from Yugoslavia, is very controversial. Greece, Bulgaria, Serbia, and Albania all lay claim to regions of Macedonia, and the name. The European Community recognizes Macedonia's independence, but only under the name "Former Yugoslav Republic of Macedonia (FYROM)."

From 1924 to 1988, a few Yugoslav Olympians were from Macedonia. The best represented sport at the Olympics among Macedonians has been wrestling. Both Šaban Trstena and Šaban Šejdi from Skopje won two wrestling medals at the Olympics between 1980 and 1988. At the 2000 Olympics, Macedonia won its first Olympic medal as an independent nation, with a bronze by Mogomed Ibragimov in light-heavyweight freestyle wrestling.

In the Ancient Olympics, it is known that Macedonians, then part of Ancient Greece, won nine championships, including four in the *stadion* (sprint) event. Two of these were consecutive by Antigonos in 292–288 B.C. The greatest Olympic champion of ancient Macedonia was Philip II, the father of Alexander the Great, who won three Olympic titles.

Madagascar [MAD]. Madagascar formed an NOC in 1964, which was recognized by the IOC that year. Madagascar made its Olympic début in the same year, and has since missed only the Games of 1976 and 1988. Madagascar has never competed at the Olympic Winter Games and no Madagascan athlete has won an Olympic medal through 1998. Its top athlete has been the sprinter, Jean-Louis Ravelomanantsoa, who finished eighth in the 100 meters in 1968, the country's best finish ever.

Malawi [MAW]. Founded in 1968, Malawi's NOC was initially granted only provisional recognition by the IOC and full recognition did not follow until 1971. Malawi has competed at the 1972, 1984, 1988, 1992, 1996, and 2000 Olympics. Malawi has never competed at the Olympic Winter Games and, through 2000, has never won an Olympic medal. In 1984, Peter Ayesu, a flyweight boxer, won two matches and lost one, to finish equal fifth of 32 competitors, the best finish ever by a Malawian Olympian.

Malaya. *See* MALAYSIA.

Malaysia [MAS, formerly MAL]. Malaysia has competed in the Olympics since 1956, missing only the 1980 Moscow Olympics. Its National Olympic Committee was formed in 1953 and recognized by the IOC in 1954. In 1956 and 1960, the country competed as *Malaya*. In 1963, Malaya joined with Singapore (q.v.), North Borneo (q.v.) (now Sabah) and Sarawak to form the Federation of Malaysia. In 1964, Singapore competed as a part of the Malaysian team, but Singapore separated from Malaysia in 1965, and since then Singapore has competed on its own. Malaysia has never competed in the

Olympic Winter Games. It won its first Olympic medal, a bronze in men's badminton, its national sport, in 1992, and has won three Olympic medals, one silver and two bronzes, all in badminton.

Maldives [MDV]. The Maldives NOC was founded and recognized by the IOC in 1985. The Maldives has competed at the 1988, 1992, 1996, and 2000 Olympics. The nation has not yet competed at the Olympic Winter Games and has never won an Olympic medal.

Mali [MLI]. Mali formed an NOC in 1962, which was recognized by the IOC in 1963. In 1964, Mali made its first appearance at the Olympics and has since missed only the 1976 Olympics. It has never won a medal and it has not competed at the Olympic Winter Games. Its best Olympic performance came in 1972 when discus thrower Namakoro Niaré finished 13th of 29 men.

Mallin, Harry William [GBR–BOX]. B. 1 June 1892, Shoreditch, London. D. 8 November 1969, Lewisham, London. With victories in the middleweight division at the 1920 and 1924 Games, Harry Mallin became the first man to successfully defend an Olympic boxing title. Even in those days, the competence and partiality of the judges posed problems and Mallin only won his second gold medal after the decision giving the quarter-final bout to French hometown hero, Roger Brousse, had been overturned. Mallin's record was incomparable; he was unbeaten in more than 300 fights and won five British amateur titles.

Malta [MLT]. Malta first competed at the Olympics in 1928. It has participated rather sporadically since then, missing the Olympic Games of 1932, 1952, 1956, 1964, and 1976. It has never competed at the Olympic Winter Games. Malta's top Olympic moment occurred in 1928 when its water polo team won one match, defeating Luxembourg 3–1, before losing to France in the second round. This placed it equal fifth, of a starting field of 14 teams.

Mangiarotti, Edoardo [ITA–FEN]. B. 7 April 1919, Renate Veduggio, Milan. Edoardo Mangiarotti was the winner of a record 13 Olympic medals (six gold, five silver, two bronze) for fencing from 1936 to 1960. He was most successful in the épée team event, winning four gold medals (1936, 1952, 1956, 1960) and a silver (1948). His other gold medals came in the épée individual (1952) and the foil team (1960). At the World Championships, he won two individual épée titles and was a member of 13 winning teams in the épée and foil. Mangiarotti later became Secretary-General of the Fédération Internationale d'Éscrime (FIE). His brother, Dario, was also a member of the Italian medal winning Olympic épée teams in 1948 and 1952.

Mäntyranta, Eero Antero [FIN–NSK]. B. 20 November 1937, Pello, Lapland. Eero Mäntyranta competed at four Olympic Games (1960–72), winning cross-country skiing medals at three of them. A member of the Finnish 4 x 10-km. relay team from 1960 to 68, he won gold in 1960, silver in 1964, and a bronze in 1968. At his peak in 1964, Mäntyranta won both the 15 km. and the 30 km., and added a silver and a bronze in these two events in 1968 to bring his total medal haul to seven. He was also world champion at 30 kilometers in 1962 and 1966. By the time of his fourth Olympic appearance in 1972, he was past his prime and was selected only for the 30 km., in which he finished 19th. His career ended soon afterward when he tested positive for drugs at the Finnish trials.

Marathon. The marathon is the longest running event conducted on the track & field athletics program at the Olympic Games. The marathon standard distance is 42,195 meters (26 miles, 385 yards), although in the early years of the Olympics, it varied from 25 miles to just under 27 miles. The standard distance was first used at the 1908 Olympic Games in London, when the race started by the gardens of Windsor Castle, so the Queen's children could watch the start. The distance from Windsor Castle to the finish line at the White City Stadium was 42,195 meters. This was adopted as the standard in the 1920s. Two marathoners have won the Olympic race twice—Abebe Bikila (ETH) (q.v.) in 1960 and 1964, and Waldemar Cierpinski (GDR) in 1976 and 1980. Although it was not always so, the men's marathon now is usually the last event on the last day of the Olympics. Women began competing in the Olympic marathon in 1984.

Marketing Commission. The Marketing Commission was formerly called the *New Sources of Financing Commission*, and was formed in

1983. The current chairman is Richard Pound (q.v.), the Canadian IOC Member who has become well known for his negotiating skills with television networks and with prospective sponsors of the Olympic Movement (q.v.). It was Pound and this commission that was responsible in 1984–1985 with forming The Olympic Programme (TOP) (q.v.), which recruits a small number of major corporations to be supporting sponsors of the Olympic Movement for each Olympiad. The current commission has 11 IOC members, with one representative each from the NOCs and IFs, and several independent members.

Marshall Islands. The application by the Marshall Islands, which is a member of the United Nations, to become an IOC member has, to date, not been successful. In 1993, their case was taken up by Paul Wallwork, formerly the IOC Member to Samoa, but the IOC's response was that, as citizens of the Marshall Islands carry U.S. passports, the United States could, in effect, send a second team to the Olympics. This incredible, and ill-founded, reply completely overlooked the fact that other territories (e.g., Guam, Puerto Rico, British Virgin Islands, Netherlands Antilles, and American Samoa) were in a similar situation, but had already been accorded membership in the IOC.

Masson, Paul [FRA–CYC]. B. 1874. D. 1945. At the first modern Olympics in 1896, Paul Masson won three cycling events — the match sprint, the one-lap time trial, and the 10,000-meter track event. The three cycling golds at one Games has been bettered only by Marcus Hurley (USA) (q.v.) in 1904 and equaled only by Robert Charpentier (FRA) (q.v.) in 1936. Masson had no significant international record prior to the 1896 Olympics. After the Olympics he turned professional, adopting the name Paul Nossam (Masson spelled backwards). His only significant performance as Paul Nossam was third in the world professional sprint championship in 1897. Paul Masson was not related to the namesake of the famous wine company.

Mathias, Robert Bruce, "Bob" [USA–ATH]. B. 19 November 1930, Tulare, California. Bob Mathias was the first of only two men to win successive Olympic decathlon titles (*See* DALEY THOMPSON). His first gold medal came in 1948 when, as a 17-year-old, he became the youngest-ever winner of an Olympic track & field event. Mathias set his third world record in defending his title in 1952, but the following year, he forfeited his amateur status by starring in a film of his life. Although a professional, he was, as a Marine officer, eligible to compete in the 1956 Inter-Services championships when he won his 11th and final decathlon competition to maintain his unbeaten record in the event. A politician later in life, Mathias was first elected as a Republican Congressman for California in 1966. He served four terms in the House of Representatives before losing out in the Democratic landslide of 1974. In 1973, he introduced legislation to amend the U.S. Olympic Charter that effectively created a Bill of Rights for amateur athletes.

Matthes, Roland [GDR–SWI]. B. 17 November 1950, Pössneck. With victories in the 100-meter and 200-meter backstrokes at both the 1968 and 1972 Games, Roland Matthes is the most successful male backstroke swimmer at the Olympics. He also won two silver and one bronze medal in the relays and added his eighth Olympic medal (a bronze) in the 1976 100-meter backstroke. Matthes set 16 world backstroke records (eight at each distance) but was also a world-class performer in other events, winning silver medals at the European Championships in the freestyle and butterfly and setting three European butterfly records. He was briefly married to Kornelia Ender (q.v.).

Mauritania [MTN]. Mauritania formed a provisional NOC in 1962, but in 1977 a more formal body was constituted. After the IOC granted provisional recognition in 1979, full recognition followed in 1980. Mauritania first competed at the Olympic Games in 1984 and has been present at each of the subsequent Olympics. It has never competed at the Olympic Winter Games and has never won an Olympic medal.

Mauritius [MRI]. Mauritius formed a National Olympic Committee in 1971, but did not compete at the Olympics until 1984 in Los Angeles. Mauritius has also competed at the Olympic Games of 1988, 1992, 1996, and 2000. Mauritius has never competed at the Olympic Winter Games and has never won an Olympic medal.

McCormick, Patricia Joan Keller (née Keller) [USA–DIV]. B. 12 May 1930, Seal Beach, California. With victories in both the springboard and platform at the 1952 and 1956 Olympics, Pat McCormick became the first diver in history to win four Olympic gold medals. Her second double victory at Melbourne came only five months after the birth of her son. Pat McCormick won 17 Amateur Athletic Union (AAU) titles at the outdoor championships, at all three levels—one-meter and three-meter springboard, and the one-meter platform—and nine indoor AAU championships. McCormick's husband was the AAU champion at both springboard and platform and her daughter, Kelly, was on the U.S. diving team at the 1983 Pan-American Games. Kelly also competed for the United States at the 1984 and 1988 Olympics, winning a silver in 1984 and a bronze in 1988, both on the springboard.

McKay, James Kenneth (né James Kenneth McManus) [USA]. B. 24 September 1921, Philadelphia, Pennsylvania. In the United States, Jim McKay achieved fame as the "Voice of the Olympics." He was host or co-host on the U.S. television network televising the Olympics an unprecedented seven times: six times for ABC Sports—1976 and 1984 for the Olympic Games, and the Olympic Winter Games consecutively from 1976 through 1988—and for CBS in 1960. McKay was not the main studio host in 1972 at Munich, but it was there that he achieved his greatest fame as an Olympics host. He was called on to broadcast the news reports of the horrific Israeli hostage massacre, and was on the air in the United States for over 15 consecutive hours. He was the one who eventually told the world, in his own poignant words, "They're all gone." He was awarded an Emmy for that broadcast, one of 10 individual Emmys won by McKay, nine for sportscaster of the year, and one for lifetime achievement.

Meagher, Mary Terstegge [USA–SWI]. B. 27 October 1964, Louisville, Kentucky. Mary T. Meagher is the greatest female butterfly swimmer ever, and for her feats she earned the nickname of "Madame Butterfly." Meagher won three gold medals at the 1984 Olympics, in both butterfly events, and on the 4 x 100-meter medley relay. In 1988, by then past her prime, she earned a bronze in the 200-meter butterfly and a silver with the medley relay. Meagher would likely have won both butterfly events in 1980 had the United States not boycotted (q.v.) the Moscow Olympics. She was World Champion in 1982 over 100 meters and in 1986 over 200 meters. She set two world butterfly records over 100 meters, and five over 200 meters, beginning in 1979. Her performance at the 1981 U.S. Nationals remains her greatest effort when she set world records of 57.93 for 100 meters, and 2:05.96 for 200 meters, both of which lasted until the late 1990s.

Medical Commission. The Medical Commission is the oldest permanent IOC Commission, having been formed in 1966. The current chairman is Prince Alexandre de Merode, a Belgian IOC member. The vice chairman is a Belgian IOC member, the orthopaedic surgeon Dr. Jacques Rogge, himself a former Olympic yachtsman. The commission has several consultant members, along with members from the NOCs, IFs, and the OCOGs (qq.v.). The Medical Commission's primary responsibility is the fight against doping and writing and re-writing the medical by-laws to the *Olympic Charter* (q.v.), as well as determining the list of proscribed medications. This commission has also dealt with the question of determining female identity, originally called *sex testing*, but now known as *gender identification* (q.v.).

Medved, Aleksandr Vasilyevich (né Oleksander Medvid [Ukraine]) [URS/UKR–WRE]. B. 16 September 1937, Belaya Tserkov, Kiev Oblast. With victories in the freestyle light-heavyweight (1964), heavyweight (1968), and super-heavyweight (1972) divisions, Aleksandr Medved was the first wrestler to win gold medals at three successive Olympic Games. He also won seven world titles. Medved's record was remarkable for the fact that his physique seldom matched that of his opponents and on his way to the Olympic super-heavyweight title in 1972, he overcame the giant American bronze medalist, Chris Taylor, who enjoyed an incredible weight advantage of almost 100 pounds (45 kg). His World Championships came at light-heavyweight (1962, 1963, and 1966), and at super-heavyweight (1967, 1969, 1970, and 1971). Medved was European champion in 1966, 1968, and 1972, competing less often at that meet.

Mexico [MEX]. Mexican athletes first competed at the 1900 Olympic Games when several polo players of mixed Mexican/Spanish ancestry played at Paris. Mexico did not compete again at the Olympics until 1924, but it has competed since without fail. Mexico sent five bobsled competitors to the 1928 Winter Olympics and in 1932 they entered another bobsled team, but it did not compete. Its other Winter Olympic appearances have come in 1984, 1988, 1992, and 1994. Mexico has won 48 Olympic medals, 10 of them gold, all at the Games of the Olympiad. Mexico also hosted the Games of the XIXth Olympiad at Mexico City in 1968.

Meyer, Deborah "Debbie" (later Reyes) [USA–SWI]. B. 14 August 1952, Haddonfield, New Jersey. With victories in the 200-meter, 400-meter, and 800-meter freestyles in 1968, Debbie Meyer became the first woman swimmer to win three individual gold medals at one Olympic Games. She won each event by a large margin and achieved her unique Olympic treble despite the fact that she was handicapped by a severe upset stomach in Mexico City. Between 1967 and 1970, Meyer set 15 world records and retired before her abilities had been fully extended.

Micronesia, Federated States of [FSM]. After becoming a member of the United Nations in 1991, the Federated States of Micronesia formed an NOC in 1995. The IOC recognized Micronesia in 1997. Micronesia first competed at the 2000 Olympic Games in Sydney, represented by five athletes—two in track & field (one man/one woman), two in swimming (one man/one woman), and one in weightlifting (one man).

Military Ski Patrol. A military ski patrol event was held at the Winter Olympics in 1928, 1936, and 1948 as a demonstration sport. The event was also contested at the 1924 Olympic Winter Games in Chamonix and, until recently, has always been considered a demonstration event. But more recent evidence makes it clear that this was a full medal event in 1924 and not a demonstration. Military ski patrol is an event similar to team biathlon (q.v.), in which all the team members ski together over a course, stopping periodically to shoot at targets.

Milon of Kroton [GRE–WRE]. *fl ca.* 540–508 B.C. The son of the well-known athlete, Diotimos, Milon of Kroton was the greatest wrestler of ancient Greece and the Ancient Olympic Games (q.v.). He was champion six times at the Olympic Games (540 B.C. in boys' wrestling, and 532–516 B.C. in wrestling), seven times at the Pythian Games, 10 times at the Isthmian Games and nine times at the Nemean Games. In four

Olympiads, he was *periodonikes,* meaning he won all of the four major festival titles. The base of his statue at Ancient Olympia reads, ". . . he had never been brought to his knees." Milon's strength was supposedly developed when he was a young boy and began carrying a wild heifer on his shoulders. As the heifer grew, Milon continued to carry it for exercise and his strength became legendary, but it eventually killed him. One day in a forest, he saw a tree that had been cut open with wedges in it. He decided to pull open the trunk with his massive hands, but when he did this the wedges flew out and the trunk trapped his hands. He was caught in the tree and wild beasts tore him to pieces that night.

Mitchell Report. *See* OLYMPIC BRIBERY SCANDAL.

Mittermaier, Rosi (later Neurather) [FRG–ASK]. B. 5 August 1930, Reit-im-Winkel. Rosi Mittermaier had a long career in international skiing, winning 10 individual World Cup races between 1969 and 1976. In 1976, she was the world champion in Alpine combined and led the overall World Cup, although she did not lead in any of the individual disciplines. Mittermaier's greatest fame came at the 1976 Olympic Winter Games when she won the slalom and downhill. With the giant slalom still to come, she had a chance to equal the feats of Toni Sailer and Jean-Claude Killy (qq.v.) by winning all three available Alpine ski events. However, in the giant slalom, she finished second, losing out by 12/100th's of a second to Canada's Kathy Kreiner. Mittermaier later married Christian Neurather, another German Olympic skier.

Miyake, Yoshinobu [JPN–WLT]. B. 24 November 1939. Yoshinobu Miyake was Japan's greatest weightlifter ever. He finished second in the 1960 Olympic bantamweight class, but won gold medals at the 1964 and 1968 Olympics as a featherweight. He also won World Championships in 1962–1963 and 1965–1966. Miyake set 25 world records, including 10 consecutive records in the snatch and nine consecutive total records in the 60-kg. class.

Modern Pentathlon. Modern pentathlon is a sport invented by the founder of the Olympic Games, the Baron Pierre de Coubertin (q.v.). It is better termed the *military pentathlon* because it supposedly mimics the skills needed by a soldier. He must first ride a horse and then fight off an enemy with a sword. He must then swim a river to escape, then fight off more enemies with a pistol, and finally, effect the final escape by running a cross-country course.

Coubertin was able to get the sport on the Olympic program in 1912. The order of the events has varied, but the current order is as in the soldier's trial: riding, fencing, swimming, shooting, and cross-country running. The riding is a cross-country steeplechase course. Fencing is a series of one-touch bouts done with épée swords. Shooting is done with an air pistol from 10 meters, but was formerly performed with a rapid-fire pistol. The swim is now a 200-meter freestyle (formerly 300 meters) and the run is a 3,000-meter cross-country event (formerly 4,000 meters). The final event is now arranged such that the runners leave the start in the order of their positions after four events. Further, the starts are arranged such that the time intervals correspond to the number of points separating the competitors. Thus, the finishing order in the run now corresponds exactly to the finishing order of the entire pentathlon, adding to the drama of the event. Beginning at the 1995 World Championships and the 1996 Olympics, the modern pentathlon was changed so that all the events are now contested in one day.

Modern pentathlon was originally dominated by the Swedes. After World War II, the Hungarians and the Soviets became the top countries. Scoring was originally on a points-for-place system with the lowest score winning, but the competition is now scored using tables for each of the five events.

Modern pentathlon is governed by the Union Internationale de Pentathlon Moderne (UIPM), which was founded in 1948 and currently has 94 members. Originally, biathlon (q.v.) and modern pentathlon were governed together, by the Union Internationale de Pentathlon Moderne at Biathlon (UIPMB), but the federation split into two separate groups in 1993, with the International Biathlon Union governing that sport. A modern pentathlon event for women (q.v.) débuted on the Olympic program at Sydney in 2000.

Moldova [MLD]. Moldova was formerly the Soviet Republic of Moldavia, which achieved independence after the Soviet break-up of 1991. Its National Olympic Committee was formed shortly thereafter and recognized by the IOC in 1993. Though the smallest of the former Soviet Republics, a few Moldavan athletes competed from 1952 to 1988 for the Soviet Union, and Moldavan athletes were present at Barcelona in 1992 as members of the Unified Team (q.v.). Moldova first competed at the Olympics as an independent nation in 1994 at Lillehammer, represented by one male and one female biathlete. They first competed at the Summer Olympics in Atlanta in 1996, and also competed in 1998 at Nagano and the 2000 Olympics in Sydney. To date, Moldova has won four Olympic medals.

Monaco [MON]. Monaco competed at the 1920 Olympic Games and has since missed only the Games of 1932, 1956, and 1980. Since first competing at the Olympic Winter Games in 1984, they have been represented at each of the subsequent Winter Olympics. The country has been represented in the bobsled events by Albert Grimaldi, Prince of Monaco, an IOC member and the son of Prince Rainier and Princess Grace. No Monegasque athlete has won a medal in a sporting event, but in 1924 Julien Médecin won a bronze medal in the architecture portion of the now-defunct Art Contests (q.v.).

Mongolia [MGL]. Mongolia has competed at the Olympic Games since 1964, its only absence being the 1984 Los Angeles Olympics, which it boycotted. Its first Olympic appearance was at the 1964 Winter Olympics and it has since missed only the 1976 Olympic Winter Games. Mongolia claims the unusual distinction of having won the most Olympic medals of any country that has not yet won a gold medal (14 through 2000, all in the Olympic Games).

Monti, Eugenio [ITA–BOB]. B. 23 January 1928, Dobbiaco, Bolzano. Eugenio Monti is considered the greatest bobsled driver in history. After winning two Olympic silver medals in 1956, he was deprived of the opportunity of further honors in 1960 as the bobsled was not included in the program at Squaw Valley. At his second Olympics in 1964, he won two bronze medals and, in 1968, Monti took the gold medals in both events. The bobsled events at the 1968 Winter Games also carried the status of the World Championships and, including his Olympic victories, Monti won the world title in the two-man event eight times and was the world four-man champion three times. He retired after the 1968 Olympics and became the Italian team manager. In addition to his championships, he is known for his sportsmanship at the 1964 Innsbruck Winter Olympics. Trailing the British team of Anthony Nash and Robin Dixon going into the final run, he lent them a bolt off his own sled when theirs failed. Nash and Dixon won the gold medal, but for this magnanimous action, Monti was awarded the International Fair Play Award. At the victory ceremony, Nash and Dixon pulled Monti up to the top step of the podium, to join in their victory.

Morelon, Daniel [FRA–CYC]. B. 24 July 1944, Bourg-en-Bresse. Between 1966 and 1975, Daniel Morelon won a record nine world amateur sprint titles and three Olympics gold medals. He won the Olympic match sprint in 1968 and 1972 to become the first of only two men to claim a repeat victory in the event. In 1968, he also won the tandem match sprint partnered by Pierre Trentin. Together, they had also won the world title in 1966. Morelon won a total of 14 French titles and set a world indoor record for 500 meters in 1976. He was essentially a track sprinter and saw no need to turn professional. After retirement, he became the French sprint cycling coach.

Morocco [MAR]. Morocco has competed at nine Olympic Games. First appearing in 1960, it has since missed only the 1980 Games. Morocco has sent athletes to the Olympic Winter Games in 1968, 1984, 1988, and 1992. Through 2000, Moroccan athletes have won 16 Olympic medals: 13 in track & field athletics and three in boxing.

Morrow, Bobby Joe [USA–ATH]. B. 15 October 1935, Harlingen, Texas. Bobby Joe Morrow was the winner of gold medals in the 100 meters, 200 meters, and the 4 x 100-meter relay at the 1956 Games. In winning the 200 meters, he became the first man to set an official world record for this distance at the Olympic Games. He also equaled the world record for 100 meters three times during the Olympic year, equaled the world 100 yards record in 1957, and was a member of six world record-breaking teams in the sprint relays (4 x 100 and 4 x 200, or the Imperial equivalents). Morrow won four Amateur Athletic Union (AAU) titles between 1955 and 1958, but he failed to make the 1960 U.S. Olympic team.

Moses, Edwin Corley [USA-ATH]. B. 31 August 1955, Dayton, Ohio. Edwin Moses dominated the 400-meter hurdles like few athletes have ever dominated an event. He won the Olympic gold medal in 1976 and 1984, and only the American boycott of the Moscow Olympics in 1980 prevented him winning a third gold medal. In 1988, he competed again, but past his prime, he won a bronze medal. Moses set the first of his four world records in the event in the 1976 Olympic final, and at one stage of his career, he won 122 successive races, including the first World Championships in 1983. Moses took the oath on behalf of the competitors at the Opening Cermony of the 1984 Olympic Games. He was also briefly a member of the U.S. World Cup bobsled team in 1990–1991.

Motorboating. Motorboating was contested at the Olympics only in 1908. Motorboating will not be appearing on the Olympic program in the near future and, in fact, the *Olympic Charter* (q.v.) precludes the sport, as Rule 52.4.2 states, "Sports, disciplines or events in which performance depends essentially on mechanical propulsion are not acceptable." However, the Union International Motonautique (UIM) does have provisional IOC recognition, although it is not clear why, since the rules do not allow motorboating on the Olympic Program. It should be noted, however, that aeronautics, automobile racing, and motorcycling also have International Federations (IFs) that have been granted provisional IOC recognition. Founded in 1922, the UIM currently has 60 members.

Motorcycling. Motorcycling has never been contested at the Olympics, even as a demonstration sport (q.v.). It is highly unlikely that motorcycling will be on the Olympic program at anytime in the foreseeable future as the *Olympic Charter* (q.v.) actually precludes the sport. Rule 52.4.2 states, "Sports, disciplines or events in which performance depends essentially on mechanical propulsion are not acceptable." However, the Fédération Internationale de Motocyclisme (FIM) does have provisional IOC recognition, although it is not clear why, since the *Olympic Charter* would preclude motorcycling from appearing on the Olympic Program. It should be noted, however, that aeronautics, automobile racing, and motorboating also have International Federations (IFs) that have been granted provisional IOC recognition. Founded in 1904, the FIM currently has 79 members.

Mozambique [MOZ]. Since making its Olympic début in 1980, Mozambique has competed at each of the subsequent Olympic Games. Mozambique has not yet competed at the Olympic Winter

Games. Their only medal winner has been the female middle-distance running phenomenon, Maria Lurdes Mutola, who won bronze in the women's 800 meters in 1996, and succeeded to the gold medal in that event in 2000.

Much Wenlock Olympian Games. The Much Wenlock Olympian Games were one of the various attempts at revival of the Ancient Olympic Games which preceded Pierre de Coubertin's (q.v.) successful attempt. Much Wenlock is a small town in Shropshire, England, 12 miles south of Shrewsbury and 40 miles west of Birmingham. On 22 October 1850, these Games were held for the first time. They were the brainchild of British sports enthusiast, Dr. William Penny Brookes (1809–1895) (q.v.).

The Games were only national in nature and the events were those of a British medieval country fair enriched by modern athletic sports disciplines. The original events in 1850 consisted of cricket, 14-a-side football, high and long jumping, quoits, a hopping race, and a running race. However, several athletic events were added in the next few editions. In 1855, a popular event was the blindfolded wheelbarrow race. In 1858, a pig race was contested in which the pig "led its pursuers over hedge and ditch right into the town, where it took ground in the cellar of Mr. Blakeway's house; and where it was captured by a man called William Hill." The most popular event became tilting-at-the-ring, which was first held in 1858. The competitors, compulsorily dressed in medieval costume, rode down a straight course and used their lances to spear a small ring, suspended from a bar over the course.

The Much Wenlock Olympian Games, altogether 45 in number up to 1895, achieved their high point in the 1860s and 1870s. In those years, representatives of the German Gymnastic Society (which was based in London) competed regularly. In 1859, Brookes contacted the Greeks and donated a £10 prize to the Zappas Olympic Games (q.v.). The winner of the long footrace at the 1859 Zappas Olympics, Petros Velissariou, was made an honorary member of the Much Wenlock Olympian Society.

In 1860, 1861, 1862, and 1864, Brookes also organized the Shropshire Olympian Games on a regional level in, respectively, Much Wenlock, Wellington, Much Wenlock, and Shrewsbury. These were followed by the Games organized by the National Olympic Association: 1866 (London), 1867 (Birmingham), 1868 (Wellington), 1874 (Much Wenlock), 1877 (Shrewsbury), and 1883 (Hadley).

The Much Wenlock Olympian Games were held more sporadically after Brookes' death in 1895, but they are actually still held today, sponsored by the Much Wenlock Olympian Society, which celebrated the 100th Much Wenlock Olympian Games in 1986. The Much Wenlock Olympian Games are important in the history of Olympic revivals because of their influence on Pierre de Coubertin. Coubertin knew of Brookes' efforts and visited the Much Wenlock Olympian Games as a guest of honor in October 1890. In 1891, he donated a gold medal that was given to the winner of tilting-at-the-ring. However, as early as 1881, William Penny Brookes was the first person ever to propose that an International Olympic Festival be staged in Athens.

Musiol, Bogdan [GDR/GER–BOB]. B. 25 July 1957, Swielochowice, Poland. Bogdan Musiol was the winner of an Olympic gold medal with the GDR four-man bobsled team in 1980, when he also won a bronze medal in the two-man. He went on to win silver medals in 1984 and 1988 at both the two-man and four-man and in 1992, he won his silver medal in the two-man. In 1989, Musiol won the world two-man title as the brakeman for Wolfgang Hoppe, with whom he won an Olympic silver in 1988.

Myanmar [MYA]. As *Burma* (name change in May 1989), Myanmar competed at all Olympics from 1948 through 1988, with the exception of the 1976 Olympics. As *Myanmar*, the nation has also competed at the 1992, 1996, and 2000 Olympics. It has never attended the Olympic Winter Games nor has it won a medal. Its best finishes by men at the Olympics have been fifth in 1972 flyweight weightlifting by Gyi Aung and equal fifth in 1964 by featherweight boxer Tun Tim. But in 2000 at Sydney, Win Kay Thi finished fourth in women's 48-kg. class weightlifting.

– N –

Naber, John Phillips [USA–SWI]. B. 20 January 1956, Evanston, Illinois. At the 1976 Games, John Naber won four gold medals, each in world record time, and his records in the 100- and 200-meter back-strokes remained unbeaten for seven years. He also won gold in the 4 x 100-meter freestyle relay and the medley relay and won a silver in the 200-meter freestyle. Perhaps the greatest of these fine performances came in the 200-meter backstroke when Naber became the first man to break two minutes for the distance. After winning three gold medals at the 1977 Pan-American Games, he retired from international competition.

Nadi, Nedo [ITA–FEN]. B. 9 June 1894, Livorno. D. 29 January 1940, Rome. Nedo Nadi was the most versatile fencer in history, who uniquely won an Olympic title with each of the three weapons at the same Games. In 1912, he won the individual foil title. In 1920, he produced one of the greatest of all Olympic performances. He won the individual foil and sabre titles and led the Italians to victory in all three team events. His brother, Aldo, also won a gold medal in each of the three team events. After the 1920 Olympics, Nedo Nadi taught as a professional in South America, but on his return, he was reinstated as an amateur and served as president of the Italian Fencing Federation.

Namibia [NAM]. Namibia's Olympic Committee was recognized by the IOC at its summer session in 1991. It competed at the 1992 and 1996 Olympics, where sprinter Frank Fredericks won two silver medals at each Olympics, earning all of Namibia's four Olympic medals. Namibia has not yet competed at the Olympic Winter Games. Namibia also competed in 2000 at Sydney.

National Governing Bodies [NGBs]. Each sport on the Olympic Program is governed by an International Federation (IF) (q.v.). Each nation competing at the Olympic Games must have a properly formed National Olympic Committee (NOC) (q.v.). In each nation, the various sports have National Governing Bodies (NGBs) that are responsible for the administration of that sport in that nation. The NGBs are invariably members of both their own NOC and the respective IF. As an example, the governing body of track & field athletics in the United States is USA Track & Field (USATF), which is a member of the United States Olympic Committee (USOC) and the International Amateur Athletic Federation (IAAF).

National Olympic Academies [NOAs]. *See* INTERNATIONAL OLYMPIC ACADEMY.

National Olympic Committees [NOCs]. National Olympic Committees (NOCs) are the bodies responsible for the Olympic Movement in their respective countries. The *Olympic Charter* (q.v.) states that their mission "is to develop and protect the Olympic Movement in their respective countries, in accordance with the *Olympic Charter*." National Olympic Committees have not always been representative of autonomous national regions. Currently, Puerto Rico, which is a Commonwealth of the United States, has its own NOC. In the early part of this century, Bohemia was represented on the IOC, even though it was only a part of the Austro-Hungarian Empire. For the most part, however, NOCs represent independent nations. They are recognized by the IOC at the IOC sessions. Currently 199 National Olympic Committees are recognized by the IOC, with one under suspension as of 2000 (Afghanistan).

NOCs are very important to the athletes competing in the Olympic Games. Specifically, athletes may not enter the Olympic Games independently or as individual competitors, but may only represent an NOC, and they must be entered by their NOC. In addition, NOCs often provide financial assistance for training and allowing athletes to compete internationally.

NOCs are supposed to be autonomous and resist political pressures and influences of any kind, but that principle has been recognized more in word than deed. Notably, prior to the fall of the Soviet Bloc, all the Eastern European Communist nations had NOCs that basically were puppets of their governments. And, in 1980, the United States Olympic Committee (USOC) was coerced into boycotting (q.v.) the Moscow Olympics (against its wishes) by the U.S. President and Government to protest the Soviet invasion of Afghanistan.

Nauru [NRU]. Nauru's Olympic Committee was recognized by the IOC at the 1994 Olympic Congress after having been given provisional recognition earlier in 1994. Nauru first competed in the Olympics in 1996 when they were represented by three weightlifters. At Sydney, one male and one female weightlifter represented Nauru.

Neckermann, Josef [FRG–EQU]. B. 5 June 1912, Würzburg. D. 13 January 1992, Dreieich. Josef Neckermann was an extremely wealthy man, who earned his money from his mail-order and department store businesses. His wealth allowed him and his family to pursue their passion for equestrian sports. Neckermann competed in the dressage at four Olympic Games (1960–1972) and won a medal on each occasion. To his gold medals in the team event in 1964 and 1968, he added two silver and two bronze medals. His daughter, Eva-Maria Pracht, won a team bronze representing Canada in 1988 and her daughter, Martina—Neckermann's granddaughter—also represented Canada at the 1992 Olympics.

Nehmer, Meinhard [GDR–BOB]. B. 13 January 1941, Boblin. A former nationally ranked javelin thrower, Meinhard Nehmer only took up bobsledding after retiring from athletics. Although well past the age of 30, he formed a formidable partnership with Bernhard Germeshausen (q.v.) and they won the 1976 Olympic two-man and were both members of the winning four-man crew in 1976 and 1980. Nehmer and Germeshausen share the record for the most gold medals won by bobsledders. Nehmer also won an Olympic bronze medal in the two-man in 1980 with Bogdan Musiol, and he was coach of the U.S. bobsled team for the 1992 Olympics.

Nemean Games. The Nemean Games were one of the four great Panhellenic sporting festivals, along with the Olympic Games, Isthmian Games, and Pythian Games (qq.v.). They were held biennially, with the first-known Nemean Games being contested in 573 B.C. The Nemean Games were held in honor of Zeus. They were held in July in the Nemean sanctuary in Argolis. The Nemean sanctuary was near the site on the Peloponnesus where Hercules killed and skinned the Nemean Lion, the first of his famed 12 labors. Winners in the Nemean Games were crowned with a wreath of fresh wild celery.

Nepal [NEP]. The Nepalese Olympic Committee was founded in 1962 and recognized by the IOC in the following year. Nepal first competed at the Olympic Games in 1964 and since then they have missed only the 1968 Olympics. This Himalayan country has still not competed in the Olympic Winter Games.

Netball. Netball has never been contested at the Olympic Games, even as a demonstration sport (q.v.). However, its governing body, the International Federation of Netball Associations (IFNA), is recognized by the IOC. Founded in 1960, it currently has 40 affiliated nations.

Netherlands, The [NED, formerly HOL]. The Netherlands sent 27 athletes to the 1900 Paris Olympics. After missing the 1904 St. Louis Olympics, the Netherlands has never missed another Olympic Games, although in 1956 it competed only at the Equestrian Games in Stockholm, boycotting (q.v.) the 1956 Olympic Games in protest of the Soviet invasion of Hungary. At the Winter Games, the Netherlands appeared first in 1928, missed the 1932 Lake Placid Games, but has appeared continuously since. In the Summer Games, the Netherlands has had a variety of successes in different sports, but has never dominated any sport. In the Winter Olympics, however, the Netherlands has always been one of the very top nations in speed skating. The Netherlands has won 274 Olympic medals, 80 of them gold. Of these, 61 medals and 19 gold medals were won at the Olympic Winter Games. The Netherlands hosted the Games of the IXth Olympiad in Amsterdam in 1928.

Netherlands Antilles [AHO]. Known as *Curaçao*, the name of the capital city, until 1948, the Netherlands Antilles formed an NOC in 1931 with a view to participating in the 1932 Los Angeles Olympics. Although recognized by the IOC in 1931, representation at the 1932 Olympics did not materialize, and there was little Olympic activity in the nation for many years. IOC recognition was re-confirmed in 1950, and the Netherlands Antilles first competed at the Olympics in 1952, when they were represented by a football (soccer) team. The nation did not travel to Melbourne in 1956, and boycotted (q.v.) the 1980 Olympics, but has otherwise competed at every Olympic Games since 1952. The Netherlands Antilles made its Olympic Winter début in 1988 at Calgary and also competed in 1992 at Albertville. The Netherlands Antilles has won one Olympic medal, a silver by Jan Boersma in boardsailing in 1988.

New Zealand [NZL]. New Zealand was first represented at the 1908 Olympic Games. In that year, it formed a combined team with Australia as *Australasia*. One New Zealander competitor, Harry Kerr, a walker, won a bronze in the 3,500-meter walk. In 1912, three New Zealanders competed with Australasia. Finally, in 1920 at Antwerp, New Zealand took part in the Olympic Games as a separate nation, and it has never missed an Olympic Games since. New Zealand competed at its first Olympic Winter Games in 1952 at Oslo. It missed the Winter Games of 1956 and 1964, but has competed at all the others since. New Zealand has had its greatest success in track & field and several of its middle-distance runners have become Olympic champions. New Zealand has won 75 Olympic medals, 30 of them gold.

Nicaragua [NCA]. Although the IOC recognized their NOC in 1959, Nicaragua did not compete at the 1960 or 1964 Olympics, and it was not until 1968 that they first competed at the Olympic Games. Apart from missing the 1988 Olympics in Seoul, Nicaragua's Olympic participation has been continuous since 1968. The country has never competed in the Olympic Winter Games. Its best Olympic performance occurred in 1992 when flyweight weightlifter Alvaro Marenco Ramos finished 11th of 17 lifters in his class.

Niemann-Stirnemann-Kleemann, Gunda (née Gunda Kleemann) [GER-SSK]. B. 7 September 1966, Sondershausen. Gunda Niemann-Stirnemann has won eight Olympic medals and three golds at the Olympics Winter Games of 1992, 1994, and 1998, equaling the marks of fellow German Karin Kania-Enke. Primarily a distance skater, her golds came at 3,000-meters in 1992 and 1998 and at 5,000-meters in 1992. At the World All-Around championships, Niemann-Stirnemann has won seven championships (1991–1993 and 1995–1998), breaking Kania-Enke's record of five titles. She also won the World Cup title at 1,500 meters in 1991–1993 and 1995–1998, and at distances (3K and 5K) in 1992–1996 and 1998. She has set 14 world records (through February 2000)—six at 3,000 meters; four at 5,000 meters; and four in the combined all-around. Through 2001, Niemann-Stirnemann continues to compete and will possibly participate at Salt Lake City in 2002.

Niger [NIG]. After recognition by the IOC early in 1964, Niger made its Olympic début in Tokyo later that year when they were represented by one boxer. Niger did not take part in the 1976 or 1980 Olympics, but has competed at all the other Olympics since 1964. Niger has never competed at the Olympic Winter Games. To date, Issaka Daborg has won the only Olympic medal for this country in 1972 when he finished third in light-welterweight boxing.

Nigeria [NGR]. The Nigerian NOC was formed in 1951 and recognized by the IOC in the same year. Nigeria first competed in the Olympics in 1952. It has since missed only the 1976 Games, owing to the African boycott. Nigeria has not yet competed at the Olympic Winter Games. Nigerians have won 17 Olympic medals, including two golds. Six of these have come in boxing, nine in track & field athletics, one in weightlifting, and one from their 1996 soccer football team.

Nordic Games. The Olympic Winter Games formally began in 1924 at Chamonix, although they were originally known as the *Semaine internationale des sports d'hiver* (International Winter Sports Week). Prior to that time, winter sports events had been held during the Summer Games of 1908 (figure skating) and 1920 (figure skating and ice hockey). But there existed an earlier international winter sports festival, the Nordic Games, which began in 1901. Suggested by Sweden's Professor E. Johan Widmark, the initiative to hold Nordic Games was taken in 1899, the first ones being arranged in 1901. After this inaugural event in Stockholm, Sweden, Nordic Games were held in 1905, 1909, 1913, 1917, 1922, and 1926, always during February, mostly in Stockholm. They began, and were perpetuated, largely by the work of the influential Swedish sports administrator, Viktor Gustaf Balck. The Nordic Games were not without political problems, nor were they originally planned as precursors to the Olympic Winter Games, as often stated. In fact, despite Balck's influential status on the IOC, he and other Swedish and Norwegian sporting leaders opposed early suggestions to start Olympic Winter Games. The Olympic Winter Games themselves began only after several heated IOC debates concerning their merits. The Nordic Games ended after 1926, partly because of the growth of the Olympic Winter Games, partly because of Balck's death and the loss of his leadership, and partly because of the growth of the Fédération Internationale de Ski.

Nordic Skiing. Nordic skiing has been practiced in the Scandinavian countries since the 18th century, and competitions are known from the early 19th century. The sport has been on the Olympic program since the Chamonix games of 1924. The international governing body is the Fédération Internationale de Ski (FIS), which was founded in 1924 and has 100 members (2000).

Nordic skiing consists of three major disciplines: cross-country skiing, ski jumping, and Nordic combined, combining elements of both cross-country and ski jumping. All three disciplines have been contested at all Winter Olympics. Women (q.v.) compete only in cross-country skiing and first began to do so in 1952. Nordic skiing has been dominated, not surprisingly, by the Scandinavian countries and the Soviet Union and Russia.

Cross-country skiing consists of races varying from 10 to 50 kilometers for men, and from 5 to 20 kilometers for women, as well as relay races. The skiers race in time-trial fashion, starting at intervals. Match sprint racing over 1,500 meters will be added to the Olympic program in 2002. Ski jumping is contested on two hills, a 90-meter and a 120-meter hill, called the *normal hill* and the *large hill*. The size of the hill is not necessarily 90 or 120 meters, but those figures refer to the expected length of the jumps measured to the "norm" point of the hill. Nordic combined consists of a cross-country ski race and ski jumping, with the results determined by a points table. In 1988, team events for men in both Nordic combined and ski jumping were added to the Olympic program.

In the 1980s, cross-country skiing underwent a revolution that was started by Bill Koch, the first American to be a top international skier. He changed from the classic cross-country of alternating legs and arms with the stride being pushed straight backward, remaining in the ski track, to a style similar to skating on skis. The FIS was pushed to ban this style by the north Europeans, but it was decided instead to allow two styles. However, races are now designated as either "classic" or "freestyle," with skating being allowed in freestyle races. Men's 50-km. and women's 20-km. racers were permitted to use any style. In the relays, the classical style must be used for the first 100 meters, for safety reasons, as the relays are a mass start, but after that the racers may use the skating technique.

Norelius, Martha [USA-SWI]. B. 20 January 1908, Stockholm, Sweden. D. 23 September 1955. Martha Norelius was America's first great female swimmer. She was originally coached by her father, Charles Norelius, who swam for Sweden at the 1906 Olympics. She was the top U.S swimmer from 1924 to 1929, with her fame resting primarily on her Olympic accomplishments. In 1924 at Paris, she won the 400-meter freestyle event, and in 1928 she defended that championship, winning the final with a world record of 5:42.8. She is the only woman to have defended the 400-meter event at the Olympics. At the 1928 Olympics, Norelius won her third gold medal when she swam on the 4 x 100-meter freestyle relay team.

Norelius won 11 individual Amateur Athletic Union (AAU) titles between 1925 and 1929. Between 1925 and 1928, she set 19 world records and 30 American records. In 1929 Norelius, was suspended by the AAU for giving an exhibition in the same pool as some professionals. She therefore decided to turn professional herself and won the $10,000 Wrigley Marathon in Toronto. While there, she met Joe Wright, one of Canada's greatest rowers. Wright had won an Olympic silver medal for Canada in the 1928 double sculls, and also played professional football with the Toronto Argonauts of the Canadian Football League. Norelius and Wright were subsequently married on 15 March 1930.

North Borneo. Borneo is one of the world's largest islands, bordering the South China Sea. The northern section of the island was formerly an independent state called *North Borneo*. North Borneo competed at the Olympic Games one time only, at Melbourne in 1956. The northern part of the island is now divided into two states of Malaysia, Sabah, Sarawak, and the independent sultanate of Brunei. The southern part of the island is ruled by Indonesia and is known as *Kalimantan. See also* BRUNEI, INDONESIA, and MALAYSIA.

Northern Rhodesia. *See* ZAMBIA.

Norway [NOR]. Norway competed at the Olympics of 1900 and has since missed only the 1904 and the 1980 Olympic Games. Norway has competed at every Olympic Winter Games. Until 1984, Norway could claim to be the top nation at the Olympic Winter Games in terms of medals and gold medals won. In that year, however, the Soviet

Union surpassed Norway in both categories. With the demise of the Soviet Union, Norway again tops the list of most medals won by a single country at the Olympic Winter Games with 239, 83 of them gold medals. Norway shares with Liechtenstein and Austria the unusual distinction of having won more medals in the Winter Games than in the Summer Olympics. Norway has twice hosted the Olympic Winter Games, in 1952 in Oslo and in 1994 in Lillehammer.

Novikov, Igor Aleksandrovich [URS/ARM–MOP]. B. 19 October 1929, Drezna, Moscow Oblast. Igor Novikov was one of the most consistent performers in the modern pentathlon. At the 1952–1964 Olympics, he finished fourth, fourth, fifth, and second in the individual event. In the team event, Novikov won two gold medals (1956 and 1964) and a silver (1960). He was heavily favored to win the individual gold medal in 1960, based on his string of world titles (1957–1959 and later in 1961), but he finished fifth because of difficulty in the riding sequence. Strong at all five disciplines, Novikov set a world pentathlon best for the fencing section when he won the 1957 world championship. Novikov became a coach and held several administrative positions in sports.

Nurmi, Paavo Johannes [FIN–ATH]. B. 13 June 1897, Turku. D. 2 October 1973, Helsinki. Paavo Nurmi was an Olympic legend whose dedication to a rigorous training schedule and mastery of pace judgment brought a new dimension to distance running. Between 1920 and 1928, he won a record nine Olympic gold medals (seven individual; two team) and three individual silver medals. His medals came in a wide range of events: 1,500 meters, 3,000 meters (team), 5,000 meters, 10,000 meters, steeplechase, and cross-country. In 1932, Nurmi was banned for alleged professionalism and missed the chance to add the 1932 marathon, for which he was one of the favorites, to his list of Olympic successes. Although subsequently reinstated as an amateur for domestic races, he continued to be excluded from international competition, a decision that left him embittered for the rest of his life. However, Nurmi returned to the Olympic arena in 1952 when he carried the torch at the Opening Ceremony. The incomparable "Flying Finn" set 22 official and 13 unofficial world records, and statues (done by Waino Aaltonen in 1925) honoring his feats stand in his hometown of Turku, outside the Olympic stadium in Helsinki, and in the park of the Olympic Museum (q.v.) in Lausanne.

Nykänen, Matti Ensio [FIN–NSK]. B. 17 July 1963, Jyvaskyla. Matti Nykänen was the winner of a record four Olympic gold medals for ski jumping. At the 1984 Winter Games, Matti Nykänen won on the large hill and placed second on the normal hill before winning both events in 1988 when he won a further gold medal in the newly introduced team event. He was also the World Champion on the large hill in 1982 and won four World Cup titles between 1983 and 1988. A controversial and often ill-tempered individual, Nykänen earned considerable respect for his sporting talents, but little for his general behavior. In 1991, he launched a career as a pop singer.

– O –

Oceania National Olympic Committees [ONOC]. The Oceania National Olympic Committees, headquartered in Fiji, is a confederation of 14 National Olympic Committees from Oceania and is one of the recognized organizations of the International Olympic Committee (q.v.). It was created on 25 September 1981 to promote the Olympic Movement and its ideals in Oceania, and to encourage and assist in the promotion and development of Olympic Sports in Oceania. The presidents of ONOC have been Harold Austad (NZL) (1981–1983), Sir Lance Cross (NZL) (1983–1989), and currently, IOC member Kevan Gosper of Australia (1989–2000).

Oerter, Alfred Adolph [USA–ATH]. B. 19 September 1936, Astoria, New York. Al Oerter, a discus thrower, was the first track & field athlete to win four successive Olympic titles, a feat since equalled by Carl Lewis in the long jump. Oerter took the gold medal in the discus in 1956, 1960, 1964, and 1968, setting a new Olympic record on each occasion, although he was never the favorite to win the event. His third victory in 1964 was remarkable for the fact that he overcame neck and rib injuries but still managed to set a career best. He also won the Pan-American title in 1959 and set four world records, the first of which in 1962 gave him the distinction of being the first man to record a legal throw of over 200 feet (60.96 meters).

Official Reports. At the end of every Olympic Games and Olympic Winter Games, the Organizing Committee of the Games is required to compile a comprehensive report of the organization, planning, finances, and results of the Olympic Games. The *Olympic Charter* (q.v.) requires that the official report be published in at least French and English. It is now common that the Report is published in French and English, and the language of the host nation, and often in Spanish and German as well. Some of the reports are compiled as one book, with parallel texts in differing languages, but the more recent ones, which are larger, tend to be published as separate editions by language. There have only been a few instances in which an official report was not issued. In 1900, the report consisted of the report of the physical culture section of the *Exposition Universalle*. In 1904, there were two reports, neither of which would be considered comprehensive by today's standards. In 1924, the report of the Olympic Winter Games was not issued separately, but published at the end of the report of the 1924 Paris Olympic Games. Reports were issued by the scheduled host cities for the 1916 Olympic Games and the 1940 Olympic Games and Olympic Winter Games. No reports were ever issued for the scheduled 1944 Olympics.

Olympiad. An Olympiad is a measure of time, designating a period of four consecutive years beginning with the opening of one edition of the Games of the Olympiad and ending with the opening of the following edition. The term is based on the Greeks, who used the term *Olympiad* to measure the time between Olympic Games. *Olympiad* might be the Olympic term most misused by the public, the media, and broadcasters. Specifically, the Olympic Games are not an "Olympiad." They are correctly termed the "Games of the Olympiad."

Olympic Anthem. *See* OLYMPIC HYMN.

Olympic Bribery Scandal. On 24 November 1998, the Salt Lake City (Utah) television station, KTVX, reported that the Salt Lake Olympic Organizing Committee for the Olympic Winter Games of 2002 (SLOC) had been paying for Sonia Essomba to attend American University in

Washington D.C. Sonia Essomba was the daughter of René Essomba, the late International Olympic Committee (IOC) (q.v.) member (1978–1998) to Cameroon. The payments, it would be revealed, were part of a larger scheme set up by SLOC to award scholarships to the family members and friends of IOC members in an effort to win their votes to become the host city. Within a few days after the revelation of the Essomba "scholarship," the media reported that, beginning in 1991, shortly after Salt Lake City had lost the 1998 Winter Olympic bid to Nagano, 13 individuals had received scholarship assistance worth almost $400,000 from the Salt Lake Bid Committee or SLOC. Of these 13 individuals, at least six were close relatives of IOC members.

Shortly thereafter, at the close of the IOC Executive Board (q.v.) on 12 December 1998, Swiss IOC member Marc Hodler spoke openly to the press, stating that at least 5 to 7 percent of IOC members had taken or solicited bribes by bid cities. Within a few days, all manner of revelations were published by the media, which descended like sharks on a feeding frenzy. Shortly before Hodler's interview, upon the recommendation of the Juridical Commission, president Juan Antonio Samaranch (q.v.) had already formed an ad hoc commission to look into the allegations and accusations made against the host cities and bid cities. Canada's Dick Pound was named to head the inquiry, usually called the *Pound Commission*.

At the beginning of 1999, investigating the IOC and the bid city process seemed to be all the rage. In addition to the Pound Commission, the SLOC formed its own Board of Ethics to investigate its own practices. The United States Olympic Committee (USOC) also formed an investigative panel, headed by the former U.S. Senator from Maine, George Mitchell. Concurrently, the Federal Bureau of Investigation (FBI) began its own inquiry into the SLOC to determine if any federal laws were violated relating to bribery and the Foreign Corrupt Practices Act. Of note, only the Pound Commission actually interviewed the IOC members under investigation, allowing them a chance to answer the charges before them.

New announcements from Salt Lake City appeared in the press almost daily in January 1999. On 7 January, the Associated Press reported that IOC member Jean-Claude Ganga of the Republic of the Congo had earned a $60,000 profit on a land deal arranged by a member of SLOC. On 8 January 1999, the president and CEO of SLOC, G.

Frank Joklik, resigned, as did his Senior Vice president, Dave Johnson. At his press conference, Joklik described some of the transgressions of the bid committee and SLOC, and said, "Therefore, I have today obtained the resignation of David Johnson, who was a vice president of the Bid Committee, and has been acting as senior vice president of the Organizing Committee until today. I have recommended the appointment of a new Chief Operating Officer. The other two principal members of the Bid Committee, Tom Welch, who was Chief Executive Officer and Craig Peterson, who was the Chief Administrative Officer, are no longer employees of the corporation . . . Finally, to ensure that the Games go immediately forward, I must take steps of my own. Although I had no knowledge of these improper payments during my tenure as the volunteer Chairman of the Board of Trustees of the Bid Committee, in order to assure the people of Salt Lake City, the State of Utah, and the world that the Organizing Committee is distinct from the Bid Committee and is off to a fresh start, I have tendered my resignation today."

Tom Welch was the main impetus behind the Salt Lake City bid to host the 2002 Winter Olympics. Though no longer in an administrative position with SLOC, he was on their payroll as a consultant when the scandal hit. Joklik stated that Welch's consulting agreement was terminated as of his announcement. Over the next few months, Welch was a marked man, and a reclusive one, who made no public statements, but spoke only through his lawyers.

On 15 January 1999, Samaranch called for an extraordinary IOC session to be held in Lausanne on 17–18 March, but he also stated that he would not resign, despite frequent calls in the media for him to do so. On 19 January, Finnish IOC member Pirjo Häggmann resigned. She was one of the first two female members of the IOC, having served since 1981. But her "crime" was that her ex-husband had worked for the Salt Lake City bid committee and had also worked for the Toronto Bid Committee when that city bid to host the 1996 Olympics. The second IOC member to resign was the Libyan, Bashir Mohamed Attarabulsi, who did so on 22 January. It was revealed that his son had attended an English language center at Brigham Young University in Salt Lake City, with tuition paid by SLOC and the son was provided with $700/month by the organizing committee. The Sydney bid for the 2000 Olympics, to this time, had been relatively unscathed. But on the same day that Attarabulsi resigned, John Coates, who had headed the Sydney bid, admitted that he had made last-minute offers of $70,000 to two African IOC officials, but said the action was legitimate.

On 23 January, the IOC Executive Board met in Lausanne to discuss the preliminary findings of the Pound Commission and make some early decisions. At the end of the meeting, Samaranch announced that the IOC had made mistakes, that they were responsible, and that it must never happen again. Six IOC members were suspended, pending the final Pound Report, with a vote to be taken on their possible expulsion at the special IOC session in March.

The six IOC members suspended (and eventually expelled) were Lamine Keita of Mali, Agustin Arroyo of Ecuador, Charles Mukora of Kenya, Zein El-Abdin Mohamed Ahmed Abdel Gadir of Sudan, Sergio Santander Fantini of Chile, and the aforementioned Jean-Claude Ganga. A third member resigned voluntarily, David Sibandze of Swaziland, while investigations continued into the status of other members.

On 8 February 1999, the Board of Ethics of the Salt Lake Organizing Committee for the Olympic Winter Games of 2002 was released. It described a litany of indiscretions by the bid committee and SLOC. These included payment of hundreds of thousands of dollars to IOC members and their families, usually in the form of "scholarship assistance." As an example, the revelations that began the scandal, the payments to Sonia Essomba, were noted to total $108,350. The Board of Ethics report also revealed direct monetary payments to IOC members, often in the form of sports-assistance programs for their NOCs.

The Board of Ethics also noted that "Many witnesses before the Board of Ethics described Mr. [Jean-Claude] Ganga as the IOC member who most took advantage of the Bid Committee's and the community's generosity." The report then gave details of a litany of indiscretions concerning Ganga and the Salt Lake City Bid Committee.

On 1 March 1999, the Mitchell Commission released its report. The Mitchell Report was more encompassing, dealing with several arms of the Olympic Movement (q.v.). It looked at the bidding process, the IOC structure, and the USOC itself. Its 50 pages of documentation ended with seven pages of conclusions and recommendations, aimed both at revamping the structure of the IOC and the bid city selection process.

The IOC extraordinary session was planned for 17–18 March. Before this meeting, the Executive Board met again and the final Pound Commission report was released. The Pound Report began with a short description of the conclusions of the Board of Ethics Report and the Mitchell Report. It then made its final recommendations near the beginning of the document, although these recommendations were supported by almost 50 pages of documentation describing the transgressions of certain IOC members. The report recommended expelling six IOC members: Agustin Arroyo, Zein El-Abdin Mohamed Ahmed Abdel Gadir, Jean-Claude Ganga, Lamine Keita, and Sergio Santander Fantini, and Paul Wallwork of Samoa. Charles Mukora, whose expulsion had been recommended earlier, had since resigned. Nine other IOC members had been investigated, but were given only warnings with no recommendations of expulsion.

After describing its recommendations concerning the IOC members, the Pound Report made several conclusions. It noted that the IOC must take action to correct the problems within its membership, and it must implement reforms to be certain these problems could never occur again. The Commission also noted that the IOC should have done more to avoid the problems concerning Salt Lake City's candidacy. The Pound Report then recommended changes in the host city selection provess, limitations on travel by IOC members to bid cities, and creation of an IOC Ethics Commission (q.v.).

The IOC met in full session a few days later. It voted to expel the members as recommended by the Pound Report, meaning that fully 10 members of the IOC lost their position in the scandal. But more importantly, the IOC voted to form two new commissions to help reform the structure of the IOC and the Olympic Movement and to ensure that such problems would never happen again.

The two commissions were the Ethics Commission and the IOC 2000 Commission (q.v.). The IOC 2000 Commission was charged with reforming the entire structure of the Olympic Movement into the next millennium to help prevent such ethical breaches in the future. The IOC 2000 Commission was made up of 82 members, with less than half of them IOC members, and with an Executive Board of 26 members, of whom 13 were IOC members. The commission produced an intermediary report in June 1999 and its final report was released in November 1999, although early leaks of information were available. Altogether, the IOC 2000 Commission (q.v.) studied more than 100 possible ideas concerning reform of the Olympic Movement, and eventually made 50 separate recommendations to the IOC.

The Ethics Commission's primary focus was to address the responsibilities of the IOC and oversee the selection process of host cities, and set guidelines for future conduct by members of the Olympic Movement. The Ethics Commission produced an IOC Code of Ethics, in the spring of 1999, which addressed many of the concerns voiced by the public and in the media relating to the recent actions of several IOC members and the Organizing Committees.

During 1999, the United States Congress also began hearings into the conduct of the IOC. The House Commerce Subcommittee on Oversight and Investigation also requested an investigation into the Atlanta Bid for the 1996 Olympic Games. This was assigned to the Atlanta law firm of King & Spaulding, and was headed by former U.S. Attorney General Griffin B. Bell. Its final document, termed the *Bell Report*, was released on 15 September 1999.

The IOC met in extraordinary session in Lausanne on 11–12 December, to vote on the recommendations made by the IOC 2000 Commission. At this historic session, the IOC voted to enact all the recommendations made by the commission. The most important changes implemented were:

1. an age limit of 70 for IOC members
2. term limits of eight years for most IOC members
3. creation of four categories of IOC members
   a athletes
   b National Olympic Committee (NOC) presidents
   c International Federation (IF) presidents
   d individual members
4. eliminating visits by IOC members to the bid cities
5. a complete change in the process of selecting host cities
6. opening IOC sessions to the media via closed-circuit television
7. much more transparency in the financial transactions of the IOC, the bid cities, and the OCOGs

In the end, all 50 recommendations of the IOC 2000 Commission were approved, most of them unanimously.

After the implementation of the numerous IOC reforms, IOC president Juan Antonio Samaranch testified before the House Commerce Subcommittee on Oversight and Investigations on 15 December 1999. It was a somewhat contentious appearance as the members of the subcommittee were underwhelmed by the IOC's reform process. Representative Joe Barton (R-Texas) asked him to resign on the spot. However, Samaranch was supported by former Senators Howard Baker and George Mitchell, who had been involved in the reform process, as noted. Both stated that the IOC was cleaning house and Mitchell noted that the IOC had even gone beyond the recommendations made by his commission.

Why did the Olympic scandal occur and why did these problems seemingly hit all at once? As has been well documented elsewhere, the IOC was once in dire financial straits, and it was only in the 1980s that it began to achieve financial independence. But all this happened quickly, too quickly for the IOC to adjust. And it is unlikely that the problems described here began only with the Salt Lake City bid. There were similar allegations going back to the mid-1980s. During his testimony before the United States House of Representatives on 14 October 1999, the IOC Director-General, François Carrard, said, "Unfortunately, while the Games evolved, our organizational structure did not keep up with the pace of change. In effect, we did not realize we were going through a growth crisis. The result of an old-fashioned structure managing modern Games was not corruption, but a situation in which some of the less-responsible members—a small minority—showed poor judgment and abused the system. Our problems were caused by weak people, structures, and procedures."

Will the new reforms undertaken by the IOC at its December 1999 session be adequate to address the problems? The media have been critical of these reforms and skeptical that they will truly solve these problems. Some of the criticisms are valid, but as George Mitchell noted, in many ways, the IOC has either enacted all of his Commission's recommendations, or in some cases, gone even further than recommended. The IOC seems willing to change and they are doing so. The end to this story has not yet been written.

Olympic Ceremonies. A number of ceremonies accompany the Olympic Games, notably the Opening, Closing, Victory, Medals, and

Diplomas Ceremonies. These ceremonies are conducted according to strict protocols defined in Rule 69 of the *Olympic Charter* (q.v.) (Opening and Closing Ceremonies) and Rule 70 of the *Olympic Charter* (Victory, Medals, and Diplomas Ceremonies).

The Opening Ceremonies begin with the Head of State of the host country (normally) entering the stadium, accompanied by the president of the International Olympic Committee (IOC) and the president of the Organizing Committee of the Games. The parade of nations then follows, with the nations of all participating countries entering the stadium. The nations march in alphabetical order, using the alphabetical designation of the language of the host country. However, Greece always enters the stadium first, as the founding nation of the Ancient Olympic Games (q.v.), and the last nation to enter is always the host country. Each nation is led by a flag bearer carrying the flag of the nation or the National Olympic Committee (q.v.).

The president of the Organizing Committee then speaks for no more than three minutes. The IOC president then speaks briefly and ends by inviting the Head of State of the host country to open the Olympic Games. He or she gives no speech, but opens the Games by stating "I declare open the Games of . . . (name of city) celebrating the . . . Olympiad of the Modern Era (or the . . . Olympic Winter Games)."

The Olympic Torch is then brought into the stadium and the Olympic Flame (q.v.) is lit by the final runner, followed by a symbolic release of pigeons, signifying peace. The flag bearers then form a semi-circle around the main rostrum and a competitor and an official of the host country take the Olympic Oath (q.v.) on behalf of all competitors and officials. The national anthem of the host country is then played, after which an artistic program entertaining the spectators is held. This program is usually designed to have some symbolic nature, representing both the Olympic Movement (q.v.) and the national features of the host country.

The Closing Ceremonies end the Olympic Games. The flag bearers of each nation first march into the stadium, followed by the athletes of all nations. The athletes march in no order and typically intermingle, signifying the friendships developed during the Olympic Games. (This change to the closing ceremony was suggested by John Ian Wing, a young British boy of Chinese origin, to the organizers of the 1956 Olympic Games in Melbourne.)

The president of the IOC and the Organizing Committee mount the rostrum in the center of the stadium. Three flags are then raised in the following order: the Greek flag on the right flagpole, the flag of the host country on the center flagpole, and the flag of the host country of the next Olympic Games (or Olympic Winter Games) on the left flagpole. All are raised to the playing of their respective national anthems.

The mayor of the host city then hands the official Olympic flag (q.v.) to the IOC president, who in turn hands it to the mayor of the host city of the next Olympic Games. The president of the Organizing Committee gives a brief speech. The IOC president then speaks briefly and ends the Olympic Games by stating, "I declare the Games of the . . . Olympiad (or the . . . Olympic Winter Games) closed and, in accordance with tradition, I call upon the youth of the world to assemble four years from now at . . . (next host city) to celebrate with us there the Games of the . . . Olympiad (or the . . . Olympic Winter Games)." A fanfare then sounds, the Olympic Flame is extinguished and while the Olympic Hymn (q.v.) is played, the Olympic flag is lowered from the flagpole.

The Victory, Medals, and Diplomas Ceremonies consist of the awarding of these respective items. The medals are to be presented by the IOC president or an IOC member designated by him. In reality, the IOC president now awards only a very few medals. The three place winners mount the victory platform, the winner on the highest step. Their names are announced and the medals are awarded to them. The national flags of the three medal winners are raised, the national flag of the winner on the central flagpole. While the flags are raised, the national anthem of the champion is played, usually in a shortened version.

Olympic Charter. The *Olympic Charter* is, effectively, the constitution of the International Olympic Committee (IOC) and the Olympic Movement (qq.v.). It sets out, basically in an outline form, the principles, rules, and by-laws that govern the workings of both the IOC and the Olympic Movement, and stipulates the conditions for the celebration of the Olympic Games. The *Olympic Charter* was first adopted in 1908, based on a handwritten set of rules created by Pierre de Coubertin (q.v.) shortly after the formation of the IOC. The 1908 list of rules was not called the *Olympic Charter,* but rather *Comité In-*

ternational Olympique: Annuaire (in French only). Since that time, the International Olympic Committee's governing rules have been published under multiple names, including *Olympic Rules, Protocol, Olympic Statutes, Olympic Statutes,* and *Rules,* being first published officially as the *Olympic Charter* only in 1978.

Though the *Olympic Charter* is often held to be inviolate, it is, in fact, fairly easily modified and has been changed many times since its inception. Modifications, or amendments, can be made according to Rule 22.4 governing the sessions, which states, "The Session is the supreme organ of the IOC. It adopts, modifies, and interprets the *Olympic Charter.*"

The *Olympic Charter* underwent major changes at the end of 1999, based on recommendations made by the IOC 2000 Commission (q.v.) in response to the Olympic Bribery Scandal (q.v.). The changes were sweeping and made significant structural changes to the Olympic Movement, many of which are discussed in various entries in this Dictionary. Specifically, the changes made to the *Olympic Charter* at the IOC session in Lausanne in December 1999 relate to the following recommendations of the IOC 2000 Commission. Details of these recommendations can be found in the entry for IOC 2000 Commission.

- Recommendation 1: IOC Members
- Recommendation 2: Procedure for Selecting and Electing IOC Members
- Recommendation 3: Nationality of IOC Members
- Recommendation 4: Terms of Office of IOC Members
- Recommendation 5: Age Limit for IOC Members
- Recommendation 6: Rights and Responsibilities of IOC Members
- Recommendation 7: Honorary IOC Members
- Recommendation 8: IOC Executive Board (q.v.)
- Recommendation 9: IOC President
- Recommendation 13: Participation of All NOCs at the Olympic Games
- Recommendation 17: Definition of an Active Olympic Athlete
- Recommendation 34: Amending the Olympic Oath (q.v.) to Include Anti-Doping (q.v.)
- Recommendation 38: Eliminating Sports Not Supporting IOC Anti-Doping Code
- Recommendation 50: New Candidature Procedure

Olympic Code. *See* OLYMPIC CREED.

Olympic Collectors Commission. The Olympic Collectors Commission was formed on 14 June 1993 by combining three associations that were recognized by the IOC—the Fédération International de Philately Olympique (FIPO), the Fédération Internationale de Numismatic Olympique (FINO), and the Association of Collectors of Olympic Memorabilia (ACOM). President Juan Antonio Samaranch (q.v.), an avid stamp collector, chairs this commission. The Olympic Collectors Commission now sponsors an annual Olympic Collectors World Fair and an Olympic stamp show, Olymphilex.

Olympic Congresses. Olympic Congresses are gatherings of all the various bodies and individuals involved in the Olympic Movement (q.v.). The *Olympic Charter* (q.v.) now states that they are to be held, in principle, every eight years at a place and date determined by the International Olympic Committee (IOC) (q.v.). This has not always been the case. Baron Pierre de Coubertin (q.v.) intended Olympic Congresses to be held from "time-to-time" to discuss the Olympic Movement. However, a gap of 43 years occurred from the 9th Olympic Congress until the 10th Olympic Congress in 1973. The Olympic Congress has no official power to make rules concerning the Olympic Games or to modify the *Olympic Charter*, but only acts as a consultant to the Olympic Movement.

To date, 12 Olympic Congresses have been held. They have been as follows, with their themes following the name of the host city:

1st	16–24 June 1894	Paris	Re-establishment of the Olympic Games
2nd	23–31 July 1897	Le Havre	Sports hygiene and pedagogy
3rd	9–14 June 1905	Brussels	Sport and physical education
4th	23–25 May 1906	Paris	Art, literature, and sport
5th	7–11 May 1913	Lausanne	Sports psychology and physiology
6th	15–23 June 1914	Paris	Olympic regulations
7th	2–7 June 1921	Lausanne	Olympic regulations

8th	29 May–4 June 1925	Prague	Sports pedagogy and Olympic regulations
9th	25–30 May 1930	Berlin	Olympic regulations
10th	30 September–4 October 1973	Varna	Sport for a world of peace—the Olympic Movement and its future
11th	23–28 September 1981	Baden-Baden	1. The future of the Olympics Games; 2. International cooperation; 3. The future of the Olympic Movement
12th	29 August–3 September 1994	Paris	1. The Olympic Movement's contribution to modern society; 2. The contemporary athlete; 3. Sport in its social context; 4. Sport and the media

As of early 2001, there are no current plans for the next Olympic Congress.

Olympic Council of Asia [OCA]. The Olympic Council of Asia is a confederation of the National Olympic Committees (q.v.) from Asia, which was formed in November 1982. The OCA is in overall charge of sports in Asia, coordinates the activities of Asian countries in sports at the regional and international level, and conducts the Asian Games every four years. It is headquartered in Kuwait and, as of 2000, its president is Sheikh Ahmad Al-Fahad Al-Sabah of Kuwait. There are currently 43 affiliated nations.

Olympic Credo. *See* OLYMPIC CREED.

Olympic Creed. "The most important thing in the Olympic Games is not to win but to take part, just as the most important thing in life is not the triumph, but the struggle. The essential thing is not to have conquered but to have fought well."

This is the current form of the Olympic Creed (also termed the *Olympic Code*, the *Olympic Credo*, an alternative *Olympic Motto*, or the *Olympic Competition Motto. See* OLYMPIC MOTTO) as it appears on the scoreboard at the Opening Ceremony of the Olympic Games, although many permutations of this basic message have been seen. The exact origin of this phrase is not clear, but it is possible that Pierre de Coubertin (q.v.) adopted this creed after hearing Ethelbert Talbot, the Bishop of Central Pennsylvania, speak at St. Paul's Cathedral on 19 July 1908, during the London Olympics. The service was given for the Olympic athletes who were all invited.

Talbot was in London for the fifth Conference of Anglican Bishops. During the conference, many of the visiting bishops spoke in various churches. Talbot actually did not say anything close to the exact words during his speech, stating instead, "The only safety after all lies in the lesson of the real Olympia—that the Games themselves are better than the race and the prize. St. Paul tells us how insignificant is the prize. Our prize is not corruptible, but incorruptible, and though only one may wear the laurel wreath, all may share the equal joy of the contest."

However, Coubertin heard Talbot speak and, at a banquet at the Grafton Galleries on 24 July 1908, he echoed Bishop Talbot's words as follows, "L'important dans ces Olympiades, c'est moins d'y gagner que d'y prendre part." ("The important thing at these Olympiads is not so much to win as to take part.") He then went on to say that these very words were the foundation of a clear and sound philosophy: "L'important dans la vie ce n'est point le triomphe mais le combat. L'essentiel ce n'est pas d'avoir vaincu mais de s'être bien battu." ("The important thing in life is not the triumph but the struggle. The essential thing is not to have won but to have fought well.")

More recent research by Prof. David C. Young indicates that Coubertin probably had this thought in mind prior to hearing the speech of the Bishop of Central Pennsylvania. Young attributes the phrase to Ovid's *Metamorphoses,* which Coubertin had read in school. A sentence in that work reads, "Nec tam turpe fuit vinci quam contendisse decorum est," which can be translated as, "It was not so shameful to be beaten as it is honorable to have contended." Coubertin's knowledge of this statement is supplemented by a speech he gave in November 1894, given to the Parnassus Literary Society in Athens, in which he said, "Le déshonneur ne consisterait pas ici à être battu: il consisterait à ne pas se battre." This is literally translated as, "The dishonor here would consist not of being beaten, it would consist of not contending."

In connection with the Olympic Games in Stockholm 1912 and Antwerp 1920, Coubertin again spoke of the words of the Bishop of Central Pennsylvania, but it did not attract any notice. At the Olympic Games in 1924 and 1928, no reference was made to Bishop Talbot's sermon in St. Paul's Cathedral in 1908. However, at the Olympic Games in Los Angeles (1932), the message appeared during the Opening Ceremonies on the great scoreboard of the Los Angeles Memorial Coliseum. It was finally established at the 1936 Olympic Games in Berlin when, at the Opening Ceremony, Pierre de Coubertin's voice was heard over the loudspeaker, in a recording, delivering his message, "Important aux Jeux Olympiques, ce n'est pas tant d'y gagner que d'y avoir pris part; car l'essentiel dans la vie, ce n'est pas tant de conquérir que d'avoir bien lutté. "("Important in the Olympic Games is not winning but taking part; for the essential thing in life is not conquering but fighting well.")

Olympic Cup. The Olympic Cup was instituted by Baron Pierre de Coubertin (q.v.) in 1906. It is awarded to an institution or association with a general reputation for merit and integrity that has been active and efficient in the service of sport and has contributed substantially to the development of the Olympic Movement (q.v.). The Olympic Cup is one of the two awards currently given by the International Olympic Committee outside of the Olympic Games. *See* OLYMPIC ORDER and Appendix V for a list of recipients of the Olympic Cup.

Olympic Diplomas. Diplomas are given to the first eight finishers of all events at an Olympic Games. It is not well known that the first three finishers receive, in addition to their medals, these diplomas. In team events, the members of the first eight teams also all receive diplomas.

Olympic Films. Numerous Olympic films and movies have been produced. The Organizing Committee of each Olympic Games now produces its own official Olympic Film celebrating in motion pictures "its" Olympics. This began with the 1936 Olympic Games in Berlin

when German film producer Leni Riefenstahl, at the behest of Adolf
Hitler, produced the most famous and haunting of all Olympic Films,
Olympia. Prior to that, the filmed record of the Olympics came from
cinema newsreels. Other famous official Olympics films have been
Tokyo Olympiad, celebrating the 1964 Olympic Games in Tokyo, and
Visions of Eight, celebrating the 1972 Olympic Games in Munich.

In addition to official Olympic films, many independent producers
produce Olympic movies: The American television network that tel-
evises the Olympics now usually produces a cinematic summary of
the Olympics and their coverage is often available to be bought and
viewed on videocassette recorders.

The most prominent producer of Olympic films has been the
American Bud Greenspan, who was initially assisted by his late wife,
Cappy Greenspan. Greenspan has produced a remarkable series of
Olympic movies termed "The Olympiad Series." In addition, he has
been the producer of the official Olympic film seven times: in 1984
(Los Angeles), 1988 (Calgary and Seoul), 1992 (Barcelona), and
1994 (Lillehammer), 1996 (Atlanta), and 1998 (Nagano).

Olympic Flag. The Olympic flag has a plain white background with no
border. In the center is the Olympic symbol, which consists of five in-
terconnected rings. They form two rows of three rings above, and two
below. The rings of the upper row are, from left to right, blue, black,
and red. The rings of the lower row are yellow and green. The rings
are thought to symbolize the five continents—Europe, Asia, Africa,
Australia, and America. The colors of the rings are thought to have
been chosen because at least one of these colors can be found in the
flag of every nation.

The origin of the flag's design is in some dispute. It is thought to
be Baron Pierre de Coubertin (q.v.) who designed the symbol to
honor and represent the 1914 Olympic Congress in Paris. Some
sources state that de Coubertin saw the rings at Delphi in 1913, but
classics scholars believe this is highly unlikely and that they are of
his own, modern invention. The idea of a flag was raised by the IOC
in 1910 and a special committee worked to plan it. Several suggestions were made, notably by Theodore Cook (GBR) and Clarence
von Rosen (SWE), but little progress was made until de Coubertin
came up with his design. He commented in the August 1913 edition

of *Revue Olympique,* "These five rings represent the five parts of the world from this point on won over to Olympism and given to accepting fruitful rivalry. Furthermore, the six colors [including the white background] thus combined reproduce the colors of all the nations, with no exception." The flag was first flown at Chatsby Stadium in Alexandria, Egypt, for the Pan-Egyptian Games on 5 April 1914. It was presented to the International Olympic Committee (IOC) (q.v.) by de Coubertin at the Olympic Congress (q.v.) in 1914 at the Sorbonne in Paris, where it was officially approved on 15 June 1914. The flag was also flown in 1915 at the San Francisco Exhibition and at the 1919 IOC session in Lausanne, before it made its début at the Olympic Games in 1920 at Antwerp, Belgium. The "primary" Olympic flag was thus known as the *Antwerp flag,* and was the main Olympic flag flown at the stadium at all Olympic Games through 1984. In 1984, Seoul presented a new Olympic flag to the IOC, made of fine Korean silk, which was first flown at the 1988 Olympics. A second "primary" Olympic flag is used for the Olympic Winter Games, which was donated in 1952 by the host city of Oslo, Norway.

The Olympic flag is raised at the Opening Ceremonies and flies over the main stadium throughout the Olympic Games. It is lowered at the Closing Ceremonies of the Olympic Games. The mayor of the Olympic host city then presents the Olympic flag to the mayor of the next Olympic host city. The flag is to be kept in the town hall of the host city until the next Olympic Games. *See* OLYMPIC CEREMONIES.

Olympic Flame, Olympic Torch, and Torch Relay. The Olympic flame is a symbol reminiscent of the Ancient Olympic Games (q.v.), in which a sacred flame burned at the altar of Zeus throughout the Olympic Games. The flame was first used at the modern Olympics in Amsterdam in 1928, and again was lit throughout the 1932 Los Angeles Olympics, but this marked the last time the flame was kindled at the site of the Games.

In 1936, Carl Diem (q.v.), chairman of the organizing committee for the Berlin Olympics, proposed the idea of lighting the flame at Ancient Olympia, and transporting it to Berlin via a torch relay. This was done and has been repeated at every Olympics since.

The flame for the Olympic Games is lit in the altis of the Ancient Olympic stadium at Ancient Olympia, on the Greek Peloponnesus.

The flame is lit during a ceremony by women dressed in robes similar to those worn by the ancient Greeks. The flame is lit naturally by the rays of the sun at Olympia, reflected off a curved mirror, and the high priestess then presents the torch to the first relay runner.

The flame for the Olympic Winter Games has not always been lit in Olympia. In 1952 and 1960, the flame for the Olympic Winter Games was lit at the hearth of Sondre Nordheim, the father of modern skiing, at his ancient home in Morgedal, Norway. In 1956, it was lit at the Temple of Jupiter in Rome for the Games in Cortina d'Ampezzo, Italy. Since 1964, the flame for the Olympic Winter Games has also been lit in Ancient Olympia. In 1994, a second, unofficial flame was lit in Morgedal for the Lillehammer Olympics, which greatly upset the Greeks, who claim proprietary rights to the Olympic flame.

Olympic Games. The Olympic Games refer to the sporting festival that is held in the summer months, and is often referred to as the Summer Olympics. The proper name of the sporting celebration is the Games of the . . . th Olympiad. The Games of the . . . th Olympiad are always held during the first year of the Olympiad (q.v.) that they celebrate. The Olympic Games are entrusted to a single host city, which is now elected seven years in advance of the scheduled Olympic Games. *See* discussions of the various Olympic Games in the section "Chronology of the Olympic Games and Olympic Winter Games."

Olympic Hymn and Anthem. An Olympic Hymn, also called the *Olympic Anthem*, was composed for the 1896 Olympic Games by Greek composer Spyros Samaras (1863–1917), with words added by his colleague Kostis Palamas. The Olympic Hymn was first played at the 1896 Olympic Opening Ceremonies, performed by nine bands and a chorus. It was used again in 1906. Thereafter, a variety of musical offerings provided the background to the Opening Ceremonies until 1960. In 1954, the IOC launched a worldwide competition for a new version of an Olympic Hymn. From the 392 scores presented, the first prize went to Michael Spisak for his ultra-modern atonal work, with lyrics extracted from Pindar's (q.v.) odes. It was never terribly popular and Spisak's demands for excessive royalties led it to not be chosen as the official Olympic Hymn. It was elected to return to the Samaras/Palamas composition as the official Olympic Hymn.

The Samaras/Palamas hymn was played and sung at the 55th IOC session in 1958 in Tokyo. It was such an impressive demonstration that IOC member Prince Axel (DEN) suggested that it should be adopted as the official hymn. This was unanimously approved, although two years of legal work then took place dealing with the heirs of Samaras and Palamas.

The Olympic Hymn was first used in that regard at the Opening Ceremonies in Rome three years later, since which time it has become an established part of the Olympic ceremonies. The *Olympic Charter* (q.v.) currently terms this the *Olympic Anthem*.

Olympic Identity Card. The Olympic Identity Card is an important political document. It is given to all members of the Olympic Family, i.e., athletes, officials, International Olympic Committee (IOC) (q.v.) members and delegates, National Olympic Committee (NOC) (q.v.) members and delegates, and International Federation (IF) (q.v.) members and delegates. The importance of the Olympic Identity Card is that it establishes the identity of the holder and, with an appropriate national passport, is supposed to allow free passage into the country in which the host Olympic city is situated. Thus the card serves as, and supplants, a travel visa. Host cities are required agree to recognize the right of all members of the Olympic Family to enter the country of the host city, based on a valid passport and the Olympic Identity Card, and not require a further visa.

Olympic Literature. The literature surrounding the Olympic Games is voluminous. The International Olympic Committee (IOC) (q.v.) now publishes multiple magazines, journals, press releases, and books. Each National Olympic Committee (NOC) (q.v.) and International Federation (IF) (q.v.) also may publish literature concerning the Olympic Games and often does so. The Organizing Committees publish a great deal of official information, in addition to press releases and packets.

Private authors have also developed an enormous amount of Olympic literature. Books on the Olympics are now produced prior to and after each Olympic Games, in most of the major languages of the world. With the advent of advanced technology, some are now being produced on CD-ROMs to be read via computers.

No current up-to-date bibliography of Olympic literature exists. The two most complete and most recent are currently 18 years old. They are *The Olympics: A Bibliography,* compiled by Bill Mallon (New York: Garland Press, 1983) and *Bibliography: Geschichte der Leibesübungen, Bandfive, Olympische Spiele* (second edition), compiled by Karl Lennartz (Bonn: Verlag Karl Hofmann, 1983). *See also* OLYMPIC MESSAGE and OLYMPIC REVIEW.

Olympic Medals. Olympic Medals are given as awards for finishing in the first three places in the events of the Olympic Games. The champion receives a gold medal, the runner-up a silver medal, and the third place finisher a bronze medal. At the 1896 Olympics, the winner received only a silver medal and the runner-up a bronze medal.

The medals must be at least 60 mm. in diameter and three mm. thick. They are designed by the Organizing Committee of the Olympic Games, upon approval by the IOC Executive Board (q.v.). The "gold" medal is actually silver gilt that must be gilded with at least six grams of pure gold. In 1908 and 1912, the gold medallists received true gold medals for the only times. The metal for the first- and second-place medals must be silver of at least 925/1000 grade.

Olympic Medals are given to the medallists at ceremonies at the conclusion of their events. The medals are draped around the athlete's necks, hung from a ribbon or other decorative necklace. This custom did not begin, however, until 1960 in Rome. Prior to that time, the medals were handed to the athlete's in specially designed boxes.

Olympic Message. The *Olympic Message* was a publication of the International Olympic Committee (IOC) (q.v.). It was first published in May 1982, and was published three or four times per year. Its publication was discontinued as of the December 1994 issue (Volume 40). The *Olympic Message* was different from the *Olympic Review* in that each issue usually studied in detail a single theme of the Olympic Movement.

Olympic Motto. The official Olympic Motto is *"Citius, Altius, Fortius,"* a Latin phrase meaning swifter, higher, stronger. The Olympic Motto was adopted by Baron Pierre de Coubertin (q.v.) for the International Olympic Committee (IOC) (q.v.) after hearing of its use by

Reverend Father Henri Martin Didon of Paris, a Dominican friar and teacher. Didon, head master of Arcueil College, used the phrase while describing the athletic accomplishments of his students at that school. He had previously been at the school Albert Le Grand, where the Latin words were carved in stone above the main entrance. Coubertin used the motto in the very first issue of *Revue Olympique*. *See also* OLYMPIC CREED.

Olympic Movement. The Olympic Movement is a phrase often used by the International Olympic Committee (IOC) (q.v.) and practitioners and administrators of international sport. However, it is not well defined. The *Olympic Charter* (q.v.) states simply that "The Olympic Movement, led by the IOC, stems from modern Olympism (q.v.)." The IOC has, however, defined the phrase more fully in some of its press releases. It has stated that the Olympic Movement encompasses the International Olympic Committee (IOC), the International Sports Federations (IFs) (q.v.), and the National Olympic Committees (NOCs) (q.v.) and that the IOC is the supreme authority of the Olympic Movement. In addition, the IOC has stated its purpose and its fundamental principles as "to contribute to building a peaceful and better world by educating youth through sport practiced without discrimination of any kind and in the Olympic spirit, which requires mutual understanding with a spirit of friendship, solidarity, and fair play. The activity of the Olympic Movement is permanent and universal. It reaches its peak with the bringing together of the athletes of the world at the great sport festival, the Olympic Games."

Olympic Museum. An Olympic Museum had been a dream of the International Olympic Committee (IOC) (q.v.) for many years. In 1915, Pierre de Coubertin (q.v.) announced his intention to set up an Olympic Museum in Lausanne to store the archives of the IOC and to become a public information center on the Olympic Movement (q.v.). IOC president Juan Antonio Samaranch (q.v.) made the dream a reality. He began his plans for an Olympic Museum in 1981, shortly after his election as IOC president, when the IOC bought a building at 18 avenue Ruchonnet in Lausanne and established a provisional museum. In 1984, the IOC acquired two plots of land in the Ouchy section of Lausanne, overlooking Lake Geneva (Lake Léman). Construction on the permanent Olympic Museum began on this land in 1988. On 23 June 1993, the Olympic Museum was inaugurated on the 99th anniversary of the creation of the IOC. The Olympic Museum is intended to be the universal depository of the written, visual, and graphic memory of the Olympic Games. Samaranch has stated that "the Olympic Museum will be a global source of information on the impact of the Olympic tradition on art, culture, the economy, and world peace. The focal point of the meaning of the Olympic Games and their role in modern society, the Olympic Museum will be both a witness and a center for reflection."

Olympic Oath. The Olympic Oath is a pledge to uphold the spirit of sportsmanship and is spoken at the Opening Ceremonies by representatives of the host country on behalf of all competitors and officials. In the July 1906 edition of the *Revue Olympique,* Pierre de Coubertin (q.v.) referred to the urgent need to introduce into the few but very important Olympic ceremonies an athlete's oath of fairness and impartiality. The protocol was first introduced at Antwerp in 1920 when the noted Belgian fencer, Victor Boin, performed the ceremony. A similar ceremony was conducted at the first Olympic Winter Games at Chamonix in 1924 when all competitors took the oath collectively, although they were led by France's Camille Mandrillon. The first woman (q.v.) to take the oath was the Italian skier Giuliana Chenal-Minuzzo at the 1956 Olympic Winter Games in Cortina d'Ampezzo. The first woman to take the oath at the Olympic Games was German track & field athlete Heidi Schüller at the 1972 Olympic Games in Munich.

Boin initially recited the following words: "We swear that we will take part in the Olympic Games in a spirit of chivalry, for the honor of our country and for the glory of sport." This oath was modified slightly in 1961, when the word "swear" was replaced by "promise," and "the honor of our country" by "the honor of our teams," in an obvious desire to eliminate nationalism from the Games.

In 1999, the IOC 2000 Commission (q.v.) recommended a change to the Olympic Oath that was enacted by the IOC session. This change added a statement to the oath in which the Olympic athletes would renounce the use of drugs in sport. The current edition of the *Olympic Charter* (q.v.) establishes the following text for the Athletes'

Oath: "In the name of all the competitors I promise that we shall take part in these Olympic Games, respecting and abiding by the rules which govern them, committing ourselves to a sport without doping (q.v.) and without drugs, in the true spirit of sportsmanship, for the glory of sport and the honor of our teams." Since 1972, the judges have also sworn an oath, the text of which, in conformity with the current *Olympic Charter*, is as follows: "In the name of all the judges and officials, I promise that we shall officiate in these Olympic Games with complete impartiality, respecting and abiding by the rules which govern them, in the true spirit of sportsmanship." *See also* OLYMPIC CEREMONIES, OLYMPIC REVIEW, and Appendix VII for the list of those who have spoken the Olympic Oath at the Opening Ceremonies of the Olympic Games.

Olympic Order. The Olympic Order is the supreme individual honor accorded by the International Olympic Committee (IOC) (q.v.). It was created in 1974 and is to be awarded to "Any person who has illustrated the Olympic Ideal through his/her action, has achieved remarkable merit in the sporting world, or has rendered outstanding services to the Olympic cause, either through his/her own personal achievement(s) or his/her contribution to the development of sport." Originally, the Olympic Order was separated into three categories: gold, silver, and bronze. Currently, there is only a gold and silver category. *See* Appendix V for a list of recipients of the Olympic Order in Gold.

Olympic Programme, The. The Olympic Programme (TOP) is a fundraising program administered by the International Olympic Committee (IOC) (q.v.) that began in the 1980s. It is used to generate revenue for the IOC and has been very successful. TOP works by soliciting only a few sponsors, no more than 12 at a time to date, guaranteeing them exclusive marketing rights to the Olympic Symbol (q.v.) within their market niche, and providing that guarantee for a complete Olympiad (q.v.). Each TOP edition thus lasts for four years. To date, there have been TOP I, TOP II, TOP III, and TOP IV. Because of the exclusivity of the program, the IOC has been able to command very large revenues from the sponsors, which has guaranteed the success of TOP.

Olympic Review. The *Olympic Review* is the official journal of the International Olympic Committee. It has been published under various titles relatively continuously since 1894. Originally published by Pierre de Coubertin (q.v.), its first title was *Bulletin du Comité International des Jeux Olympiques.* From 1901 to 1914, it first took its current name in French, *Revue Olympique.* From 1938 to 1944, it was published in Berlin with the German title *Olympische Rundschau,* although French and English editions were also available. Other titles used during its publishing history include *Bulletin du Comité International Olympique, Bulletin Officiel du Comité International Olympique, Pages de critique et d'histoire,* and *Lettre d'information/Newsletter/Carta información.* It is now published monthly in English, French, German, and Spanish. Since 1970, the official title has remained *Olympic Review, Revue Olympique, Olympische Rundschau,* and *Revista Olimpica.*

Olympic Solidarity. Olympic Solidarity is a program in which the International Olympic Committee (IOC) (q.v.) helps the sporting development of underprivileged nations. Certain IOC fundraising is distributed via Olympic Solidarity to the National Olympic Committees (NOCs) (q.v.) that the IOC recognizes to be in the greatest need. This has taken the form of coaching assistance, technical assistance, and funds to help athletes travel to the Olympic Games and other international sporting events. The goals of Olympic Solidarity are quoted in the *Olympic Charter* (q.v.) to be "promoting the fundamental principles of the Olympic Movement; developing the technical sports knowledge of athletes and coaches; improving the technical level of athletes and coaches; training sports administrators; and collaborating with the various IOC commissions."

Olympic Solidarity began in 1961 as the International Olympic Aid Committee at the suggestion of Jean, Count de Beaumont (FRA). In 1968, this Committee became a Commission of the IOC while retaining the same name. In 1971, Adriaan van Karnebeek (NED) took the initiative for further developments by setting up an Olympic Solidarity Commission through the Permanent General Assembly of National Olympic Committees. (*See* ASSOCIATION DES COMITÉS NATIONAUX OLYMPIQUES [ACNO]) In 1972, the two groups merged to become what is now known as *Olympic Solidarity.* It was originally headquartered in Rome, but in 1979, at the 81st IOC session, Olympic Solidarity was moved to its present headquarters in Lausanne. In 1982, Anselmo López became its first full-time director, a position he held through 1995. He remains the honorary director, with the post of director being held since 1995 by Pere Miró.

Olympic Solidarity Commission. *See* OLYMPIC SOLIDARITY.

Olympic Symbol. *See* OLYMPIC FLAG.

Olympic Torch and Torch Relay. *See* OLYMPIC FLAME.

Olympic Truce. It is often stated that in ancient Greece, a sacred Olympic Truce, or *ekecheiria*, existed such that all wars ceased during the Olympic Games. In addition, all persons traveling to or from the Olympic Games were guaranteed free passage to Olympia, in the city-state of Elis—even if passing through lands or city-states that were at war. It is not certain if, in fact, the Olympic Truce existed fully in this form, and recent research by classical scholars indicates that this may be an oversimplification of the facts. It has been noted that the Olympic Truce "never stopped a war, nor indeed were the Eleans so foolishly utopian as to imagine they could achieve that" (Finley and Pleket, *The Olympic Games*, p. 98 [London: Chatto & Windus, 1976]). Apparently, the Olympic law only forbade open warfare against the Eleans, and the truce was specifically meant only not to disrupt the Olympic Games.

In 1992, the International Olympic Committee (IOC) (q.v.) made steps to re-institute this important part of Olympic lore, by creating the Olympic Truce Project. Contact was made by IOC president Juan Antonio Samaranch with all of the National Olympic Committees (NOCs) (q.v.), many nongovernmental organizations, and the United Nations General Assembly, in which he proposed an Olympic Truce to take place during the period of and surrounding the Olympic Games. This was eventually approved by the United Nations General Assembly in Resolution A/Res/48/11 on 25 October 1993 at their 36th Plenary Meeting.

Samaranch's appeal for the Olympic Truce, released from Barcelona on 21 July 1992, read as follows:

> *The International Olympic Committee,*
> *Considering* the frequency of conflicts which seriously affect the lives and future of the youth of the world;

Faithful to the mission which it has assigned itself, namely to contribute to peace;

Anxious in this respect to restore the ancient Greek tradition of *Ekecheiria* or "Olympic Truce Pledge";

Calls on:

- all States (their heads, governments, and assemblies);
- all international and national organizations;

to decide that:

1. During the period from the 7th day before the opening of the Olympic Games until the 7th day after the end of these Games, the "Olympic Truce" shall be observed;
2. During the Olympic Truce dedicated, as in ancient Greece, to the spirit of brotherhood and understanding between peoples, all initiatives shall be taken and all group or individual efforts made to begin and continue to achieve by peaceful means the settlement of conflicts, whether or not of an international nature, with a view to establish peace;
3. During this period, all armed conflicts, and any acts related to, inspired by or akin to such conflicts, shall cease, whatever the reason, cause or means of perpetration thereof.

The United Nations Resolution A/Res/48/11 reads as follows:

The General Assembly,

Considering the appeal launched by the International Olympic Committee for an Olympic Truce, which was endorsed by 184 Olympic Committees and presented to the Secretary General,

Recognizing that the goal of the Olympic Movement is to build a peaceful and better world by educating the youth of the world through sport, practiced without discrimination of any kind and in the Olympic spirit, which requires mutual understanding, promoted by friendship, solidarity, and fair-play,

Recognizing also the efforts of the International Olympic Committee to restore the ancient Greek tradition of the Ekecheiria, or "Olympic Truce," in the interest of contributing to international understanding and the maintenance of peace,

Recalling resolution CM/Res. 1472 (LVIII), which supports the appeal for an Olympic Truce, adopted by the Council of Ministers of the Organization of African Unity at its 58th Ordinary session, held in Cairo from 21 to 26 June 1993, and endorsed by the Assembly of Heads of State and government of that organisation,

Recognizing further the valuable contribution that the appeal launched by the International Olympic Committee for an Olympic Truce could make towards advancing the purposes and principles of the Charter of the United Nations,

1. Commends the International Olympic Committee, the International Sports Federations and the National Olympic Committees for their efforts to mobilize the youth of the world in the cause of peace;
2. Urges Member States to observe the Olympic Truce from the seventh day before the opening until the seventh day following the closing of each of the Olympic Games, in accordance with the appeal launched by the International Olympic Committee.
3. Notes the idea of the Olympic Truce, as dedicated in ancient Greece to the spirit of fraternity and understanding between peoples, and urges Member States to take the initiative to abide by the Truce, individually and collectively, and to pursue in conformity with the purposes and principles of the Charter of the United Nations the peaceful settlement of all international conflicts;
4. Calls upon all Member States to cooperate with the International Olympic Committee in its efforts to promote the Olympic Truce;
5. Requests the Secretary General to promote the observance of the Olympic Truce among Member States, drawing the attention of world public opinion to the contribution such a truce would make to the promotion of international understanding and the maintenance of peace and goodwill, and to cooperate with the International Olympic Committee in the realization of this objective.

Olympic Village. At each Olympics since 1924, the Organizing Committees have provided an Olympic Village, which houses the athletes. In recent years with the spread of the Games over very large areas, many Organizing Committees have provided several Olympic Villages. Recently, the host cities to the Olympic Games have used the

Olympic Villages to provide low-cost housing to their citizens at the end of the Olympics.

Olympic Winter Games. The Olympic Winter Games are held every four years. Originally, they were held in the same year as the Olympic Games or Games of the Olympiad. Currently, they are contested every four years, but during the second calendar year following the beginning of the Olympiad (q.v.). This ruling was made at the 91st IOC session in 1986 in Lausanne, by a vote of 78–2, specifically to take advantage of the better use of advertising and television dollars to fund the Olympic Movement. *See* discussions of the various Olympic Winter Games in the chronology.

Olympism. Olympism is a philosophy that is felt to be the cornerstone of the Olympic Movement. It is not easily defined and probably means different things to different people. The International Olympic Committee (IOC) (q.v.) defines Olympism in the *Olympic Charter* (q.v.) as follows: "Olympism is a philosophy of life, exalting and combining in a balanced whole the qualities of body, will, and mind. Blending sport with culture and education, Olympism seeks to create a way of life based on the joy found in effort, the educational value of good example, and respect for universal fundamental ethical principles. The goal of Olympism is to place everywhere sport at the service of the harmonious development of man, with a view to encouraging the establishment of a peaceful society concerned with the preservation of human dignity."

Dr. John Powell, an eminent lecturer and author on Olympic ideals, has proposed another definition, which in 1986 was adopted by the Executive Committee of the Canadian Olympic Association, "Olympism is a harmony of ideas and ideals that affirm the value of Olympic sport in promoting and developing sound physical and moral qualities in individuals, and in contributing to a better and more peaceful world by enabling representatives of nations to meet in an atmosphere of mutual respect and international amity."

Oman [OMA]. Oman formed an NOC in 1982 that the IOC recognized in the same year. Oman made its Olympic début in 1984 at Los Angeles, where it was represented in shooting, track & field athletics, and yachting. Oman also competed in 1988, 1992, and 1996. Its best Olympic finish came in 1988 when Mohammad Al-Malky finished eighth in the 400 meters in track & field athletics. Oman has never competed at the Olympic Winter Games.

Ono, Takashi [JPN–GYM]. B. 26 July 1931, Noshiro, Akita Prefecture. Takashi Ono was the first Japanese to win an individual Olympic gold medal for gymnastics. He won the horizontal bar in 1956 and 1960, shared first place in the horse vault in 1960, and won also team gold in 1956 and 1960. To his five gold medals, he added four silver and four bronze medals, highlighted by silver medals in the all-around in both 1956 and 1960. At the World Championships, Ono won four silver medals and a bronze in 1958 and won the World Championships on the horizontal bar in 1962.

Organización Deportiva Centroamericana y del Caribe [ODE-CABE]. The Organización Deportiva Centroamericana y del Caribe is a confederation of National Olympic Committees (NOCs) (q.v.) of the Central American and Caribbean region. The organization is headquartered in Mexico City and its president is José Joaquin Puello of the Dominican Republic.

Organización Deportiva Panamericana [ODEPA]. *See* PAN AMERICAN SPORTS ORGANIZATION (PASO).

Organizing Committees of the Olympic Games [OCOGs/COJOs]. The organization of each Olympic Games is entrusted by the IOC to an Organizing Committee, which is then in charge of producing the Olympic Games. The committees are formed exclusively for the purpose of putting on the Olympics and, as such, dissolve shortly after the Olympics are held. The French acronym stands *for Comité d'Organisateur des jeux Olympiques.*

Orienteering. Orienteering has never been contested at the Olympic Games, even as a demonstration sport (q.v.). However, the International Orienteering Federation (IOF) is recognized by the IOC. The IOF was founded in 1961 and currently has 49 affiliated member nations.

Osburn, Carl Townsend [USA–SHO]. B. 5 May 1884, Jacksontown, Ohio. D. 28 December 1966, Helena, California. Carl Osburn was the most successful Olympic marksman in history. At the Games of 1912, 1920, and 1924, he won five gold, four silver, and two bronze medals for a record total of 11 medals. Three of his five gold medals came in 1920. He was a career Naval officer who graduated from Annapolis in 1906 and rose to the rank of Commander. Besides his Olympic shooting success, Osburn competed internationally for the United States at the World Championships of 1921, 1922, 1923, and 1924, and at the Pan-American Matches of 1913.

Otto, Kristin [GDR–SWI]. B. 7 February 1966, Leipzig. Kristin Otto's six gold medals at one Games (1988) is a women's record for any sport. In Seoul, Otto uniquely won gold medals in three different strokes, freestyle, backstroke, and butterfly, and her overall performance at the 1988 Games ranks as one of history's greatest sporting achievements. At the World Championships (1982, 1986), she won seven gold medals. Otto set two individual world records and contributed to four relay world records in her career.

Owens, James Cleveland "Jesse" [USA–ATH]. B. 12 September 1913, Decatur, Alabama. D. 31 March 1980, Tucson, Alabama. Jesse Owens is an Olympic legend whose four gold medals at the 1936 Games (100 meters, 200 meters, 4 x 100-meters relay, and long jump) did much to undermine Hitler's myth of Aryan superiority. His place in sporting history had already been assured when he set six world records in one day (25 May 1935) and his long jump record of 26'8¼" (8.13 meters), set that day, remained a world best for more than 25 years. At the end of the 1936 season, Owens turned professional and in his later years, he traveled extensively as a speaker promoting the cause of Olympism (q.v.) and related philosophies.

– P –

Pakistan [PAK]. Pakistan first competed at the Olympic Games in 1948. It did not attend the 1980 Moscow Olympics, but has attended all Games since. It has never competed at the Olympic Winter

Games. Pakistan owes almost its entire Olympic success to one sport: field hockey. It won a medal in this sport at every celebration from 1956 through 1984, finished fourth in 1948 and 1952, fifth in 1988, third in 1992, sixth in 1996, and fourth in 2000. In 1960, it won the gold medal, defeating India in the final and ending its 32-year Olympic winning streak, a feat it repeated in both 1968 and 1984.

Palestine [PLE]. A Palestine Olympic Committee existed prior to World War II, formed in 1933. Palestine was ruled under a British mandate from 1921 through 1948. During those years, Palestine had an NOC that was recognized by the IOC, although it never competed at the Olympic Games. The Palestine Olympic Committee was titularly to represent Jews, Muslims, and Christians from the region of Palestine, but the rules of the original Palestine NOC stated that "(they) represent the Jewish National Home." Thus, that Olympic Committeee was more a precursor of the Israel Olympic Committee than of the current Palestine Olympic Committee. *See* ISRAEL.

Palestine currently has no exact geographic boundaries, but its NOC was given provisional recognition by the IOC at its annual meeting in Monte Carlo in September 1993. This occurred shortly after the historic agreement signed between the Palestine Liberation Organization (PLO) and the state of Israel in that same month. Palestine first competed at the Olympic Games in 1996 when it was represented by a single athlete, who finished last in his heat of the 10,000 meters. Palestine was represented at Sydney in 2000 by one female swimmer and one male runner.

Palau [PLW]. The Palau NOC was granted provisional recognition by the IOC in 1998 and full recognition followed in 1999. Palau made its Olympic début in 2000 at Sydney, represented by five athletes: two in track & field athletics (one male/one female), two swimmers (one male/one female), and one woman in weightlifting.

Pan American Sports Organization [PASO]. The Pan American Sports Organization (PASO) is a confederation of National Olympic Committees (NOCs) (q.v.) in the Americas. It was founded on 8 August 1948 and, in 1955, the current structure was put in place and the current name of the group was adopted. The official languages of the group are English and Spanish and its name is listed as both the Pan American Sports Organization (PASO) and the Organización Deportiva Panamericana (ODEPA). The group's goals, as listed in its charter, are "To strengthen and tighten the bonds of friendship and solidarity among the peoples of America; to further the development and growth of the Olympic Ideal; to cooperate with the NOCs of the Americas; to ensure the periodic celebration of the Pan American Games; and to coordinate the Olympic and Pan American Solidarity Programs." The organization is headquartered in Mexico City and the current president (2000) is Mario Vázquez Raña of Mexico. As of 2000, there are 42 member nations.

Panama [PAN]. Panama was represented at the Olympics in 1928, 1948, and 1952 by a single athlete. It has sent larger contingents since 1960, although the country did not attend the 1980 Moscow Olympics. It has never competed in the Olympic Winter Games. Its lone competitor in 1948 did quite well, as Lloyd LaBeach won Panama's only two Olympic medals to date, finishing third in both the 100- and 200-meter dashes.

Pankration—Ancient Olympic Sport. The pankration was a violent sport with virtually no holds barred, in which kicking played an important part. It was a very popular sport with the fans, and was actually less brutal than boxing because the pankratiasts wore no gloves that inflicted so much harm on the boxers. Plato described it as "a contest combining incomplete wrestling with incomplete boxing." The first recorded champion was Lygdamis of Syracuse in 648 B.C., and champions are recorded through Aurelius Phoibammon of Egypt in 221 A.D. Five separate athletes won at least three championships at Olympia in the pankration. A boys' pankration was held from 200 B.C. through 117 A.D. One of the most famous pankration champions, Arrikion of Figaleia, was killed while successfully defending his title in this sport. He was awarded the title posthumously when his opponent was disqualified.

Papp, László [HUN–BOX]. B. 25 March 1926, Budapest. After winning the Olympic middleweight title in 1948, László Papp won the light-middleweight crown in 1952 and 1956 to become the first boxer to win three Olympic gold medals. Possibly his finest victory in the Olympic ring came in the 1956 final when he beat José Torres (USA), a future world professional champion. A skillful, hard-punching southpaw, Papp was the first fighter from the Soviet bloc to turn professional and he won the European middleweight title in 1962. However, in 1965, the Hungarian authorities withdrew their permission for him to fight professionally and the chance of a world title bout was denied him.

Papua New Guinea [PNG, formerly NGU]. Papua New Guinea has competed at every Olympic Games since they made their début in 1976, with the exception of 1980. In 1992, Henry Kungsi posted its best Olympic performance yet. A lightweight boxer, he won one match to finish equal ninth of 29 competitors in his class. No athletes from Papua New Guinea have competed in the Olympic Winter Games.

Paraguay [PAR]. Paraguay has competed at every Olympic Games since their début in 1968, with the exception of 1980. It has not yet won a medal. Its two finest Olympic performances were in 1992 when its football (soccer) team finished sixth of 16 teams, and in 2000, when Rossana de los Rios de Neffa finished equal 9th of 64 competitors in women's singles tennis. Paraguay has not yet competed at the Olympic Winter Games.

Paralympic Games. The Paralympic Games are an international sporting event, specifially for athletes with disabilities. They typically follow the Olympic Games, usually in the same city that hosts the Olympic Games. Recent rules changes mandated by the IOC 2000 Commission have made it mandatory that the Paralympics be held just after the Olympic Games in the same city as the Olympics. The Paralympic Games are organized by the International Paralympic Committee, which is an organization recognized by the International Olympic Committee. The Paralympics trace their beginnings to shortly after World War II and the Stoke Mandeville Games. The Stoke Mandeville Hospital in England is a well-known spinal cord injury research and treatment center. The hospital began sponsoring a series of Games in 1948, called the *Stoke Mandeville Games*. The Games were originally for athletes with paralysis, and were started by Dr. Ludwig Guttman.

The Paralympics first began in 1960 at Rome, and have expanded on the Stoke Mandeville concept to include many other disabilities, including amputees and blind athletes. The International Paralympic Committee (IPC) has its headquarters in Bonn, Germany. In addition to the IPC, the IOC recognizes several other organizations for athletes with disabilities. These include the Cerebral Palsy International Sports and Recreation Association (CP-ISRA), the International Blind Sports Federation (IBSA), the International Sports Federation for Persons with an Intellectual Disability (INAS-FID), the International Sports Organization of the Disabled (ISOD), the Comité International des Sports des Sourds (CISS—Deaf Athletes), and the forerunner of them all, the International Stoke Mandeville Wheelchair Sports Federation (ISMWSF).

The Stoke Mandeville Wheelchair Games continue to be held annually in Buckinghamshire, England. The Paralympics have been expanded to include a Winter version, conducted since 1976. Like the Summer Paralympics, they are usually held in the same city as the Olympic Winter Games, with the following exceptions: 1976—Ornskoldsvik, Sweden (not Innsbruck); 1980—Geilo, Norway (not Lake Placid), and 1984—Innsbruck, Austria (not Sarajevo).

The IOC also recognizes Special Olympics International, which is an American group that organizes sporting events for athletes with disabilities. Originally, Special Olympics began as an American sports festival, but it has expanded and now includes international events as well, highlighted by the Special Olympic World Games, which are also held in both Summer and Winter Versions. The Special Olympic World Games began in 1968 in Chicago, with their most recent celebration having been held in Raleigh-Durham, North Carolina in 1999. The Special Olympics World Winter Games began in 1977 in Steamboat Springs, Colorado, with their most recent celebration occuring in 1997 at Toronto/Collingswood, Ontario, Canada.

Parisi, Angelo [GBR/FRA–JUD]. B. 3 January 1953, Italy. With four Olympic medals (one gold, two silver, one bronze), Angelo Parisi is the most successful *judoka* in Olympic history. Italian born, he won a bronze in the open class in 1972 representing Great Britain, and then represented France in 1980 and 1984, following his marriage to a French woman. In 1980, Parisi won the unlimited class title and placed second in the open class. In 1984, he won his fourth medal with a silver in the unlimited class. Parisi never managed to win at the World Championships.

Patzaichin, Ivan [ROM–CAN]. B. 26 November 1949, Tulcea. Ivan Patzaichin won 13 canoeing titles at the Olympic Games and World Championships, equaling the record for men set by Gert Fredriksson (SWE) (q.v.) and Rüdiger Helm (GDR). His Olympic record included seven medals, of which four were gold and three silver. Patzaichin competed at five Olympic Games, from 1968 through 1984, representing the Dinamo Bucharest club for Romania. His Olympic titles were the C2–1000 in 1968, the C1–1000 in 1972, the C2–1000 in 1980, and the C2–1000 in 1984. His World Championships were at C2–500 in 1979, C2–1000 in 1970, 1973, and 1981, the C1–1000 in 1977, and the C1–10K in 1978.

Pelota Basque. Pelota is a generic name for various hand-and-ball or racquet-and-ball games derived from the ancient French racquet sport of *jeu de paume.* It has similarities to the American parimutuel betting sport of jai alai. Pelota basque, the Spanish variant played in the Basque regions and contiguous provinces of France and Spain, has thrice been an Olympic demonstration sport in 1924, 1968, and 1992. In addition, at the unusual Olympic Games of 1900, a version of pelota can be considered to have been an Olympic sport. The Fédération Internationale de Pelote Basque (FIPV) was founded in 1929 and is recognized by the IOC, with 25 affiliated national members in 2000.

Pentathlon—Ancient Olympic Sport. The five events of the ancient pentathlon were jumping, a *stadion* race (sprint of about 190 meters), the discus throw, the javelin throw, and wrestling. The origin of the event is attributed to Jason (of Argonaut fame). According to mythology, Jason was to award the prizes at an ancient games, and his friend Peleus was second in all the contests. So, Jason combined the events out of a desire to honor his friend, and thus created the pentathlon.

It is unclear how the winner of the pentathlon was decided. The precise order of the events is also unclear. It is only known with certainty that the last event was wrestling. If any athlete won any three events, he was immediately declared the winner, and the ancient term *triakter* is often seen, meaning the winner of three events. However, classics and Olympics scholars have not agreed on how the victor was determined in other circumstances.

Pentathlon, Modern. *See* MODERN PENTATHLON.

People's Democratic Republic of Yemen [YMD]. *See* YEMEN.

Persia. Although Persia had two early members of the IOC, Mizzam Eddin Khoi (1921–1923) and Prince Samad Khan Momtazos Saltaneh (1923–1927), interest in Olympic matters was virtually nonexistent in the country. The fact that both of these IOC members were resident in Europe did nothing to improve matters and it was not until the 1930s, when a program of modernization began and Persia became known as *Iran* that a degree of Olympic interest developed. *See also* IRAN.

Peru [PER]. After IOC member Carlos de Candamo competed as a fencer in the 1900 Olympics, Peru's next Olympic appearance was in 1936. It has since missed only the 1952 Games in Helsinki. The country has not competed at the Olympic Winter Games. Peru has won four Olympic medals, with one gold medal. Three of these were won in shooting and one in women's volleyball. Oddly, the nation has won one medal each in 1948, 1984, 1988, and 1992.

Philippines, The [PHI]. The Philippines first competed at the Olympics in 1924, and has since missed only the 1980 Moscow Olympics. The Philippines has competed at the Olympic Winter Games of 1972, 1988, and 1992. The Philippines has won nine Olympic medals in boxing, swimming, and track & field athletics. Though the country has not yet won a gold medal in an official sport, Arianne Cerdena won the women's bowling event in that exhibition sport in 1988.

Pierre de Coubertin Commission. The Pierre de Coubertin Commission was created in 1975 and works to promulgate the teachings of Baron Pierre de Coubertin and his philosophy. It works very closely with the International Pierre de Coubertin Committee in this regard. IOC president Juan Antonio Samaranch (q.v.) serves as the Commission president. The current vice chairman is Spanish Judge Conrado Durántez, who is president of the International Pierre de Coubertin Committee. The commission and committee work closely with the International Olympic Academy (IOA) (q.v.) and various National Olympic Academies to spread Coubertin's message. The commission consists of Samaranch, one other IOC member, Nikos Filaretos (GRE), and several academicians.

Pietri, Dorando [ITA–ATH]. B. 16 October 1885, Mandrio, Reggio Emilia. D. 7 February 1942. Dorando Pietri is the most famous loser in Olympic history. Entering the stadium at the end of the 1908 Olympic marathon he held a comfortable lead over Johnny Hayes (USA), but then collapsed five times and had to be helped across the finishing line. This assistance from well-meaning officials resulted in his disqualification but, in defeat, Pietri's fame far exceeded that of the winner. Queen Alexandra presented him with a large gold cup that was an exact replica of the one awarded to the Olympic champion, and Irving Berlin wrote the popular song "Dorando" in his honor. Pietri turned professional shortly after the 1908 Olympics and enjoyed a successful career in America and Europe.

Pindar [GRE]. *fl. ca.* 520–440 B.C. Pindar was a Greek lyric poet, considered the greatest of the Greek choral lyricists. Few details remain of his life, but he was known to have been an aristocrat from Thebes who studied in Athens. Pindar is best known for his *epinicia,* which were odes celebrating athletic victories. Forty-four of these have survived, most celebrating victories in the Olympic, Isthmian, Nemean, and Pythian Games (qq.v.). The odes were usually commissioned by the victor or his family.

Poland [POL]. Poland competed continuously at the Olympic Games from 1924 through 1980, and after boycotting Los Angeles in 1984, returned to the Olympic fold in 1988 at Seoul. Prior to 1924, several Poles probably competed for other countries. In 1908, Jerzy Gajdzyk, his name Americanized to George Gaidzik, won a diving bronze medal for the United States. In 1912, the Polish-born Julius Beresford (né Wisniewski) won a silver medal with the British eight-oared crew. The 1912 Russian Olympic team included eight Poles. Poland has also competed at all the Olympic Winter Games since 1924. Through 2000, Poland has won 245 Olympic medals, 57 of them gold, with all but four of the medals.

Polo. Polo has been contested at the Olympics in 1900, 1908, 1920, 1924, and 1936. The Fédération Internationale de Polo (FIP) was founded in 1985 and is an IOC-recognized federation, currently with 48 national members.

Portugal [POR]. Portugal has competed at the Olympic Games continuously since 1912. Through 1984, Portugal had appeared at the Olympic Winter Games once with only one competitor. That was Duarte Espirito Santo Silva, who competed in Alpine skiing events in 1952 at Oslo. However, Portugal also competed at the Olympic Winter Games in 1988, 1994, and 1998. Portugal has won 17 Olympic medals through 2000, three of them gold. It has yet to win a medal at the Olympic Winter Games.

Pound Report. *See* OLYMPIC BRIBERY SCANDAL.

Pound, Richard William Duncan, Q.C. [CAN]. B. 22 March 1942, St. Catharines, Ontario. Dick Pound was a swimming finalist (sixth in the 100-meter freestyle) at the 1960 Olympic Games, who became president of the Canadian Olympic Association in 1977 and a member of the International Olympic Committee (IOC) (q.v.) the following year. In 1987, he was appointed a vice president of the IOC. In recent years, he has exerted considerable influence in the financial sphere, particularly in negotiations with sponsors and the sale of TV rights. Pound has been chairman of the IOC Finance Commission since its inception. A Montreal-based lawyer specializing in tax law, Pound earned his undergraduate and law degrees at McGill University in Montreal. His legal skills provided invaluable support to president Juan Antonio Samaranch (q.v.) in the negotiations with North Korea over the 1988 Games. He was also the Chairman of the IOC commission that oversaw the Olympic Bribery Scandal (q.v.) in 1999, and has been named Chairman of the World Anti-Doping Agency (WADA) (q.v.). Pound is expected to be one of the prime candidates to succeed Samaranch as president of the IOC in 2001.

Press Commission. The Press Commission was originally called the *Press and Public Relations Commission*, which was formed in 1967 and lasted until 1972. A separate Press Commission was formed in 1973. The current Chairman is Australian IOC member R. Kevan Gosper, a former Olympic 400-meter runner. Three other IOC members are on the commission, along with representatives of the world's sporting press. Prior to becoming IOC presidents, both Lord Killanin and Juan Antonio Samaranch (qq.v.) served as chairmen of this commission.

Protopopov, Oleg Alekseyevich [URS–FSK]. *See* BELOUSOVA, LYUDMILA.

Puerto Rico [PUR]. Puerto Rico first competed at the 1948 Olympics in London and has competed at every Olympic Games since then. Puerto Rico has also competed at the Olympic Winter Games of 1984, 1988, 1992, 1994, and 1998. Puerto Rican athletes have won one silver and five bronze medals at the Olympic Games.

Pythian Games. The Pythian Games were one of the four great Panhellenic sporting festivals, along with the Olympic Games, Isthmian Games, and Nemean Games (qq.v.). They were held in honor of Apollo at Delphi. They were the only one of the four main Greek festivals that also featured musical contests. The Pythian Games were first recorded in 582 B.C. and continued until the fourth century A.D. The Pythian Games were held quadrennially, in the third year of each Olympiad. The victors at the Pythian Games were awarded a laurel crown.

– Q –

Qatar [QAT]. Qatar made its initial Olympic appearance in Los Angeles in 1984 with a team of eight track & field athletes, a football (soccer) team, and four shooters. Qatar also competed in 1988, 1992, 1996, and 2000. Qatar won its first Olympic medal in 1992 when Mohamed Sulaiman finished third in the men's 1,500 meters in track & field athletics. In 2000, Said Asaad added another bronze, won in the 105-kg. class weightlifting. Qatar has never competed at the Olympic Winter Games.

– R –

Race in Armor—Ancient Olympic Sport. The race in armor was contested at Olympia from 520 B.C. through at least 185 A.D. It was also known as the *hoplite* event. The event was held over two laps of the stadium (about 385 meters). Leonidas of Rhodes won four championships consecutively, from 164 to 152 B.C.

Rackets. Rackets has been contested as an Olympic sport only in 1908, when a men's singles and doubles event was held in London.

Racquetball. Racquetball is decidedly different from rackets and is a very modern sport. It has not been contested at the Olympic Games, but the International Racquetball Federation (IRF) is recognized by the IOC. It was founded in 1968 and currently has 90 affiliated member nations.

Radio and Television Commission. The Radio and Television Commission has been known by various names. The first "media" commission was the Press and Public Relations Commission, which was formed in 1967 and lasted until 1972. At that time, two separate commissions, the Press Commission and the Television Commission were created. A Radio Commission existed briefly in 1984. In 1985, this was merged with the Television Commission to form the Radio and Television Commission. The current chairman of the commission is the Korean IOC member Kim Un-Yong. Six IOC members are on the commission, but the bulk of this commission is made up of representatives of the television and radio networks worldwide, as well as representatives of the OCOGs (q.v.) who deal with the electronic media.

Radmilovic, Paul [GBR–WAP]. B. 5 March 1886, Cardiff, Glamorgan, Wales. D. 29 September 1968, Weston-Super-Mare, Somerset. Paul Radmilovic won water polo gold medals at three successive Olympic Games (1908, 1912, 1920) and also swam on the British 4 x 200 freestyle relay team that won in 1908. Radmilovic competed in Olympic water polo again in 1924 and 1928. His career was marked by its extraordinary length and by the range of distances over which he excelled. He won his first national swimming title in 1901 and the last in 1929 and he won championships at distances from 100 yards to 5 miles. Radmilovic had a Yugoslavian father and an Irish mother. In 1967, he was the first Briton to be inducted into the International Swimming Hall of Fame.

Real Tennis. *See* JEU DE PAUME.

Redgrave, Stephen Geoffrey [GBR-ROW]. B. 23 March 1962, Amersham. With five Olympic gold medals and one bronze, Steve Redgrave is the most successful Olympic oarsman of all time. After winning the coxed fours in 1984, he won the coxless pairs at the next three Games (1988, 1992, 1996) and added a bronze in the coxed pairs in 1988. At Sydney in 2000, he added his fifth gold medal in the coxless fours, at which he had also been world champion in 1999. Redgrave won gold medals at the World Championships in coxless pairs in 1991, 1993, 1994, and 1995, and in the coxless fours in 1997 and 1999. In 1986, he became the first rower to win three gold medals at the Commonwealth Games. At Henley, he was Diamond Sculls champion in both 1983 and 1985. In 1989, Redgrave was also a member of the crew that won the British four-man bobsled title.

Regional International Games. In addition to the Olympic Games, numerous international sporting events are held throughout the world each year. Many of these are simply international championships in the various sports, such as the World Gymnastics Championships or the World Athletics Championships. But in addition, since the 1910s, the nations of the world have gathered together to compete in regional international multisport competitions. The International Olympic Committee (IOC) (q.v.) has encouraged this because it follows some of the principles of Olympism and the Olympic Movement (qq.v.)—bringing together the various peoples of the world in peaceful sporting competition. In addition, as the Olympic Games grow and grow, the Regional International Games often now serve as qualifying events for the Olympic Games. Thus, they have become even more important. In addition, two of the Regional Games have had definite importance to the various political battles afflicting the Olympic Movement. These are the Games of the New Emerging Forces (GANEFO) and the Goodwill Games.

The various Regional Games number probably over 100, but the most important of them are listed: African Games, Arab Games, Arctic Winter Games, Asian Games, Asian Winter Games, Baltic Sea Games, Black Sea Games, Bolivarian Games, Central American and Caribbean Games, Central American Games, Central Asian Games, Commonwealth Games (formerly the British Empire Games), East Asian Games, Far East Championships, Games of the Small Countries of Europe, Games of the New Emerging Forces (q.v.), Goodwill Games (qq.v.), Goodwill Winter Games, Indian Ocean Islands Games, Inter-Allied Games, Island Games, Mediterranean Games, Micronesian Games, Nordic Games (q.v.), Pacific Ocean Games, Pan-American Games, South American Games, South Asian Federation Games, South East Asian Games, South Pacific Games, South Pacific Mini Games, and the West Asian Games.

Revival of the Olympic Games. *See* ATTEMPTS AT REVIVAL.

Revue Olympique. *See* OLYMPIC REVIEW.

Rhodesia [RHO]. *See* ZIMBABWE.

Ritola, Viljo Eino "Ville" [FIN–ATH]. B. 18 January 1896, Peräseinäjoki. D. 24 April 1982, Helsinki. Ville Ritola was an outstanding distance runner who rivaled his legendary countryman, Paavo Nurmi (q.v.). At the 1924 Olympic Games, Ritola won the steeplechase in his first attempt at the race and improved his own 10,000-meter world record to win that event. He also won two further gold medals in the 3,000-meter team event and the team cross-country event. Ritola and Nurmi met on the track for the first time at these Olympics with Nurmi claiming the honors by winning the 5,000 meters and defeating Ritola in the cross-country and 3,000 meters. At the 1928 Amsterdam Olympics, the match-up was in the 5,000 meters with Ritola defeating Nurmi to win the gold medal. The 14th of 20 children, Ritola left home in 1913 to emigrate to the United States and eventually won 14 Amateur Athletic Union (AAU) titles, returning home in the Olympic years. He never competed in the Finnish national championships.

Robert Dover's Games [Cotswold Olimpick Games]. Robert Dover's Games, or Cotswold Olimpick Games, were probably first contested in 1612, during Whitsun (Pentecostal) Week upon the Cotswold Hills. The Games were started by Robert Dover, a local lawyer who lived nearby in the Cotswold Hills. The Games were basically a medieval country fair type of festival, but they achieved great fame. They were held from about 1612 to 1642 and were immortalized in a collection of 30 laudatory poems, entitled *Annalia Dubrensia,* and published about Robert Dover's Olimpick Games in 1636. Four of the poems were composed by great poets of the era: Ben Jonson, Michael Drayton, Thomas Heywood, and Sir William Davenant. It is slightly conjectural, but apparently even Shakespeare knew of these Games, possibly mentioning them in *Sir John Falstaff and the Merry Wives of Windsor.* "Slender: '. . . How does your fallow greyhound, sir? I heard say he was outrun on Cotsall.'"

The Cotswold Olimpicks did not end after 1642, but were simply stopped, during the Civil War in England. They were revived in the 1660s and were then held at unknown intervals for two centuries. In 1851, they were revived, but were shortly thereafter suspended again. After another century, the Cotswold Olimpicks were revived in 1951, were briefly suspended and then resumed in 1963 to continue to this day.

Though they were quite famous in their era, and though they have been contested for many centuries, the only justification to call them "Olympic" Games rests on the fact that they adopted that name and that they had been brought into contact with the Olympic, Pythian, Nemean, and Isthmian Games (qq.v.) via the *Annalia Dubrensia.* They had no significant influence on Pierre de Coubertin (q.v.) or others who attempted to revive the Olympic Games.

Rodnina, Irina Konstantinova (later Zaytsev) [URS–FSK]. B. 12 September 1949, Moscow. Irina Rodnina was the most successful pair skater in history. Olympic victories in 1972 with Aleksey Ulanov and in 1976 and 1980 with Aleksandr Zaytsev gave her a record total of three gold medals. Her record at the World Championships was even more impressive. Rodnina won the title for 10 successive years (1969–1978), the first four with Ulanov and the next six with Zaytsev. She married Zaytsev in 1973 and their successes in the latter part of their partnership were as husband and wife. Rodnina is now a figure skating coach.

Rogge, Chevalier Dr. Jacques [BEL]. B. 2 May 1942, Ghent. Jacques Rogge was an accomplished sailor, competing in three Olympic Games (1968, 1972, 1976) with his best finish in that sport being 14th in the Finn Monotype Class in 1972 at Munich. He also competed on one world championship team in sailing and was 16 times Belgian champion. In addition, he competed internationally for Belgium in rugby football, at which he was selected 10 times for the national team. Rogge is the former Chairman of the International Sailing Federation (ISAF) Medical Commission, serving in his capacity as an orthopaedic surgeon. He is the head of the Orthopaedic Surgery Department at Ghent Hospital. As a sports administrator, he became head of the Comité Olympique et Interfédéral Belge in 1989 and in 1990 became president of the European Olympic Committees (EOC). He was elected a member of the IOC in 1991 and was appointed to the Executive Board in 1998. Rogge is now considered one of the strongest candidates to succeed Juan Antonio Samaranch as president of the International Olympic Committee.

Roller Hockey. In 1992, roller hockey was contested as a demonstration sport (q.v.) at the Barcelona Olympics. Roller hockey has never been contested at the Olympics at any other time. Roller hockey is governed by the Fédération Internationale de Roller-Skating (FIRS). *See also* ROLLER SKATING.

Roller Skating. Roller skating has never been contested at the Olympic Games, although it is contested at many of the Regional Games, including the Pan-American Games. Roller skating is governed by the Fédération Internationale de Roller-Skating (FIRS), which was founded in 1924, and is recognized by the IOC. The FIRS currently has 107 affiliated member nations. *See also* ROLLER HOCKEY.

Romania [ROM]. Romania's first Olympic participant was future IOC member Gheorghe Plagino, who competed in the clay trap shooting event in 1900. They next competed at the 1924 Olympic Games, and have since missed only the 1932 and 1948 Olympics. Romania defied pressure from its neighbors and valiantly was the only Warsaw Pact country to compete at the 1984 Olympics in Los Angeles. Romania has competed at the Olympic Winter Games since their inception in

1924, missing only 1960. It is best known for its outstanding women gymnasts, and has also produced excellent canoeists. Romania has won 266 Olympic medals, 133 by its men and 128 by its women (five in mixed events), with 74 gold medals.

Roque. *See* CROQUET.

Rose, Iain Murray [AUS–SWI]. B. 6 January 1939, Nairn, Scotland. Murray Rose was a triple gold medalist at the 1956 Games; he won the 400- and 1,500-meter freestyle and was a member of the world record-breaking team in the 4 x 200-meter freestyle relay. After the Melbourne Games, Rose enrolled at the University of Southern California. At the 1960 Olympics, he retained his 400-meters title, won silver in the 1,500 meters, and a bronze in the relay. His total of six Olympic medals would surely have been greater but for the fact that he was not selected for the 1964 Games as he refused to return from California for the Australian Championships. Earlier in the year, Rose had set world records for 880 yards and 1,500 meters and would certainly have been a medal contender in Tokyo. Rose continued to enjoy competitive swimming long after his Olympic career was over. In 1981, he won the World Masters title in faster times than he recorded at the 1956 Games.

Rowing & Sculling. Rowing was first known as a means of transportation in the ancient cultures of Egypt, Greece, and Rome. Rowing as a sport probably began in England in the 17th and early 18th centuries. By the 19th century, rowing was popular in Europe and had been brought to America. Early races were usually contested by professionals, with heavy betting on races common. Competitive rowing precedes most of the other Olympic sports in its recorded modern history. The first Oxford-Cambridge race took place in 1828, and Yale and Harvard first rowed against each other in 1852.

Only in 1896 has rowing not been contested in the Olympics. It was actually on the program that year, but rough seas forced cancellation of the events. There have been multiple events for men in both sweep events (single oar used by alternate oarsmen) and sculling events (two oars used by a single sculler or by two or more scullers). Through 1992, these included races for single, double, and quadruple sculls, and in sweep events, races for two and four oarsmen/women, with and without coxswain, and the large boats with eight oarsmen/women and a coxswain. Women (q.v.) were admitted to the Olympic rowing program in 1976. They compete in a streamlined program, with only one sweep event for two and four oarswomen, but they also compete in single, double, and quad sculls, and the eight-oar sweep event. The rowing program for the 1996 Olympics underwent a drastic change with the introduction of lightweight events. The men's coxed pairs and coxed fours was discontinued, replaced by the lightweight double sculls, and lightweight coxless fours. The women's coxless pairs was also discontinued, replaced by lightweight double sculls.

The United States was the dominant nation in Olympic rowing until about 1960. The Soviet Union quickly became a power in the sport, but the German Democratic Republic (East Germany (GDR) (q.v.) was by far the pre-eminent nation in the 1970s and 1980s. The recent merger of the Germanys has changed this, although it should be noted that the Federal Republic of Germany was also a rowing power, though not on the same level as its Eastern counterpart.

The world governing body of rowing is the Fédération Internationale des Sociétés d'Aviron (FISA), which was formed in 1892 and has 110 member nations as of 2000. *See also* DRESDEN FOUR, THE GDR COXLESS FOUR ROWING TEAM [1968–1972].

Rudolph, Wilma Glodean [USA–ATH]. B. 23 June 1940, St. Bethlehem, Tennessee. D. 12 November 1994, Brentwood, Tennessee. Although born with polio and contracting scarlet fever and double pneumonia at the age of four, Wilma Rudolph overcame all these handicaps to become one of the greatest women sprinters of all time. As a 16-year-old, she won a bronze medal in the relay at the 1956 Olympics and four years later she was the heroine of the 1960 Games. After setting a world 200-meter record (22.9) at the 1960 U.S. Championships, she was a triple gold medalist at the Rome Olympics, winning the 100 meters, 200 meters, and relay. A following wind deprived her of a world record in the 100 meters, but she anchored the U.S. team to a world record in the heats of the relay. The following year, Rudolph equaled the world 100-meter record (11.3). Four days later, she posted a new record of 11.2 in addition to leading the U.S. to another world relay record. Her brilliant career ended with her retirement in 1962, after which she devoted herself to coaching and worked extensively with underprivileged children. She died fairly young from a brain tumor.

Rugby (Union) Football. Rugby Union has been contested at the Olympics in 1900, 1908, 1920, and 1924. Amazingly, the defending Olympic champions are the United States, who won the gold medals in both 1920 and 1924. The International Rugby Board (IRB) governs the sport worldwide and is recognized by the IOC. Founded in 1886, it currently has 91 member nations.

Ruiz-Conforto, Tracie [USA–SYF]. B. 4 February 1963, Honolulu, Hawaii. Tracie Ruiz-Conforto was the first Olympic star in the relatively new sport of synchronized swimming. In 1984, as *Tracie Ruiz*, she won gold medals in both the solo event and, with Candie Costie, the duet. She then retired and married a former Penn State football player. Ruiz-Conforto took up bodybuilding and competed briefly in that sport, but returned to synchronized competition in 1987. At the 1988 Olympics, she competed only in the solo event, earning a silver medal. At the Pan-American Games, she won a team gold in 1979, solo and duet golds in 1983, and a solo gold in 1987. She was 1982 World Champion in solo, and also won six U.S. Championships in the solo and four in the duet.

Ruska, Willem "Wim" [NED–JUD]. B. 29 August 1940, Amsterdam. Willem Ruska is the only *judoka* to have won two gold medals at the same Olympics. In 1972, he was the Olympic champion in the heavyweight and the open class. Ruska was also heavyweight world champion in 1967 and 1971. To this, he added seven European titles and 10 Dutch championships during his career. He was not particularly large for the unlimited or open class (110 kg. at only 1.89 meters), but was extremely muscular and cut a striking figure with his light blond hair. Ruska began his judo career at age 20 and traveled to Japan to train and learn from the Japanese masters. He retired after the 1972 Olympics.

Russia [RUS]. Prior to the Bolshevik Revolution, Russia competed at the Olympics of 1900, 1908, and 1912. Although at the first two celebrations its representation was only four and six athletes, respectively, in

1912, it sent a large team of 169 athletes. At those Olympics, Russia won one gold medal, four silver medals, and three bronze medals. After the Bolshevik Revolution, Russia became the largest republic of the Soviet Union (Union of Soviet Socialist Republics [q.v.]). The Soviet Union did not compete in the Olympics from 1920 to 1948, but returned to the Olympic Games at Helsinki in 1952, and competed in the Olympics through 1988. With the political events of 1991, Russia again became eligible to compete as an individual nation. At Albertville and Barcelona, Russia joined with other former Soviet republics to compete as the *Unified Team* (q.v.), representing the Commonwealth of Independent States (q.v.). Russia returned to the Olympic fold after an absence of 82 years in 1994 at Lillehammer. Russia has also competed at the 1996 and 2000 Olympic Games and the 1998 Olympic Winter Games. Through 2000, Russian athletes have won 198 medals at the Olympics, with 79 gold. Of these medals, 56 came in the Summer Olympics and 42 at the Winter Olympics.

Rwanda [RWA]. Rwanda first competed in the Olympics in 1984 and has since participated in 1988, 1992, 1996, and 2000. Apart from 1992, when the Rwandan team included three cyclists, and 2000, when they had one male and female swimmer, their representation has been exclusively in track & field athletics. Rwanda has not yet competed in the Olympic Winter Games and no Rwandan athlete has won an Olympic medal.

Ryskal, Inna Valeryevna [URS/AZE–VOL]. B. 15 June 1944, Baku. Inna Ryskal won four consecutive Olympic medals playing for the Soviet volleyball team from 1964 to 1976. In 1972 and 1976, she helped the Soviets to gold medals, and she won silver medals in 1964 and 1976. She also played on a World Championship team in 1970 and European Championship teams in 1963, 1967, and 1971.

– S –

Saar, The. In 1952, the Saar was recognized as a separate Olympic Committee by the IOC and competed at the Helsinki Olympics, represented by 31 athletes, but winning no medals. The Saar was reunited with the Federal Republic of Germany in 1956. Its athletes were absorbed by the combined German teams and the Saar Olympic Committee was dissolved on 20 September 1956. Its best finishes in 1952 were equal eighth by Erich Schmidt in lightweight Græco-Roman wrestling, and ninth by Therese Zenz in women's kayak singles canoeing.

Ságiné-Ujlakiné-Rejtő, Ildikő [HUN–FEN]. B. 11 May 1937. Ildikő Ságiné-Ujlakiné-Rejtő has the unusual distinction of winning Olympic medals under three different names—as *Miss Rejtő* in 1960, as *Mrs. Ujlakiné-Rejtő* in 1964 and 1968, and as *Mrs. Ságiné-Ujlakiné-Rejtő* in 1972 and 1976. She shares this with German speed skater Andrea Ehrig-Schöne-Mitscherlich (q.v.). Ildikő won seven Olympic medals, including gold in the individual and team foil in 1964. At the World Championships, she won four titles—individual foil in 1963, and team foil in 1962, 1967, and 1973.

Sailer, Anton "Toni" [AUT–ASK]. B. 17 November 1935, Kitzbühel. Toni Sailer, known as "The Blitz from Kitz," because of his hometown, was the greatest Alpine skier in Olympic history. Although his feat of winning all three Alpine events at the 1956 Winter Games was matched by Jean-Claude Killy (q.v.) 12 years later, Sailer's overall performance was far more impressive. He won the downhill by 3.5 seconds, the slalom by 4.0 seconds, and the giant slalom by a remarkable 6.2 seconds, whereas Killy's margins of victory were far narrower. Sailer was also World Champion at Alpine combination (1956, 1958) and the downhill and slalom (1958). His career at the international level lasted only four seasons before he retired to become a hotelier and an occasional film actor and singer. A national hero, he was appointed technical director of the Austrian Alpine team in 1972.

Sailing. Sailing as a competitive sport was called *yachting* until recently. The international federation changed the sport's competitive name in an attempt to limit the elitist connotation associated with the term *yachting*. The sport has been termed *yachting* at the Olympics through 1996 and *sailing*, in effect, made its Olympic début in 2000 at Sydney.

Yachting actually began as a form of sailing, which has been practiced since antiquity as a means of transportation. In the modern sense, yachting probably originated in the Netherlands, and the word seems to come from the Dutch "jaght" or "jaght schip," probably a light, fast naval craft.

Sailing sport was brought to England by King Charles II about 1660 after his exile to Holland. International yacht racing began in 1851 when a syndicate of members of the New York Yacht Club built a 101-foot schooner named *America*. The yacht was sailed to England where it won a trophy called the *Hundred Guineas Cup* in a race around the Isle of Wight under the auspices of the Royal Yacht Squadron. The trophy was renamed The America's Cup, after the yacht, not after the United States, as is commonly thought. Sailing is now governed worldwide by the International Sailing Federation (ISAF), formerly the International Yacht Racing Union (IYRU), which was formed in 1907 and currently has 121 nations.

Sailing was first contested at the 1900 Olympics. It made its next Olympic appearance in 1908 and has been on every Olympic program since that year. Sailing has had a very varied program that is usually changed every few Olympiads as the popularity of various boats waxes and wanes. Women (q.v.) have always been allowed to compete in Olympic sailing with men. In 1988, separate sailing events exclusively for women were introduced. In 1984, the popular sport of boardsailing was also added to the Olympic program, and a separate boardsailing event for women was placed on the program for the first time in 1992.

The current trend is toward smaller boats with crews of only 1–3 people aboard. At Sydney in 2000, there were three events open only to men: Mistral boardsailing (1 person), Finn Monotype (1 person), and 470 Class (2 persons); three events open only to women: Mistral boardsailing (1 person), European Monotype (1 person), and 470 Class (2 persons); and five mixed events: Laser Dinghy (1 person), 49er Open Dinghy (2 persons), Laser Class (2 persons), Star Class (2 persons), and Soling Class (3 persons).

Sailing is contested at the Olympics in a series of fleet races, with points awarded for the placement in each race. The only exception is the Soling Class. In Soling, a short series of fleet races qualifies boats for a match racing elimination tournament.

Saint Cyr, Henri Julius Révérenoy [SWE–EQU]. B. 15 March 1902, Stockholm. D. 27 July 1979. Henri Saint Cyr began his Olympic career in 1936 with the Swedish three-day team. In 1960, he ended his Olympic career, having appeared in five different Olympics with five different horses. He was the first rider to win two individual Olympic gold medals in dressage, 1952 and 1956, and he led Sweden to team gold medals at both Olympics. In 1956, he took the Oath of the Athletes at the Opening Ceremony on behalf of the competitors at the Olympic Equestrian Games in Stockholm.

Saint Kitts and Nevis [SKN]. *See* ST. KITTS AND NEVIS.

Saint Lucia [LCA]. Saint Lucia was given official recognition by the IOC in September 1993, and the country first competed at the Atlanta Olympic Games in 1996. They have not yet competed in the Olympic Winter Games.

Saint Vincent and the Grenadines [VIN]. *See* ST. VINCENT AND THE GRENADINES.

Salnikov, Vladimir Valeryevich [URS–SWI]. B. 21 May 1960, Leningrad. At the 1980 Games, Vladimir Salnikov won gold medals in the 400 meters, the 1,500 meters (with the first ever sub-15-minute time), and the 4 x 200-meter freestyle relay. He remained the world's greatest long-distance swimmer, although the Soviet boycott (q.v.) of the 1984 Games denied him the opportunity of Olympic honors in that year. But he returned from near retirement to win a stunning victory in the 1,500 freestyle at the 1988 Seoul Olympics. Salnikov set six world records at 400 meters (1979–1983), four at 800 meters (1979–1986), and three at 1,500 meters (1980–1983). At the World Championships, he won the 400 meters and 1,500 meters in both 1978 and 1982.

Salumäe, Erika [URS/EST–CYC]. B. 11 June 1962. Erika Salumäe came to sports late; she took up cycling in 1981 and made the Soviet national team in 1984. She won the 1987 and 1989 world sprint championship and in 1988 and 1992 was Olympic match sprint champion. Her victory in 1992 at the Olympics was poignant because it was the first victory for Estonia at the Olympic Games after its independence from the Soviet Union. Salumäe also set several world records for the 200 meters (flying start) and 1,000-meters time trial from a standing start.

Samaranch (Torrelo), Juan Antonio, Marquis de Samaranch [ESP]. B. 17 July 1920, Barcelona. Juan Antonio Samaranch is the current and seventh president of the International Olympic Committee (IOC) (q.v.). First appointed to the IOC in 1966, he became a vice president in 1974 before succeeding Lord Killanin as president in 1980. During this period, he was also appointed as Spanish Ambassador to the Soviet Union in 1977. His period of office as president of the IOC has been marked by the transformation of the Olympic Movement into a vast business-like organization, although not all the changes have met with the approval of the traditionalists. Ably supported by a dedicated group of vice presidents, he has taken the Olympic Movement into the modern era. Although not unique among IOC presidents in having to face situations that threatened the fabric of the Olympic Movement, his diplomatic skills were invaluable in such matters as containing the boycotts of the 1984 and 1988 Games. In 1991, he was ennobled by the King of Spain for his services to Olympism (q.v.). Samaranch's reign was marred by the Olympic Bribery Scandal (q.v.) that erupted in 1998–1999, the events of which occurred during his term of office. In mid-1999, the IOC supported Samaranch by giving him an almost unanimous vote of confidence. Samaranch will step down as president after the IOC session in July 2001.

Samoa, American. *See* AMERICAN SAMOA.

Samoa [SAM]. Formerly called *Western Samoa*, Samoa has competed at the Olympic Games of 1984, 1988, 1992, 1996, and 2000. Marcus Stephan, a 1992 featherweight weightlifter, finished ninth of 31 in his class, this being the best finish by a Samoan in the Olympics. Samoa has not yet competed at the Olympic Winter Games.

San Marino [SMR]. San Marino has competed at nine Summer Olympics—those of 1960, and all those from 1968 to 2000. It has competed at the Olympic Winter Games of 1976, 1984, 1988, 1992, and 1994, but missed 1998. The best finish by an athlete from San Marino was fifth in small-bore rifle (prone) shooting in 1984 by Francesco Nanni.

São Tomé and Príncipe [STP]. São Tomé and Príncipe was given official recognition by the IOC in September 1993, and the country first competed at the Olympic Games in Atlanta in 1996. They have not yet competed in the Olympic Winter Games.

Saudi Arabia [KSA, formerly SAU]. Recognized by the IOC in 1965, Saudi Arabia has competed at every Olympics since 1972, with the exception of 1980. It has never competed in the Olympic Winter Games. Saudi Arabia won its first Olympic medals at Sydney in 2000. Hadj Souan Somayli won a silver in the men's 400-meter intermediate hurdles, and Khaled Al-Eid won an equestrian bronze in individual show jumping.

Sautin, Dmitry [RUS/EUN-DIV]. B. 12 June 1982, Voronege. With six Olympic medals, Dmitry Sautin has won more Olympic medals than any other diver. Representing the Unified Team (Équipe Unifié) in 1992, he earned a bronze on the springboard. In 1996, he was the gold medalist on the platform, representing Russia. The addition of synchronized events in 2000 allowed Sautin to enter four diving events in Sydney and he won medals in all four events, topped by a gold medal in the synchronized platform event. Sautin was also world champion on the springboard in 1998 and the platform in 1994 and 1998, and European champion on the springboard in 1995 and 1997 and the platform in 1993.

Savón Fabré, Félix [CUB–BOX]. B. 22 September 1967. Félix Savón Fabré has likely been the greatest heavy boxer of the later 1980s and early 1990s, amateur or pro included. He began his international career winning the 1986 World Championship in the heavyweight class, and has since won that title six times consecutively: 1986, 1989, 1991, 1993, 1995, and 1997. Cuba boycotted the 1988 Olympic Games in Seoul, which prevented Savón Fabré from a certain gold medal. But in 1992, 1996, and 2000, he easily won the Olympic gold medal in the heavyweight division. Savón Fabré also won Pan-American Games gold medals in 1987, 1991, and 1995, and won the AIBA World Challenge Matches for his weight class in 1989–1990, 1992, and 1994. He has never turned professional because of Cuba's insistence on keeping their athletes amateur only, but he would certainly have been a leading contender to become professional heavyweight world champion.

Schemansky, Norbert [USA–WLT]. B. 30 May 1924, Detroit, Michigan. Norbert Schemansky is the only man in history to win four medals in Olympic weightlifting. After placing second to John Davis in the heavyweight division at the 1947 World Championships, he again finished as runner-up to Davis at the 1948 Olympics. Schemansky then won a gold medal at the 1952 Games and two bronzes in 1960 and 1964. When Schemansky won his fourth medal (1964), he had passed his 40th birthday and is the oldest man ever to win a medal in Olympic weightlifting.

Schenk, Adrianus "Ard" [NED–SSK]. B. 16 September 1944. In his 1968 Olympic début, Ard Schenk tied for second place in the 1,500-meters speed skating. Four years later, he won three gold medals (1,500 meters, 5,000 meters, 10,000 meters). Each victory was by a wide margin and he posted new Olympic records in the 5,000 meters and 10,000 meters. Schenk emphasized his superiority over his rivals two weeks later when he became one of only four men to win all four events at the World Championships. He set 18 world records at distances from 1,000 meters to 10,000 meters between 1966 and 1972, after which he turned professional.

Schmidt-Fischer, Birgit (née Fischer) [GDR/GER–CAN]. B. 25 February 1962, Brandenburg. Birgit Schmidt-Fischer is considered the greatest woman canoeist of all time. Her total of 26 gold medals (1977–1997) at the World Championships has never been approached and her 10 (7 gold) Olympic medals is also a record for women. Representing East Germany (GDR), she won the Olympic K1 title in 1980 (as *Miss Fischer*) and the K2 and K4 in 1988. After a three-year break from competition, during which she gave birth to her second child, she won the K1 in 1992 as a member of the unified German team. Her fifth Olympic gold medal came in 1996 as a member of the German K4 team. At Sydney in 2000, Schmidt-Fischer won gold medals in both the K2 and K4 events. In addition to her seven Olympic gold medals, Schmidt-Fischer also won silver medals in the 1988 K1, the 1992 K4, and the 1996 K2. Her husband, Jörg, was a World Champion and Olympic silver medalist in canoeing.

Schneider, Vreni [SUI–ASK]. B. 26 November 1964, Elm. With five medals, Vreni Schneider has won the most Alpine skiing Olympic medals of any female, a number matched among men only by Kjetil André Aamodt (NOR) and Alberto Tomba (ITA), and among women only by Katja Seizinger (GER) (qq.v.). Schneider won both the slalom and giant slalom at the 1992 Olympic Winter Games. In 1994 at Lillehammer, she won three more medals, repeating as champion in the slalom, while earning a silver in the Alpine combined, and a bronze in the giant slalom. At the World Championships, Schneider won the giant slalom in 1987 and 1989, and the slalom in 1991. She was overall World Cup champion in 1989, winning the following event championships: 1986, 1987, 1989, and 1991 giant slalom; and the 1989, 1990, 1992, and 1993 slalom. Among women, Schneider's 55 victories trails only Austria's Annemarie Moser-Proll in overall World Cup race wins.

Schollander, Donald Arthur [USA–SWI]. B. 30 April 1946, Charlotte, North Carolina. In 1964, Don Schollander became the first swimmer to win four gold medals at one Olympic Games. His victories came in the 100- and 400-meter freestyles and in both relays, and in all but the 100 meters, he set a world record. He was unfortunate that the 200 meters was not on the program at the Tokyo Games because he set nine world records at this, his best distance (1963–1968). He also posted three world records at 400 meters and shared in eight world records in the freestyle relays. At the 1968 Games, he was unable to defend his 100- and 400-meter Olympic titles as he failed to make the U.S. team at these distances, but Schollander won his fifth gold in the 4 x 200-meter freestyle relay and took the silver in the 200-meter freestyle.

Scotland [SCO]. Scotland competed as a separate country in 1908 field hockey, finishing third, and with a separate team in the 1912 cycling road race. In all other Olympics, and in all the other sports at the 1908 and 1912 Olympics, Scotland has competed as a member of the United Kingdom of Great Britain and Northern Ireland. Scotland has also hosted one Olympic event as, in 1908, the 12-meters yachting was held on the River Clyde in Glasgow.

Seizinger, Katja [GER–ASK]. B. 10 May 1972. Katja Seizinger was the top female power skiier of the 1990s, setting records at the Olympics by winning five medals, including three gold medals, matched only by Vreni Schneider (SUI) among women. Seizinger won the downhill in 1994 and 1998, becoming the first person, man or woman, to defend the Olympic downhill title. She added a third gold in the Alpine combined in the 1998 Olympic Winter Games. Her other Olympic medals were bronze in the Super-G in 1992 and in the giant slalom in 1998. Seizinger was less successful in the World Championships, winning only the 1993 Super-G. However, she posted a remarkable record in the World Cup events, winning 36 times to the end of the 1998 season. She was overall World Cup champion in 1996 and 1998, and won the following individual World Cup titles: Super-G (1993–1996 and 1998) and downhill (1992–1994 and 1998).

Senegal [SEN]. Senegal first competed at the 1964 Olympic Games and has competed at every Olympics since. It has competed at the Olympic Winter Games in 1984, 1992, and 1994. Amadou Dia Bâ won the nation's only medal to date, a silver in the 1988 400-meter hurdles in track & field athletics. Prior to Dia Bâ's medal in 1988, it can be argued that Senegal had won a medal in 1960. In that year, Abdoulaye Seye won a bronze in the 200 meters while representing France. Seye was a Senegalese national, but the country was still a French territory, so he had to compete under the French flag. The first Senegalese national to compete in the Olympics was probably Cire Samba who competed for France in the javelin throw in 1924.

Serbia. Serbia competed at the 1912 Olympics, the only time Serbia has been represented at the Olympics as an independent nation. In that year, Serbia, later the largest province in Yugoslavia (q.v.), sent two athletes to the Olympic Games. Dragutin Tomašević did not finish the marathon race, and Dušan Milošević finished third in his heat of the 100 meters. However, it is likely that Momcilo Tapavica, who competed in 1896 in wrestling and tennis and is usually listed as representing Hungary, was actually a Serbian student from Belgrade studying in Budapest. On 4 December 1918, Serbia became part of the country that was then termed the Kingdom of Serbs, Croats, and Slovenes and would later become Yugoslavia. Serbian athletes competed under that banner through 1988. With the breakup of Yugoslavia in 1991, Yugoslavia now consists solely of the former provinces of Serbia and Montenegro, with Serbia having two autonomous regions, Vojvodina and Kosovo. Thus, Serbian athletes still compete at the Olympics under the Yugoslav flag.

Sessions of the IOC. The main decision-making body of the International Olympic Committee is the annual session of the IOC. Currently, these are held once a year, although special sessions may be called by the IOC president. Every other year, one session is held immediately before either the Olympic Games or the Olympic Winter Games, at the site of those Games. Formerly, when the Olympic Games and Olympic Winter Games were held in the same year, two sessions were held in the Olympic year, one at the site of the Olympic Games and one at the site of the Olympic Winter Games, and immediately preceding those events. The session is a plenary meeting of the IOC and is considered its main rules making body. In reality, the session is usually presented with a list of decisions made by the Executive Board and these are almost universally approved; thus the Executive Board really has the authoritative power. The session also votes on the approval of prospective IOC members, but the choices of the IOC president are usually approved without dissension. The session also has the power to modify the Olympic Charter.

Sex Testing. *See* GENDER VERIFICATION.

Seychelles [SEY]. The Seychelles has competed at five Olympic Games, those of 1980, 1984, 1992, 1996, and 2000. For reasons not precisely clear, the Seychelles did not compete in 1988 at Seoul. Its best Olympic performance came in 1992 when light-heavyweight boxer Roland Raforme won two matches to finish fifth of 27 in his class, and in 1996 when another boxer, Rival Cadeau, finished fifth in the light-middleweight class. The Seychelles has never competed at the Olympic

Winter Games. A Seychelles national, Henri Dauban de Silhouette, represented Great Britain in the javelin throw at the 1924 Olympic Games.

Shakhlin, Boris [URS/UKR–GYM]. B. 27 January 1932, Ishim, Tyumen Region. Boris Shakhlin won six gold medals in individual gymnastic events, which remains an Olympic best for men, bettered only by Věra Čáslavská (q.v.). Between 1956 and 1964, he won a total of 13 Olympic medals (seven gold, four silver, two bronze) with his strongest individual event being the pommelled horse, in which he won gold in 1956 and 1960. Shakhlin also won a total of 14 medals at the World Championships. Unusually tall for a gymnast, Shakhlin's height and reach were a distinct advantage on the horizontal bar, but he was weak at the floor exercise.

Shcherbo, Vitaly [URS/EUN/BLR–GYM]. B. 13 January 1972, Minsk. Vitaly Shcherbo was the most successful gymnast at the 1992 Olympic Games, when he won six gold medals, adding four individual apparatus championships to the individual and team all-around titles. Shcherbo's record at the World Championships was also excellent. He won the all-around in 1993, the floor exercises in 1994–1995, the horizontal bar in 1994, the parallel bars in 1993 and 1995, and the horse vault in 1993–1994. Shcherbo competed again at the Olympics in 1996. He won four medals, again of the same color, this time all bronze.

Sheridan, Martin Joseph [USA–ATH]. B. 28 March 1881, Bohola, County Mayo, Ireland. D. 27 March 1918, New York. Martin Sheridan was the world's finest all-round athlete until the arrival of Jim Thorpe (q.v.), and the greatest discus thrower until Al Oerter (q.v.). In addition to winning the discus at the 1904, 1906, and 1908 Olympic Games, Sheridan won the shot in 1906 and the Greek-style discus in 1908. To these five gold medals, he added three silver medals in 1906 in the stone throw and the standing jumps and a bronze medal in the standing long jump in 1908. Between 1904 and 1911, Sheridan won 11 Amateur Athletic Union (AAU) titles at a variety of events, including three in the All-Around Championship. He was at his best before world records were officially recognized, but from 1902 to 1911, he set no less than 15 new "world bests" in the discus, although irregularities in the specification of the throwing circle would have precluded some of these performances from being officially recognized under more stringent modern conditions. Irish-born, Sheridan emigrated to the USA at the age of 16 and died from pneumonia on the eve of his 37th birthday while serving with the New York Police Department.

Shooting. Shooting originated as a means of survival, as shooting was practiced to hunt game for food. In the 19th century, as the industrial revolution occurred and hunting for food became less necessary for more people, shooting as a sport evolved. The sport was first popular in English-speaking countries, notably England and the United States, but also in Ireland and South Africa. The National Rifle Association (NRA) was formed in 1871 and provided the impetus for the development of organized shooting sport in the United States. The world governing body is the International Shooting Sport Federation (ISSF), formerly the Union Internationale de Tir (UIT), which was formed in 1907 and had 157 member nations in 2000.

Shooting has been contested at most of the Olympic Games. Baron Pierre de Coubertin (q.v.) was an avid pistol shot so he saw to it that the sport was included on the program in 1896. There were also events in 1900, but none were contested in 1904 at St. Louis. In 1928 at Amsterdam, shooting events were also not on the program.

The program has varied as much as any sport (with the possible exception of sailing). In 1908, 1912, 1920, and 1924, there were dozens of events, including multiple team events, and it was possible for shooters to win several medals at each Olympics. After the sport's hiatus in 1928, it returned to the Olympics in 1932 with only two events—one for pistols and one for rifles. Since World War II, the program has become relatively standardized.

Women were first allowed to compete in Olympic shooting in 1968. In that year, Mexico, Peru, and Poland each entered one female contestant. In 1976, Margaret Murdock (USA) won a silver medal in the small-bore rifle (three positions) event. In 1984, the UIT introduced separate events for women. Since 1984, the women's shooting program has been expanded at each Olympics, and the number of mixed events decreased. Beginning in 2000 at Sydney, men and women competed in fully separate shooting programs, with 10 events for men and 7 for women.

Shooting events at the Olympics have been held in several types of events: long-distance rifle, small-bore rifle, air pistol and rifle shooting, pistol shooting, skeet and trap shooting, and running target events. From 1908 to 1924, there were numerous team shooting events, which allowed the shooters to win many medals, but team shooting events were discontinued beginning after the 1924 Olympics.

Short-Track Speed Skating. *See* SPEED SKATING.

Sierra Leone [SLE]. In 1960, a Sierra Leone athlete, Albert Massquoi, represented Liberia in the Olympic marathon, finishing 62nd. But as an independent nation, Sierra Leone made its Olympic début in 1968, after having been recognized by the IOC in 1964. They have since missed only the 1972 and 1976 Olympic Games, but have never competed at the Olympic Winter Games. Its best Olympic performance came in 1996 when Eunice Barber finished fifth in the women's heptathlon.

Singapore [SIN]. Singapore has competed independently at 11 Olympic Games since 1948, missing only 1964 and 1980. In 1964, Singaporean athletes also competed at the Olympic Games, but under the banner of Malaysia (q.v.) in a combined team with Malaya and North Borneo (q.v.). Singapore left the Malaysian Federation in 1965. Singapore has not competed at the Olympic Winter Games. In 1960, Tan Howe-Liang won Singapore's only Olympic medal to date, a silver in lightweight weightlifting. *See also* MALAYSIA.

Singh, Udham Kullar [IND–HOK]. B. 4 August 1928. Of the seven Indian players to win three Olympic gold medals for hockey (field), only Udham Singh and Leslie Claudius (q.v.) also won a silver medal. Singh won gold in 1952, 1956, and 1964, and silver in 1960.

Skating. *See* FIGURE SKATING, ICE HOCKEY, SHORT-TRACK SPEED SKATING, and SPEED SKATING.

Skeleton. Skeleton is a sledding sport founded on the famed Cresta Run at St. Moritz, Switzerland. In skeleton, the sliders lie prone on their sleds, face-down. Skeleton was contested at the Olympic Winter Games in 1928 and 1948, when they were held in St. Moritz. Skeleton was recently approved to be returned to the Olympic program with events for men and women scheduled to be held at the 2002 Olympic Winter Games in Salt Lake City. *See also* BOBSLEDDING.

Skiing. *See* ALPINE SKIING, BIATHLON, FREESTYLE SKIING, MILITARY SKI PATROL, NORDIC SKIING, SKIJÖRING, SNOWBOARDING, and SPEED SKIING.

Skijöring. Skijöring, originally called *skid-körning*, was held as a demonstration sport at the 1928 Winter Olympics in St. Moritz. Skijöring is a sport in which skiers are towed behind horses. It was considered a military competition in Norway and Sweden, and was part of the Nordic Games in 1901, 1905, and 1909. It is today contested primarily in Switzerland and Sweden.

Ski Jumping. *See* NORDIC SKIING.

Skoblikova, Lidiya Pavlovna [URS–SSK]. B. 8 March 1939, Zlatoust, Chelyabinsk. Lidiya Skoblikova holds the record with six Olympic gold medals for speed skating. She was a world-class performer before speed skating for women was added to the Olympic program in 1960 at the Squaw Valley Games. In 1960, Skoblikova won gold medals in the 1,500 meters, with a new world record, and the 3,000 meters. At the 1964 Winter Games, she became the first woman to win all four speed-skating events at one Games, setting new Olympic records in the 500 meters, 1,000 meters, and 1,500 meters, and was only deprived of a fourth record by adverse ice conditions in the 3,000 meters. After these successes, her third Olympic appearance in 1968 was a disappointment when she finished 11th in the 1,500 meters. A teacher from Siberia, Skoblikova set world records at 1,000 meters and 3,000 meters and was the world overall champion in 1963 and 1964, winning all four events in both years.

Sledding. *See* BOBSLEDDING, LUGE, and SKELETON.

Sloane, William Milligan [USA]. B. 12 November 1850, Richmond, Ohio. D. 11 September 1928, Princeton, New Jersey. William Milligan Sloane was the pioneer of the Olympic Movement in America

and a founding member of the International Olympic Committee
(IOC) (q.v.). A close friend and supporter of Pierre de Coubertin
(q.v.), he was the driving force behind the establishment, maintenance, and development of the strong links between the Olympic
Movement and the United States. A professor of history at Princeton
University and a distinguished academician, he later held the Roosevelt Chair at Berlin University, but gave up most of his appointments after becoming ill in 1921, although it was not until 1924 that
he resigned from the IOC. His best-known academic work was his
four-volume *Life of Napoleon Bonaparte.*

Slovakia [SVK]. Slovakia, which split from Czechoslovakia (q.v.) on 1
January 1993 along with the Czech Republic (q.v.), competed in the
Olympic Games as an independent nation for the first time at Lillehammer in 1994. Prior to the division, many Czechoslovakian athletes were actually from Slovakia. A Slovakian Olympic Committee
was actually first formed in June 1939, and it attempted to revive its
activities after World War II in 1945. However, in June 1947, it was
co-opted into the Czechoslovak Olympic Committee. The Slovakian
Olympic Committee was re-created in October 1990, and was then
formed officially on 19 December 1992, before its split from the
Czech Republic on 1 January 1993. It received provisional recognition by the IOC on 16 March 1993 and official recognition at the
1993 IOC session in Monaco in September 1993. At Lillehammer,
Slovakia was represented by 34 men and eight women athletes. Slovakia has also competed at the 1996 Olympic Games, the 2000
Olympic Games, and the 1998 Olympic Winter Games.

Slovenia [SLO]. Prior to 1992, Slovenia had never competed at the
Olympics as a sovereign nation. However, many Yugoslav athletes
were natives of Slovenia, notably Leon Štukelj (from Maribor) who
won, between 1924 and 1936, more medals (six) and gold medals
(three) than any other Yugoslav Olympian. Slovenia was also responsible for all of Yugoslavia's (q.v.) medals in the Olympic Winter
Games between 1984 and 1988. Slovenia made its Olympic début at
both Albertville and Barcelona in 1992 after the Yugoslavian civil
war. It has since competed at the 1996 and 2000 Olympic Games and
the Olympic Winter Games of 1994 and 1998.

Smetanina, Raisa Petrovna [URS–NSK]. B. 29 February 1952, Mokhcha, Komi. Over a long career that encompassed five Olympics, Raisa Smetanina compiled one of the greatest records of any female cross-country skiier. Smetanina first came to international attention at the 1974 World Championships, where she helped the Soviet Union relay team to the championship. This led to her greatest Olympic performance at Innsbruck in 1976. She competed in three events, medaling in all three, with a silver at 5 km., and golds in the 10 km., and relay. Smetanina competed at the Olympic Winter Games in 1976, 1980, 1984, 1988, and 1992, retiring after the Albertville Olympics. During that time, she won 10 Olympic medals, including four gold. Two of the gold medals came in 1976, and she added another individual gold in the 1980 5 km. Smetanina's Olympic career ended after she helped the Soviet women's relay team to a gold medal at the 1992 Winter Olympics. Raisa Smetanina also won 13 medals at the World Championships. In addition to her international triumphs, she was 21 times champion of the Soviet Union and was named an Emeritus Master of Sport of the USSR.

Smith, John William [USA–WRE]. B. 9 August 1965, Del City, Oklahoma. John Smith is the most titled American wrestler ever. A freestyler, he won two National Collegiate Athletic Association (NCAA) championships while at Oklahoma State. His first major international victory was the Goodwill Games title in 1986. In 1987, he won the Pan-American Championship and the World Championship. In 1988 and 1992, he was Olympic champion; from 1989 to 1991, he won the World Championships. In 1990, he also defended his Goodwill Games gold medal. From 1986 through 1990, Smith's international record was 150–3. He also received the Sullivan Award in 1990, the only American wrestler ever so honored. He retired from competition and became coach at his alma mater where his team won the NCAA Championship in his first year of formal coaching.

Smyrna. At the 1906 Intercalated Olympics, an international team represented Smyrna in the football (soccer) tournament and won a silver medal. The athletes were actually all from Armenia, France, and Great Britain.

Soccer (Association Football). *See* FOOTBALL (ASSOCIATION FOOTBALL/SOCCER).

Softball. Softball began in the 1890s as a variant of baseball, usually played by women (q.v.). It was originally called *mushball, kittenball,* or *indoor baseball*, but acquired the name *softball* by the 1920s. In the United States, the sport became organized with the formation of the Amateur Softball Association in 1933. Several variants of the sport exist in the United States, including fast-pitch, modified fast-pitch, and slow-pitch. The international organization is the International Softball Federation (ISF), which was formed in 1952 and had 118 member nations as of December 2000. Softball (fast-pitch) made its début as a full-medal sport for women at the 1996 Olympics in Atlanta. It is the only sport on the Olympic program open only to women and not men, although two disciplines also fall in this category—synchronized swimming and rhythmic gymnastics.

Solomon Islands [SOL]. The Solomon Islands Olympic Committee was recognized by the IOC in 1983 and they made their Olympic début in 1984. They have since competed at the 1988, 1992, 1996, and 2000 Olympic Games. The Solomon Islands has never competed at the Olympic Winter Games and their athletes have yet to win a medal.

Somalia [SOM]. Somalia has competed at five Olympic Games—those of 1972, 1984, 1988, 1996, and 2000. Somalia entered the 1992 Olympics but did not compete, probably because of the famine in the country. It has competed only in track & field with 14 men competitors, and one woman who competed at Sydney in 2000. Somalia has not competed in the Olympic Winter Games and has not yet won an Olympic medal.

South Africa [RSA, formerly SAF]. With the exception of the Intercalated Games of 1906, South Africa's participation at the Olympic Games was continuous from 1904 through 1960. From 1964 to 1988, however, it was not allowed to compete at the Olympics. This was because of the country's policy of apartheid and, in particular, its use of the policy in choosing its athletic teams, which is forbidden by International Olympic Committee (IOC) (q.v.) policy. It is ironic that the first South African Olympians were two Tsuana tribesmen who ran in the 1904 marathon; named *Len Tau* and *Jan Mashiani*, both black men.

The story of South Africa's banishment from the Olympics is one of the most complex issues that has ever faced the IOC. South Africa did not always practice apartheid as a sporting policy. In the 1930s, there was frequent interracial competition, but in June 1956, a South African law was passed requiring an end to interracial sport. In 1958, IOC member Olav Ditlef-Simonsen of Norway informed IOC president Avery Brundage (q.v.) that his country would exclude an all-white South African team, if his nation were awarded the Olympics. In 1959, the Indians, Egyptians, and Soviets pressed the IOC for South Africa's ouster from the Olympics, but the IOC was content with the promise that its 1960 Olympic team would be a multiracial one. It was not.

In 1962, South Africa Interior Minister Jan de Klerk commented publicly that, "Government policy is that no mixed teams should take part in sports inside or outside the country." The IOC could scarcely ignore this message. At the 60th IOC session in Moscow in 1962, the IOC voted to suspend the South African National Olympic Committee (SANOC) ". . . if the policy of racial discrimination practiced by the government . . . does not change before our session in Nairobi, which takes place in October 1963." SANOC was eventually suspended at the 62nd IOC session in Innsbruck in January 1964.

Further problems arose in December 1966 in Bamako, Mali, when 32 African nations formed the Supreme Council for Sport in Africa (SCSA). The SCSA's stated purpose was to coordinate and promote sport, but its true objective was to attack South Africa's apartheid policies in sport. At its founding conference, the SCSA resolved: ". . . to use every means to obtain the expulsion of South African sports organizations from the Olympic Movement and from International Federations (qq.v.) should South Africa fail to comply fully with the IOC rules."

In mid-September 1967, an IOC commission visited South Africa to inspect the sporting facilities and see if the South Africa sporting groups were in violation of Olympic principles. The commission consisted of three IOC members: future IOC president Lord Killanin (Ireland) (q.v.), Reginald Alexander (Kenya, a white man), and Sir Adetokunbo Ademola (Nigeria, a black man). They presented their report to the IOC on 30 January 1968, and it was felt to be generally positive. By a mail ballot, the IOC voted to restore recognition to SANOC, allowing a multiracial South African team to compete at the 1968 Olympics.

This prompted mass boycott (q.v.) demands from the African nations, which vehemently opposed this decision. The IOC Executive Board subsequently met in Lausanne on 20 April 1968, and decided to poll the IOC members. By a postal ballot of 47–17 (with eight abstentions), the IOC reversed its course and withdrew its recognition of SANOC, preventing a huge boycott of the 1968 Olympics. In May 1970, at the 70th IOC session in Amsterdam, the South African Olympic Committee was expelled from the IOC by a vote of 35–28, with three abstentions.

In 1976, the South African question again became prominent when several African nations boycotted in protest of a New Zealand rugby team's having played several games on tour in South Africa. Ironically, rugby has not been an Olympic sport since 1924 and the New Zealand rugby team was named the *All-Blacks*.

In 1990, South Africa began to take steps to eliminate apartheid. In April 1991, the IOC, anticipating apartheid's elimination, gave provisional recognition to the South African Olympic Committee. On 9 July 1991, the International Olympic Committee granted full recognition to the South African Olympic Committee, and lifted its 21-year ban on its participation in the Olympics. In 1992 at Barcelona, South Africa competed on the Olympic stage for the first time in 32 years and the nation competed again in 1996 at Atlanta and at Sydney in 2000.

South Africa has also competed at the Olympic Winter Games in 1960, 1994, and 1998. South Africa has won 63 Olympic medals, 19 of them gold, none of them at the Olympic Winter Games. Of these, two silver medals came at South Africa's return to the Olympic stage in 1992; they also won five medals in both 1996 and 2000.

Soviet Union [URS]. *See* UNION OF SOVIET SOCIALIST REPUBLICS (USSR).

Soviet Union (USSR) Ice Hockey Teams [1956–1992]. The Soviet Union first entered the Olympic Winter Games in 1956 and immediately established itself as a dominant force in most winter sports.

However, it was in ice hockey that the Soviet Union would be most dominant over the next 36 years. From 1956 through 1992, the Soviet Union won all but two of the Olympic gold medals in ice hockey (eight in all), losing only in 1960 and 1980 to the "hometown" United States' teams. Its last gold medal in 1992 was won as the *Unified Team* (q.v.), after the dissolution of the Soviet Union. During this time, Soviet and Unified ice hockey teams posted a record of 61 wins, 6 losses, and 2 ties.

Soviet Union (USSR) Women's Gymnastics Teams [1952–1992]. The Soviet Union's women's gymnastics teams produced a nonpareil record at the Olympic Games; they never lost. From 1952 to 1988, and as the *Unified Team* (q.v.) in 1992, the Soviet Union won every women's team all-around title in gymnastics (eight consecutive and nine titles), with the lone exception of 1984, when it did not compete because of the boycott.

Spain [ESP]. In 1900, Spain was represented by 14 athletes at the Paris Olympics. A Spanish NOC was formed in 1905, at the urging of the Greeks, and 20 Spanish athletes competed at Athens in 1906. Spain next appeared on the Olympic stage in 1920, and has since missed only the 1936 Berlin Olympics. In addition, Spain did not compete at Melbourne in 1956, although Spanish riders did compete in the Olympic Equestrian Games at Stockholm in 1956. Spain's first winter appearance was in 1936 at Garmisch-Partenkirchen and it has never failed to compete in the Olympic Winter Games since. Spain has won 78 Olympic medals, 27 of them gold, with two medals having been won at the Olympic Winter Games. In 1992, Barcelona hosted the Games of the XXVth Olympiad.

Special Olympics. *See* PARALYMPIC GAMES.

Speed Skating. Speed skating emerged on the canals of Holland as early as the 13th century. Competition has been held in The Netherlands since 1676. The sport spread throughout Europe and national competitions were held in the 1870s. The first World Championships were contested in 1889, although the International Skating Union (ISU) held its first championships in 1893, one year after its formation.

Speed skating was contested at the 1924 Olympic Winter Games and has been on the Olympic Winter program since. Women first competed at the Olympics in 1932 when it was a demonstration sport (q.v.). Women's speed skating as a full medal Olympics sport began in 1960. The sport is governed by the International Skating Union, which also governs figure skating. The ISU was formed in 1892 and had 72 members (representing 55 nations) at the end of 1994.

Olympic speed skating has almost always been contested in the European system of skating time trials in two-man pairs. In 1932 at Lake Placid, the Americans convinced the ISU to hold the events in the North American style of pack racing. Many Europeans boycotted the events as a result and the Americans won all four gold medals.

Short-track speed skating, racing in a pack indoors over a smaller rink, was contested as a demonstration sport in 1988 at Calgary. It became a full medal sport for both men and women in 1992 at Albertville, and continues on the Olympic program.

Speed skating has been dominated by the Norwegians, the Dutch, and the former Soviet Union and its republics. In addition, the women of the former German Democratic Republic were outstanding speed skaters. The United States has produced excellent sprinters, winning many medals and gold medals by both men and women. In addition, in 1980, the United States' Eric Heiden (q.v.) won all five available gold medals, a dominance in speed skating matched only by the USSR's Lidiya Skoblikova (q.v.), who won all four women's events in 1964.

Speed Skiing. Speed skiing was a demonstration sport at the 1992 Olympic Winter Games in Albertville. The event was marred by the death of one of the course officials who was struck by a skier during a training run.

Spitz, Mark Andrew [USA–SWI]. B. 10 February 1950, Modesto, California. Usually considered the greatest swimmer ever, Mark Spitz remains an Olympic legend who won seven gold medals (four individual, three relay) for swimming, each in a new world record time, at the 1972 Olympics. At the 1968 Games, he had won four medals (two gold, one silver, one bronze) and his overall total of 11 Olympic medals has only been matched by Matt Biondi (q.v.) among male swimmers. Spitz set 26 individual world records and six in the relays. He returned to competition in 1991 with the aim of making the 1992 Olympic team but, as he was over 40 years of age, it was a forlorn hope and an unfortunate end to a career of unrivaled achievements.

Sport and Environment Commission. The Sport and Environment Commission was formed after the 1994 Lillehammer Olympic Winter Games, in response to the Norwegian policy of conducting a "Green" Olympics—quite a feat at the Olympic Winter Games. But the International Olympic Committee (IOC) (q.v.) thought the Lillehammer policies toward the environment were important and formed the commission to help institute similar policies in international sport. The Chairman is Pál Schmitt of Hungary. The commission has seven IOC members, members from the National Olympic Committees, the International Federations, and the athletes, and 14 independent members, who act as consultants on the environment.

Sport and Law Commission. The Sport and Law Commission was formed in 1996 with Judge Kéba Mbaye as its only Chairman to date. It consists of three other International Olympic Committee (IOC) (q.v.) members, all trained as lawyers: Anita DeFrantz (USA), Marc Hodler (SUI), and Richard Pound (CAN) (q.v.); along with representatives of the National Olympic Committees and International Federations, three athletes, and several independent members who act as legal consultants.

Sport for All Commission. The International Olympic Committee (IOC) (q.v.) formed a Sport for All Working Group in 1983. In 1985, the IOC formed the Mass Sport Commission, which was renamed the *Sport for All Commission* in 1986. The concept of the availability of Sport for All was a basic tenet of Baron Pierre de Coubertin's (q.v.) philosophy of Olympism. The concept attempts to provide sport as a human right for all individuals, regardless of race, social class, and sex, and encourages the practice of sport by people of all ages, sexes, and social and economic conditions. The current chairman is Walther Tröger of Germany. The commission consists of eight IOC members, members from both the National Olympic Committees and International Federations, several athletes, and five independent members.

In 1987, the Sport for All Commission developed the concept of an Olympic Day Run, held on 23 June each year (the anniversary of the founding of the IOC at the 1894 Sorbonne Congress).

Squash Rackets. This sport is different from both rackets and racquetball but it has never been contested at the Olympic Games, even as a demonstration sport (q.v.). However, the World Squash Federation (WSF) is recognized by the IOC, with 115 affiliated members as of 2000.

Sri Lanka [SRI]. Sri Lanka, as *Ceylon*, competed at the Olympics from 1948 through 1968. After its name change to *Sri Lanka* (on 22 May 1972), it has competed at the Olympics of 1972, 1980, 1984, 1988, 1992, 1996, and 2000. Sri Lanka has yet to compete in the Olympic Winter Games. The first Ceylonese national to compete at the Olympics was Carl Van Geyzel, who competed for Great Britain in the 1928 high jump. In 1948, Duncan White won a silver medal in the 400-meter hurdles in track & field athletics for Ceylon. The other medal for this nation was a bronze in the women's 200 meters in 2000 by Susanthika Jayasinghe.

St. Kitts and Nevis [SKN]. St. Kitts and Nevis was given official recognition by the IOC in September 1993, and competed at the Olympic Games in 1996 and 2000, when it was represented on both occasions by two track & field athletes: one female and one male. The country has not yet competed at the Olympic Winter Games.

St. Vincent and the Grenadines [VIN]. St. Vincent and the Grenadines first competed in the Olympics in 1988 at Seoul, when it was represented by six track & field athletes: five male and one female. The nation also competed in 1992, 1996, and 2000, but has not competed at the Olympic Winter Games. The nation has not yet won any Olympic medals.

Stadion Race—Ancient Olympic Sport. The *stadion* race was the original Olympic event. It is a simple sprint of length of the Ancient Olympic stadium of approximately 192 meters. From this event, our modern word for stadium is derived. The first known champion was Coroebus of Elis in 776 B.C. The last known champion of the *stadion* was Dionysios of Alexandria in 269 A.D. It is possible that, in the earliest Ancient Olympic Games (q.v.), the *stadion* was the only event contested. Leonidas of Rhodes won four consecutive titles in this event from 164 to 152 B.C. Five other athletes are known to have won at least three titles.

Stevenson Lorenzo, Téofilo [CUB–BOX]. B. 29 March 1952, Dcilias. Téofilo Stevenson is one of only three men to win three Olympic gold medals for boxing (*See also* LÁSZLÓ PAPP and FÉLIX SAVÓN FABRÉ). On his way to winning the heavyweight title in 1972, 1976, and 1980, he had 12 scheduled bouts; one of his opponents withdrew and he won nine of his 11 Olympic fights by a knock out. His devastating punching power resulted in all four of his bouts at the 1976 Games ending in a knock out. At his peak, he was undoubtedly the best heavyweight in the world, but he resisted many lucrative offers to fight professionally. Had he done so, there is little doubt that he would have been the world champion. And had Cuba not boycotted the 1984 Olympics, Stevenson would have been the favorite to win his fourth gold medal. He was world amateur champion in 1974, 1978, and 1986.

Strickland de la Hunty, Shirley Barbara (née Strickland) [AUS–ATH]. B. 18 July 1925, Guildford, Western Australia. With seven Olympic medals Shirley Strickland de la Hunty set a record for women's track & field that, although subsequently equaled by Irena Szewińska, has never been beaten. The Australian sprinter-hurdler won three gold medals in the 80-meters hurdles (1952, 1956) and the 4 x 100-meters relay (1956). Strickland de la Hunty also won one silver and three bronze medals in three Olympic appearances (1948–1956). She also competed in the 1950 British Empire Games, winning silver medals in both the 100 and 200 meters.

Sudan [SUD]. Sudan formed a National Olympic Committee in 1956, which was recognized by the IOC in 1959. Since making its Olympic début in 1960, Sudan has missed only the Olympics of 1964, 1976, and 1980. It has never competed at the Olympic Winter Games. Its best Olympic performance came in 1984 when Omar Khalifa finished eighth in the men's 1,500 meters in track & field athletics.

Süleymanoğlu, Naim (né Naim Suleimanov, aka Naum Shalamanov) [BUL/TUR–WLT]. B. 23 January 1967, Ptichar, Bulgaria. It is likely that Naim Süleymanoğlu is the strongest man who has ever lived, pound-for-pound. He set his first world record at age 15, and at the 1984 European Championships he became the second man to lift three times his bodyweight overhead. Süleymanoğlu was also the first man to snatch two-and-a-half times his own bodyweight (27 April 1988). He was born in Bulgaria, but defected to Turkey at the 1986 World Cup finals. Born Naim Suleimanov and of Bulgarian Turkish descent, he was quite upset when the Bulgarians changed his name to Naum Shalamanov in 1985, to remove vestiges of its Turkish origins. Once in Turkey, he changed the name again to a more Turkish one, and at the 1988 Olympics, Süleymanoğlu was absolutely dominant. He was World Champion at 60 kg. in 1985, 1986, 1989, and 1991, and at 64 kg. in 1993–1995. He did not compete in 1987 because of his defection. Süleymanoğlu also did not compete in 1990, retiring briefly before making a successful comeback. In 1992 at Barcelona, he defended his Olympic championship and he won again in 1996 at Atlanta. His 10 championships at the Olympics and World Championships is an all-time best, as are his three Olympic gold medals. Süleymanoğlu retired after Atlanta, but returned to compete in Sydney, although he failed to make a successful lift at the 2000 Olympics.

Sumo Wrestling (Japanese Wrestling). Sumo, the Japanese traditional form of wrestling, was contested as a demonstration sport (q.v.) at the 1964 Olympic Games in Tokyo, as part of the *budo* demonstration, along with *kendo* (fencing) and *kyudo* (archery). Sumo wrestling is governed internationally by the International Sumo Federation (IFS), which was founded in 1946 and is recognized by the IOC. The IFS currently has 81 affiliated member nations. *See also* BUDO.

Surfing. Surfing has never been on the Olympic program, and it is unlikely that it will be, because surfing can only be contested at oceanside locations. However, the International Surfing Association (ISA) was founded in 1976 and is recognized by the IOC, with 43 affiliated member nations as of early 2000.

Suriname [SUR]. Suriname has competed at eight Olympic Games since its début in 1968, missing only the 1980 Moscow Olympics. In

1960, Suriname sent one athlete to the Olympics, Wym Essajas. Essajas was entered in the 800 meters but, after being told the heats were in the afternoon, slept through the heats, which were held that morning. One Suriname athlete, Anthony Nesty, is responsible for both medals won at the Olympics by Suriname. A swimmer, Nesty won a gold medal in the 1988 100-meter butterfly and a bronze medal in the same event in 1992.

Svan, Gunde Anders [SWE–NSK]. B. 12 January 1962, Skamhed, Vansbro. Prior to Norway's Bjørn Dæhlie (q.v.) in the 1990s, Gunde Anders Svan was the most bemedalled international cross-country skier ever. Svan began his Olympic career in 1984, winning gold in the 15 km. and relay, silver at 50 km., and bronze in the 30 km. He returned to the Olympics to win gold in 1988 at 50 km. and in the relay, giving him four gold and six Olympic medals. Svan was World Cup champion five times (1984–1986 and 1988–1989), placing in the top three for eight consecutive years (1983–1990). He won five individual World Championships: 1989 15 km., 1985 and 1991 30 km., and 1985 and 1989 50 km. Overall, he won 372 of 615 races at the national and international level from 1965–1991, won 30 World Cup races, and was Swedish national champion 16 times.

Swahn, Alfred Gomer Albert "Alf" [SWE–SHO]. B. 20 August 1879, Uddevalla. D. 16 March 1931, Stockholm. Alfred Swahn was the son of Oscar Swahn, who holds the record as the oldest medallist and gold medallist in Olympic history. Together, father and son competed for Sweden at the 1908, 1912, and 1920 Olympic Games. Alfred Swahn also competed again in 1924. Alfred won nine Olympic medals, three of which were gold. He specialized in the running deer events and was certainly helped by the proliferation of shooting events on the Olympic program, especially team events, in the era in which he competed. His Olympic medals were as follows: 1908: Running deer shooting (single shot team) (1). 1912: Running deer shooting (single shot) (1); Running deer shooting (single shot team) (1). 1920: Running deer shooting (single shot) (2); Running deer shooting (double shot team) (2); Trap shooting (team) (3). 1924: Running deer shooting (single shot team) (2); Running deer shooting (double shot) (3); and Running deer shooting (double shot team) (3).

Swaziland [SWZ]. Swaziland has competed at six Olympic Games—those of 1972, 1984, 1988, 1992, 1996, and 2000, and one Olympic Winter Games, 1992. Swaziland has not yet won an Olympic medal.

Sweden [SWE]. With the exception of the 1904 St. Louis Olympics, Sweden has competed at every Olympic Games and every Olympic Winter Games. In addition to having been one of the top countries in the Winter Games, it has also been outstanding in equestrian sport, sailing, shooting, and wrestling at the Summer Olympics. Sweden has won 572 Olympic medals, 175 of them gold medals. Stockholm, Sweden, hosted the Games of the Vth Olympiad in 1912. Stockholm also hosted the Equestrian Games of the XVIth Olympiad in 1956 when Australia was unable to hold the equestrian events in Melbourne because of the country's strict quarantine laws.

Swimming. Swimming is an ancient practice as prehistoric man had to learn to swim in order to cross rivers and lakes. There are numerous references in Greek mythology to swimming, the most notable being that of Leander swimming the Hellespont (now the Dardenelle Straits) nightly to see his beloved Hero.

Swimming as a sport probably was not practiced widely until the early 19th century. The National Swimming Society of Great Britain was formed in 1837 and began to conduct competitions. Most early swimmers used the breaststroke or a form of it. In the 1870s, a British swimming instructor named *J. Arthur Trudgeon* traveled to South America, where he saw the natives using an alternate arm overhand stroke. He brought it back to England as the famous trudgeon stroke—a crawl variant with a scissors kick.

In the late 1880s, an Englishman named Frederick Cavill traveled to the South Seas, where he saw the natives there performing a crawl with a flutter kick. Cavill settled in Australia, where he taught the stroke that was to become the famous Australian crawl.

Swimming has been held at every Olympic Games. The early events were usually only conducted in freestyle (crawl) or breaststroke. Backstroke was added later. In the 1940s, breaststrokers discovered they could go much faster by bringing both arms overhead together. This was banned in the breaststroke shortly thereafter, but became the butterfly stroke, which is now the fourth stroke used in competitive swimming. Women's swimming was first held at the 1912 Olympics. It has since been conducted at all the Olympics.

The current program has events for men and women in freestyle, backstroke, breaststroke, butterfly, individual medley, and relays. Both men and women compete in freestyle over 50, 100, 200, and 400 meters. The long-distance event for women is 800 meters and for men is 1,500 meters. Backstroke, breaststroke, and butterfly events are contested over both 100 and 200 meters. The individual medley is held at 200 and 400 meters. Men and women now compete in the same three relays: 4 x 100-meter freestyle relay, 4 x 100-meter medley relay, and 4 x 200-meter freestyle relay.

The United States has been by far the dominant nation in this sport at the Olympics. At various times, Australia, Japan, and previously the German Democratic Republic women (GDR, East Germany), have made inroads into that dominance. The governing body is the Fédération Internationale de Natation Amateur (FINA), which was formed in 1908 and had 176 member nations as of December 2000.

Swimming, Underwater. *See* UNDERWATER SWIMMING.

Switzerland [SUI]. Switzerland first competed at the 1896 Olympic Games when it was represented by Louis Zutter, a gymnast from Neuchâtel. Switzerland also competed at the first Olympic Winter Games in 1924, and was represented before that in 1920 at Antwerp in both the figure skating and ice hockey events. It has been represented at every Olympic Games and every Olympic Winter Games, one of only three countries to make this claim (Great Britain and France are the others). Switzerland has really never been the dominant country in any sport. In the early Games, it had top-notch gymnasts. Until the GDR became dominant, it was the top nation in bobsledding in the Winter Games. Switzerland has won 270 medals, 76 gold, with 93 medals and 30 gold at the Olympic Winter Games. St. Moritz, Switzerland, hosted the 2nd Olympic Winter Games in 1928 and the 5th Olympic Winter Games in 1948.

Synoris—Ancient Olympic Sport. The *synoris* was a two-horse chariot race, lasting for eight circuits of the hippodrome (*circa*

9,000 meters). Champions are known from 408 B.C. (Euagoras of Elis) through 60 B.C. (Menedernos of Elis).

Syria [SYR]. Syria sent one athlete to the 1948 Olympic Games. In 1960, the United Arab Republic (Egypt and Syria) (UAR) competed at Rome with 74 athletes. Syria was a member of the UAR at that time but only three of the 74 athletes were Syrian. Syria and Egypt dissolved their political alliance in 1961 and Syria did not compete in the 1964 Olympic Games. It returned to the Olympic fold in 1968, and has since missed only 1976. It has yet to compete at an Olympic Winter Games. In 1984, Joseph Atiyeh won Syria's first Olympic medal, a silver in heavyweight freestyle wrestling. In 1996, Ghada Shouaa won Syria's first gold medal in the women's heptathlon event.

Szewińska-Kirszenstein, Irena (née Kirszenstein) [POL–ATH]. B. 24 May 1946, Leningrad, USSR. With a total of seven Olympic medals in track & field, Irena Szewińska-Kirszenstein equaled the record of Australian Shirley Strickland, a record since broken only by Jamaica's Merlene Ottey (q.v.). She won gold medals in the 4 x 100-meter relay (1964), the 200 meters (1968), and the 400 meters (1976), and she also won two silver and two bronze medals. Her Olympic career ended in 1980 when, in her fifth Games, she pulled up with a muscle strain in the semi-finals of the 400 meters. Szewińska-Kirszenstein's tally of 13 world records included her Olympic victories of 1968 (200 meters) and 1976 (400 meters) and at the European Championships she won a record 10 medals (five gold, one silver, four bronze). Born to Polish parents in the Soviet city of Leningrad, she returned to Poland at an early age and during an outstanding career, set 38 Polish records. In 1967, she married her coach, Janusz Szewińska. In 1998, Irena Szewińska was co-opted as a member of the International Olympic Committee (IOC) (q.v.).

– T –

Table Tennis. Table tennis was developed in the late 19th century, though its origins are not well documented. Several different sources for its invention are credited, but the modern game is said to have started with the introduction of the celluloid ball circa 1891. This development can be attributed to the Englishman, James Gibb, a world-record holding distance runner, who discovered the celluloid ball during a visit to America. This ensured the success of the game as a domestic pastime, from which a competitive game emerged.

The sport is widely practiced throughout the world. However, it made an unusual entry into the Olympic program. Table tennis made its Olympic début as a full medal sport in 1988 at Seoul. It was never contested at the Olympics as a demonstration sport (q.v.), which the IOC usually required of new sports. Men and women compete in four Olympic events, singles and doubles for men and women. Since the late 1950s, the Chinese have been by far the dominant factor in table tennis, although they are closely pushed by the Koreans. The governing body of the sport is the International Table Tennis Federation (ITTF), which was formed in 1926 and had 186 nations at the end of 2000.

Taekwondo. Taekwondo was contested as a demonstration sport (q.v.) at the 1988 and 1992 Olympics. The World Taekwondo Federation (WTF) was recognized by the IOC in 1973 and currently has 157 members. The sport made its Olympic début in 2000 at Sydney, with four weight classes for men and four for women.

Taiwan. *See* CHINESE TAIPEI.

Tajikistan [TJK]. As a former member of the Soviet Union, a few Tajikistani athletes competed from 1952 to 1988 for the Soviet Union. Tajikistani athletes were also present at Barcelona in 1992 as members of the Unified Team. Tajikistan made its Olympic début as an independent nation in 1996, but has not yet competed at the Olympic Winter Games.

Tanganyika. *See* TANZANIA.

Tanzania [TAN]. Tanganyika sent three athletes to the 1964 Olympic Games. In late 1964, the former nations of Tanganyika and Zanzibar merged to form Tanzania. Tanzania has competed at every Olympic Games since 1968, except for those of 1976. It has never competed at the Olympic Winter Games. In 1980 at Moscow, Filbert Bayi won a silver medal in the steeplechase. In 1976, Bayi had been a co-favorite with New Zealand's John Walker in the 1,500 meters and the battle between them was anticipated to be one of the great races in track history. It never occurred as Tanzania joined the 1976 African boycott (q.v.) in protest of a New Zealand rugby team playing in South Africa. Tanzania's other Olympic medal occurred in 1980 when Suleiman Nyambui finished second in the 5,000 meters in track & field athletics.

Team Handball. *See* HANDBALL (TEAM HANDBALL).

Television. Television is the method by which most of the world watches the Olympic Games. The rights fees paid by television are also crucially important to the continued success of the Olympic Movement (q.v.) because they are the primary method of financing the Olympic Games and the activities of the International Olympic Committee. The Olympic Games were televised for the first time in 1936, but with only a few viewers in Germany. The next few Olympiads also saw Olympic Games telecast within the host country, but with no significant rights fees. Television first began worldwide broadcasts in 1960 at Rome, with most of Europe seeing the Games live, and the United States viewing them on tape delay. The rights fee paid by the U.S. host television network, CBS (Columbia Broadcasting System), was $395,000. By contrast, NBC (National Broadcasting Company), which televised the 1996 Atlanta Olympic Games in the United States, paid $456,000,000 for the rights to the Games. Worldwide rights for the 1996 Olympics totaled $902,087,500. The rights fees for upcoming Games are as follows: 2000 Sydney—U.S. $715 million and worldwide $1.338 billion; 2002 Salt Lake City—U.S. $545 million and worldwide $738 million.

Although only one country was able to watch the Olympic Games of 1936, 1948, and 1956 on television, 21 nations watched the 1960 Olympics on television, and that number increased to over 200 for the 1996 Olympics. It was estimated that the gross cumulative television audience for the 1992 Olympics was 24.6 billion people, and that 2.3 billion people (85% of all those with televisions) watched the 1992 Olympics at some time.

Tennis (Lawn Tennis). Tennis, originally lawn tennis, was invented by Major Walter Wingfield, a British army officer, in 1873. The original name was *sphairistike*. However, tennis variants are much older than that. Court tennis, royal tennis, real tennis, or jeu de paume, was known to have been played in the Middle Ages.

Tennis was contested at every Olympic Games from 1896 through 1924 as a regular medal sport. It was then discontinued although it was on the schedule as a demonstration sport in 1968 and 1984. The reasons for dropping tennis as an Olympic sport probably were two: the IOC was upset that many of the top tennis players, though considered amateurs, infringed upon its strict definition of amateurism; and the tennis establishment, especially in Britain, was concerned that the Olympic events might become more important than Wimbledon and did not wish that to occur.

Tennis returned to the Olympics as a full medal sport in 1989 and almost certainly will remain on the Olympic program. Full-scale professionals now compete in the Olympics, with no other qualifications. There are four Olympic events, singles and doubles, for both men and women. Mixed doubles is not currently contested on the Olympic Program. The governing body of the sport is the International Tennis Federation (ITF), which was founded in 1913 and had 191 members at the end of 2000.

Tethrippon—Ancient Olympic Sport. The *tethrippon* was a four-horse chariot race that was contested over 12 laps of the hippodrome (circa 14,000 meters). Champions are known from 680 B.C. (Pagondas of Thebes) through 241 A.D. (Titus Domitius Prometheus of Athens). Euagoras of Sparta was the only three-time champion in this event (548–540 B.C.).

Thailand [THA]. Competing in the Olympics since 1952, Thailand has missed only the 1980 Moscow Olympics. It has never competed in the Olympic Winter Games. Thai athletes have won nine Olympic medals, two gold, one silver, and six bronze. Eight of the medals have been won in boxing, and one in weightlifting.

Theagenes of Thasos [GRE–BOX/WRE]. *fl. ca.* 480–460 B.C. Theagenes is credited with more than 1,400 victories in various sporting festivals in ancient Greece. Theagenes won at Olympia in 480 B.C. in boxing and in 476 B.C. in the pankration. He and

Kleitomachos of Thebes are the only two athletes to have won the boxing and pankration at Olympia.

The Thasians erected a statue to Theagenes in the town. A former athlete, who hated Theagenes, attacked the statue one night and it fell on him and killed him. The Thasians followed Draconian law and threw the statue into the sea. A great drought fell upon the island of Thasos, and crops suffered, with many animals dying as a result. The oracle at Delphi told them this could be corrected by bringing back to the country all their exiles. They did this but the drought and famine continued. They then consulted the wise Pythia at Delphi, who told them, "You have forgotten your great Theagenes, whom you threw in the sand, where he now lies, though before he won a thousand prizes." Several Thasian fishermen hauled the statue back in their nets, it was re-erected in its former position, and the drought ended. Later, the Thasians sacrificed to Theagenes as a hero of healing.

Thessalonika (Thessaloniki) [TSL]. At the 1906 Intercalated Olympics, a football (soccer) team represented Thessalonika and won a bronze medal. This is the only independent Olympic appearance by this province and city of Greece, which was then under control of the Turkish Ottoman Empire. However, many of the athletes representing Thessalonika were actually Greek nationals.

Thompson, Francis Morgan "Daley" [GBR–ATH]. B. 30 July 1958, Notting Hill, London. Daley Thompson shares with Bob Mathias the distinction of successfully defending an Olympic decathlon title. Thompson won his Olympic gold medals in 1980 and 1984, setting his fourth and final world record at the Los Angeles Games. He also competed in the 1976 and 1988 Olympics and is one of only two decathletes to have taken part in four Games. Thompson was also the World (1983), European (1982, 1986), and British Commonwealth (1978, 1982, 1986) champion. He set four world records in the decathlon.

Thompson, Jennifer Beth [USA-SWI]. B. 26 February 1973, Danvers, Massachusetts. With 10 medals and eight gold medals, Jenny Thompson has won more swimming medals and gold medals than any woman in Olympic history. But all eight of her gold medals came in relays, and this immensely talented swimmer has been frustrated in her attempt to win an individual Olympic gold medal. Her only individual medals were a silver in the 1992 100 freestyle and a bronze in the same event in 2000. Twenty-three times a national champion, she was more successful individually at the World Championships, winning the 100 free and 100 fly at the 1998 worlds. At the other major international event, the Pan-Pacifics, Thompson also won the 50 free four times (1989, 1991, 1993, 1999), the 100 free four times (1993–1999), and the 100 fly three times (1993, 1997–1999). Among all female Olympians, Thompson's eight gold medals are surpassed only by Larisa Latynina's (q.v.) nine.

Thorpe, James Francis (né Wa-tho-huck [Sac-and-Fox Indian name meaning "Bright Path"]) [USA–ATH]. B. 28 May 1888, Bellemont, Oklahoma. D. 28 March 1953, Lomita, California. Jim Thorpe is often described as the greatest all-round athlete in history. The accolade is well merited when judged by his superiority over his contemporaries. At the 1912 Olympics, he won the pentathlon and decathlon by huge margins, setting world records in both events. The following year, his name was struck from the roll of Olympic champions after it was revealed that he had earlier been paid for playing minor league baseball. The amount involved was minuscule ($15 [US] per week), but it was not until 1982 that the IOC reversed its decision and, after an interval of 70 years, the medals were returned, posthumously, to the family of their rightful owner. Part French and Irish, and part Sac-and-Fox Indian, he attended Carlisle Indian School, where he established an awesome reputation as a football player, being voted All-American in 1911 and 1912. Thorpe later played professionally for the Canton Bulldogs and played major league baseball for the New York Giants, Boston Braves, and Cincinnati Reds.

Thunberg, Clas Arnold Robert [FIN–SSK]. B. 5 April 1893, Helsinki. D. 28 April 1973, Helsinki. Clas Thunberg's record of five Olympic gold medals for speed skating was equaled by Eric Heiden (q.v.) in 1980 but has never been bettered. In 1924, he won the 1,500 meters, 5,000 meters, and the combined event, placed second in the 10,000 meters, and third in the 500 meters. Four years later, he won the 500 meters and successfully defended his 1,500-meters crown.

Further Olympic honors seemed likely at the 1932 Games but, like many leading European skaters, Thunberg refused to compete at Lake Placid as a protest against the mass-start style of racing. An unusual character, he made his World Championship début in 1922 at the age of 28 and his final appearance was in 1935, aged 42. During this period, he missed three Championships (1926, 1930, 1935), but still won 14 individual titles and was the overall champion five times. Thunberg set five world records, the last in 1931 at the age of 38. He later became a Member of the Finnish Parliament.

Tikhonov, Aleksandr Ivanovich [URS/RUS–BIA]. B. 2 January 1947, Chelyabinsk Oblast. During his Olympic biathlon career, which ran from 1968 to 1980, Aleksandr Tikhonov won five medals, of which four were gold medals. All of his gold medals, however, came as a member of the winning Soviet relay teams, winning that event four times consecutively. He is the only athlete to have won a gold medal in the same event at four consecutive Winter Olympics. To his team gold medals, Tikhonov added a silver medal over 20 kilometers in the 1968 individual event. He also finished fourth in that event in 1972 and fifth in 1976. At the World Championships, he won individual titles in 1969–1970 and 1973 over 20 kilometers and over 10 kilometers in 1977. Tikhanov won a further six relay gold medals at the World Championships, giving him a total of 13 biathlon gold medals at the Olympic and World Championships.

Timmons, Stephen Dennis [USA–VOL]. B. 29 November 1958, Newport Beach, California. With three Olympic medals, two of them gold, Steve Timmons shares the record for Olympic volleyball medals won by a man. Timmons led the U.S. to Olympic gold medals in both 1984 and 1988, being named most valuable player of the 1984 Olympic team. Between Olympics, he helped the U.S. win the 1986 World Championship and the 1985 World Cup. Timmons left the national team in 1989 to play professional volleyball for Il Messaggero in Rome. Timmons and Kiraly led Il Messaggero to the 1991 World Club Championship. He then returned to the national team to help the U.S. win a bronze medal at the 1992 Olympics. Timmons owns a beach sportswear company, and was briefly married to the former Jeanne Buss, the daughter of the owner of the Los Angeles Lakers.

Togo [TOG]. Togo has competed at five Olympic Games—those of 1972, 1984, 1988, 1992, 1996, and 2000. The nation's best Olympic performance came in 1988 when welterweight boxer Abdoukerim Hamidou won one match to place equal ninth of 44 in his class. Togo has never competed at the Olympic Winter Games.

Tomba, Alberto [ITA–ASK]. B. 19 December 1966, San Lazzaro di Savena, Bologna. An Olympic gold medalist in the slalom and giant slalom in 1988, Alberto Tomba successfully defended his giant slalom title in 1992 when he also took the silver medal in the slalom. At his third Winter Games in 1994, he placed second in the slalom, giving him a total of five Olympic medals: a record for Alpine skiing, which he shares with Kjetil André Aamodt, Vreni Schneider, and Katja Seizinger (qq.v.). Had Tomba chosen to compete regularly in the downhill and super giant slalom events, he would surely have won even more medals. Surprisingly, in view of his Olympic successes, he had a poor record at the World Championships, where he won a solitary bronze medal in 1987. In contrast, he enjoyed a superb record in the World Cup, winning the slalom in 1988, 1992, and 1994–1995; the giant slalom in 1988, 1991–1992, and 1995; and the overall title in 1995. A flamboyant, dashing character, both on and off the slopes, he was the idol of the Italian sporting public, to whom he was known as "La Bomba."

Tonga [TGA]. Tonga has competed at the 1984, 1988, 1992, 1996, and 2000 Olympics. Tonga has never competed at the Olympic Winter Games. Tonga's one Olympic medal to date came in 1996 when boxer Paea Wolfgram finished second in the unlimited class.

TOP [The Olympic Programme]. *See* OLYMPIC PROGRAMME, THE.

Torres, Dara Grace [USA-SWI]. B. 15 April 1967, Beverly Hills, California. Dara Torres has had the longest successful career of any Olympic swimmer, one which has seen her win nine Olympic medals and four gold medals. Torres began her career in 1984, winning a gold medal in the 4 x 100 freestyle relay. She added a silver and bronze in relays in 1988, and seemingly ended her swimming career with another gold in the 4 x 1 free relay in 1992. Tall and strikingly

252 • TORVILL, JAYNE (LATER MRS. CHRISTENSEN)

attractive, Torres then began a career as a model, becoming the first athlete to appear in *Sports Illustrated*'s swimsuit issue. She also achieved notice as a commercial spokeswoman on an infomercial for a fitness training method. But in late 1998, she elected to return to competitive swimming. With seemingly little time to prepare, she returned to the Olympic pool at Sydney, and won five medals, including two golds in relays. She won three individual bronze medals at Sydney—in the 50 free, the 100 free, and the 100 fly.

Torvill, Jayne (later Mrs. Christensen) B. 7 October 1957, Nottingham; and **Dean, Christopher Colin** B. 27 July 1958, Nottingham. **[GBR–FSK].** The ice dance partnership of Jayne Torvill and Christopher Dean produced one of the legendary performances in Olympic history. Their interpretation of Ravel's "Bolero" at the 1984 Winter Games in Sarajevo drew the maximum score of 6.0 for artistic impression on all nine judges' scorecards. They were clear winners of the Olympic gold medal and set a new standard against which ice dancing was to be judged in the future. Only four weeks later, they repeated their own superlative Olympic performance to win their fourth consecutive world title. A successful and lucrative professional career followed but, after Olympic eligibility had been restored, they took the bronze medal at the 1994 Olympic Winter Games, having earlier won the 1994 European title. Dean has twice been married to figure skating world champions: first to Isabelle Duchesnay, French pair world champion (1991), and currently to the 1990 world ladies' champion, Jill Trenary (USA).

Track & Field. *See* ATHLETICS (TRACK & FIELD).

Trampoline. Trampolining was never contested at the Olympic Games as a demonstration sport. However, the Fédération Internationale de Trampoline (FIT) has been recognized by the International Olympic Committee (IOC) (q.v.). Trampoline made its Olympic début on the 2000 Olympic program as a discipline within the gymnastics program, with one event for men and one for women. *See also* GYMNASTICS.

Tretyak, Vladislav Aleksandrovich [URS–ICH]. B. 25 April 1952, Moscow Oblast. Of the six ice hockey players to have won three

Olympic gold medals, Vladislav Tretyak is the only one to have added a silver medal to his collection. Recognized as one of the greatest goalkeepers of all time, he won Olympic gold in 1972, 1976, and 1984, and silver in 1980 when the Americans defeated the Soviets in a major upset. Tretyak was also on the winning team at nine World Championships and his talents attracted the attention of many National Hockey League (NHL) clubs. The Montreal Canadiens drafted him, but the authorities in the USSR refused to let him play abroad, although he later coached the Chicago Black Hawks goaltenders. Tretyak enjoys the distinction of being the first Soviet player in the Hockey Hall of Fame.

Triathlon. Triathlon is a relatively new sport that consists of running, swimming, and cycling. Its origins date to the 1970s when the first major triathlon, the Ironman Race, was first held in Hawaii. Triathlon is governed by the International Triathlon Union (ITU), which was recognized by the IOC in 1989, currently with 94 members. Triathlon appeared on the Olympic program at the 2000 Olympic Games, with two events: one for men and one for women. The Olympic triathletes race over what is termed the "Olympic distance," 1,500-meter swim, 40-km. cycling, and 10-km. running.

Trinidad and Tobago [TRI]. Trinidad and Tobago has competed continuously at the Olympics since its debut in 1948, competing only as Trinidad through 1956 and in 1964. In 1960, it had one cyclist and one track & field athlete competing in a combined team with Jamaica and Barbados under the name of the *West Indies Federation,* termed the *Antilles* by the Rome organizing committee. Although the West Indies Federation won two medals, no Trinidad athlete was a medal winner in 1960. Trinidad and Tobago competed in the Olympic Winter Games for the first time in 1994 at Lillehammer and competed again in 1998 at Nagano. Trinidad and Tobago has won 11 Olympic medals, eight in track & field athletics and three in weightlifting. Its only gold medal occurred in 1976 when Hasely Crawford won the men's 100 meters in track & field athletics.

Tug-of-War. In 1900, 1904, 1906, 1908, 1912, and 1920, tug-of-war was contested as a part of the track & field athletics program. The sport has not returned to the Olympics since. Three British athletes, Frederick Humphreys, Edwin Mills, and James Shephard, won three tug-of-war medals, two of them gold. The sport is governed internationally by the Tug-of-War International Federation (TWIF), which is provisionally recognized by the IOC.

Tunisia [TUN]. Tunisia has competed at the Olympic Games since 1960, missing only the 1980 Olympic Games. It has never competed at the Olympic Winter Games. Tunisia has won six Olympic medals, four of them by Mohamed Gammoudi, a distance runner, and two in boxing.

Turishcheva, Lyudmila Ivanovna (later Borzova) [URS–GYM]. B. 7 October 1952, Grozny, Checheno-Ingushskaya. Lyudmila Turishcheva ranks with Larisa Latynina (q.v.) as one of the two greatest Soviet female gymnasts ever. But Turishcheva never won the fans' affections that were often reserved during her career for her teammates Olga Korbut and Nelli Kim (qq.v.). Turishcheva won nine Olympic medals, four of them gold. She was all-around champion at the 1972 Olympics, 1970 and 1974 World Championships, 1971 and 1973 European Championships and at the first World Cup in 1975, when she uniquely won all five individual events. She later married Soviet sprint great Valery Borzov and became coach of the Soviet gymnastics teams.

Turkey [TUR]. Turkey was first represented at the Olympic Games of 1906 when an Armenian student at Robert College in Constantinople (now Istanbul) competed in the 800 and 1,500-meter track events. It is often claimed that during a visit to Turkey in 1907, Pierre de Coubertin (q.v.) invited his guide, Aleko Mulas, to take part in the gymnastic events at the 1908 Olympics, but there is no evidence that Mulas competed or was even officially entered. The two Turkish entrants at the 1912 Olympics were again Armenians. Turkey could be said to have really made its Olympic début in 1924 when they sent a 21-man team to the Paris Olympics. Since then, it has missed only the Games of 1932 and 1980. Turkey first competed at the Olympic Winter Games in 1936 and has since missed only the Winter Games of 1952, 1972, and 1980. Turkey has won 64 Olympic medals. Turkish wrestlers account for an outstanding 52 of these, with 27 wrestling gold medals.

Turkmenistan [TKM]. As a former member of the Soviet Union, Turkmenistani athletes competed from 1952 to 1988 on the former Soviet Union teams, and their athletes were present at Barcelona in 1992 as members of the Unified Team. Turkmenistan first competed independently at the 1996 Olympic Games, but it has not yet participated in the Olympic Winter Games.

Turner, Cathy Ann [USA–STK]. B. 10 April 1962, Rochester, New York. Cathy Turner began her speed-skating career in the 1970s, winning the 1979 U.S. short-track title. But she retired in 1980 to pursue a singing and songwriting career. When short-track speed skating became an Olympic sport in 1992, she came out of retirement and won the only individual event on the program, the 500 meters. She defended that title in 1994 at Lillehammer, and added relay medals (silver in 1992 and bronze in 1994) to give her four short-track medals in all. She was one of the few speed skaters to appear in Ice Capades, which she did in 1992, skating and singing. She also appeared on television as one of the American Gladiators.

– U –

Ueberroth, Peter Victor [USA]. B. 2 September 1937, Evanston, Illinois. After the financial disaster of the 1976 Games and the boycott (q.v.) in 1980, there was no longer any great enthusiasm among cities to host the Olympic Games. Los Angeles was the only city to apply to stage the 1984 Games and under Peter Ueberroth's able direction as president of the Organizing Committee, they proved a great success. Although the Games had no public funding, a successful drive for corporate sponsorship and the sale of TV rights resulted in a surplus of more than $220 million. This resulted in a worldwide revival of interest in hosting future editions of the Games. Although the European press initially vilified Ueberroth's methods, his marketing ideas have been adopted by the IOC, and subsequent organizing committees, and are now considered *de rigueur.* Ueberroth later served as commissioner of baseball in the United States, but after he lost the support of the owners, he did not seek re-election for a second term.

Uganda [UGA]. Uganda competed at the Olympics for the first time in 1956. Its participation was continuous through 1972—the highlight that year being John Akii-Bua winning the first Ugandan gold medal with his world record performance in the 400-meter hurdles. In 1976, after the overthrow of Idi Amin, and joining in the African boycott, Uganda did not participate at Montréal. It did compete, however, in both 1980 and 1984. Uganda has never competed at the Olympic Winter Games. Ugandan athletes have won six Olympic medals, two in track & field athletics and four in boxing.

Ukraine [UKR]. As a separate nation, Ukraine had never competed at the Olympics until its début in 1994 at Lillehammer at the Olympic Winter Games and in 1996 at the Olympic Games in Atlanta. This is due mostly to the fact that, until the Soviet revolution of 1991, the Ukraine had only been truly independent in the 20th century for a brief period around the time of the Bolshevik Revolution (and was at civil war for most of that time). Many Ukrainians competed for the Soviet Union at the Olympic Games, however. The Ukraine was second only to Russia among Soviet republics in terms of medals won. Ukrainian athletes were present at Albertville and Barcelona in 1992 as members of the Unified Team (q.v.). At Lillehammer, the Ukraine accounted for two Olympic medals, highlighted by the gold-medal-winning performance of Oksana Baiul in women's figure skating. The Ukraine has never hosted an Olympic Games, but in 1980 several preliminary football (soccer) matches were held in Kiev. Through 2000, the Ukraine has won 49 Olympic medals, 13 of them gold.

Ulvang, Vegard [NOR–NSK]. B. 10 October 1963, Kirkenes. After achieving only modest success at the 1988 Winter Games, Vegard Ulvang dominated cross-country skiing at the 1992 Games. At Calgary in 1988, he won a bronze medal in the 30 km. but four years later at Albertville, he won three golds (10 km., 30 km., and relay) and a silver (combined pursuit). In 1994, he was no longer a major contender for individual honors, but won his sixth Olympic medal with a silver in the relay. He competed injured in 1994, and also shortly after the trauma of his younger brother being lost and dying while running in the woods in the autumn of 1993.

Underwater Swimming. Underwater swimming has never been contested as a separate sport at the Olympic Games, even as a demonstration sport (q.v.). However, the Confédération Mondiale des Activités Subaquatiques (CMAS) is recognized by the IOC. Founded in 1959, it currently has 94 affiliated member nations. In 1900 at Paris, the swimming program did include an underwater swimming event and the 1904 Olympic swimming program included a plunge for distance event.

Unified Team (Équipe Unifié) (aka CIS) [EUN]. Because of the Soviet revolution of 1991, the Unified Team represented the Commonwealth of Independent States (q.v.) at the 1992 Olympics in both Albertville and Barcelona. At Albertville, the Unified Team was a loose confederation of five former Soviet republics—Russia, Belarus (formerly Byelorussia), the Ukraine, Kazakstan, and Uzbekistan. At Barcelona, the Unified Team had representatives from all the former Soviet republics, save for the Baltic states of Estonia, Latvia, and Lithuania, which competed independently. The Unified Team at Barcelona also included athletes from Georgia, which had not joined the Commonwealth of Independent States. In 1994, the republics began to compete independently.

Union of Soviet Socialist Republics (USSR) [URS]. The Soviet Union has had two distinct periods of Olympic participation. From 1900 through 1912, it competed at the Olympics as *Russia*. However, after the Bolshevik Revolution, the Soviet Union withdrew from international sport until the late 1940s. After World War II, it competed in the European Championships in track & field athletics in 1946, but it did not return to the Olympics until 1952 at Helsinki. It made its inaugural Olympic Winter Games appearance in 1956 at Cortina. It competed at every Olympics from 1956 to 1988, with the exception of the 1984 Los Angeles Olympics. In 1992, its constituent republics competed as the *Unified Team (EUN)* (q.v.). After returning to the Olympics, the Soviet Union was a dominant force in almost all Olympic sports. The Soviet Union was disbanded in late 1991 after the August revolution. It no longer competes as a single nation at the Olympics because its 15 former republics now compete as independent nations. The Soviet Union hosted the Games of the XXIInd Olympiad in Moscow in 1980.

United Arab Emirates [UAE]. The United Arab Emirates has competed at the Olympics in 1984, 1988, 1992, 1996, and 2000. It is no surprise that the United Arab Emirates, a desert nation, has never competed at the Olympic Winter Games.

United Arab Republic [UAR]. *See* EGYPT and SYRIA.

United States of America [USA]. The United States has competed at every Olympic Games, with the exception of the 1980 Moscow Games, and has never failed to be represented at the Olympic Winter Games. In addition, it had skaters present in both 1908 and 1920, when those events were held with the summer celebration. It has been the dominant country in terms of medals won since the inception of the Games. However, in the era from 1952 to 1988, the Soviet Union won slightly more medals, and the German Democratic Republic threatened this dominance prior to its merger with West Germany in October 1990. The United States has also been host to the Olympic Games more than any other country. Four times the Games of the Olympiad have been held in the United States: 1904 in St. Louis, 1932 in Los Angeles, 1984 in Los Angeles, and 1996 in Atlanta. The Olympic Winter Games have also been held in the United States three times: 1932 in Lake Placid, 1960 in Squaw Valley, and 1980 in Lake Placid. The 2002 Olympic Winter Games will be held in Salt Lake City, Utah.

United States Basketball Team—1960. The United States 1960 Olympic basketball team was one of the greatest basketball teams ever assembled. It is almost certainly the greatest amateur team ever and its line-up would match up well with almost any professional team ever. The team easily won the gold medal at Rome in 1960. The team members were Burdette Haldorson, Jay Arnette, Walter Bellamy, Robert Boozer, Terry Dischinger, Darrall Imhoff, Allen Kelley, Lester Lane, Jerry Lucas, Oscar Robertson, Adrian Smith, and Jerry West. The starting line-up usually consisted of Robertson and West as guards. As professionals, they would later be considered the two finest guards of their era.

United States Basketball Team—1984. The United States 1984 Olympic basketball team rivaled the United States 1960 team as a great amateur unit. The team was coached by Bob Knight of Indiana University, and was never challenged in winning the gold medal. It was led by Michael Jordan (q.v.) of the University of North Carolina, who would later be considered the greatest professional player ever. The team members were Steve Alford, Leon Wood, Patrick Ewing, Vern Fleming, Alvin Robertson, Michael Jordan, Joseph Kleine, Jon Koncak, Wayman Tisdale, Chris Mullin, Samuel Perkins, and Jeffrey Turner. Ewing, Jordan, and Mullin would also later play on the 1992 Dream Team.

United States' Virgin Islands [ISV]. Since making its Olympic début in 1968, the U.S. Virgin Islands has only missed the Olympics Games of 1980. It has competed at every Olympic Winter Games since 1984. Peter Holmberg won a silver medal in 1988 Finn monotype yachting, the only medal yet won by an athlete from the U.S. Virgin Islands.

Uphoff, Nicole [FRG/GER–EQU]. B. 25 January 1967, Duisburg. A dressage rider, Nicole Uphoff won her first international event in 1987 aboard Rembrandt. It presaged her dominance of dressage for the coming years. In both 1992 and 1996, she won the individual dressage gold medal and helped Germany to the team title at the Olympics. She repeated her double victories at the 1989 Europeans and 1990 World Championships. She retired after the 1996 Olympic Games, marrying German Olympic show jumper Otto Becker.

Upper Volta [VOL]. *See* BURKINA FASO.

Uruguay [URU]. Uruguay first competed at the 1924 Olympics in Paris and has competed at every Games since, with the exception of the 1980 Games in Moscow. It had only one competitor in 1932, but he did quite well; Douglas Guillermo won a silver medal in the single sculls rowing. Uruguay first competed in the Olympic Winter Games in 1988 when it was represented by one alpine skier. Uruguay has won 10 Olympic medals. Two of these were gold, the outstanding victories by the Uruguayan football (soccer) teams in 1924 and 1928.

Uruguay Football Teams [1924 and 1928]. In both 1924 and 1928, Uruguay won the gold medal in the Olympic football (soccer) tournament. This was considered a major upset in 1924 because Uruguay had never before even entered the Olympic football (soccer) tournament. In fact, since 1928, Uruguay has not even competed in the Olympic football tournament. In 1930, the Uruguay team revealed its greatness when several of its Olympic players helped Uruguay to win the inaugural World Cup in football. The players who played on both the World Cup team and at least one of Uruguay's gold medal teams were: Héctor Castro (1924, 1928 Olympic, 1930 World Cup), Pedro Cea (1928 Olympic, 1930 World Cup), José Nasazzi (1924, 1928 Olympic, 1930 World Cup), José Andrade (1924, 1928 Olympic, 1930 World Cup), Lorenzo Fernández (1928 Olympic, 1930 World Cup), Alvaro Gestido (1928 Olympic, 1930 World Cup), and Hector Scarone (1924, 1928 Olympic, 1930 World Cup).

Uzbekistan [UZB]. Many Uzbeki athletes competed from 1952 to 1988 for the Soviet Union, and Uzbeki athletes were present at Barcelona and Albertville in 1992 as members of the Unified Team. As an independent nation, Uzbekistan competed at the Olympic Winter Games of 1994 and 1998, and at the 1996 and 2000 Olympic Games. Lina Cheryazova won a gold medal in 1994 freestyle skiing aerials, the only medal won by Uzbekistan to date at the Olympic Winter Games. Uzbekistan has won seven Olympic medals, two gold.

– V –

Val Barker Award. The Val Barker Award is given at each Olympic Games to the boxer who is judged to be the best overall technical boxer. It is named in honor of Val Barker of Great Britain, a former president of the Association Internationale de Boxe Amateur (AIBA), and was first awarded in 1936. Though typically it is given to one of the boxing gold medalists, three times it has been awarded to a non-champion, as follows: 1936 flyweight bronze medalist Louis Lauria (USA); 1968 featherweight bronze medalist Philip Waruinge (KEN); and 1988 light-middleweight silver medalist Roy Jones (USA).

Välbe, Yelena (née Trubizina) [EUN/RUS–NSK]. B. 24 April 1968, Magadan, Siberia. With 16 victories at the Olympic Games and

World Championships, Yelena Välbe has won more major championships than any other female cross-country skier. She was World Cup champion in 1989 and 1991–1992 and was favored to win multiple medals at the 1992 Olympic Winter Games. She succeeded in earning a medal in every event, but in the four individual events, she won four bronze medals. She has three Olympic gold medals in the 1992, 1994, and 1998 relay. Her greatest performance came at the 1997 Worlds when she won a gold medal in all five cross-country events for women. At the World Championships, she won the following titles: 1989—10 km. and 30 km.; 1991—10 km. and 15 km.; 1993—15 km. and relay; 1995—30 km. and relay; and 1997—5 km., 15 km., 30 km., pursuit, and relay.

Van Innis, Hubert [BEL–ARC]. B. 24 February 1866, Elewyt. D. 25 November 1961, Zemst. Hubert Van Innis must be considered the supreme Olympic archer who won a record six gold medals and a record total of 10 medals at the Games of 1900 and 1920. Although the exceptional number of archery events at these Games clearly helped him toward his record medal total, this advantage was countered by his absence from the 1904 and 1908 Games and by the fact that archery events were not held at the 1912 Games. After his successes in 1920, archery was never again an Olympic sport during his lifetime. In 1933, at the age of 67, Van Innis won a team gold medal at the World Championships and in all probability would have won further Olympic medals, had he been given the opportunity. Van Innis was an architect by profession.

Vanuatu [VAN]. Vanuatu made its Olympic début in 1988 at Seoul and also competed in 1992, 1996, and 2000. Vanuatu has not yet competed at the Olympic Winter Games and its athletes have not yet won a medal.

Venezuela [VEN]. Venezuela formed a National Olympic Committee in 1935 and achieved IOC recognition in the same year. However, it was not until 1948 that Venezuelans competed at the Olympics. The Venezuelans have been represented at the Olympic Games without fail since 1948. It first competed in the Olympic Winter Games in 1998 when it was represented by a single lugeist. Venezuela has won eight Olympics medals, five in boxing, and one each in men's track & field athletics, men's shooting, and men's swimming.

Vietnam [VIE]. The original NOC for Vietnam was founded on 25 November 1951 and was recognized by the International Olympic Committee (IOC) (q.v.) in 1952. After the Vietnam War, the committee was restructured on 20 December 1976 and waited four years for IOC recognition. Since making its Olympic début in 1952, Vietnam has only missed the Olympics of 1976 and 1984. It has never competed at the Olympic Winter Games. Vietnam won its first Olympic medal in 2000 at Sydney, when Tran Hieu Ngan finished second in women's 57-kg. class taekwondo.

Vikelas, Demetrios [GRE]. B. 6 June 1835, Syra. D. 7 July 1908, Athens. Demetrios Vikelas was the first International Olympic Committee (IOC) (q.v.) president (1894–1896). Vikelas was better known as a writer and for his interest in literature and the arts than for his sporting inclinations. But because he lived in Paris and was well acquainted with Pierre de Coubertin (q.v.), he represented Greece and the Pan-Hellenic Gymnastic Club at the 1894 Olympic Congress in Paris. It was felt that the IOC president should come from the country hosting the next Games and with Athens being awarded the 1896 Games, Vikelas was appointed president. Despite his lack of experience in sports administration, he proved an able and enthusiastic president before handing the office over to Coubertin at the successful conclusion of the 1896 Games.

Virén, Lasse Artturi [ATH-FIN]. B. 27 July 1949, Myrsklä. At Munich in 1972, Lasse Virén became, only the fourth man to win the Olympic 5,000 and 10,000 meters at the same Games. Virén repeated this feat in 1976, a unique double-double. Despite falling early in the 1972 10,000 meters, his time was a new world record. Attempting to emulate Zátopek's 1952 triple that included a marathon victory, Virén entered the 1976 marathon as well, finishing fifth. Virén also competed at the 1980 Olympic Games, finishing fifth in the 10,000, and failing to finish the marathon. Virén was less successful at other major meets, with his best efforts at the European Championships being a fourth in the 5,000 meters and third in the 10,000 meters in 1974.

Virgin Islands, British [IVB]. *See* BRITISH VIRGIN ISLANDS.

Virgin Islands, U.S. [ISV]. *See* UNITED STATES' VIRGIN IS-LANDS.

Volleyball. Volleyball, like basketball, is a sport whose origin is known almost to the day. Oddly, both sports were invented at the same college and within a few years of one another. Volleyball was invented in 1895 by William G. Morgan, a student at Springfield College and a director of the YMCA at Holyoke, Massachusetts. The game was originally called *minonette*.

Volleyball quickly spread around the world and became more popular in other countries than in the United States. The sport was introduced in the Olympics in 1964 by the Japanese, although it was never contested as a demonstration sport (q.v.) at the Olympics. No country has been truly dominant in volleyball, although the Soviet Union has won the most medals. Originally, the Japanese had the world's best women's players and the United States had the best men's team in the world for most of the 1980s.

Volleyball has now reached great heights of popularity in the United States, spurred on by beach volleyball, a two-man outdoor sport played by the ocean or on any sand-covered court. In 1993, the IOC approved beach volleyball as an Olympic sport that was contested at the 1996 Atlanta Olympics. Two-person beach volleyball for men and women remained on the Olympic program in 2000. It has been called "*Baywatch* with a medal ceremony."

The international governing body of volleyball is the Fédération Internationale de Volleyball (FIVB), which was formed in 1947 and had 218 member nations as of December 2000. This makes volleyball the international federation with the most affiliated nations worldwide.

Volleyball, Beach. *See* VOLLEYBALL.

von Halmay, Zoltán [HUN–SWI]. B. 18 June 1881. D. 20 May 1956. Zoltán von Halmay was the first great swimmer from Continental Europe, winning nine Olympic medals (three gold, five silver, one bronze) between 1900 and 1908 at distances ranging from 50 yards to 4,000 meters. His gold medals came in the 50- and 100-yard freestyle in 1904 and the 4 x 250-meter relay in 1906. His 1904 50-yard freestyle victory came in a second race after the judges declared a dead heat in the first race between von Halmay and J. Scott Leary of the United States. Von Halmay swam mostly with his arms, without any leg movements, but in 1905 he set what is considered the inaugural record for 100 meters. The record remained unbeaten for more than four years, a remarkable length of time during a period of rapid development in the sport.

– W –

Waldo, Carolyn [CAN–SYF]. B. 11 December 1964, Montreal, Quebec. At the 1984 Olympics, Carolyn Waldo finished second in the solo synchronized swimming event behind Tracie Ruiz (USA) (q.v.). But Waldo then displaced her as the top synchronized performer, winning the 1986 World Championships in solo and duet, partnered by Michelle Cameron, and competing on the winning team. She had also earned a team gold at the 1982 Worlds. At the 1988 Olympic Games in Seoul, Waldo won the solo gold medal and, together with Cameron, added the duet gold medal as well. Waldo won "triples," the solo, duet, and team championships, at the 1985 FINA Cup, 1986 World Championships, and the 1987 Pan-Pacific Meet. She also competed on winning teams at the 1981 Pan-Pacifics and the 1983 Pan-American Games.

Wales. Wales competed as a separate country in 1908 field hockey, finishing third. In all other Olympics, and in all the other sports at the 1908 Olympics, Wales has competed as a member of the United Kingdom of Great Britain and Northern Ireland.

Walter-Martin, Steffi (née Martin) [GDR–LUG]. B. 17 September 1962, Schlema. Steffi Walter-Martin is the only woman to win two Olympic gold medals for luge. She took the title in 1984 and 1988 and on both occasions led the East Germans to a clean sweep of the medals. She was also the World Champion in 1983 and 1985, and won the World Cup in 1984.

Watanabe, Osamu [JPN–WRE]. B. 21 October 1940. It is possible that Osamu Watanabe is the greatest wrestler ever, pound-for-pound. He had a very short career but he was never beaten. It is known that he won at least 187 consecutive matches until his victory in the 1964 Olympics at Tokyo when he won the feather-weight freestyle gold medal. In that tournament, Watanabe won all of his matches without sacrificing a single point. This followed Watanabe's victories in the 1962 and 1963 World Championships. He was not immensely strong, but was very quick and his technical skills were unmatched in his era.

Water Polo. Water polo was developed in Europe and the United States as two separate sports. In the United States it was termed *softball water polo* because the ball was an unfilled bladder and the sport was very rough, often degenerating into numerous fights. In 1897, Harold Reeder of New York formulated the first rules for that sport, which were intended to decrease the excessive roughness of the game. The European style of water polo predominated and today is the form of the game practiced universally. It is more scientific, faster, and less dangerous than the American game.

Water polo was played at the Olympics of both 1900 and 1904. It was not on the 1906 Olympic program, but has been contested at all Games since. Great Britain won four of the first five Olympic tournaments, but by far the greatest exponents of water polo have been the Hungarians. Between 1928 and 1980, Hungary never failed to medal in the sport at the Olympics. Hungary did not compete in 1984 and failed to medal in 1988 and 1992.

Women's World Championships are held in water polo, and women competed in water polo at the 2000 Olympic Games for the first time. Water polo, like swimming and diving, is governed by the Fédération Internationale de Natation Amateur (FINA), which was formed in 1908 and has 176 affiliated nations.

Water Skiing. Water skiing was a demonstration sport at the 1972 Olympics. The sport is governed by the International Water Ski Federation (IWSF), which was formed in 1946 and is recognized by the IOC. There are currently 80 affiliated member nations. It was thought that water skiing might possibly be added to the Olympic Program for the 2004 Olympic Games in Athens, but that was voted down by the Executive Board in December 2000.

Weightlifting. Weightlifting in various forms has been popular for centuries. Strongmen of all types often performed at various fairs in the Middle Ages. In the 19th century, professional strongmen often toured with carnivals or vaudeville shows. However, weightlifting as a sport became organized only in the late 19th century. The governing body is the International Weightlifting Federation (IWF), which had 167 member nations in late 2000. The first governing body of weightlifting was founded in 1905 as the Amateur Athleten Weltunion. The current Federation was founded in 1920 as *the Fédération Internationale Haltérophile*, and adopted the current name in 1972.

Weightlifting has been on the program of the Olympics, except in the years of 1900, 1908, and 1912. The program has varied little except for the addition of more and more weight classes in recent years. Originally, there were no weight classes, only an open competition. In 1920 and 1924, there were also one-handed lifts. Beginning in 1928, the three Olympic lifts were standardized as the military press, the snatch, and the clean & jerk. Because of difficulties judging the press, and because there was some concern that the lift was biomechanically dangerous to lifters' backs, it was eliminated from international competition after the 1972 Olympics. Today, lifters compete only in the snatch and the clean & jerk at the Olympics. Women (q.v.) made their Olympic début in weightlifting at the 2000 Olympic Games in Sydney, with separate events for seven weight classes.

Weightlifting has been dominated by the Soviet Union and its republics since its entry to the Olympics in 1952. In the 1970s and 1980s, Bulgaria challenged that dominance, although a number of its lifters ran afoul of drug testing, notably in 1992. The United States was once a weightlifting power, but has won only one Olympic medal since 1968 (and none since 1976), with the exception of the 1984 Olympics, which were not attended by the East European nations.

Beginning in 1993, the weight classes in international weightlifting have been changed, with a completely new set of world records. This is to eliminate the possibility of earlier records having been set by drug users prior to stricter drug controls.

Weissmuller, Johnny (né Petr Jánós Weiszmüller) [USA–SWI/WAP]. B. 2 June 1904, Freidorf, then Hungary. D. 20 January 1984, Acapulco, Mexico. Johnny Weissmuller was the winner of the 100-meter freestyle in 1924 and 1928, the 400-meter freestyle in 1928, and a member of the winning relay team in both years. He set 28 world records and such was his margin of superiority over his contemporaries that some authorities still rate him ahead of Mark Spitz (q.v.) as the greatest swimmer of all time. Because of the limited number of events available to Weissmuller, his Olympic record cannot be fairly compared with that of Spitz, but the longevity of his records is testament to his greatness. His 1927 world record for the 100-yard freestyle was unbeaten for 17 years, a remarkable length of time during a period of rapid development in the sport. Much of his success was due to his revolutionary high-riding stroke, flutter kick, and head-turning breathing. Invited for a screen test for the role of Tarzan, Weissmuller was preferred to 150 other applicants and went on to become the most famous screen Tarzan of all, playing the role in 19 movies between 1934 and 1948.

Wenzel, Hanni [LIE–ASK]. B. 14 December 1956, Staubirnen, Germany. With a total of four medals, Hanni Wenzel trails only Vreni Schneider and Katja Seizinger (qq.v.) as the most successful of all women Olympic Alpine skiers. After winning a bronze medal in the slalom in 1976, Wenzel won gold in the slalom and giant slalom and a silver in the giant slalom in 1980. Born in Germany, Wenzel moved to Liechtenstein as an infant and was granted citizenship after winning the slalom at the 1974 World Championships. Both her brother and sister were Olympic Alpine skiers.

West Indies Federation. In 1960, Jamaica, Barbados, and Trinidad competed as a combined team, representing the West Indies Federation. The Rome organizing committee called the "nation" the *Antilles*, a term that has, unfortunately, been often copied in many books. The West Indies team consisted of 12 athletes in 1960, one from Barbados, four from Trinidad, and seven from Jamaica (qq.v.), who competed in track & field athletics, cycling, sailing, shooting, and weightlifting. Since 1960, the three constitutent nations have competed independently as separate nations.

Westergren, Carl Oscar "Calle" [SWE–WRE]. B. 13 October 1895, Malmö. D. 5 August 1958. Prior to the 1990s, Carl Westergren was the most successful Olympic wrestler in the Græco-Roman style, and his Olympic records in that discipline have been equaled only by Russia's Aleksandr Karelin (q.v.). A four-time Olympian, he won gold in 1920 (middleweight), 1924 (light-heavyweight), and 1932 (unlimited), but in 1928, when he was defending his light-heavyweight title, he was surprisingly defeated in the first round by Onni Pellinen of Finland and withdrew from the competition. His total of three Olympic gold medals is a record shared with Ivar Johansson (SWE), Aleksandr Medved (URS) (qq.v.), and Karelin. Westergren was a three-time European champion and was the world middleweight champion in 1922.

Western Samoa [SAM]. *See* SAMOA.

Winkler, Hans Günter [FRG–EQU]. B. 24 July 1926, Wuppertal-Barmen. Hans Günter Winkler has the finest record ever of any German show jumper and his overall record internationally is rivaled only by France's Pierre Jonquères d'Oriola and Italy's Raimondo D'Inzeo (q.v.). Winkler won seven Olympic medals (five gold, one silver, one bronze), but only one in the individual event. That individual medal, a gold, came in 1956 when Winkler won the show jumping at the Melbourne Olympics. He led Germany to team golds in 1956, 1960, 1964, and 1972, a bronze in 1968, and a silver in 1976. Winkler's 1956 championship was his third consecutive internationally. In 1954 and 1955, he won the first two World Championships in show jumping.

Winter Pentathlon. In 1948 at St. Moritz, a winter pentathlon event was held as a demonstration sport (q.v.). The events of the winter pentathlon were cross-country skiing, shooting, downhill skiing, fencing, and horse riding.

Witt, Katarina [GDR/GER–FSK]. B. 3 December 1965, Karl-Marx-Stadt (now Chemnitz). As a gold medalist in 1984 and 1988 Katarina Witt became the first woman figure skater to retain an Olympic title since Sonja Henie (q.v.). She was also a four-time World Champion

(1984–1985, 1987–1988). After taking the Olympic and world titles in 1988, she turned professional. With the return to Olympic eligibility of certain professionals, Witt took part in the Winter Games for a third time in 1994, but some of the magic of the earlier days had gone and she finished in seventh place. Witt became enormously wealthy because of her talent, but also because of her beauty, which attracted many commercial endorsements.

Women at the Olympics. The first connection between women and the Olympic Games can be traced back to the 10th century B.C. when the Herean Games, a sporting and religious festival exclusively for women, were held at Olympia, although not as part of the Ancient Olympic Games (q.v.). The Herean Games were held quadrennially in honor of Hera, the wife of Zeus. There was only one event, a footrace of about 160 meters, but it was divided into three age categories, allowing young girls to compete. The women were given crowns of olive, similar to the Olympic prizes, and they also received a portion of a heifer that was sacrificed to Hera.

The first recorded Ancient Olympic Games occurred in 776 B.C., although it is considered that their origins date to the 12th century B.C. Discrimination against women in sport is as old as these Games themselves, as women could not take part in the Ancient Olympic Games. In fact, with few exceptions, they were not even allowed as spectators. Strangely, young girls could watch, although the athletes were competing nude. Pausanias noted, "They do not prevent virgins from watching." Only one adult woman was allowed to witness the Games, that being the Priestess of Demeter Chamyne, who was awarded this honorary office every four years from the Eleans. The penalty for women watching the Olympic Games was severe. Any woman caught watching the Games, or even crossing the River Alpheios on the days the Olympics were held, would be put to death by being tossed from the cliffs of Mount Typaion.

The Olympic boxing crown in 404 B.C. was won by Eukles, who was the son of Akousilaos and the grandson of Diagoras, who won the Olympic boxing championships in 464 and 448 B.C. To this time, legend has it that women were put to death if they were discovered watching the events. However, Eukles' mother, Kallipateira, attended his matches, disguised as a trainer. When he won, she leaped over the barrier behind the trainer's station and exposed herself as a woman. The judges withheld the death penalty "out of respect for her father and her brothers and son" (Finley and Pleket, *The Olympic Games: The First Thousand Years*, pp. 45–46). A rule was then enacted requiring all trainers to thereafter attend all Olympic contests fully naked, like the athletes.

In 396 B.C., the first female Olympic champion was crowned when Princess Kyniska of Sparta, the daughter of Sparta's King Archidamos, won the tethrippon, a four-horse chariot race. But it should be mentioned that in the Ancient Olympics, the winners of the chariot races were considered to be the owners of the chariots and horses, not the drivers.

No females officially competed in the first modern Olympics in 1896. There is fairly good evidence, however, that a woman ran the marathon course near the time of the Olympic race after she was not allowed to compete in the actual race. The Greek woman runner's name was Stamata Revithi, but this has only recently been discovered. For years, she has been known as *Melpomene*, a name chosen by the Greek media to honor the Greek muse of tragedy.

The 1900 Olympic Games were very odd, as they were held in conjunction with a large world's fair, the Paris International Exposition. It is not precisely certain which events conducted at the fair should be considered "Olympic" and years later, many athletes did not even know that had competed in the 1900 Olympic Games. But the Games of 1900 are important for they saw the first official female Olympic participants, when a total of 19 competitors from Bohemia, France, Great Britain, Switzerland, and the United States took part in croquet, golf, sailing, and tennis. The first known woman to compete in the Olympics was a Swiss yachtswoman, Hélène de Pourtalès, who crewed on her husband's yacht in the 1- to 2-ton class. By winning the tennis singles and mixed doubles on 11 July 1900, Charlotte Cooper of Great Britain became the first individual female champion at the modern Olympic Games. There was a women's golf competition, won by Margaret Abbott of the United States, although in later life, Ms. Abbott did not even know she had competed at the Olympic Games. Women also competed in ballooning competition at the fair, although again, it is uncertain if this was an Olympic event. It is interesting to note that at the 1900 Paris Exposition, a Feminist Congress was held within the walls of the Exposition.

Over the next few Olympics, women gradually were allowed to compete in a few Olympic sports. A detailed list of how women's sports have been added to the Olympic program follows. Briefly, in 1904 at St. Louis, there was a women's archery event. In 1908, women competed at London in figure skating and motorboating. A big step forward occurred in 1912 when women competed in swimming and diving at the Olympic Games, the first truly "athletic" events at the summer Olympics.

Through the 1924 Olympics, women were not allowed to compete in track & field athletics, the most publicized sport at the Olympic Games. In response, women formed their own organization, the Fédération Sportive Feminine Internationale (FSFI), which sponsored the "Women's Olympics" in Paris in 1922 and the "Second International Ladies' Games" in Göteborg, Sweden, in 1926. Only after these events proved that women could turn in credible athletic performances did the International Amateur Athletic Federation (IAAF) agree to allow them to compete in the 1928 Games, albeit only in five events.

All went well, except in the 800 meters, when Lina Radke, the German winner, left a field of exhausted runners sprawled in various stages of collapse behind her. The International Olympic Committee (IOC) (q.v.) then banned women from any events beyond 200 meters, on the grounds that they were not physically equipped to run long distances. The ban remained in effect for 32 years, until the 1960 Olympics, when the 800-meters women's event was reinstated, with longer races to follow, beginning in 1972.

Why was there so much resistance to allowing women to compete at the Olympic Games? Much of the problem can be traced to the founder of the modern Olympic Games, Baron Pierre de Coubertin (q.v.). He did not want women to compete on Olympian fields, and his philosophy toward woman and sports is the greatest stain on his remarkable achievements. Although Coubertin has been deified by some followers of the Olympic Movement (q.v.), others have not treated him so kindly because of his views on women in sports. Jean-Marie Brohm wrote of him, "It is indeed confusion to declare Coubertin a great humanist when his written texts or his quoted remarks are clearly those of a blind reactionary for anyone who knows how to read them, [consisting of] elitism and sexism . . ."

Coubertin wrote a great deal during his life, and his writings on women in sports, when read in the 21st century, do not reflect well on him. Note the following, "With regard to boys ... sporting competition ... is vital with all its consequences and all its risks. Feminized, it becomes something monstrous." And, "I still . . . think that . . . feminine athletics ... are bad and that these athletics should be excluded from the Olympic programme—that the Olympiads have been restored for the rare and solemn glorification of the [male adult]."

Since 1928, women have seen their presence in the Olympic stadium increase almost at every Olympic Games, although they do not yet have an equal role with men. Since 1900, only in 1920, 1932, 1956, and 1972 has the women's program at the Olympics not been enlarged in some way. It is instructive to look at some of the numbers regarding women's participation at the Olympics. In 1912, 15 sports were open exclusively to men, three for women, and two mixed sports. Men could compete in 143 events, while women only in 21, 14 of those mixed events. At Sydney in 2000, there were 300 events in 28 sports, with 25 sports open to women. Of these 300 events, there were 168 events for men only, 120 for women only, and 12 mixed events. Women now actually compete at the Olympics in three sports or disciplines not open to men: rhythmic gymnastics, synchronized swimming, and softball.

The Olympic Winter Games are even better, and near equality is upon us on the snow and ice. At Salt Lake City in 2002, there will be 78 events in 6 sports and 14 disciplines, of which all sports and disciplines will be open to women. Of these 78 events, 42 events will be for men only, 34 for women only, and 2 mixed events in figure skating. Women and men have equal programs in Alpine skiing, biathlon, figure skating, freestyle skiing, ice hockey, short-track speed skating, snowboarding, and speed skating. Women still lag slightly with fewer events than men in bobsledding (1 vs. 2), luge (1 vs. 2), and primarily, Nordic skiing, in which the men will have 12 events, and the women 6. This discrepancy exists because women do not yet compete at the Olympics in the Nordic disciplines of ski jumping and Nordic combined.

As noted, the list of sports, disciplines, and events in which women compete at the Olympic Games has increased almost at every Olympics. The following list of sports have been added to the

Olympic program for women and the years in which they have been added:

	Olympic Games	Winter Games/Sports
1900	Croquet, Golf, Tennis, Sailing	—
1904	Archery	—
1908	Motorboating	Figure Skating
1912	Diving, Swimming	—
1924	Fencing	—
1928	Gymnastics, Track & Field	—
1936	—	Alpine Skiing
1948	Canoe & Kayaking	—
1952	Equestrian Events	Nordic Skiing
1960	—	Speed Skating
1964	Volleyball	Luge
1968	Shooting*	—
1976	Basketball, Handball, Rowing	—
1980	Hockey (Field)	—
1984	Cycling, Shooting†	—
1988	Table Tennis, Sailing§	—
1992	Badminton, Judo	Biathlon
1994	***	—
1996	Football (Soccer), Softball	***
1998	***	Curling, Ice Hockey
2000	Modern Pentathlon, Taekwondo Triathlon, Weightlifting	***
2002	***	Bobsled, Skeleton

*Women were admitted to shooting in 1968 as mixed events.
†Separate shooting events for women began in 1984.
§Separate sailing events for women began in 1988.
*** Games not held in that year.

Women play other roles in the Olympic Movement. In 1956 at Cortina, Italian skier Giuliana Chenal Minuzzo was the first woman to take the Athletes' Oath (q.v.) on behalf of the competitors. At Mexico City in 1968, Enriqueta Basilio de Sotelo became the first woman to light the main Olympic Torch in the stadium, although Sweden's

Karin Lindberg lit one of the torches in 1956 at the Equestrian Olympic Games. Heidi Schüller (FRG) was the first woman to take the Athletes' Oath at the Summer Olympics in 1972 at Munich.

The IOC resisted female membership for a long time. It was not until 1981 that the first women became members of the IOC. Two were elected in that year—Flor Isava-Fonseca (VEN) and Pirjo Vilmi-Häggman (FIN). Three women to date have served on the IOC Executive Board (q.v.), which really has the power within the IOC. One is Anita DeFrantz of the United States, who was elected as a vice president in 1997, and in 2000 advanced to 1st vice president. Ms. DeFrantz was also an Olympic medallist, winning a bronze medal in rowing eights in 1976. The first female Executive Board member was Ms. Isava-Fonseca, serving from 1990 to 1994. They were joined in 2000 by Sweden's Gunilla Lindberg, who was elected to the Executive Board.

The IOC has publicly stated that it is committed to bringing more and more women into the highest levels of sports administration. In 1996, the IOC mandated that National Olympic Committees (NOCs) (q.v.), International Federations (IFs) (q.v.), and other members of the Olympic Movement should reach a goal of 10 percent of women in administrative positions by the year 2000, with that percentage increasing to 20 percent by 2005. Through 2000, the full list of women elected to the IOC is as follows:

Dates of Service	Name [Nation]
1981–1999	Pirjo Vilmi-Häggman [FIN]
1981–	Flor Isava-Fonseca [VEN]
1982–1993	Dame Mary Alison Glen Haig [GBR]
1984–	Her Royal Highness Princess Nora [LIE]
1986–	Anita Luceete DeFrantz [USA]
1988–	Princess Anne, Her Royal Highness the Princess Royal [GBR]
1990–2001	Carol Anne Letheren [CAN]
1995–	Věra Čáslavská [CZE]
1996–	Gunilla Lindberg [SWE]
1996–	Princess Doña Pilar de Borbon [ESP/FEI]
1996–	Lu Shengrong [CHN]
1998–	Irena Szewińska-Kirszenstein [POL]
1998–	Nawal El-Moutawakel Bennis [MAR]

1999–2000	Hassiba Boulmerka [ALG/Athlete]
1999–	Charmaine Crooks [CAN/Athlete]
1999–	Manuela Di Centa [ITA/Athlete]
2000–	Susan O'Neill [AUS/Athlete]

World Anti-Doping Agency [WADA]. In 1999, the International Olympic Committee (IOC) (q.v.) announced the formation of a new entity in the world of sports administration, the World Anti-Doping Agency. WADA was formed in response to the proliferation of doping (drug use) in sports. Its express purpose is to oversee drug testing in sports, educate athletes against the use of drugs, and to eventually eliminate doping. In mid-1999, it was announced that the Canadian IOC member Dick Pound (q.v.) would be the first head of WADA.

Wrestling. Wrestling is the most ancient known competitive sport. Wrestling was introduced into the Ancient Olympic Games (q.v.) in 708 B.C., shortly after the Games' recorded history begins in 776 B.C. Ancient Olympic champions are recorded from Eurybatos of Sparta (708 B.C.) through Aurelius Aelix of Phoenicia (213 A.D.). The most titled champions at Olympia were Milon of Kroton, who won five titles in wrestling (532–516 B.C.) and one in boys' wrestling (540 B.C.), and Hipposthenes of Sparta, who also won five wrestling titles (624–608 B.C.) and one boys' wrestling title (632 B.C.) at Ancient Olympia.

Only in 1900 has wrestling not been on the Olympic program. The four main forms of amateur competitive wrestling practiced in the world are: Græco-Roman wrestling, freestyle wrestling, judo wrestling, and sombo wrestling. Judo is considered a separate sport at the Olympics. Sombo is a combination of freestyle and judo and is most popular in the Asian republics of the former Soviet Union, but it has not yet been contested in the Olympics. Currently, both freestyle and Græco-Roman wrestling are contested at the Olympics and both have been held since 1920. Prior to that (except in 1908), only one form was used, usually Græco-Roman. Freestyle wrestling is similar to American collegiate style (folkstyle wrestling). Holds are relatively unlimited, provided that they are not dangerous and can be applied to any part of the body. Græco-Roman wrestling limits holds to the upper body.

The dominant country in wrestling has been the Soviet Union and its former republics—especially in Græco-Roman style. The United States is close to the Soviets in freestyle, however. Other nations that produce good wrestlers include Iran, Turkey, and Mongolia. The wrestling international federation is the Fédération Internationale de Luttes Associées (FILA), which was formed in 1912 and had 142 affiliated nations as of December 2000.

Wushu. Wushu is a Chinese martial art. "Wu" in Chinese refers to the military or warfare, while "shu" refers to the method of performing an activity. Wushu has never been on the Olympic Program, but the International Wushu Federation (IWUF) was recognized by the IOC in 1999. As of 2000, the IWUF had 77 member nations.

– Y –

Yachting. *See* SAILING.

Yegorova, Lyubov [EUN/RUS–NSK]. B. 5 May 1966. Lyubov Yegorova was the winner of a female record six gold medals for Nordic skiing. She won three golds in 1992 (15 km., combined pursuit, and relay), and a further three in 1994 (5 km., combined pursuit, and relay). Additionally, she won two silver medals in 1992 (5 km. and 30 km.) and one in 1994 (15 km.). Yegorova was less successful in the World Championships, winning only one individual title, the 30-km. freestyle event in 1991.

Yemen [YEM]. Yemen was formed on 22 May 1990 by combining the nations of the People's Democratic Republic of Yemen and the Yemen Arab Republic. It was shortly thereafter recognized by the IOC. Yemen has since competed at the Olympic Games of 1992, 1996, and 2000. Prior to the merger, the People's Democratic Republic of Yemen competed in 1988 at Seoul, and the Yemen Arab Republic competed at both the 1984 Los Angeles Olympics and the 1988 Seoul Olympics.

Yemen Arab Republic (North) [YAR]. *See* YEMEN.

Yemen Democratic Republic (South) [YMD]. *See* YEMEN.

Yugoslavia [YUG]. Yugoslavia first competed at the Olympics in 1920, although Serbia (q.v.) was represented by two athletes in 1912 at Stockholm. Since 1920, Yugoslavia has appeared at every Summer Olympic celebration. In 1932, it was represented by a lone track & field athlete. It first appeared at the Olympic Winter Games at their inception in 1924 and has returned every four years with the exception of 1932, 1960, and 1994. Recent civil unrest in Yugoslavia caused the secession of many of the individual republics. Both Croatia and Slovenia (qq.v.) competed at the Olympic Games of 1992, 1996, and 2000 and in the Olympic Winter Games of 1992, 1994, and 1998. Bosnia-Herzegovina (q.v.) was also present at Barcelona in 1992, Atlanta in 1996, and Sydney in 2000, and first competed at the Olympic Winter Games in 1994. The Former Yugoslav Republic of Macedonia (FYROM) (q.v.) competed at the Olympic Games in 1996 and 2000, and the Olympic Winter Games in 1998. Yugoslavia now consists of only the former republics of Serbia and Montenegro, with Serbia consisting of two autonomous regions of Vojvodina and Kosovo, the latter under UN control. Yugoslavia has won 97 Olympic medals, 28 of them gold. In 1984, Yugoslavia hosted the 14th Olympic Winter Games in Sarajevo, which is actually the capital of the former Yugoslav republic of Bosnia-Herzegovina, now an independent nation only recently torn by civil war.

– Z –

Zaire [ZAI]. *See* CONGO, DEMOCRATIC REPUBLIC OF THE.

Zambia [ZAM]. Formerly Northern Rhodesia, this nation took the name *Zambia* on 24 October 1964. Zambia has competed at the Olympic Games of 1968, 1972, 1980, 1984, 1988, and 1992. In addition, the country competed at Tokyo in 1964 as *Northern Rhodesia*. Zambia has never competed at the Olympic Winter Games. In 1984, Keith Mwila won a bronze medal in light-flyweight boxing, the first medal won by a Zambian athlete at the Olympics. The nation's second Olympic medal came in 1996, when Samuel Matete finished second in the men's 400-meter intermediate hurdles.

Zanzibar. In 1964 Zanzibar united with Tanganyika to form the United Republic of Tanzania. Zanzibar never competed at the Olympic Games under its own name but since the 1964 Olympic games, its athletes have been eligible to represent Tanzania.

Zappas, Evangelos [GRE]. B. 1800, in what is now Albania. D. 1865. Evangelos Zappas was a wealthy landowner and businessman of Greek background, but he never set foot in Athens, where he would become famous for sponsoring an early effort at Olympic revival. He lived most of his life in Romania, settling there after fighting for Greece in the Greek War of Independence. In early 1856, Zappas proposed to the Greek government a permanent revival of the Olympic Games, and offered to finance the project. The first of the Zappas Olympic Games (q.v.) was held in 1859. Zappas had earmarked funds for restoration of the ancient Panathenaic Stadium, but this was not done for the 1859 Games. After his death, his will provided ample money to support a permanent revival of the Ancient Olympic Games and for restoration of the stadium. Prior to the 1870 Zappas Olympics, the Panathenaic Stadium was restored, thanks to Zappas' largesse.

Zappas Olympic Games. Numerous attempts at revival of the Olympic Games occurred prior to the successful efforts of Baron Pierre de Coubertin. (*See* ATTEMPTS AT REVIVAL) Perhaps the most significant of these were the Zappas Olympic Games. They are today usually called by this name, although in the 19th century, the Greeks termed them "Olympic Games for Greece."

The Zappas Olympic Games were conducted four times, in 1859, 1870, 1875, and 1889. They were held in Athens. The Games were the brainchild of Panagiotis Soutsos, but were sponsored by Evangelos Zappas, a wealthy Greek, who then lived in Romania. In 1856, he wrote to King Otto and offered to fund the entire Olympic revival himself. In early November 1859, a series of three festivals was conducted. The first was a series of agri-industrial contests. One week later, chariot races were conducted for professionals and laymen (the word "amateur" in reference to sports had not yet been invented).

On 15 November 1859, the athletic Games were conducted at Plateia Loudovikou, a city square on the edge of town. There were sprint races, a 1,500-meter race, two javelin throws (one for distance, the other for accuracy), and two discus throws (one for distance and one for accuracy). The winner of the 1,500 meters was Petros Velissariou, who came from Smyrna, and won a first prize of 280 drachmas, the largest prize of the first Zappas Olympics, because Brookes' Much Wenlock prize of £10 was included. *See* MUCH WENLOCK OLYMPIAN GAMES.

In 1870, the Zappas Olympics were moved to the ancient Panathenaic Stadium in the center of Athens. The stadium had been restored at Zappas' expense, although he had died in 1865. These Games, held on 15 November 1870, were the most successful of the Zappas Olympics, with the newspapers calling them a resounding success. Over 30,000 spectators attended these Games.

The 1875 Zappas Olympics are termed by classics scholar David Young a "disaster." In 1870, the winner of the 400 meters had been Evangelis Skordaras, a butcher, and the wrestling winner was Kardamylakes, a manual laborer. Several of Athens' elite then suggested that the Games be restricted only to athletes from the upper class and that the general public be banned. This early attempt at elitism and using the early British concepts of amateurism proved highly detrimental to the Zappas Olympics. Only 24 athletes took part in 1875, with a small crowd that left large sections of the stadium empty.

The 1889 Zappas Olympics took place in May in a small gym, rather than in the stadium, and were not well organized. In fact, they were scheduled, begun, canceled, and then conducted again a few days later. Again, only a few privileged, upper-class athletes competed, and the crowd was much smaller. In 1891 and 1893, Panhellenic Gymnastic Society Games were contested, which were not organized by the Zappas Committee. Interestingly, several Greek athletes who competed in 1893 also competed at the 1896 Olympics.

The Zappas Olympic Games rank with the Much Wenlock Olympian Games as the most significant attempts to revive the Ancient Olympic idea. They probably surpass the Much Wenlock Games because they were national sporting contests. Though he later denied any knowledge of them, Coubertin was keenly aware of the efforts of the Zappas Committee to hold Olympic Games, having been told of them by Demetrios Vikelas, who would later be the first IOC president.

The Games themselves were fairly successful in 1859, and especially in 1870, but were "ruined" by elitism, anti-athleticism, bigotry, and attempts to apply an amateur-type code imposed on the athletes. The Zappas Olympics never had the international flavor that Coubertin would instill in the modern Olympic Games. But they were the closest attempt to that point of a true Olympic revival.

Zátopek, Emil [TCH–ATH]. B. 19 September 1922, Koprivnice, Moravia. D. 22 November 2000, Prague. Emil Zátopek was a supreme distance runner whose rugged training regimen was rewarded with unprecedented success. At the 1948 Olympics, he won the gold medal in the 10,000 meters and finished second in the 5,000 meters. Then at Helsinki in 1952, he produced one of the greatest performances in distance running history. He won the 5,000 meters, successfully defended his 10,000 meters title, and then took his third gold medal in his first-ever marathon race to complete a "triple," which remains unique in Olympic history. Zátopek closed his Olympic career four years later, when he placed sixth in the marathon in Melbourne. Between 1949 and 1954, he set 18 world records at every distance from 5,000 meters to 30,000 meters, a remarkable display of versatility at the very highest level. His wife, Dana (née Ingrova), was the Olympic gold medalist in the javelin in 1952.

Zátopek's life was remarkable. Under the Soviet régime, his athletic feats earned him and his wife many perquisites not available to other Czech citizens. But despite that, after the Soviet tanks attacked Prague in 1968, he spoke out against the Soviet invasion, for which he paid dearly. For that, he lost most of the favors bestowed upon him and he spent much of the rest of his life as a trash collector, his status only restored after the fall of the Iron Curtain.

Železný, Jan [CZE/TCH-ATH]. B. 16 June 1966, Mladá Bolaslav. Jan Železný is considered the greatest javelin thrower in track & field history. At the 1988 Olympic Games, he narrowly missed winning the gold medal, settling for silver. But he has since won the gold medal at the 1992, 1996, and 2000 Olympic Games. He was also World

Champion with the javelin in both 1993 and 1995. Although the javelin specifications have changed twice during his career, he can claim six world records with the various spears. In December 1999, Železný was elected a member of the IOC as an athlete member, having previously been a member of the Athletes' Commission (q.v.).

Zijlaard-van Moorsel, Leontine Martha Henrica Petronella "Leontien" [NED-CYC]. B. 22 March 1970, Boekel. Leontien Zijlaard first competed at the Olympic Games in 1992, as *Leontien van Moorsel*, finishing 8th in individual pursuit and 23rd in the road race. This was somewhat disappointing, considering her record to that time at the World Championships. Van Moorsel was world road champion in 1991 and 1993, and won the individual pursuit in 1990. But van Moorsel was tortured by other demons, suffering from anorexia and bulimia, an eating disorder, and shortly thereafter lost 20 kg. (44 lbs.) from a frame not considered obese. Her cycling career suffered, but she returned to prominence in the late 1990s, winning the individual time trial World Championship in both 1998 and 1999. At the Sydney Olympics in 2000, she had the most successful Olympics ever by a woman cyclist. She won the individual pursuit in world record time, won the road race and the individual time trial, and added a silver medal on the track in points race.

Zimbabwe [ZIM]. Zimbabwe was formerly Rhodesia, a British colony that was self-governing from 1923, and as *Rhodesia*, competed at three Olympic Games: 1928, 1960, and 1964. On 11 November 1965, Rhodesian Prime Minister Ian D. Smith announced his nation's unilateral declaration of independence from Great Britain. Britain termed the act illegal and demanded that Rhodesia broaden voting rights to provide for eventual rule by majority Africans. In May 1968, the United Nations Security Council condemned the white-dominated Rhodesian government, asking that Rhodesian passports not be accepted for international travel. Rhodesia (q.v.) did not compete at the 1968 Olympics, one reason being that the International Olympic Committee (IOC) (q.v.) did not recognize its independent status, another being that Mexico honored the U.N. Security Council ruling.

At the 71st IOC session in Luxembourg in 1971, the IOC decreed that Rhodesian athletes could compete at the 1972 Olympics under the same conditions as in 1968—using British uniforms, the Union Jack as a flag, and with "God Save the Queen" as an anthem. Initially, this placated the African nations. However, shortly before the 1972 Munich Olympics, the African nations threatened a mass boycott (q.v.) if Rhodesia was allowed to compete. The petition stated that the Rhodesians had entered Germany not on British passports, as still required by the U.N. Security Council, but using the Olympic Identity Card. Two days before the 1972 Opening Ceremonies, the IOC voted narrowly (36–31, with three abstentions) to withdraw the invitation to Rhodesia for the 1972 Olympics.

In 1975, the IOC sent a three-member contingent to visit Rhodesia to inspect the sporting facilities and groups. Led by Major Sylvio Magalhães de Padilha of Brazil, this commission of inquiry was not kind to Rhodesian sports, and the IOC expelled the Rhodesian Olympic Committee, by a 41–26 vote.

After changing its constitution to allow black rule and normalizing relations with Great Britain, Rhodesia became Zimbabwe on 18 April 1980. Zimbabwe first appeared at the Olympics in 1980 at Moscow and the highlight of its appearance was the gold medal performance of its women's hockey (field) team. This remains the only medal won by Zimbabwe at the Olympics. It has not competed at the Olympic Winter Games. Zimbabwe also competed at the 1984, 1988, 1992, 1996, and 2000 Olympic Games.

Zimyatov, Nikolay [URS/RUS–NSK]. B. 28 June 1955, Rumyant-sevo, Moscow Oblast. Nikolay Zimyatov is the greatest Soviet or Russian male cross-country skier. His fame rests primarily on his performance at the 1980 Olympics in Lake Placid, when he won three gold medals in the 30 km., 50 km., and on the Soviet relay team. He added two further Olympic medals in 1984, defending his 30-km. title, and helping the Soviets win a silver in the relay. At other events, he was much less successful, winning only one World Championship, and that in the 1982 relay event. His best individual finish at a World Championship was second in the 1978 30 km. at Lahti.

Appendix I: Presidents of the International Olympic Committee

1894–1896	Demetrios Vikelas [Greece]
1896–1924*	Pierre Frédy, Baron de Coubertin [France]
1925–1942§	Count Henri de Baillet-Latour [Belgium]
1946–1952	J[ohannes] Sigfrid Edström [Sweden]
1952–1972	Avery Brundage [United States]
1972–1980	Sir Michael Morris, The Lord Killanin of Dublin and Spiddal [Ireland]
1980–date	Juan Antonio Samaranch Torello, Marqués de Samaranch [Spain]

*During World War I, between December 1915 and February 1917, Baron Godefroy de Blonay of Switzerland served as an interim President of the IOC. This was at the request of Baron de Coubertin, who felt that the IOC President should represent a country that was neutral during the war.

§The IOC Presidency was technically vacant from 1942 to 1946; however, J. Sigfrid Edström served as *de facto* President during that time.

Appendix II: The Games of the Olympiads: Sites, Dates, Nations, Athletes

	Site	Dates	Nations	Athletes	Men/Women	
1896	Athens	6–15 Apr	14	245	245	-
1900	Paris	20 May–28 Oct	26	1,225	1,206	19
1904	St. Louis	1 Jul–23 Nov	13	687	681	6
1906	Athens	22 Apr–2 May	20	826	820	6
1908	London	27 Apr–31 Oct	22	2,035	1,999	36
1912	Stockholm	5 May–27 Jul	27	2,383	2,330	53
1920	Antwerp	23 Apr–12 Sep	29	2,668	2,591	77
1924	Paris	4 May–27 Jul	44	3,072	2,941	131
1928	Amsterdam	17 May–12 Aug	46	3,014	2,724	290
1932	Los Angeles	30 Jul–14 Aug	37	1,408	1,281	127
1936	Berlin	1–16 Aug	49	4,066	3,738	328
1948	London	29 Jul–14 Aug	59	4,099	3,714	385
1952	Helsinki	19 Jul–3 Aug	69	4,925	4,407	518
1956	Total		72	3,342	2,958	384
	Stockholm	10–17 Jun	29	158	145	13
	Melbourne	22 Nov–8 Dec	67	3,184	2,813	371

1960	Rome	25 Aug–11 Sep	83	5,346	4,736	610
1964	Tokyo	10–24 Oct	93	5,140	4,457	683
1968	Mexico City	12–27 Oct	112	5,530	4,749	781
1972	Munich	26 Aug–11 Sep	121	7,123	6,065	1,058
1976	Montreal	17 Jul–1 Aug	92	6,026	4,779	1,247
1980	Moscow	19 Jul–3 Aug	80	5,217	4,092	1,125
1984	Los Angeles	28 Jul–12 Aug	140	6,797	5,230	1,567
1988	Seoul	17 Sep–5 Oct	159	8,465	6,279	2,186
1992	Barcelona	25 Jul–9 Aug	169	9,367	6,659	2,708
1996	Atlanta	20 Jul–4 Aug	197	10,310	6,797	3,513
2000	Sydney	14 Sep–1 Oct	199	10,592	6,559	4,033

Appendix III: The Olympic Winter Games: Sites, Dates, Nations, Athletes

	Site	Dates	Nations	Athletes	Men/Women	
1908	London	28–29 Oct	6	21	14	7
1920	Antwerp	23–29 Apr	10	86	74	12
1924	Chamonix	25 Jan– 4 Feb	16	258	245	13
1928	St. Moritz	11–19 Feb	25	464	438	26
1932	Lake Placid	4–15 Feb	17	252	231	21
1936	Garmisch- Partenkirchen	6–16 Feb	28	668	588	80
1948	St. Moritz	30 Jan– 8 Feb	28	669	592	77
1952	Oslo	14–25 Feb	30	694	585	109
1956	Cortina d'Ampezzo	26 Jan– 5 Feb	32	820	688	132
1960	Squaw Valley	18–28 Feb	30	665	522	143
1964	Innsbruck	29 Jan– 9 Feb	36	1,091	891	200
1968	Grenoble	6–18 Feb 14 Aug	37	1,158	947	211
1972	Sappro	3–13 Feb	35	1,006	800	206
1976	Innsbruck	4–15 Feb	37	1,123	892	231
1980	Lake Placid	13–24 Feb	37	1,072	839	233
1984	Sarajevo	8–19 Feb	49	1,274	1,000	274
1988	Calargy	13–28 Feb	57	1,423	1,110	313
1992	Albertville	8–23 Feb	64	1,801	1,313	488
1994	Lillehammer	12–27 Feb	67	1,737	1,217	520
1998	Nagano	17–22 Feb	72	2,175	1,389	786

Appendix IV: Members of the International Olympic Committee

Dates of Service	*Member [Nation]*
1894–1895	Ferdinando Lucchesi Palli [ITA]
1894–1897	Demetrios Vikelas [GRE]
1894–1898	Arthur Oliver Russell, Lord Ampthill [GBR]
1894–1898	Duke Riccardo d'Andria Carafa [ITA]
1894–1900	General Aleksey Butowsky [RUS]
1894–1901	Count Maxime de Bousies [BEL]
1894–1905	Leonard Albert Cuff [NZL]
1894–1906	Charles Herbert [GBR]
1894–1907	Dr. Ferenc Kémény [HUN]
1894–1907	José Benjamin Zubiaur [ARG]
1894–1913	Ernst Callot [FRA]
1894–1921	General Viktor Gustaf Balck [SWE]
1894–1924	Professor William Milligan Sloane [USA]
1894–1925	Pierre Frédy, Baron Pierre de Coubertin [FRA]
1894–1943	Dr. Jiří Guth-Jarkovský [BOH/TCH]
1896–1909	Karl August Willibald Gebhardt [GER]
1897–1919	Count Eugenio Brunetta d'Usseaux [ITA]
1897–1925	Count Alexandros Merkati [GRE]
1897–1927	Reverend Robert Stuart de Courcy Laffan [GBR]
1898–1924	Baron Frederik Willem Christiaan Hendrik van Tuyll van Serooskerken [NED]
1899–1902	Prince Gheorghe Bibesco [ROM]
1899–1903	Count Archambauld Talleyrand de Perigord [GER]
1899–1906	Niels Vilhelm Sophus Holbeck [DEN]
1899–1937	Baron Godefroy de Blonay [SUI]
1900–1903	Theodore Stanton [USA]
1900–1904	Caspar Whitney [USA]
1900–1908	Prince Sergey Beloselsky-Belotsersky [RUS]

1900–1911	Henri Hébrard de Villeneuve [FRA]
1900–1916	Count Nikolao Ribeaupierre [RUS]
1900–1948	Count Carl Clarence von Rosen [SWE]
1901–1903	Robert François Joseph Nicolas Ghislain Reyntiens [BEL]
1901–1905	Prince Eduard Max Vollrath Friedrich of Salm-Horstmar [GER]
1901–1908	Sir Charles Edward Howard Vincent [GBR]
1901–1931	Miguel de Beistegui [MEX]
1902–1921	Antonio de Mejorada del Campo, Marquis de Villamejor [ESP]
1903–1908	James Hazen Hyde [USA]
1903–1914	Count Caesar Erdmann von Wartensleben Carow [GER]
1903–1942	Count Henri de Baillet-Latour [BEL]
1904–1920	Count Albert Bertier de Sauvigny [FRA]
1905–1907	Henrik August Angell [NOR]
1905–1909	Alexander, Prince von Solms Braunfels [AUT]
1905–1909	Count Egbert Hoyer von der Asseburg [GER]
1905–1913	William Henry Grenfell, Lord Desborough of Taplow [GBR]
1905–1922	Don Carlos F. de Candamo [PER]
1905–1932	Richard Coombes [AUS]
1906–1912	Dimitri Tzokov [BUL]
1906–1912	Duke Antonio de Lancastre [POR]
1906–1912	Torben Grut [DEN]
1907–1908	Thomas Thomassen Heftye [NOR]
1907–1910	Manuel de la Quintana [ARG]
1907–1938	Count Géza Andrassy [HUN]
1908–1909	Prince Scipione Borghese [ITA]
1908–1910	Prince Simon Trubetskoy [RUS]
1908–1919	Baron Reinhold Felix von Willebrand [FIN]
1908–1920	Allison Vincent Armour [USA]
1908–1927	Johan Tidemann Sverre [NOR]
1908–1930	Selim Sirri Bey Tarcan [TUR]
1908–1939	Count Albert Gautier Vignal [MON]
1908–1949	Gheorghe A. Plagino [ROM]
1909–1914	Attilio Brunialti [ITA]

1909–1914	Baron Karl von Wenningen-Ullner von Diepburg [GER]
1909–1915	Sir Theodore Andrea Cook [GBR]
1909–1938	Jigoro Kano [JPN]
1909–1946	Gyula von Muzsa [HUN]
1910–1919	Count Adalbert von Francken-Sierstorpff [GER]
1910–1929	Jean-Maurice Pescatore [LUX]
1910–1933	Prince Léon Durusov [RUS]
1910–1963	Angelos Khristos Bolanaki [EGY]
1911–1914	Abel Ballif [FRA]
1911–1914	Oscar N. Garcia [CHI]
1911–1917	Evert Jansen Wendell [USA]
1911–1919	Otto, Prince zu Windisch-Gritz [AUT]
1911–1919	Rudolf, Count Colloredo-Mansfield [AUT]
1911–1921	John Hanbury-Williams [CAN]
1912–1921	Fritz Hansen [DEN]
1912–1940	Count José Carlos Peñha Garcia [POR]
1912–1949	Svetomir V. Đukić [SER/YUG]
1913–1915	Georges Aleksandrovich Duperron [RUS]
1913–1919	Count Adolf von Arnim-Muskau [GER]
1913–1920	Algernon St. Maur Somerset, Duke of Somerset [GBR]
1913–1929	Dimitri Stanciov [BUL]
1913–1938	Baron Edouard-Émile de Laveleye [BEL]
1913–1938	Raul de Rio Branco [BRA]
1913–1944	Albert Glandaz [FRA]
1914–1919	Sydney Howard Farrar [RSA]
1914–1939	Carlo Montu [ITA]
1914–1950	Marquis Melchior de Polignac [FRA]
1918–1922	Bartow Sumter Weeks [USA]
1918–1929	Eduardo Dorn y de Alsua [ECU]
1918–1940	Pedro Jaime de Matheu [ESA/Central America]
1919–1922	Carlos Silva-Vildosola [CHI]
1919–1925	Arthur Marryatt [NZL]
1919–1929	Marquis Giorgio Guglielmi [ITA]
1919–1933	Count Justinien de Clary [FRA]
1920–1927	Sir Dorabji Jamsetji Tata [IND]
1920–1943	Henry Nourse [RSA]

1920–1946	Franjo Bučar [YUG]
1920–1948	Ernst Edvard Krogius [FIN]
1921–1923	Henrique Echevarrieta [ESP]
1921–1923	Nizzam Eddin Khon [IRI]
1921–1932	Marcelo T. de Alvear [ARG]
1921–1933	Reginald John Kentish [GBR]
1921–1936	Francisco Ghigliani [URU]
1921–1946	James George Bower Merrick [CAN]
1921–1952	Johannes Sigfrid Edström [SWE]
1921–1954	Baron Guell de Santiago [ESP]
1921–1957	Wang Chengting [CHN]
1922–1924	Prince Stefan Lubomirski [POL]
1922–1931	Ivar Nyhölm [DEN]
1922–1936	Charles Hitchcock Sherrill [USA]
1922–1948	William May Garland [USA]
1922–1951	John Joseph Keane [IRL]
1923–1924	José Carlos Rincon Gallardo, Marquis de Guadalupe [MEX]
1923–1927	Joseph Pentland Firth [NZL]
1923–1927	Prince Samad Khan Momtazos Saltaneh [IRI]
1923–1929	Gerald Oakley, Earl of Cadogan [GBR]
1923–1936	Porfirio Franca y Alvarez de la Campa [CUB]
1923–1939	Jorgé Matte Gormaz [CHI]
1923–1949	Ricardo Camillo Aldao [ARG]
1923–1957	Alfredo Benavides [PER]
1923–1961	Arnaldo Guinle [BRA]
1923–1962	José Ferreira Santos [BRA]
1924–1927	David Kinley [USA]
1924–1927	Fernando Alvarez, Duke d'Alba [ESP]
1924–1927	Jorgé Gomez de Parada [MEX]
1924–1928	Dr. Martin Haudek [AUT]
1924–1929	Oskar Ruperti [GER]
1924–1930	Prince Kasimierz Lubomirski [POL]
1924–1933	Seichi Kishi [JPN]
1924–1938	Theodor Lewald [GER]
1924–1944	James Taylor [AUS]
1924–1957	Pieter Wilhelmus Scharroo [NED]
1925–1943	Baron Alphert Schimmelperminck van der Oye [NED]

1925–1953	Count Alberto Bonacossa [ITA]
1926–1930	Giorgios Averof [GRE]
1926–1947	Jānis Dikmānis [LAT]
1926–1956	Duke Adolf Friedrich von Mecklenburg-Schwerin [GER]
1927–1933	George Kemp, Lord Rochdale [GBR]
1927–1936	Ernest Lee Jahncke [USA]
1927–1950	Sir Thomas Fearnley [NOR]
1928–1930	Bernard Cyril Freyberg [NZL]
1928–1930	Marquis François Manuel de Pons [ESP]
1928–1932	Friederik Akel [EST]
1928–1932	Miguel Moises Saenz [MEX]
1928–1938	Theodor Schmidt [AUT]
1928–1939	Ignasz Matuszewski [POL]
1928–1939	Sir George McLaren Brown [CAN]
1929–1933	Don Alfredo Ewing [CHI]
1929–1944	Stepan G. Shaprachikov [BUL]
1929–1957	Clarence Napier Bruce, Lord Aberdare of Duffryn [GBR]
1929–1964	Karl Ferdinand Ritter von Halt [GER]
1930–1931	Augusto Turati [ITA]
1930–1932	Kremalettin Sami Pascha [TUR]
1930–1933	Nikolaos Politis [GRE]
1931–1933	Cecil J. Wray [NZL]
1931–1945	Stanisław Rouppert [POL]
1931–1952	Count Federico Suarez de Vallelano [ESP]
1932–1952	Horacio Bustos Moron [ARG]
1932–1958	Axel Kristian George, Prince of Denmark [DEN]
1932–1964	Count Paolo Thaon di Revel [ITA]
1932–1966	Guru Dutt Sondhi [IND]
1933–1936	Jotaro Sugimoura [JPN]
1933–1950	Sir Francis Noel Curtis Bennett [GBR]
1933–1951	Sir Harold Daniel Luxton [AUS]
1933–1952	Rechid Saffet Atabinen Bey [TUR]
1933–1981	David George Brownlow Cecil, Lord Burghley, The 6th Marquess of Exeter [GBR]
1934–1948	Count Michimasa Soyeshima [JPN]
1934–1966	François Piétri [FRA]
1934–1967	Lord Arthur Espie Porritt [NZL]

1934–1968	Mohamed Taher Pascha [TUR]
1934–1973	Segura Marte Rodolfo Gomez [MEX]
1936–1939	Prince Iesato Tokugawa [JPN]
1936–1942	Joakhim Puhk [EST]
1936–1972	Avery Brundage [USA]
1936–1980	His Royal Highness Prince Franz-Josef II [LIE]
1936–1980	Jorgé B. Vargas [PHI]
1937–1939	Henri Guisan [SUI]
1937–1948	Frédéric René Coudert [USA]
1937–1956	Joaquin Serratosa Cibils [URU]
1938–1942	Walther von Reichenau [GER]
1938–1955	Antonio Prado [BRA]
1938–1967	Johan Wilhelm Rangell [FIN]
1938–1969	Miguel Angel de los Dolores Amado de Jesus Moenck y Peralta [CUB]
1939–1939	Albert Victor Lindbergh [RSA]
1939–1948	Miklós von Horthy [HUN]
1939–1949	Giorgio Vaccaro [ITA]
1939–1950	Matsuzo Nagai [JPN]
1939–1955	Kong Xiangxi [CHN]
1939–1957	Baron Gaston de Trannoy [BEL]
1939–1967	Shingoro Takaishi [JPN]
1946–1951	Sydney Charles Dowsett [RSA]
1946–1954	John Coleridge Patteson [CAN]
1946–1955	Rodolphe William Seeldrayers [BEL]
1946–1956	José Joaquim Fernandes Pontes [POR]
1946–1964	Charles Ferdinand Pahud de Mortanges [NED]
1946–1965	Ioannis Ketseas [GRE]
1946–1965	Josef Gruss [TCH]
1946–1966	Benedikt G. Waage [ISL]
1946–1968	Albert Roman Mayer [SUI]
1946–1970	Armand Émile Massard [FRA]
1946–1975	Hugh Richard Weir [AUS]
1946–1982	Reginald Honey [RSA]
1946–1998	His Royal Highness Grand Duke Jean [LUX]
1947–1958	Shou Tungyi [CHN]
1947–1967	Sidney Dawes [CAN]
1947–1969	Manfred Mautner Ritter von Markhof [AUT]

1947–1992	Raja Bhalindra Singh of Patiala [IND]
1948–1952	Enrique O. Barbosa Baeza [CHI]
1948–1952	Miguel Ydigoras Fuentes [GUA]
1948–1959	Stanko Bloudek [YUG]
1948–1961	Ferenc Mező [HUN]
1948–1961	Jerzy Loth [POL]
1948–1965	Bo Daniel Ekelund [SWE]
1948–1967	Olaf Christian Ditlev-Simonsen [NOR]
1948–1968	John Jewett Garland [USA]
1948–1976	Erik von Frenckell [FIN]
1949–1950	Rainier Grimaldi III, Prince of Monaco [MON]
1949–1956	Ahmed E. H. Jaffer [PAK]
1950–1951	James Brooks Bloodgood Parker [USA]
1950–1964	Pierre Grimaldi, Prince of Monaco [MON]
1950–1968	Ryotaro Azuma [JPN]
1951–1974	Lewis Luxton [AUS]
1951–1988	Ian St. John Lawson-Johnston, The Lord Luke of Pavenham [GBR]
1951–1988	Konstantin Andrianov [URS]
1951–1990	Count Jean Robert Maurice Bonin de la Bonninie de Beaumont [FRA]
1951–1992	Giorgio de Stefani [ITA]
1952–1959	Enrique Alberdi [ARG]
1952–1967	Augustin A. Sosa [PAN]
1952–1968	Julio B. Bustamente [VEN]
1952–1970	Gustaf Peder Wilhelmsson Dyrssen [SWE]
1952–1971	Aleksey Romanov [URS]
1952–1971	José de Jesús Clark de Flores [MEX]
1952–1980	Sir Michael Morris, The Lord Killanin of Dublin and Spiddal [IRL]
1952–1984	Douglas Fergusson Roby [USA]
1952–1985	Pedro Ybarra y McMahon, The Second Marquis de Guell [ESP]
1952–1986	Julio Gerlein Comelin [COL]
1952–1987	Sheik Gabriel Gemayel [LIB]
1952–1987	Vladimir D. Stoychev [BUL]
1955–1960	Lee Ki-Poong [KOR]
1955–1980	Prince Gholam Reza Pahlavi [IRI]

1955–1984	Suat Erler [TUR]
1955–1985	Alejandro Rivera Bascur [CHI]
1955–1998	Alexandru Siperco [ROM]
1956–1991	Willi Daume [GER]
1957–1962	Saul Cristovão Ferreira Pires [POR]
1958–1964	His Royal Highness Prince Albert of Liege [BEL]
1958–1977	Ivar Emil Vind [DEN]
1958–1982	Eduardo Dibos de Lima [PER]
1959–1996	Syed Wajid Ali [PAK]
1960–1974	Mario Luis Jose Negri [ARG]
1960–1987	Boris Bakrač [YUG]
1960–1990	Reginald Stanley Alexander [KEN]
1960–1993	Ahmed El-Demerdash Touny [EGY]
1961–1997	Mohamed Ben Hadj Addelouahed Benjelloun [MAR]
1961–1996	Włodzimierz Reczek [POL]
1963–1974	His Majesty King Konstantinos [GRE]
1963–1975	Alfredo Inciarte [URU]
1963–1985	Sir Adetokunbo Ademola [NGR]
1963–1989	Raúl Cordiero, Pereira de Castro [POR]
1963–	João Marie Godefrois Faustin Havelange [BRA]
1963–	Marc Hodler [SUI]
1964–1966	Lee Sang-Beck [KOR]
1964–1977	Jonkheer Herman Adriaan van Karnebeek [NED]
1964–1983	Arpád Csánadi [HUN]
1964–1983	Giulio Onesti [ITA]
1964–	Prince Alexandre de Merode [BEL]
1964–1995	Sylvio Magalhães de Padilha [BRA]
1965–1969	Amadou Barry [SEN]
1965–1981	František Kroutil [TCH]
1965–1981	Pyrros Lappas [GRE]
1965–1996	Gunnar Lennart Vilhelm Ericsson [SWE]
1965–	Mohamed Mzali [TUN]
1966–1971	Georg von Opel [FRG]
1966–1971	His Royal Highness, Prince George Wilhelm von Hanover [IOA]
1966–1980	Heinz Schöbel [GDR]
1966–	Juan Antonio Samaranch Torrelo, Marquis de Samaranch [ESP]

1967–1977	Chang Key-Young [KOR]
1967–1981	Paavo Honkajuuri [FIN]
1967–1981	Prince Tsuneyoshi Takeda [JPN]
1967–1989	James Worrall [CAN]
1967–2000	Jan Staubo [NOR]
1968–1971	Henri René Rakotoke [MAD]
1968–1976	Hamengku Buwono, IX [INA]
1968–1981	José A. Bercasa [VEN]
1968–1982	Abdel Mohamed Halim [SUD]
1968–1999	Agustin Carlos Arroyo Yeroui [ECU]
1969–1976	Rudolf Nemetschke [AUT]
1969–1988	Sir Cecil Lancelot Stewart Cross [NZL]
1969–1989	Masaji Kiyokawa [JPN]
1969–1991	Raymond Gafner [SUI]
1969–1994	Virgilio E. de Léon [PAN]
1969–1999	Louis Guirandou-N'Diaye [CIV]
1970–1976	Sven Alfred Thofelt [SWE]
1970–1988	Henry Heng Hsu [TPE]
1970–1994	Maurice Herzog [FRA]
1971–1974	Prabhas Charusathiara [THA]
1971–1987	Ydnekatcheu Tessema [ETH]
1971–	Vitaly Smirnov [URS/RUS]
1972–1988	Berthold Beitz [GER]
1972–1994	Pedro Ramírez Vázquez [MEX]
1973–1993	Manuel Gonzalez Guerra [CUB]
1973–2000	Ashwini Kumar [IND]
1973–	Kéba M'Baye [SEN]
1973–2000	Roy Anthony Bridge [JAM]
1974–1981	David Henry McKenzie [AUS]
1974–1986	Julian Kean Roosevelt [USA]
1974–1990	Dawee Chullasapya [THA]
1974–1991	Eduardo Hay [MEX]
1974–	Mohamed Zerguini [ALG]
1975–1977	Epaminondas Petralias [GRE]
1976–1993	Matts Wilhelm Carlgren [SWE]
1976–1994	Kevin Patrick O'Flanagan [IRL]
1976–1995	José Dalmiro Vallarino Veracierto [URU]
1976–	Peter Julius Tallberg [FIN]
1977–1983	Kim Taik-Soo [KOR]

1977–1986	Cornelis Lambert "Kees" Kerdel [NED]
1977–1999	Roberto Guillermo Peper [ARG]
1977–1989	Dadang Suprayogi [INA]
1977–1990	German Rieckehoff [PUR]
1977–1999	Bashir Mohamed Attarabulsi [LBA]
1977–1999	Lamine Keita [MLI]
1977–	Niels Holst-Sørensen [DEN]
1977–2000	Philipp von Schöller [AUT]
1977–	Richard Kevan Gosper [AUS]
1977–	Shagdarjav Magvan [MGL]
1978–1986	Nikolaos Nissiotis [GRE]
1978–1994	Kim Yu-Sun [PRK]
1978–1998	René Essomba [CMR]
1978–	Honorable Tan Seri Hamzah Bin Haji Abu Samah [MAS]
1978–	Richard William Duncan Pound [CAN]
1981–1990	Sheik Fahad Al-Ahmad Al-Sabah [KUW]
1981–1992	Günther Heinze [GDR/GER]
1981–1999	Pirjo Vilmi-Häggman [FIN]
1981–	Flor Isava-Fonseca [VEN]
1981–	He Zhenliang [CHN]
1981–	Nikolaos Filaretos [GRE]
1981–	Vladimir Cernušak [TCH/SVK]
1982–1993	Dame Mary Alison Glen Haig [GBR]
1982–	Chiharu Igaya [JPN]
1982–	Franco Carraro [ITA]
1982–	Ivan Dibos [PER]
1982–	Philip Walter Coles [AUS]
1983–1999	Zein El-Abdin Mohamed Ahmed Abdel Gadir [SUD]
1983–1999	His Royal Highness Prince Faisal Fahd Abdul Aziz [KSA]
1983–	Anani Matthia [TOG]
1983–	Pál Schmitt [HUN]
1983–	Roque Napoleon Muñoz Peña [DOM]
1984–1985	Park Chong-Kyu [KOR]
1984–1988	Turgut Atakol [TUR]
1984–1999	David Sikhulumi Sibandze [SWZ]

1984–	Her Royal Highness Princess Nora [LIE]
1985–1991	Robert Hanna Helmick [USA]
1985–1998	Carlos Ferrer Salat [ESP]
1985–	Albert Grimaldi, Prince of Monaco [MON]
1985–	Francisco J. Elizalde [PHI]
1985–	Henry Edmund Olufemi Adefope [NGR]
1986–1999	Jean-Claude Ganga [CGO]
1986–	Anita Luceete DeFrantz [USA]
1986–	Kim Un-Yong [KOR]
1986–	Lambis V. Nikolaou [GRE]
1987–1999	Seuili Paul Wallwork [SAM]
1987–	Antonius Johannes Geesink [NED]
1987–	Ivan Borissov Slavkov [BUL]
1987–	Slobodan Filipović [YUG]
1988–1992	Marat V. Gramov [URS/RUS]
1988–	Borislav Stanković [YUG]
1988–	Fidel Mendoza Carrasquilla [COL]
1988–	Francis Were Nyangweso [UGA]
1988–	Princess Anne Windsor, Her Royal Highness the Princess Royal [GBR]
1988–	Rampaul Ruhee [MRI]
1988–	Sinan Erdern [TUR]
1988–	Tennant Edward "Tay" Wilson [NZL]
1988–	Willi Kaltschmitt Lujan [GUA]
1988–	Wu Ching-Kuo [TPE]
1989–	Fernando F. Lima Bello [POR]
1989–	Walther Tröger [GER]
1990–1996	Philippe Chatrier [FRA/ITU]
1990–1999	Charles Nderitu Mukora [KEN]
1990–	Antonio Rodriguez [ARG]
1990–2001	Carol Anne Letheren [CAN]
1990–	Nat Indrapana [THA]
1990–	Richard L. Carrion [PUR]
1990–	Shun-Ichiro Okano [JPN]
1991–	Denis Oswald [SUI]
1991–	Dr. Jacques Rogge [BEL]
1991–	Mario Vázquez Raña [MEX]
1991–	Thomas Bach [GER]

1992–1994	Olaf Poulsen [NOR]
1992–1999	Sergio Santander Fantini [CHI]
1992–1999	Primo Nebiolo [ITA/IAAF]
1992–	Sheik Fahad Al-Ahmad Al-Sabah [KUW]
1994–	Alex Gilady [ISR]
1994–	Alpha Ibrahim Dialio [GUI]
1994–	Arne Ljungqvist [SWE]
1994–	Austin L. Sealy [BAR]
1994–	Craig Reedie [GBR]
1994–	Gerhard Heiberg [NOR]
1994–	James Leland Easton [USA]
1994–	Mario Pescante [ITA]
1994–	Mohamed Hasan [INA]
1994–	Robin Mitchell [FIJ]
1994–	Shamil Tarpichev [RUS]
1994–	Valery Borzov [UKR]
1995–1996	Yury Titov [RUS/FIG]
1995–	Antun Vrdoljak [CRO]
1995–	Jean-Claude Killy [FRA]
1995–	Mustapha Urfaoui [ALG/FINA]
1995–	Olegario Vázquez Raña [MEX]
1995–	Patrick Hickey [IRL]
1995–	René Fasel [SUI/IIHF]
1995–	Reynaldo González López [CUB]
1995–	Sam Ramsamy [RSA]
1995–	Toni Khouri [LIB]
1995–	Věra Čáslavská [CZE]
1996–1998	George Killian [USA/FIBA]
1996–	Gunilla Lindberg [SWE]
1996–	Guy Drut [FRA]
1996–	Hein Verbruggen [NED/UCI]
1996–	Julio Cesar Maglione [URU]
1996–	Lee Kun-Hee [KOR]
1996–	Lu Shengrong [CHN]
1996–	Ottavio Cinquanta [ITA/ISU]
1996–	Princess Doña Pilar de Borbon [ESP/FEI]
1996–	Syed Shahid Ali [PAK]
1996–	Tomas Sithole [ZIM]

1996–	Ung Chang [PRK]
1998–	His Royal Highness Prince Henri [LUX]
1998–	His Royal Highness Prince of Orange [NED]
1998–	Irena Szewińska-Kirszenstein [POL]
1998–	Leopold Wallner [AUT]
1998–	Melitón Sanchez Rivas [PAN]
1998–	Mohammad Samih Moudallal [SYR]
1998–	Mounir Saleh Sabet [EGY]
1998–	Nawal El-Moutawakel Bennis [MAR]
1998–	Ser Miang Ng [SIN]
1999–	Roland Barr [GER/Athlete]
1999–2000	Hassiba Boulmerka [ALG/Athlete]
1999-	Sergey Bubka [UKR/Athlete]
1999-	Charmaine Crooks [CAN/Athlete]
1999-	Robert Ctvrtlik [USA/Athlete]
1999-	Manuela Di Centa [ITA/Athlete]
1999–	Johann Olav Koss [NOR/Athlete]
1999–	Aleksandr Popov [RUS/Athlete]
1999–	Vladimir Smirnov [KAZ/Athlete]
1999–	Jan Železný [CZE/Athlete]
1999–	Josep S. Blatter [SUI/FIFA]
1999–	Lamine Diack [SEN/IAAF]
2000–	Ruben Acosta [MEX/FIVB]
2000–	Tamas Ajan [HUN/IWF]
2000–	Alfredo Goyeneche [ESP/Spain OC]
2000–	Bruno Grandi [SUI/FIG]
2000–	Seyed Mostafa Hashemi Taba [IRI/Iran OC]
2000–	Paul Henderson [CAN/ISAF]
2000–	William J. Hybl [USA/United States OC]
2000–	Gian-Franco Kasper [SUI/AIWF]
2000–	Kipchoge Keino [KEN/Kenya OC]
2000–	Carlos Arthur Nuzman [BRA/Brazil OC]
2000–	Lassana Palenfo [CIV/Côte d'Ivoire OC]
2000–	Henri Serandour [FRA/France OC]
2000–	Robert Steadward [CAN/IPC]
2000–	Yu Zaiqing [CHN/China OC]
2000–	Giovanni Agnelli [ITA/Honor]
2000–	Alain Danet [FRA/Honor]

2000–	Kurt Furgler [SUI/Honor]
2000–	Henry Alfred Kissinger [USA/Honor]
2000–	Yoshiaki Tsutsumi [JPN/Honor]
2000–	Susan O'Neill [AUS/Athlete]
2000–	Manuel Estiarte Duocastella [ESP/Athlete]

Appendix V: Awards of the International Olympic Committee

The International Olympic Committee has given out several awards, outside of the medals and diplomas given to Olympic athletes. Currently, the IOC presents only two awards, the Olympic Order and the Olympic Cup. Other awards by the IOC were discontinued at the 75th IOC Session in Vienna in 1974. These included the Olympic Diploma of Merit (first awarded in 1905), the Sir Thomas Fearnley Cup (donated in 1950), the Mohammed Taher Trophy (donated in 1950), the Count Alberto Bonacossa Trophy (presented in 1954), the Tokyo Trophy (presented in 1964), and the Prix de la Reconnaissance Olympique (presented in 1972).

RECIPIENTS OF THE OLYMPIC ORDER

The Olympic Order is the supreme individual honor accorded by the International Olympic Committee. It was created in 1974 and is to be awarded to "Any person who has illustrated the Olympic Ideal through his/her action, has achieved remarkable merit in the sporting world, or has rendered outstanding services to the Olympic cause, either through his/her own personal achievement(s) or his/her contribution to the development of sport." Originally, the Olympic Order was separated into three categories: gold, silver, and bronze. The bronze Olympic Order was discontinued in 1984; currently, there is only a gold and a silver category. Only the recipients of the Olympic Order in gold are listed. Through 2000, there have been almost 800 recipients of the Olympic Order in Silver, and 111 recipients of the Olympic Order in Bronze.

GOLD [70]

1975	Avery Brundage	USA
1980	Lord Killanin of Dublin and Spiddal	IRL
1981	Lord Burghley, the Marquess of Exeter	GBR
	His Majesty King Olaf of Norway	NOR
	Amadou Mahtar M'Bow	SEN
	Pope John Paul II	VAT
1982	His Majesty King Pertuan Agung of Malaysia	MAS
1983	Indira Gandhi	IND
1984	François Mitterrand	FRA
	Peter Victor Ueberroth	USA
	Branko Mikuliç	YUG
1985	His Majesty King Juan Carlos de Borbon	ESP
	Erich Honecker	GDR
	Nicolae Ceauçescu	ROM
1986	Li Wan	CHN
1987	Todor Zhivkov	BUL
	His Majesty King Bhumibol Adulyadej	THA
	His Excellency Kenan Evren	TUR
1988	Frank W. King	CAN
	Mario Vázquez Raña	MEX
	His Royal Highness Prince Rainier III	MON
	His Royal Highness Prince Bertil Bernadotte	SWE
1989	Chevalier Raoul Mollet	BEL
	His Imperial Majesty Emperor Akihito	JPN
	His Excellency Raphael Hernandez Colon	PUR
1990	Giulio Andreotti	ITA
1991	Count Jean de Beaumont	FRA
	Yoshiaki Tsutsumi	JPN
	Willi Daume	FRG
1992	Josep Miguel Abad	ESP
	Michel Barnier	FRA
	Javier Gomez-Navarro	ESP
	Jean-Claude Killy	FRA
	Pasqual Marragal	ESP
	Jordi Pujol	ESP
	Leopoldo Rodes	ESP
	Carlos Salinas de Gortari	MEX

	Narcis Serra	ESP
	Javier Solaña	ESP
	Boris Yeltsin	RUS
1994	Joaquin Leguina	ESP
	Richard von Weizsäcker	GER
	Dr. Mauno Koivisto	FIN
	His Majesty King Harald of Norway	NOR
	Gerhard Heiberg	NOR
	Her Majesty Queen Sonja of Norway	NOR
1995	Arpád Goncz	HUN
	Robert Mugabe	ZIM
1996	Konstantino Stephanopoulo	GRE
	Adolphus Drewery "A. D." Frazier	USA
	Andrew Young	USA
	William Porter Payne	USA
	Islam Karimov	UZB
1997	Blaise Compaore	BUR
	El-Hadj Omar Bongo	GAB
	Nursultan Nazarbaev	KAZ
	Elias Hrawi	LIB
	Ernesto Zedillo Ponce de Léon	MEX
	Aleksander Kwaśniewski	POL
	Suleyman Demirel	TUR
1998	Eishiro Saito	JPN
	Grand Duke Jean	LUX
1999	Eduardo Shevardnadze	GEO
	Helmut Kohl	GER
	Petru Lucinschi	MDA
	Yury Luzhkov	RUS
2000	Michael Knight	AUS
	David Richmond	AUS
	Adolf Ogi	SUI

RECIPIENTS OF THE OLYMPIC CUP

The Olympic Cup was instituted by Baron Pierre de Coubertin in 1906. It is awarded to an institution or association with a general reputation for merit and integrity that has been active and efficient in the service

of sport and has contributed substantially to the development of the
Olympic Movement.

1906	Touring Club de France
1907	Henley Royal Regatta
1908	Sveriges Centralförening för ldrottens Främjande
1909	Deutsche Turnerschaft
1910	Česka obec Sokolska
1911	Touring Club Italiano
1912	Union des Sociétés de Gymnastique de France
1913	Magyar Athletikai Club
1914	Amateur Athletic Union of America
1915	Rugby School, England
1916	Confrérie Saint-Michel de Gand
1917	Nederlandsche Voetbal Bond
1918	Equipes Sportives du Front Interallié
1919	Institut Olympique de Lausanne
1920	YMCA International, Springfield, Massachusetts, USA
1921	Dansk Idræts Forbund
1922	Amateur Athletic Union of Canada
1923	Associación Sportiva de Cataluña
1924	Finnish Gymnastic and Athletic Federation
1925	National Physical Education Committee of Uruguay
1926	Norges Skiforbund
1927	Colonel Robert M. Thomson [USA]
1928	Junta Nacional Mexicana
1929	Y.M.C.A. World's Committee
1930	Association Suisse de Football et d'Athlétisme
1931	National Playing Fields Association, Great Britain
1932	Deutsche Hochschule für Leibesübungen
1933	Société Fédérale Suisse de Gymnastique
1934	Opera Dopolavoro Roma
1935	National Recreation Association of the USA
1936	Union of Hellenic Gymnastics and Athletics Associations, Athens
1937	Österreichischer Eislauf Verband
1938	Königlich Akademie für Körpererziehung in Ungam
1939	"Kraft durch Freude"
1940	Svenska Gymnastik – och Idrottsföreningarnas Riksförbund

1941	Finnish Olympic Committee
1942	William May Garland [USA]
1943	Comité Olímpico Argentino
1944	City of Lausanne
1945	Norges Fri Idrettsførbund, Oslo
1946	Comité Olímpico Colornbiano
1947	J. Sigfrid Edström [SWE] – IOC President
1948	The Central Council of Physical Recreation, Great Britain
1949	Fluminense Football Club, Rio de Janeiro
1950	Comité Olympique Belge
	New Zealand Olympic and British Empire Games Association
1951	Académie des Sports, Paris
1952	City of Oslo
1953	City of Helsinki
1954	Ecole Fédérale de Gymnastique et de Sports, Macolin [SUI]
1955	Organizing Committee of the Central American and Caribbean Games, Mexico
	Organizing Committee of the Pan-American Games, Mexico
1956	Not awarded
1957	Federazione Sport Silenziosi d'Italia, Milano
1958	Not awarded
1959	Panathlon Italiano, Génève
1960	Centro Universitario Sportivo Italiano
1961	Helms Hall Foundation, Los Angeles
1962	IV Juegos Deportivos Bolivarianos, Barranquilla
1963	Australian British Empire and Commonwealth Games Association
1964	City of Tokyo
1965	Southern California Committee for the Olympic Games [USA]
1966	Comité International des Sports Silencieux, Liège [BEL]
1967	Juegos Deportivos Bolivarianos
1968	City of Mexico
1969	Polish Olympic Committee
1970	Organizing Committee of the Asian Games in Bangkok [THA]
1971	Organizing Committee of the Pan-American Games in Cali [COL]
1972	Turkish Olympic Committee
	City of Sapporo

1973   Population of Munich
1974   Bulgarian Olympic Committee
1975   Comitato Olímpico Nazionale Italiano (CONI)
1976   Czechoslovak Physical Culture and Sports Association
1977   Comité Olympique Ivoirien
1978   Comité Olympique Hellenic
1979   Organizing Committee of the 1978 World Rowing Champion-
           ships in New Zealand
1980   Ginasio Clube Português
1981   Confédération Suisse/International Olympic Academy
1982   Racing Club de France
1983   Puerto Rico Olympic Committee
1984   Organizing Committee of the 1st World Championships in
           Athletics at Helsinki
1985   Chinese Olympic Committee
1986   City of Stuttgart
1987   *L'Équipe* (French sporting daily newspaper)
1988   The People of Australia
1989   City of Calgary
           City of Seoul
           La Gazzetta dello Sport (Italian sporting daily newspaper)
1990   Panhellenic Athletic Club of Athens
1991   Japanese Olympic Committee
1992   Département de la Savoie (Région Rhône-Alpes)
           City of Barcelona
1993   Comité Olympique Monégasque
1994   Comité National Olympique et Sportif Français and the
           Norwegian People
1995   Korean Olympic Committee
1996   City of Baden-Baden (GER)
1997   not awarded
1998   People of Nagano (JPN)
1999   Leon Štukelj (YUG/SLO)
2000   His Majesty, King Bhumibol Adulyadej (THA)
           People of Sydney

Appendix VI: Final Olympic Torch Bearers

(within the Olympic Stadium)

GAMES OF THE OLYMPIADS

1936	Fritz Schilgen [GER]
1948	John Mark [GBR]
1952	Paavo Nurmi [FIN]
	Hannes Kolehmainen [FIN]
1956	Ron Clarke [AUS]
1960	Giancarlo Peris [ITA]
1964	Yoshinori Sakai [JPN]
1968	Enriqueta Basilio de Sotelo [MEX]
1972	Günter Zahn [FRG]
1976	Stéphane Prefontaine [CAN]
	Sandra Henderson [CAN]
1980	Sergey Belov [URS]
1984	Rafer Johnson [USA]
	Gina Hemphill [USA]
1988	Sohn Kee-Chung [KOR]
	Lim Chun-Ae [KOR]
	Chung Sun-Man [KOR]
	Kim Won-Tak [KOR]
	Sohn Mi-Chung [KOR]
1992	Herminio Menéndez Rodriguez [ESP]
	Juan Antônio San Epifanio Ruiz [ESP]
	Antônio Rebollo (archer) [ESP]
1996	Muhammad Ali [USA]
	Janet Evans [USA]
	Paraskevi "Voula" Patoulidou [GRE]
	Evander Holyfield [USA]
	Al Oerter [USA]

2000   Catherine Freeman [AUS]
           Raelene Boyle [AUS]
           Betty Cuthbert [AUS]
           Shirley Strickland de la Hunty [AUS]
           Dawn Fraser [AUS]
           Shane Gould [AUS]
           Debbie Flintoff-King [AUS]

OLYMPIC EQUESTRIAN GAMES

1956   Hans Wikne [SWE]
           Karin Lindberg [SWE]
           Henry Eriksson [SWE]

OLYMPIC WINTER GAMES

1952   Eigil Nansen [NOR]
1956   Guido Caroli [ITA]
1960   Kenneth Henry [USA]
1964   Joseph Rieder [AUT]
1968   Alain Calmat [FRA]
1972   Hideki Takada [JPN]
1976   Christl Haas [AUT]
           Josef Feistmantl [AUT]
1980   Charles Morgan Kerr [USA]
1984   Sandra Dubravčić [YUG]
1988   Robyn Perry [CAN]
1992   Michel Platini [FRA]
           François-Syrille Grange [FRA]
1994   Crown Prince Haakon Magnus [NOR]
           Stein Gruben (ski jumper) [NOR]
           Catherine Nottingnes [NOR]
1998   Midori Ito [JPN]
           Hiromu Suzuki [JPN]
           Takanori Kono [JPN]
           Masaki Chiba [JPN]
           Chris Moon [NZL]

Appendix VII: Speakers of the Olympic Oath

GAMES OF THE OLYMPIADS–ATHLETES

1920	Victor Boin [Water Polo/Fencing]
1924	Georges André [Athletics]
1928	Harry Dénis [Football]
1932	George Calnan [Fencing]
1936	Rudolf Ismayr [Weightlifting]
1948	Donald Finlay [Athletics]
1952	Heikki Savoläinen [Gymnastics]
1956	John Landy [Athletics]
1960	Adolfo Consolini [Athletics]
1964	Takashi Ono [Gymnastics]
1968	Pablo Garrido [Athletics]
1972	Heidi Schüller [Athletics]
1976	Pierre St. Jean [Weightlifting]
1980	Nikolay Andrianov [Gymnastics]
1984	Edwin Moses [Athletics]
1988	Huh Jae [Basketball]
	Son Mi-Na [Handball]
1992	Luis Doreste Blanco [Yachting]
1996	Teresa Edwards [Basketball]
2000	Rechelle Hawkes Hockey (Field)]

OLYMPIC EQUESTRIAN GAMES–ATHLETE

1956	Henri Saint Cyr [Equestrian]

OLYMPIC WINTER GAMES–ATHLETES

1924	Camille Mandrillon [Nordic Skiing]
1928	Hans Eidenbenz [Nordic Skiing]
1932	Jack Shea [Speed Skating]
1936	Wilhelm Bögner [Alpine Skiing]
1948	Riccardo "Bibi" Torriani [Ice Hockey]
1952	Torbjørn Falkanger [Ski Jumping]
1956	Guilliana Chenal-Minuzzo [Alpine Skiing]
1960	Carol Heiss [Figure Skating]
1964	Paul Aste [Bobsledding]
1968	Leo Lacroix [Alpine Skiing]
1972	Keichi Suzuki [Speed Skating]
1976	Werner Delle Karth [Bobsledding]
1980	Eric Heiden [Speed Skating]
1984	Bojan Križaj [Alpine Skiing]
1988	Pierre Harvey [Nordic Skiing]
1992	Surya Bonaly [Figure Skating]
1994	Vegard Ulvang [Nordic Skiing]
1998	Kenji Ogiwara [Nordic Combined]

GAMES OF THE OLYMPIADS–OFFICIALS

1972	Heinz Pollay [Equestrian official]
1976	Maurice Fauget [Track & Field Athletics official]
1980	Aleksandr Medved [Wrestling official]
1984	Sharon Weber [Gymnastics official]
1988	Lee Hak-Rae [Judo official]
1992	Eugeni Asensio [Water Polo official]
1996	Hobie Billingsley [Diving official]
2000	Peter Kerr [Water Polo official]

OLYMPIC WINTER GAMES–OFFICIALS

1972	Fumio Asaki [Ski Jumping official]
1976	Willi Köstinger [Nordic Skiing official]

1980	Terry McDermott [Speed Skating official]
1984	Dragan Perović [Alpine Skiing official]
1988	Suzanne Morrow-Francis [Figure Skating official]
1992	Pierre Bornat [Alpine Skiing official]
1994	Kari Karing [Nordic Skiing official]
1998	Junko Hiromatsu [Figure Skating official]

Appendix VIII: Official Openings of the Olympic Games

GAMES OF THE OLYMPIADS

1896	King Giorgios I [Greece]
1900	none
1904	President David Rowland Francis [Louisiana Purchase Exposition/United States]
1906	King Giorgios I [Greece]
1908	King Edward VII [United Kingdom]
1912	King Gustaf V (Sweden)
1920	King Albert I [Belgium]
1924	President Gaston Doumergue [France]
1928	His Royal Highness Prince Hendrik [The Netherlands]
1932	Vice President Charles Curtis [United States]
1936	Reichsführer Adolf Hitler [Germany]
1948	King George VI [United Kingdom]
1952	President Juho Kusti Paasikivi [Finland]
1956	His Royal Highness Philip, The Duke of Edinburgh [United Kingdom]
1960	President Giovanni Gronchi [Italy]
1964	Emperor Hirohito [Japan]
1968	President Dr. Gustavo Díaz Ordaz [Mexico]
1972	President Dr. Gustav Heinemann [Federal Republic of Germany]
1976	Queen Elizabeth II [United Kingdom]
1980	President Leonid Ilyich Brezhnev [Soviet Union]
1984	President Ronald Wilson Reagan [United States]
1988	President Roh Tae-Woo [Korea]
1992	King Juan Carlos I [Spain]

1996   President William Jefferson Clinton [United States]
2000   Governor-General Sir William Patrick Deane [Australia]

OLYMPIC EQUESTRIAN GAMES

1956   King Gustaf VI Adolf [Sweden]

OLYMPIC WINTER GAMES

1924   Under-Secretary for Physical Education Gaston Vidal [France]
1928   President Edmund Schulthess [Switzerland]
1932   Governor Franklin Delano Roosevelt [New York, United States]
1936   Reichsführer Adolf Hitler [Germany]
1948   President Enrico Celio [Switzerland]
1952   Her Royal Highness Princess Ragnhild [Norway]
1956   President Giovanni Gronchi [Italy]
1960   Vice-President Richard Milhous Nixon [United States]
1964   President Dr. Adolf Schärf [Austria]
1968   President General Charles de Gaulle [France]
1972   Emperor Hirohito [Japan]
1976   President Dr. Rudolf Kirchschläger [Austria]
1980   Vice-President Walter Frederick Mondale [United States]
1984   President Mika Spiljak [Yugoslavia]
1988   Governor-General Jeanne Sauvé [Canada]
1992   President François Mitterrand [France]
1994   King Harald V [Norway]
1998   Emperor Akihito [Japan]

Appendix IX: Most Olympic Medals Won: Summer, Men

Medals	Athlete [Nation-Sport]
15	Nikolay Andrianov [URS-GYM]
13	Edoardo Mangiarotti [ITA-FEN]
13	Takashi Ono [JPN-GYM]
13	Boris Shakhlin [URS-GYM]
12	Sawao Kato [JPN-GYM]
12	Paavo Nurmi [FIN-ATH]
12	Aleksey Nemov [RUS-GYM]
11	Matthew Biondi [USA-SWI]
11	Viktor Chukarin [URS-GYM]
11	Carl Osburn [USA-SHO]
11	Mark Spitz [USA-SWI]
10	Aleksandr Dityatin [URS-GYM]
10	Raymond Ewry [USA-ATH]
10	Aladár Gerevich [HUN-FEN]
10	Carl Lewis [USA-ATH]
10	Akinori Nakayama [JPN-GYM]
10	Vitaly Shcherbo [EUN/BLR-GYM]
10	Hubert Van Innis [BEL-ARC]
9	Giulio Gaudini [ITA-FEN]
9	Zoltán von Halmay [HUN-SWI]
9	Eizo Kenmotsu [JPN-GYM]
9	Aleksandr Popov [EUN/RUS-SWI]
9	Heikki Savolainen [FIN-GYM]
9	Martin Sheridan [USA-ATH]
9	Alfred Swahn [SWE-SHO]
9	Yury Titov [URS-GYM]
9	Mitsuo Tsukahara [JPN-GYM]
9	Mikhail Voronin [URS-GYM]

Appendix X: Most Olympic Medals Won: Summer, Women

Medals	Athlete [Nation-Sport]
18	Larisa Latynina [URS-GYM]
11	Věra Čáslavská [TCH-GYM]
10	Polina Astakhova [URS-GYM]
10	Ágnes Keleti [HUN-GYM]
10	Birgit Schmidt-Fischer [GDR/GER-CAN]
10	Jennifer Thompson [USA-SWI]
9	Nadia Comăneci [ROM-GYM]
9	Dara Torres [USA-SWI]
9	Lyudmila Turishcheva [URS-GYM]
8	Shirley Babashoff [USA-SWI]
8	Kornelia Ender [GDR-SWI]
8	Dawn Fraser [AUS-SWI]
8	Sofiya Muratova [URS-GYM]
8	Susan O'Neill [AUS-SWI]
8	Merlene Ottey [JAM-ATH]
8	Margit Plachyné-Korondi [HUN-GYM]
8	Franziska Van Almsick [GER-SWI]
7	Simona Amanar [ROM-GYM]
7	Agneta Andersson [SWE-CAN]
7	Krisztina Egerszegi [HUN-SWI]
7	Mariya Gorokhovskaya [URS-GYM]
7	Dagmar Hase [GER-SWI]
7	Karin Janz [GDR-GYM]
7	Elisabeta Lipa-Oleniuc [ROM-ROW]
7	Ildikó Ságiné-Ujlakiné-Rejtő [HUN-FEN]
7	Shirley Strickland de la Hunty [AUS-ATH]
7	Irena Szewińska-Kirszenstein [POL-ATH]
7	Shannon Miller [USA-GYM]

Appendix XI: Most Olympic Gold Medals Won: Summer, Men

Golds	Athlete [Nation-Sport]
10	Raymond Ewry [USA-ATH]
9	Carl Lewis [USA-ATH]
9	Paavo Nurmi [FIN-ATH]
9	Mark Spitz [USA-SWI]
8	Matthew Biondi [USA-SWI]
8	Sawao Kato [JPN-GYM]
7	Nikolay Andrianov [URS-GYM]
7	Viktor Chukarin [URS-GYM]
7	Aladár Gerevich [HUN-FEN]
7	Boris Shakhlin [URS-GYM]
6	Gert Fredriksson [SWE-CAN]
6	Rudolf Kárpáti [HUN-FEN]
6	Reiner Klimke [FRG-EQU]
6	Pál Kovács [HUN-FEN]
6	Edoardo Mangiarotti [ITA-FEN]
6	Nedo Nadi [ITA-FEN]
6	Akinori Nakayama [JPN-GYM]
6	Vitaly Shcherbo [EUN/BLR-GYM]
6	Hubert Van Innis [BEL-ARC]

Appendix XII: Most Olympic Gold Medals Won: Summer, Women

Golds	Athlete [Nation-Sport]
9	Larisa Latynina [URS-GYM]
8	Jennifer Thompson [USA-SWI]
7	Věra Čáslavská [TCH-GYM]
7	Birgit Schmidt-Fischer [GDR-CAN]
6	Kristin Otto [GDR-SWI]
6	Amy Van Dyken [USA-SWI]
5	Polina Astakhova [URS-GYM]
5	Nadia Comăneci [ROM-GYM]
5	Ágnes Keleti [HUN-GYM]
5	Nelli Kim [URS-GYM]
5	Krisztina Egerszegi [HUN-SWI]

Appendix XIII: Most Medals Won: Winter, Men

Medals	Athlete [Nation-Sport]
12	Bjørn Dæhlie [NOR-NSK]
9	Sixten Jernberg [SWE-NSK]
7	Ivar Ballangrud [NOR-SSK]
7	Veikko Hakulinen [FIN-NSK]
7	Eero Mäntyranta [FIN-NSK]
7	Bogdan Musiol [GDR-BOB]
7	Clas Thunberg [FIN-SSK]
7	Vladimir Smirnov [URS/RUS-NSK]
6	Johan Grøttumsbråten [NOR-NSK]
6	Wolfgang Hoppe [GDR-BOB]
6	Roald Larsen [NOR-SSK]
6	Eugenio Monti [ITA-BOB]
6	Gunde Anders Svan [SWE-NSK]
6	Vegard Ulvang [NOR-NSK]
6	Mika Myllylä [FIN-NSK]
6	Harri Kirvesniemi [FIN-NSK]

Appendix XIV: Most Olympic Medals Won: Winter, Women

Medals	Athlete [Nation-Sport]
10	Raisa Smetanina [EUN/URS-NSK]
9	Lyubov Yegorova [EUN/RUS-NSK]
8	Karin Kania-Enke [GDR-SSK]
8	Galina Kulakova [URS-NSK]
8	Gunda Niemann-Stirnemann-Kleemann [GER-SSK]
7	Andrea Ehrig-Schöne-Mitscherlich [GDR-SSK]
7	Marja-Liisa Kirvesniemi-Hämäläinen [FIN-NSK]
7	Manuela Di Centa [ITA-NSK]
7	Stefania Belmondo [ITA-NSK]
7	Yelena Välbe [EUN/URS/RUS-NSK]
7	Larisa Lazutina [EUN/RUS-NSK]
6	Bonnie Blair [USA-SSK]
6	Lidiya Skoblikova [URS-SSK]
6	Ursula "Uschi" Disl [GER-NSK]
5	Alevtina Kolchina [URS-NSK]
5	Anfisa Reztsova [EUN/URS-BIA/NSK]
5	Vreni Schneider [SUI-ASK]
5	Helena Takalo [FIN-NSK]
5	Chun Lee-Kyung [KOR-STK]
5	Katja Seizinger [GER-ASK]
5	Claudia Pechstein [GER-SSK]

Appendix XV: Most Olympic Gold Medals Won: Winter, Men

Golds	Athlete [Nation-Sport]
8	Bjørn Dæhlie [NOR-NSK]
5	Eric Heiden [USA-SSK]
5	Clas Thunberg [FIN-SSK]
4	Ivar Ballangrud [NOR-SSK]
4	Yevgeny Grishin [URS-SSK]
4	Sixten Jernberg [SWE-NSK]
4	Johann Olav Koss [NOR-SSK]
4	Matti Nykänen [FIN-NSK]
4	Gunde Anders Svan [SWE-NSK]
4	Aleksandr Tikhonov [URS-BIA]
4	Thomas Wassberg [SWE-NSK]
4	Nikolay Zimyatov [URS-NSKI

Appendix XVI: Most Olympic Gold Medals Won: Winter, Women

Golds	Athlete [Nation-Sport]
6	Lidiya Skoblikova [URS-SSK]
6	Lyubov Yegorova [EUN/RUS-NSK]
5	Bonnie Blair [USA-SSK]
5	Larisa Lazutina [EUN-NSK]
4	Galina Kulakova [URS-NSKI
4	Raisa Smetanina [EUN/URS-NSK]
4	Chun Lee-Kyung [KOR-STK]
3	Klavdiya Boyarskikh [URS-NSK]
3	Yvonne van Gennip [NED-SSK]
3	Sonja Henie [NOR]FSK]
3	Karin Kania-Enke [GDR-SSK]
3	Marja-Liisa Kirvesniemi-Hämäläinen [FIN-NSK]
3	Anfisa Reztsova [EUN-BIA]
3	Irina Rodnina [URS-FSK]
3	Vreni Schneider [SUI-ASK]
3	Gunda Niemann-Stirnemann-Kleemann [GER-SSK]
3	Yelena Välbe [EUN/RUS-NSK]
3	Katja Seizinger [GER-ASK]
3	Deborah Compagnoni [ITA-ASK]
3	Nina Gavrylyuk [URS-NSK]

Appendix XVII: List of All Positive Drug Tests at the Olympic Games

Listed after each athlete's name is his or her country, sport and event, finish before disqualification, and the name of illegal drug detected.

1968 Mexico City [1]

Hans-Gunnar Liljenvall [SWE]   Modern pentathlete; 3rd Alcohol.

1972 Sapporo [1]

Alois Schröder [FRG]   Ice hockey; 7th   Ephedrine. [Note: The team doctor, Franz Schlickenrieder, was disqualified from serving in that capacity for life.]

1972 Munich [5]

Bakhaava Buida [MGL]   Judo, 63-kg. class; 2nd   drug unknown.

Miguel Coli [PUR]   Basketball; 6th   Ephedrine.

Richard DeMont [USA]   Swimming, 400 meter freestyle; 1st Ephedrine.

Jamie Huelamo [ESP]   Cycling, individual road race; 3rd Coramine.

Walter Legel [AUT]   Weightlifting, 67½-kg. class; 15th Amphetamines.

1976 Innsbruck [2]

Galina Kulakova [URS]   Nordic skiing, 5 km.; 3rd   Ephedrine.

[Note: Kulakova also finished 3rd in the 10 km. and 1st on the 4- x 5-km. relay team at these Olympic Winter Games, but was allowed to keep those medals.]

František Pospíšil [TCH]   Ice hockey; 2nd   Codeine.

[Note: The team doctor, Treffný, was disqualified from serving in that capacity for life.]

1976 Montreal [11]

Blagoi Blagoev [BUL]   Weightlifting, 82½-kg. class; 2nd
Anabolic steroids.

Mark Cameron [USA]   Weightlifting, 110-kg. class; 5th
Anabolic steroids.

Paul Cerutti [MON]   Shooting, Trap shooting; 43rd
Amphetamines.

Valentin Khristov [BUL]   Weightlifting, 110-kg. class; 1st
Anabolic steroids.

Dragomir Ciorislan [ROM]   Weightlifting, 75-kg. class; 5th
Fencanfamine.

Phillip Grippaldi [USA]   Weightlifting, 90-kg. class; 4th
Anabolic steroids.

Zbigniew Kaczmarek [POL]   Weightlifting, 67½-kg. class; 1st
Anabolic steroids.

Lorne Leibel [CAN]   Yachting, Tempest class; 7th
Phenylpropanolamine.

Ame Norback [SWE]   Weightlifting, 60-kg. class; eliminated
Anabolic steroids.

Petr Pavlagek [TCH]   Weightlifting, 110-kg. class; 6th   Anabolic
steroids.

Danuta Rosani-Gwardecka [POL]   Track & field athletics, Discus
throw; 14th in qualifying (DNQ)   Anabolic steroids.

1980 Lake Placid and Moscow [0]

No positive drug tests at either Games.

1984 Saraievo [1]

Purevjalyn Batsukh [MGL]   Nordic skiing, 15 km.; 69th/ 30 km.;
65th/ 4- x 10-km. relay/15th   Methandienone.

1984 Los Angeles [12]

Serafim Grammatikopoulos [GRE]   Weightlifting, Unlimited
class; did not finish   Nandrolone.

Vesteinn Hafsteinsson [ISL]   Track & field athletics, Discus
throw; 14th in qualifying round   Nandrolone.

Thomas Johansson [SWE]   Wrestling, Unlimited Graeco-Roman
class; 2nd   Methenolone.

Stefan Laggner [AUT]   Weightlifting, Unlimited class; 4th
Nandrolone.

Göran Petterson [SWE]   Weightlifting, 110-kg. class; 6th
Nandrolone.
EIji Shimomura [JPN]   Volleyball; 7th   Testosterone.
Mikiyasu Tanaka [JPN]   Volleyball; 7th   Ephedrine.
[Note: The trainer of the Japanese volleyball team was banned from
the Olympics for life.]
Ahmed Tarbi [ALG]   Weightlifting, 56-kg. class; 9th   Nandrolone.
Mahmoud Tarha [LBA]   Weightlifting, 52-kg. class; 4th
Nandrolone.
Gian-Paolo Urlando [ITA]   Track & field athletics, Hammer
throw; 4th   Testosterone.
Martti Vainio [FIN]   Track & field athletics, 10,000 meters; 2nd
Methenolone.
Anna Verouli [GRE]   Track & field athletics, Javelin throw; 13th
in qualifying round   Nandrolone.

1988 Calgary [1]
Jaroslav Morawiecki [POL]   Ice hockey; 10th   Testosterone.

1988 Seoul [11]
Alidad [AFG]   Wrestling, 62-kg. freestyle class; eliminated third
round   Furosemide.
Kerrith Brown [GBR]   Judo, 71-kg.; 3rd   Furosemide.
Kálmán Csengeri [HUN]   Weightlifting, 75-kg. class; 4th
Stanozolol.
Angel Genchev [BUL]   Weightlifting, 67½-kg. class; 1st
Furosemide.
Mitko Grablev [BUL]   Weightlifting, 56-kg. class; 1st
Furosemide.
Ben Johnson [CAN]   Track & field athletics, 100 meters; 1st
Stanozolol.
Fernando Mariaca [ESP]   Weightlifting, 67½-kg. class; 13th
Pemoline.
Jorge Quezada [ESP]   Modern pentathlon; 24th   Propranolol.
Andor Szányi [HUN]   Weightlifting, 100-kg. class; 2nd
Stanozolol.
Alexander Watson [AUS]   Modern pentathlon; 61st   Caffeine.
Sergiusz Wolczaniecki [POL]   Weightlifting, 90-kg. class; 3rd
Stanozolol.

1992 Albertville [0]

No positive drug tests.

1992 Barcelona [5]

Madina Biktagirova [EUN]   Track & field athletics, Marathon; 4th   Norephedrine.

Bonnie Dasse [USA]   Track & field athletics, Shot put; 14th in qualifying round   Clembuterol.

Judson Logan [USA]   Track & field athletics, Hammer throw; 4th Clembuterol.

Nijole Medvedeva [LTU]   Track & field athletics, Long jump; 4th Meziocarde (a stimulant).

Wu Dan [CHN]   Volleyball; 7th   Stimulant with a strychnine base.

1994 Lillehammer [0]

No positive drug tests.

1996 Atlanta [0]

No positive drug tests. There were actually six positive tests, but five of these were for the controversial drug Bromantan. These five athletes were originally disqualified, but on appeal, all were reinstated because the drug was new, it was not certain if it was an ergogenic aid, and it had not been announced in advance. A sixth positive test for phenylpropanolamine was announced, but the athlete was given only a warning because that drug is commonly found in cold medications. Two persons were disqualified, a coach and physician to the Lithuanian cycling team, because several of their athletes did test positive for Bromantan.

1998 Nagano [0]

There were no drug disqualifications. However, in men's giant slalom snowboarding, the winner, Ross Rebagliati [CAN], was disqualified two days after winning the event, when he tested positive for marijuana use. He was reinstated as the gold medalist on 12 February after a ruling by the Court of Arbitration for Sport (CAS).

2000 Sydney [10]

Fritz Aanes [NOR]   Wrestling, 85-kg. Graeco-Roman; 4th Nandrolone.

Ashot Danielyan [ARM]   Weightlifting, Unlimited class; 3rd Stanozolol.

Izabela Dragneva [BUL]   Weightlifting, 48-kg. class; 1st Furosemide.

Ivan Ivanov [BUL]   Weightlifting, 56-kg. class; 2nd Furosemide.

Alexander Leipold [GER]   Wrestling, 76-kg. freestyle; 1st Nandrolone.

Svetlana Pospelova [RUS]   Track & field athletics; 400 metres; 4th in heat of round one   Stanozolol.

Oyunbileg Puervbaatar [MGL]   Wrestling; 58-kg. freestyle; 5th Furosemide.

Andreea Raducan [ROM]   Gymnastics; Individual all-around; 1st Pseudoephedrine.

Andris Reinholds [LAT]   Rowing; Single sculls; 8th Nandrolone.

Minchev Angelov Sevdalin [BUL]   Weightlifting; 62-kg. class; 3rd   Furosemide.

Appendix XVIII: Attempts at Olympic Revival Prior to 1896

1612   Robert Dover's Games, also known as the *Cotswold Olimpick Games*, are first contested in the Cotswold Hills in England, during Whitsun (Pentecostal) Week. The Games continued to 1642 and then are discontinued until the 1660s. They are held intermittently from the 1660s to the 1850s. Resumed again a few decades later, they continue to be held sporadically. Rather than true sporting contests, the Games resemble more a medieval country fair.

1834   Ramlösa, Sweden (near Helsingborg) "Olympic Games" organized under the initiative of Professor Gustav Johann Schartau of the University of Lund.

1836   Ramlösa, Sweden   Second, and last, Swedish attempt at revival.

1830–1840s   Olympic-type festivals held in Montréal, Quebec, Canada.

1850   First Much Wenlock Olympian Games held in Much Wenlock, a small town near Shrewsbury, Shropshire, England. Altogether, 45 in number were held consecutively, failing only 1874, through 1895. They were later held sporadically and continue to the 1990s.

1859   First Zappas Olympic Games in Athens, Greece, sponsored by the Greek philanthropist Evangelis Zappas.

1860   First Shropshire Olympic Games organized in Much Wenlock, England, by the Shropshire Olympic Society.

1861   Second Shropshire Olympic Games held in Wellington, Shropshire, England.

1862   Third Shropshire Olympic Games held in Much Wenlock, Shropshire, England.

	First Grand Olympic Festival held in Liverpool, England, sponsored by the Liverpool Olympian Society.
1863	Second Grand Olympic Festival held in Liverpool, England, sponsored by the Liverpool Olympian Society.
1864	Fourth, and last, Shropshire Olympic Games held in Much Wenlock, England.
	Third Grand Olympic Festival held in Liverpool, England, sponsored by the Liverpool Olympian Society.
1866	First Olympic Games sponsored by England's National Olympian Association, held in London, England.
	Fourth Grand Olympic Festival held in Llandudno, Wales, sponsored by the Liverpool Olympian Society.
1867	Second Olympic Games sponsored by the National Olympian Association, held in Birmingham, England.
	Fifth, and last, Grand Olympic Festival held in Liverpool, England, sponsored by the Liverpool Olympian Society.
1868	Third Olympic Games sponsored by the National Olympian Association, held in Wellington, Shropshire, England.
1870	Second Zappas Olympic Games in Athens, Greece.
1873	First Morpeth Olympic Games held in Morpeth, England. The Games were held almost annually until 1958.
1874	Fourth Olympic Games sponsored by the National Olympian Association, held in Much Wenlock, England.
1875	Third Zappas Olympic Games in Athens, Greece.
1877	Fifth Olympic Games sponsored by the National Olympian Association, held in Shrewsbury, England.
1880	Olympic Games at Lake Palić, held from 1880 to 1914 in Palić, a spa eight kilometers east of Subotica, then in Hungary, and now in the Vojvodina province of Serbia. The Games were held sporadically until 1914.
1883	Sixth, and last, Olympic Games sponsored by the National Olympian Association, held in Hadley, Shropshire, England.
1889	Fourth Zappas Olympic Games in Athens, Greece.

1891   First Panhellenic Gymnastic Society Games, modeled after the Zappas Olympics, held in Athens.

1893   Second Panhellenic Gymnastic Society Games, modeled after the Zappas Olympics, held in Athens.

April 1896 Games of the Ist Olympiad, celebrating the First Olympiad of the Modern Era, held in Athens, Greece, signaling the final rebirth of the Olympic Games after 15 centuries.

Bibliography

Within each section, the books are listed first by Olympic Games, then alphabetically, and then chronologically, in cases where one author has several books listed. Also included are dissertations specifically concerned with the Olympic Games or certain aspects of them. In addition, a very few pertinent articles are listed, where no comprehensive book on a certain subject is available. All transliterated titles are from the native alphabet, using the *Encyclopaedia Britannica* as the source of the transliteration table.

OFFICIAL REPORTS OF THE GAMES OF THE OLYMPIAD

Current official reports (at least since 1960) are issued in both English and French, and usually in the language of the host nation. These are sometimes issued with parallel texts, and sometimes as separate editions for each language. In the following, COJO is the acronym that stands for Comité d'Organisateur des Jeux Olympiques, the French name for the Organizing Committee.

1896

The Baron de Coubertin; Philemon, Timoleon; Lambros, Spiridon P.; and Politis, Nikolaos G., editors. *The Olympic Games 776 B.C–1896 A.D.; With the approval and support of the Central Council of the International Olympic Games in Athens, under the Presidency of H. R. H. the Crown Prince Constantine.* Athens: Charles Beck, 1896. This was issued in various versions, including several in parallel texts, as follows: Greek/English; Greek/French; Greek/French/English; and German/English. Also, multiple reprints of this first Official Report have been produced, most notably a 1966 edition with English/French/Greek parallel texts published by the Hellenic Olympic Committee, and also a 1971 German edition entitled *Die Olympischen Spiele 1896–Offizieller Bericht,* published by the Carl-Diem-Institut in Cologne, Germany.

1900

Merillon, Daniel, editor. *Concours Internationaux d'Exercices Physiques et de Sport: Rapports Publiés sous la Direction de M. D. Merillon, Délégué Général.* 2 vols. Paris: Imprimerie Nationale, 1901 (Vol. 1) and 1902 (Vol. 2). Strictly speaking, this was a report of the physical culture section of l'Exposition Internationale in Paris in 1900.

1904

Lucas, Charles J. P. *The Olympic Games 1904.* St. Louis: Woodward & Tiernan Printing Co., 1905.

Sullivan, James E., compiler. *Spalding's Official Athletic Almanac for 1905: Special Olympic Number, Containing the Official Report of the Olympic Games of 1904.* New York: American Sports Publishing, 1905.

1906

Savvidis, Panagiotis S., editor. *Leukoma ton en Athenais B'Diethnon Olympiakon Agonon 1906/Jeux Olympiques Internationaux 1906.* Athens: Estia, K. Maisner, N. Kargadouris, 1907.

1908

Cook, Theodore Andrea, editor. *The Fourth Olympiad: Being the Official Report of the Olympic Games of 1908 Celebrated in London Under the Patronage of His Most Gracious King Edward VII and by the Sanction of the International Olympic Committee.* London: British Olympic Council, 1909.

1912

Bergvall, Erik, editor. *The Official Report of the Olympic Games of Stockholm 1912* and *V. Olympiaden. Officiel redogorelse for olympiska spelen i Stockholm 1912.* Stockholm: Wahlstrom & Widstrand, 1913.

1916

COJO Berlin 1916. *Denkschrift zur Vorbereitung der VI. Olympiade 1916, veranstaltet im Deutschen Stadion zu Berlin.* Berlin: author, n.d.

1920

Verdyck, Alfred, editor. *Rapport officiel des Jeux de la VIIème Olympiade, Anvers 1920.* Brussels: COJO Antwerp 1920, 1922.

1924

Avé, M.A., editor. *Les Jeux de la VIIIè Olympiade Paris 1924. Rapport officiel du Comité Olympique Français.* Paris: Librairie de France, 1925.

1928

Rossem, George van, editor. *IXe Olympiade. Officiel gedenkboek van de spelen der IXe Olympiade Amsterdam 1928; The Ninth Olympiad – Being the Official Report of the Olympic Games of 1928 Celebrated at Amsterdam Issued by the Netherlands Olympic Committee;* and *Olympiade Amsterdam 1928. Rapport officiel des Jeux de la IXè Olympiade Amsterdam 1928.* Amsterdam: J. H. de Bussy, 1930. Separate editions were published in Dutch, English, and French.

1932

Browne, Frederick Granger, editor. *The Games of the Xth Olympiad, Los Angeles, 1932: Official Report.* Los Angeles: COJO Los Angeles 1932, 1933.

1936

COJO Berlin 1936. *XI Olympiade, Berlin 1936: Amtlicher Bericht; Les XIè Jeux Olympiques, Berlin 1936. Rapport official;* and *The XIth Olympic Games, Berlin 1936. Official Report.* Berlin: W. Limpert, 1937. Separate editions were published in German, French, and English.

1940

COJO Tokyo 1940. *XIIth Olympic Games, Tokyo, 1940. Report of the Organizing Committee on Its Work for the XII Olympic Games of 1940 in Tokyo until the Relinquishment.* Tokyo: Isshiki, 1940.

COJO Helsinki 1940. *XII Olympiad Helsinki 1940;* and *Olympische Vorbereitungen für die Feier der 12. Olympiade Helsinki 1940.* Helsinki; author, 1940. Separate editions were issued in English and German.

1944

No report was ever issued.

1948

Lord Burghley, editor. *The Official Report of the Organizing Committee for the XIV Olympiad.* London: McCorquodale & Co., Ltd., 1951.

1952

Kolkka, Sulo, editor. *The Official Report of the Organizing Committee for the Games of the XV Olympiad Helsinki 1952; Le Rapport officiel du comité d'organisateur pour les Jeux Olympiques de la XVè Olympiade Helsinki 1952;* and *XV Olympiakisat Helsingissa 1952. Jarjestelytoimikunnan virallinen kertomus.* Porvoo, Finland: Werner Soderström Osakeyhtio, 1955. Three separate editions published in English, French, and Finnish.

1956

Doyle, E. A., editor. *The Official Report of the Organizing Committee for the Games of the XVI Olympiad, Melbourne 1956.* Melbourne: W. M. Houston, Government Printer, 1958.

1956 Equestrian Games

COJO Stockholm 1956. *Ryttaroolympiaden: The Equestrian Games of the XVIth Olympiad, Stockholm 1956.* Stockholm: Esselte Aktiebolag, 1959. Parallel texts in Swedish and English.

1960

Giacomini, Romolo, editor. *The Games of the XVII Olympiad, Rome 1960; Giochi della XVII Olimpiada Roma 1960;* and *Les jeux de la XVIIè Olympiade, Rome 1960.* 2 volumes. Rome: COJO Rome 1960, 1960. Three separate editions were published in English, Italian, and French.

1964

COJO Tokyo 1964. *The Games of the XVIII Olympiad, Tokyo 1964. The Official Report of the Organizing Committee.* 2 vols. Tokyo: author, 1964.

1968

Trueblood, Beatrice, editor. *Mexico 1968. Mémoire officiel des Jeux de la XIX Olympiade/Commemorative Volumes of the Games of the XIX Olympiad.* 4 vols. Mexico City: COJO Mexico City 1968, 1968. Two separate editions were issued, one with parallel texts in French and English and one with parallel texts in Spanish and German. A fifth volume was also issued, which contained entry tickets, programs, and other memorabilia. A supplement was also issued to the second volume.

1972

Diem, Liselott, and Ernst Knoesel, editors. *Die Spiele: The Official Report of the Organizing Committee for the Games of the XXth Olympiad, Munich 1972.* 3 vols. Munich: ProSport, 1974. Separate editions of volumes 1 and 2 were issued in English, German, and French. Volume 3 (the results) was issued with parallel texts in English, French, and German.

1976

Rousseau, Roger, editor. *Games of the XXI Olympiad, Montreal 1976: Official Report,* and *Jeux de la XXIè Olympiade, Montréal 1976. Rapport officiel.* 3 vols. Montreal: COJO Montreal 1976, *ca.* 1978. Separate editions were issued in English and French.

1980

Novikov, I. T., editor. *Games of the XXIInd Olympiad Moscow 1980: Official Report of the Organizing Committee of the Games of the XXIInd Olympiad;* and *Jeux de la XXIIè Olympiade Moscou 1980: Rapport officiel du Comité d'organisation des Jeux de la XXIIè Olympiade. 3 vols.* Moscow: Fitzkultura i Sport, *1981.* Separate editions were issued in English and French.

1984

Perelman, Richard B., editor. *Official Report of the Games of the XXIIIrd Olympiad Los Angeles, 1984.* 2 vols. Los Angeles: COJO Los Angeles 1984, 1985. Separate editions were issued in French and English.

1988

Roh Sang-Kook; Lee Kyong-Hee; and Lee Bong-Jie, editors. *Official Report: Games of the XXIVth Olympiad Seoul 1988.* 2 vols. Seoul: Korean Textbook Co., Ltd., *1989.* Separate editions were issued in French, English, and Korean.

1992

Cuyàs, Romà, editor. *Official Report: Games of the XXV Olympiad Barcelona 1992.* 4 vols. Barcelona: COJO Barcelona 1992, 1992. Separate editions were issued in English, French, Castilian Spanish, and Catalan Spanish. Note that this Official Report, unlike most of them, did not contain complete results. Volume Four of the Official Report listed results, but only the top eight finishers in each event. The results were issued as a separate volume, entitled *Games of the XXV Olympiad Barcelona 1992: The Results*, with the same editor and publisher. The results text was issued in parallel texts of English, French, Castilian Spanish, and Catalan Spanish.

1996

Watkins, Ginger T., editor. *The Official Report of the Centennial Olympic Games.* 3 vols. Atlanta: Peachtree Publishers, 1997. Separate editions were issued in English, French, Spanish, and German.

OFFICIAL REPORTS OF THE OLYMPIC WINTER GAMES

1924

No separate official report of the Chamonix Winter Olympics was ever issued. The report is found at the end of the report for the 1924 Olympic Games in Paris, *Les Jeux de la VIIIè Olympiade Paris 1924. Rapport officiel du Comité Olympique Français.* See above.

1928

Swiss Olympic Committee. *Rapport général du Comité Exécutif des IIèmes Jeux Olympiques d'Hiver et documents officiels divers.* Lausanne: author, 1928. Results were not included in this report but were issued in a separate volume as follows: Swiss Olympic Committee. *Résultats des Concours des IIèmes Jeux Olympiques d'Hiver organisés à St. Moritz.* Lausanne: author, 1928.

1932

Lattimer, George M., editor. *Official Report: III Olympic Winter Games, Lake Placid 1932.* Lake Placid: COJO Lake Placid 1932, 1932.

1936

COJO Garmisch-Partenkirchen 1936. *IV. Olympische Winterspiele 1936. Garmisch-Partenkirchen 6. bis 16. Februar: Amtlicher Bericht.* Berlin: Reichssportverlag, 1936.

1940

Diem, Carl, editor. *Vorbereitungen zu den V. Olympischen Winterspiele 1940 Garmisch-Partenkirchen.* Munich: Knorr und Hirth, 1939. The Games did not take place. They were originally scheduled for Sapporo, Japan, and were later scheduled for St. Moritz, Switzerland, before being rescheduled to Garmisch-Partenkirchen. Sapporo and St. Moritz did not issue reports.

1944

No report was ever issued.

1948

Swiss Olympic Committee. *Rapport Général sur les Vès Jeux Olympiques d'Hiver St-Moritz 1948.* Lausanne: author, 1951.

1952

Petersen, Rolf, editor. *VI Olympiske Vinterleker/Olympic Winter Games: Oslo 1952.* English translation by Margaret Wold and Ragnar Wold. Oslo: Kirstes Boktrykkeri, 1956. Parallel texts in English and Norwegian.

1956

Comitato Olimpico Nazionale Italiano. *VII Giochi Olimpici Invernali/VII Olympic Winter Games: Rapporto ufficiale/Official Report.* Rome: author, ca. 1957. Parallel texts in Italian and English.

1960

Rubin, Robert, editor. *VIII Olympic Winter Games, Squaw Valley, California 1960: Final Report.* Sacramento: California Olympic Commission, 1960. Issued in English only.

1964

Wolfgang, Friedl, and Berd Neumann, editors. *Offizieler Bericht der IX. Olympischen Winterspiele Innsbruck 1964; Official Report of the IXth Olympic Winter Games, Innsbruck 1964;* and *Rapport du comité d'organisation des IXème Jeux Olympiques d'Hiver 1964.* Vienna: Osterreichischer Bundesverlag, 1967. Separate editions were issued in German, French, and English.

1968

COJO Grenoble 1968. *Xème Jeux Olympiques d'Hiver: Grenoble 1968/Xth Olympic Winter Games Grenoble 1968: Official Report/X. Olympischen Winterspiele*

Grenoble 1968. Amtlicher Bericht. Grenoble: author, 1968. Parallel texts in French, English, and German.

1972

COJO Sapporo 1972. *Les XI Jeux Olympiques d'Hiver: Sapporo 1972. Rapport official;* and *The 11th Olympic Winter Games: Sapporo 1972. Official Report.* Sapporo: author, 1972. Separate editions were published in French and English.

1976

Neumann, Bertl, editor. *Endbericht herausgegeben vom Organisationskomitee der XII. Olympischen Winterspiele Innsbruck 1976/Rapport final publié par le Comité d'Organisation des XIIèmes Jeux Olympiques d'Hiver 1976 à Innsbruck/Final Report Published by the Organizing Committee for the XIIth Winter Olympic Games 1976 at Innsbruck.* Innsbruck: COJO Innsbruck 1976, 1976. Parallel texts in German, French, English, and Russian.

1980

Madden, Robert, and Edward J. Lewi, editors. *Final Report/Rapport Final. XIII Olympic Winter Games/XIII Jeux Olympiques d'Hiver. Lake Placid, NY.* New York: Ed Lewi Associates, 1981. Parallel texts in English and French. Oddly, no results were given in the Official Report, as is common now, but they were issued separately, with no publishing information given, as:
Official Result/Résultats Officiels/Offizielle Ergebnisse. No real text, but titles were given in English, French, and German.

1984

COJO Sarajevo 1984. *Final Report Published by the Organising Committee of the XIVth Winter Olympic Games 1984 at Sarajevo/Rapport Final publié par le Comité d'Organisateur des XIVèmes Jeux Olympiques d'Hiver 1984 a Sarajevo/Završni Izvještaj Organizacionoh komiteta XIV zimskih olimipijskih igara Sarajevo, 1984.* Sarajevo: Oslobodjenje, 1985. Parallel texts in English, French, and Serbo-Croatian (but written in Latin alphabet, thus Croatian as opposed to Serbian, which is written in the Cyrillic alphabet).

1988

COJO Calgary 1988. *Rapport officiel des XVes Jeux Olympiques d'hiver/XV Olympic Winter Games Official Report.* Calgary: author, 1988. Parallel texts in French and English.

1992

Blanc, Claudie, and Jean-Marc Eysseric, editors. *Rapport officiel des XVIes Jeux Olympiques d'hiver d'Albertville et de la Savoie/Official Report of the XVI Olympic Winter Games of Albertville and Savoie.* Albertville: COJO Albertville 1992, 1992. Parallel texts in French and English.

1994

Aune, Tor; Fjellheim, Tom; Mjelde, Helge; and Verde, Linda, eds. *Official Report of The XVII Olympic Winter Games Lillehammer 1994.* 4 vols. Lillehammer: COJO Lillehammer 1994.

1998

COJO Nagano 1998. *The XVIII Olympic Winter Games. Official Report.* 3 vols. A separate case volume containing a CD-ROM of the report was also issued. Nagano: COJO Nagano 1998, 1999. Separate editions were issued in English, French, Spanish, German, and Japanese.

ANCIENT OLYMPIC GAMES

Diem, Carl. *Die Olympischen Spiele in Altertum und Gegenwart.* Eulau: n.p., 1933.

Finley, M. I., and H. W Pleket. *The Olympic Games: The First Thousand Years.* London: Chatto & Windus, 1976.

Gardiner, E. Norman. *Athletics of the Ancient World.* Chicago: Ares, 1930.

Harris, H. A. *Sport in Greece and Rome.* Ithaca, New York: Cornell University Press, 1972.

Matz, David. *Greek and Roman Sport: A Dictionary of Athletes and Events from the Eighth Century B.C. to the Third Century A.D.* Jefferson, North Carolina: McFarland, 1991.

Raschke, Wendy J., editor. *The Archaeology of the Olympics.* Madison, Wisconsin: University of Wisconsin Press, 1988.

Renson, Roland; Limmer, Manfred; Riordan, James; and Chassiotis, Dimitrios, editors. *The Olympic Games Through the Ages: Greek Antiquity and Its Impact on Modern Sport.* Athens: Hellenic Sports Research Institute, 1991.

Swaddling, Judith. *The Ancient Olympic Games.* London: British Museum Publications, 1980.

West, Gilbert. *Odes of Pindar, with Several Other Pieces in Prose and Verse, to Which Is Added a Dissertation on the Olympick Games.* London: R. Dodsley, 1753.

Young, David C. *The Myth of Greek Amateur Athletics.* Chicago: Ares, 1984.

ATTEMPTS AT REVIVAL

Burns, Francis. *Heigh for Cotswold! A History of Robert Dover's Olimpick Games.* Chipping Campden, England: Robert Dover's Games Society, 1981.

Kivroglou, A. "Die Bemühungenn von Ewangelos Sappas um die Wiedereinführung der Olympischen Spiele in Griechenland unter besonderer Berücksichtigung der Spiele von 1859." Unpublished Diplomarbeit, Deutsche Sporthochschule Köln, 1981.

Lennartz, Karl. *Kenntnisse und Vorstellungen von Olympia und den Olympischen Spielen in der Zeit von 393–1896.* Schorndorf: Verlag Karl Hofmann, 1974.

Mullins, Sam. *British Olympians: William Penny Brookes and the Wenlock Games.* London and Birmingham: Birmingham Olympic Council and British Olympic Association, 1986.

Neumüller, B. "Die Geschichte der Much Wenlock Games." Unpublished Diplomarbeit, Deutsche Sporthochschule Köln, 1985.

Redmond, Gerald. *The Caledonian Games in Nineteenth-Century America.* Rutherford, New Jersey: Fairleigh Dickinson University Press, 1971.

Rühl, Joachim K. *Die "Olympischen Spiele" Robert Dovers.* Heidelberg: Carl Winter Universitätsverlag, 1975.

Svahn, Åke. "'Olympiska Spelen' i Helsingborg 1834 och 1836," In: *Idrott Historia och Samhalle,* (1983), pp. 77–105. Text in Swedish, but with an English summary.

Young, David C. *The Modern Olympics: A Struggle for Revival.* Baltimore: Johns Hopkins University Press, 1996.

Young, David C. "Origins of the Modern Olympics," *International Journal of the History of Sport, 4* (1987), pp. 271–300.

WORKS ON SPECIFIC OLYMPIC GAMES

1896

Georgiadis, Konstantinos. "Die Geschichte der ersten Olympischen Spiele 1896 in Athen—ihre Entstehung, Durchführung und Bedeutung." Unpublished Diplomarbeit, Johannes Gutenberg Universität Mainz, 1986/87.

Kluge, Volker, ed. *1896 Athens: The Pictures of the First Olympiad.* Berlin: Brandenburgisches Verlaghaus, 1996.

Lennartz, Karl. *Geschichte der Deutschen Reichsaußchußes für Olympische Spiele: Heft 1—Die Beteiligung Deutschlands an den Olympischen Spielen 1896 in Athen.* Bonn: Verlag Peter Wegener, 1981.

Lennartz, Karl, and Walter Teutenbergr. *Die deutsche Olympia-Mannschaft von 1896.* Frankfurt am Main: Kasseler Sportverlag, 1992.

Mallon, Bill, with Ture Widlund. *The 1896 Olympic Games: Results for All Competitors in All Events, with Commentary*. Jefferson, North Carolina: McFarland, 1998.
Mandell, Richard D. *The First Modern Olympics*. Berkeley: University of California Press, 1976.
Tsolakidis, Elias. "Die Olympischen Spiele von 1896 in Athen: Versuch einer Rekonstruktion." Unpublished Diplomarbeit, Deutsche Sporthochschule Köln, 1987.

1900

Bijkerk, Ton. *Nederlandse Deelnemers aan de Tweed Olympische Spelen. Tijdens de Wereldtentoonstelling Parijs 1900*. Haarlem, NED: De Vrieseborch, 2000.
Lennartz, Karl. *Geschichte des Deutschen Reichsaußchußes für Olympische Spiele: Heft 2—Die Beteiligung Deutschlands an den Olympischen Spielen 1900 in Paris und 1904 in St. Louis*. Bonn: Verlag Peter Wegener, 1983.
Lennartz, Karl, and Walter Teutenberg. *II. Olympische Spiele 1900 in Paris. Darstellung und Quellen*. Berlin: Agon Sportverlag, 1995.
Mallon, Bill. *The 1900 Olympic Games: Results for All Competitors in All Events, with Commentary*. Jefferson, North Carolina: McFarland, 1998.

1904

Lennartz, Karl. *Geschichte der Deutschen Reichsaußchußes für Olympische Spiele: Heft 2—Die Beteiligung Deutschlands an den Olympischen Spielen 1900 in Paris und 1904 in St. Louis*. Bonn: Verlag Peter Wegener, 1983.
Lucas, Charles J. P. *The Olympic Games 1904*. St. Louis: Woodward & Tiernan, 1905.
Mallon, Bill. *A Statistical Summary of the 1904 Olympic Games*. Durham, North Carolina: author, 1981.
Mallon, Bill. *The 1904 Olympic Games: Results for All Competitors in All Events, with Commentary*. Jefferson, North Carolina: McFarland, 1999.

1906

Lennartz, Karl, and Walter Teutenberg. *Die Olympischen Spiele 1906 in Athen*. Kassel: Kasseler Sportverlag, 1992.
Mallon, Bill. *The 1906 Olympic Games: Results for All Competitors in All Events, with Commentary*. Jefferson, North Carolina: McFarland, 1999.

1908

Lennartz, Karl, with Ian Buchanan, Volker Kluge, Bill Mallon, and Walter Teutenberg. *Olympische Spiele 1908 in London*. Berlin: Agon Sportverlag, 1999.

Mallon, Bill, and Ian Buchanan. *The 1908 Olympic Games: Results for All Competitors in All Events, with Commentary.* Jefferson, North Carolina: McFarland, 2000.

1912

Mallon, Bill, and Ture Widlund. *The 1912 Olympic Games: Results for All Competitors in All Events, with Commentary.* Jefferson, North Carolina: McFarland, 2001.

1916

Lennartz, Karl. *Die VI. Olympischen Spiele Berlin 1916.* Cologne: Barz & Beienburg, 1978.

1920

Mallon, Bill. *The Unofficial Report of the 1920 Olympics.* Durham, North Carolina: MOST Publications, 1992.

Mallon, Bill. *The 1920 Olympic Games: Results for All Competitors in All Events, with Commentary.* Jefferson, North Carolina: McFarland, 2002.

Renson, Roland. *The Games Reborn: The VIIth Olympiad Antwerp 1920.* Antwerp: Pandora, 1996. Also published in French as *La VIIiéme Olympiade Anvers 1920. Les Jeux Ressuscités*, in 1995.

1932

Pieroth, Doris H. *Their Day in the Sun: Women of the 1932 Olympics.* Seattle: University of Washington, 1996.

1936

Graham, Cooper. *Leni Riefenstahl and Olympia.* Metuchen, New Jersey: Scarecrow Press, 1986.

Hart-Davis, Duff. *Hitler's Games: The 1936 Olympics.* London: Century, 1986.

Holmes, Judith. *Olympiad 1936: Blaze of Glory for Hitler's Reich.* New York: Ballantine, 1971.

Mandell, Richard D. *The Nazi Olympics.* New York: Macmillan, 1971.

1956

Lechenperg, Harald. *Olympische Spiele 1956: Cortina, Stockholm, Melbourne.* Munich: Copress-Verlag, 1957.

1960

Lechenperg, Harald. *Olympische Spiele 1960: Squaw Valley, Rome.* Munich: Co-press-Verlag, 1960; and Zurich: Schweizer Druckerei und Verlagshaus, 1960. Also published in English as *Olympic Games 1960: Squaw Valley – Rome.* New York: A.S. Barnes, 1960.

1964

Lechenperg, Harald. *Olympische Spiele 1964: Innsbruck, Tokyo.* Munich: Copress-Verlag, 1964; Zurich: Schweizer Druckerei und Verlagshaus, 1964; and Linz, Austria: Trauner, 1964. Also published in English as *Olympic Games 1964: Innsbruck – Tokyo.* New York: A.S. Barnes, 1964.

1968

Lechenperg, Harald. *Olympische Spiele 1968.* Munich: Copress-Verlag, 1968.

1972

Groussard, Serge. *The Blood of Israel: The Massacre of the Israeli Athletes: The Olympics, 1972.* New York: Morrow, *1975.*
Lechenperg, Harald. *Olympische Spiele 1972.* Munich: Copress-Verlag, 1972.
Leebron, Elizabeth Joanne. "An Analysis of Selected United States Media Coverage of the 1972 Munich Olympic Tragedy." Northwestern University, Unpublished Ph.D. Thesis, 1978.
Mandell, Richard D. *A Munich Diary: The Olympics of 1972.* Chapel Hill, North Carolina: University of North Carolina Press, 1991.
Reeve, Simon. *One Day in September.* New York: Arcade Publishing, 2000.

1976

Ludwig, Jack. *Five Ring Circus: The Montreal Olympics.* Toronto: Doubleday, 1976.
Auf der Maur, Nick. *The Billion Dollar Game: Jean Drapeau and the 1976 Olympics.* Toronto: J. Lorimer, 1977.

1980

Barton, Laurence. "The American Olympic Boycott of 1980: The Amalgam of Diplomacy and Propaganda in Influencing Public Opinion." Boston University, Unpublished Ph.D. Thesis, 1983.

Booker, Christopher. *The Games War: A Moscow Journal.* London: Faber & Faber, 1981.

Hulme, Derick L., Jr. "The Viability of International Sport as a Political Weapon: The 1980 U.S. Olympic Boycott (United States)." Fletcher School of Law and Diplomacy (Tufts University), Unpublished Ph.D. Thesis, 1988.

Hulme, Derick L., Jr. *The Political Olympics: Moscow, Afghanistan, and the 1980 U.S. Boycott.* New York: Praeger, 1990.

Wilson, Harold Edwin, Jr. "'Ours Will Not Go.' The U.S. Boycott of the 1980 Olympic Games." The Ohio State University, Unpublished Master's Thesis, 1982.

1984

Perelman, Richard B. *Olympic Retrospective: The Games of Los Angeles.* Los Angeles: COJO Los Angeles 1984, 1985.

Reich, Kenneth. *Making It Happen: Peter Ueberroth and the 1984 Olympics.* Santa Barbara, California: Capra Press, 1986.

Shaikin, Bill. *Sport and Politics: The Olympics and the Los Angeles Games.* New York: Praeger, 1988.

Ueberroth, Peter V., with Richard Levin and Amy Quinn. *Made in America: His Own Story.* New York: Morrow, 1985.

Wilson, Harold Edwin, Jr. "The Golden Opportunity: A Study of the Romanian Manipulation of the Olympic Movement During the Boycott of the 1984 Los Angeles Olympic Games." The Ohio State University, Unpublished Ph.D. Thesis, 1993.

1988

Kim Un-Yong. *The Greatest Olympics.* Seoul: Si-sa-yong-o-sa, 1990.

King, Frank W. *It's How You Play the Game: The Inside Story of the Calgary Olympics.* Calgary: Script, 1991.

Park She-Jik. *The Seoul Olympics: The Inside Story.* London: Bellew, 1991.

Pound, Richard W. *Five Rings Over Korea.* Boston: Little Brown, 1994.

1992

Brunet, Ferrán. *Economy of the 1992 Barcelona Olympic Games.* Barcelona: Centre d'Estudis Olímpics Universitat Autónoma de Barcelona, 1993.

1994

Klausen, Arne Martin, ed. *Olympic Games as Performance and Public Event: The Case of the XVII Winter Olympic Games in Norway.* New York: Berghahn, 1999.

2000

McGeoch, Rod, with Glenda Korporaal. *The Bid: How Australia Won the 2000 Games*. Melbourne: William Heinemann Australia, 1994.

GENERAL SPORTING HISTORIES OF THE OLYMPIC GAMES

Andersen, P. Chr., and Vagn Hansen. *Olympiadebogen. De Olympiske Lege 1896–1948*. Copenhagen: Samlererns Forlag, 1948.

Associated Press and Grolier. *The Olympic Story: Pursuit of Excellence*. New York: Franklin Watts, 1979.

Gillmeister, Heiner. *Olympisches Tennis: Die Geschichte der olympischen Tennisturniere (1896–1992)*. Sankt Augustin: Academia Verlag, 1993.

Greenberg, Stan. *The Guinness Book of Olympics Facts & Feats*. Enfield, Middlesex, England: Guinness, 1983. Second edition issued as *Olympic Games: The Records*, same publisher, 1987. Third edition issued as *The Guinness Olympics Fact Book*, same publisher, 1991.

Gueorguiev, Nikolay. *Analyse du programme Olympique 1896–1996*. Lausanne: IOC, 1995.

Gueorguiev, Nikolay. *Analyse du programme des Jeux Olympiques d'hiver 1924–1998*. Lausanne: IOC, 1995.

Gynn, Roger, and David Martin. *The Olympic Marathon*. Champaign, Illinois: Human Kinetics, 2000.

Henry, Bill. *An Approved History of the Olympic Games*. Four editions, those of 1948, 1976, 1981, and 1984. The last three editions were edited by Henry's daughter, Patricia Henry Yeomans. First edition: New York: G.P. Putnam, 1948. Second edition: New York: G.P. Putnam, 1976. Third/Fourth editions: Sherman Oaks, California: Alfred Publishing, 1981 and 1984.

Kahlich, Endre; Papp, László Gy.; and Subert, Zoltán. *Olympic Games 1896–1972*. Budapest: Corvina, 1972.

Kaiser, Rupert. *Olympia Almanach: Geshichten, Zahlen, Bilder. 90 Jahre Olympische Winterspiele*. Kassel, Germany: 1998.

Kaiser, Rupert. *Olympia Almanach: Geshichten, Zahlen, Bilder. 100 Jahre Olympische Spiele*. Kassel, Germany: 1996.

Kamper, Erich. *Lexikon der Olympischen Winterspiele*. Stuttgart: Union Verlag, 1964. Parallel texts in German, French, English, and Swedish.

Kamper, Erich. *Enzyklopädie der Olympischen Spiele*. Dortmund: Harenberg, 1972. Parallel texts in German, French, and English. American edition issued as *Encyclopaedia of the Olympic Games* by McGraw-Hill (New York) in 1972.

Kamper, Erich. *Lexikon der 12,000 Olympioniken*. Graz, Austria: Leykam-Verlag, 1975. Second edition issued as *Lexikon der 14,000 Olympioniken*, same publisher, 1983.

Kamper, Erich, and Bill Mallon. *The Golden Book of the Olympic Games.* Milan: Vallardi, 1993.

Kamper, Erich, and Herbert Soucek. *Olympische Heroen: Portraits und Anekdoten von 1896 bis heute.* Erkrath, Germany: Spiridon Verlag, 1991.

Lord Killanin and John Rodda, editors. *The Olympic Games.* London: Queen Anne Press, 1976. Second edition published as *The Olympic Games 1984: Los Angeles and Sarajevo,* Salem, New Hampshire: Michael Joseph, 1983.

Lovett, Charlie. *Olympic Marathon: A Centennial History of the Games' Most Storied Race.* Westport, Connecticut: Prager, 1997.

Kluge, Volker. *Die Olympischen Spiele von 1896 bis 1980.* Berlin: Sportverlag, 1981.

Kluge, Volker. *Winter Olympia Kompakt.* Berlin: Sportverlag, 1992.

Kluge, Volker. *Olympische Sommerspiele: Die Chronik I. Athen 1896–Berlin 1936.* Berlin: Sportverlag, 1997.

Kluge, Volker. *Olympische Sommerspiele: Die Chronik II. London 1948–Tokyo 1964.* Berlin: Sportverlag, 1998.

Kluge, Volker. *Olympische Sommerspiele: Die Chronik III. Mexico 1968–Los Angeles 1984.* Berlin: Sportverlag, 2000.

Kluge, Volker. *Olympische Sommerspiele: Die Chronik IV. Seoul 1988–Atlanta 1996.* Berlin: Sportverlag, 2000.

Mallon, Bill. *The Olympic Record Book.* New York: Garland, 1987.

Mallon, Bill. *Total Olympics.* New York: Total Sports, 2001.

Maritchev, Gennadi. *Who Is Who at the Summer Olympics 1896–1992.* 4 vols. Riga: Demarko Sport Publishing, 1996.

Messinesi, Xenophon. *The History of the Olympic Games.* New York/London: Drake, 1976.

Mező, Ferenc. *The Modern Olympic Games.* Budapest: Pannonia Press, 1956. Multiple editions were issued, in English, French, German, Spanish, and Hungarian.

Page, James A. *Black Olympian Medalists.* Englewood, Colorado: Libraries Unlimited, 1991.

Petrov, Prof. Raiko. *Olympic Wrestling Throughout the Millennia.* Lausanne: FILA, 1993.

Schaap, Richard [Dick]. *An Illustrated History of the Olympics.* Three editions, those of 1963, 1967, and 1975. Last two editions list author's name as Dick Schaap. New York: Alfred A. Knopf, 1963, 1967, 1975.

Soames, Nicolas, and Roy Inman. *Olympic Judo: History and Techniques.* Swindon, England: Crowood, Press, 1990.

Wallechinsky, David. *The Complete Book of the Olympics.* Five editions, followed by a separate edition for the Winter Olympics (following). First edition: Middlesex, England: Penguin Books, 1983. Second edition: New York: Viking Penguin, 1988. Third edition: London: Aurum, 1991. Fourth edition: Boston: Little Brown, 1996. Fifth edition: Woodstock, NY: Overlook Press, 2000.

Wallechinsky, David. *The Complete Book of the Winter Olympics.* Boston: Little, Brown, 1993. 2nd edition: Woodstock, New York: Overlook, 1998.

Wasner, Fritz. *Olympia-Lexikon.* Bielefeld, Germany: Verlag E. Gunglach Aktiengesellschaft, 1939.

Weyand, Alexander M. *Olympic Pageant.* New York: Macmillan, 1952.

zur Megede, Ekkehard. *The Modern Olympic Century 1896–1996.* Berlin: Deutsche Gesellschaft für Leichtathletik-Dokumentation e.V., 1999.

GENERAL POLITICAL AND SOCIOLOGICAL HISTORIES OF THE OLYMPIC GAMES

Clark, Stanley James. "Amateurism, Olympism, and Pedagogy: Cornerstones of the Modern Olympic Movement." Stanford University, Unpublished Ed.D. Thesis, 1975.

Daniels, Stephanie, and Anita Tedder. *A Proper Spectacle: Women Olympians 1900–1936. Celebrating 100 Years of Women in the Olympics.* Houghton Conquest, England: ZeNaNa Press, 2000.

Diem, Carl. *Ewiges Olympia.* Minden: np, 1948.

Espy, Richard. *The Politics of the Olympic Games.* Berkeley: University of California Press, 1979.

Findling, John E., and Kimberly D. Pelle. *Historical Dictionary of the Olympic Movement.* Westport, CT: Greenwood, 1996.

Fuoss, Donald E. "An Analysis of the Incidents in the Olympic Games from 1924 to 1948, with Reference to the Contribution of the Games to International Understanding." Columbia University, Unpublished Ph.D. Thesis, 1952.

Gafner, Raymond, and Norbert Müller. *The International Olympic Committee— One Hundred Years. The Idea—The Presidents—The Achievements.* 3 vols. Lausanne: IOC, 1995.

Graham, Peter J., and Horst Ueberhorst, editors. *The Modern Olympics.* Cornwall, New York: Leisure Press, ca. 1975.

Guttmann, Allen. *The Olympics: A History of the Modern Games.* Urbana, Illinois: University of Illinois Press, 1992.

Hill, Christopher R. *Olympic Politics: Athens to Atlanta 1896–1996.* 2nd ed. Manchester: Manchester University Press, 1996. First edition issued as *Olympic Politics,* same publisher, in 1992.

Hoberman, John. *Olympic Crisis: Sport Politics and the Moral Order.* New Rochelle, New York: Caratzas, 1986.

Jennings, Andrew. *The New Lords of the Rings.* New York: Pocket, 1996. (See Simson, Vyv, and Andrew Jennings for the first edition.)

Kanin, David B. *A Political History of the Olympic Games.* Boulder, Colorado: Westview Books, 1981.

Landry, Fernand; Landry, Marc; and Yerles, Magdeleine, editors. *Sport: The Third Millennium/Le troisième millénaire.* Sainte-Foy, Quebec: Les presses de l'université Laval, 1991. A collection of papers with text in either French or English. Abstracts are provided in both languages.

Leiper, Jean Marion. "The International Olympic Committee: The Pursuit of Olympism, 1894–1970." University of Alberta (Canada), Unpublished Ph.D. Thesis, 1976.

Lucas, John. *The Modern Olympic Games.* New York: A.S. Barnes, 1980.

Lucas, John. *The Future of the Olympic Games.* Champaign, Illinois: Human Kinetics, 1992.

Lyberg, Wolf. *The Book of Facts on the Olympic Winter Games 1924–1992: Part I: The Participants, The Medals, The Spectators.* Lausanne: IOC, 1992.

Lyberg, Wolf. *Fabulous 100 Years of the IOC: Facts—Figures—and Much, Much More.* Lausanne: IOC, 1996.

Lyberg, Wolf. *The History of the IOC Sessions.* 3 vols. Lausanne: IOC, 1994.

Lyberg, Wolf. *The Seventh President of the IOC: Facts and Figures.* Lausanne: IOC, 1997.

Messinesi, Xenophon Leon. *A Branch of Wild Olive.* New York: Exposition Press, 1973. Second edition issued as *A History of the Olympics,* published in 1976 by Drake Publishers of New York.

Miller, Geoffrey. *Behind the Olympic Rings.* Lynn, Massachusetts: H.O. Zimman, 1979.

Multi-Media Partners, Ltd. *Grace & Glory: A Century of Women in the Olympics.* Chicago: Triumph, 1996.

Okafor, Udodiri Paul. "The Interaction of Sports and Politics as a Dilemma of the Modern Olympic Games." The Ohio State University, Unpublished Ph.D. Thesis, 1979.

Platt, Alan R. "The Olympic Games and Their Political Aspects: 1952 to 1972." Kent State University, Unpublished Ph.D. Thesis, 1976.

Plowden, Martha Ward. *Olympic Black Women.* Gretna, Louisiana: Pelican, 1996.

Segrave Jeffrey O., and Donald Chu editors. *The Olympic Games in Transition.* Champaign, IL: Human Kinetics, 1988.

Senn, Alfred E. *Power, Politics, and the Olympic Games.* Champaign, Illinois: Human Kinetics, 1999.

Simson, Vyv, and Andrew Jennings. *Lords of the Rings: Power, Money & Drugs in the Modern* Olympics. London: Simon & Schuster, 1991. Published in the United States as *Dishonored Games: Corruption, Money & Greed at the Olympics.* New York: S.P.I. Books, 1992. (*See also* Jennings, Andrew for the second edition.)

Sun Byung-Kee; Lee Sei-Kee; Kim Sung-Kyu; and Kogh Young-Lee, editors. *Olympics and Politics.* Seoul: Hyung-Seul, *ca.* 1984.

Tait, Robin. "The Politicization of the Modern Olympic Games." University of Oregon, Unpublished Ph.D. Thesis, 1984.

Tomlinson, Alan, and Garry Whannel, editors. *Five Ring Circus: Money, Power, and Politics at the Olympic Games.* London: Pluto Press, 1984.

HISTORIES OF NATIONAL PARTICIPATION AT THE OLYMPIC GAMES

Australia

Atkinson, Graeme. *Australian & New Zealand Olympians: The Stories of 100 Great Champions.* Canterbury, Victoria: Five Mile Press, 1984.

Blanch, John, and Paul Jenes. *Australia at the Modern Olympic Games.* Coogee, New South Wales: John Blanch Publishing, 1984.

Gordon, Harry. *Australia and the Olympic Games.* St. Lucia: University of Queensland Press, 1994.

Howell, Reet, and Max Howell. *Aussie Gold: The Story of Australia at the Olympics.* South Melbourne: Brooks Waterloo, 1988.

Lester, Gary. *Australians at the Olympics: A Definitive History.* Sydney: Lester-Townsend Publishing, 1984.

Phillips, Dennis H. *Australian Women at the Olympic Games.* Kenthurst, New South Wales: Kangaroo Press, 1992.

Bulgaria

Tsigur Petfur Beron. *Olimpiyskite Igry 1896–1980 Shravochnyuk.* [Transliterated title] Sofia: Meditsina i fizkultura, *ca.* 1982.

Canada

Bryden, Wendy. *The Official Sports History and Record Book: Canada at the Olympic Winter Games.* Edmonton: Hurtig Publishers, 1987.

Cosentino, Frank, and Glynn Leyshon. *Olympic Gold: Canadian Winners of the Summer Games.* Toronto: Holt, Rinehart and Winston, 1975.

Cosentino, Frank, and Glynn Leyshon. *Winter Gold: Canada's Winners in the Winter Olympic Games.* Markham, Ontario: Fitzhenry & Whiteside Limited, 1987.

Roxborough, Henry. *Canada at the Olympics.* Three editions in 1963, 1969, and 1975. Toronto: Ryerson Press, 1963, 1969, 1975.

Czechoslovakia

Klír M., Kössl; Jiří, and Martíkovi; AaM. *Almanach Ceskoslovenskych Olympionikü.* Prague: Stráz, 1987.

Kössl, Jiří, ed. *Český Olympijský Výbor. Olympijská knihovnička. Dokumentace K Dějinám Českého Olympismu.* Prague: Czech Olympic Committee, 1998. Two volumes. Volume one covers 1891–1918, and volume two covers 1918–1945.

Estonia

Kivine, P. *Estonikie sportsmeny prisery Olimpiyskikh/Estonian Olympic Medal Winners/Die estnischen Olympiamedaillen-gewinner/Les Médaillés olympiques d'Estonie.* Tallinn: Perioodika, 1980. Parallel texts in Estonian, English, German, and French.

France

Charpentier, Henri. *La Grande Histoire des Médaillés Olympiques Français de 1896 à 1988.* Paris: Editions Robert Laffont, ca. 1989.
Pellissard-Darrigrand, Nicole. *La Galaxie Olympique.* Biarritz: CNOSF, 1995.
Pellissard-Darrigrand, Nicole. *La Galaxie Olympique d'Hiver.* Biarritz: CNOSF, 1998.

German Democratic Republic

Gilbert, Doug. *The Miracle Machine.* New York: Coward, McCann & Geoghegan, Inc., 1980.

Great Britain

Buchanan, Ian. *British Olympians: A Hundred Years of Gold Medallists.* London: Guinness, 1991.

Greece

Tarasouleas, At[hanassios]. *Helliniki Simmetokhi Stis Sinkhrones Olympiades.* [Transliterated title] Athens: author, 1990.

Hungary

Mező, Ferenc. *Golden Book of Hungarian Olympic Champions/Livre d'Or des Champions Olympiques Hongrois.* Budapest: Sport Lap. És Könyvkiadö, 1955. Parallel texts in English and French.

India

Sanyal, Saraduni. *Olympic Games and India.* New Delhi: Metropolitan Book, 1970.

Ireland

Naughton, Lindie, and Johnny Watterson. *Irish Olympians.* Dublin: Blackwater Press, 1992.

New Zealand (*see also* Australia)

Atkinson, Graeme. *Australian & New Zealand Olympians: The Stories of 100 Great Champions.* Canterbury, Victoria, Australia: Five Mile Press, 1984.

Poland

Gluszek, Zygmunt. *Polscy Olimpijczycy 1924/1984.* 2nd ed. Warsaw: Sport i Tu-rystyka, 1988. First edition published in 1980 as *Polscy Olimpijczycy 1924/1976.*

Slovenia

Levovnik, Tomo; Racic, Marko; and Rozman, Marko. *1920–1988. Nasi olimpijci.* Ljublana: Grafos, 1992.

Soviet Union

Brokhin, Yury. *The Big Red Machine: The Rise and Fall of Soviet Olympic Champions.* New York: Random House, 1977 and 1978.
Khavin, B[oris]. *Vsyo ob Olimpiyskikh Igrakh.* [Transliterated title] Moscow: Fizkultura i sport, 1979.
Pavlov, S. P. *Olimpiyskaya Entsiklopediya.* [Transliterated title] Moscow: Fizkultura i sport, 1980.
Pavlov, S. P. *Olimpiyskaya Komanda SSSR.* [Transliterated title] Moscow: Fizkultura i sport, 1980.

Sweden

Glanell, Tomas; Huldtén, Gösta; et al., editors. *Sverige och OS.* Stockholm: Brunnhages Förlag, 1987.
Pettersson, Ulf, editor. *1896–1980 Guldboken om alla Våra Olympiamästare.* Stockholm: Brunnhages Förlag, 1980.

Ukraine

Zinkewych, Osyp. *Ukrainian Olympic Champions.* 3rd ed. Baltimore: V. symonenko Smoloskyp Publishers, 1984.

United States

Bortstein, Larry. *After Olympic Glory: The Lives of Ten Outstanding Medalists.* New York: Frederick Warne, 1978.
Carlson, Lewis H., and John J. Fogarty. *Tales of Gold: An Oral History of the Summer Olympic Games Told by America's Gold Medal Winners.* Chicago: Contemporary, 1987.
Johnson, William O[scar], Jr. *All That Glitters Is Not Gold: An Irreverent Look at the Olympic Games.* New York: Putnam, 1972.

Mallon, Bill, and Ian Buchanan. *Quest for Gold: The Encyclopaedia of American Olympians.* New York: Leisure, 1984.

BIOGRAPHIES OF AND BY IOC PRESIDENTS

Demetrios Vikelas

Young, David C. "Demetrios Vikelas: First President of the IOC." In: *Stadion,* (1988), pp. 85–102.

Pierre de Coubertin

Boulongne, Yves-Pierre. *La vie et l'œuvre de Pierre de Coubertin.* Ottawa, Quebec: Lemeac, 1975.

Durántez, Conrado. *Pierre de Coubertin: The Olympic Humanist.* Lausanne: IOC, 1994.

Durry, Jean. *Le Vrai Pierre de Coubertin.* Paris: Comité français Pierre de Coubertin, 1994.

Éyquem, MarieThérése. *Pierre de Coubertin. L'Épopée Olympique.* Paris: Calman-Lévy, 1966.

Lucas, John Apostal. "Baron Pierre de Coubertin and the Formative Years of the Modern International Olympic Movement 1883–1896." University of Maryland, Unpublished Ed.D. Thesis, 1962.

MacAloon, John J. *This Great Symbol: Pierre de Coubertin and the Origins of the Modern Olympic Games.* Chicago: University of Chicago Press, 1981.

Müller, Norbert, editor. *Pierre de Coubertin: Textes Choisis.* 3 vols. Zurich: Weidmann, 1986.

Navacelle, Geoffroy de. *Pierre de Coubertin: Sa vie par l'Image.* Lausanne: IOC, 1986.

Henri de Baillet-Latour

Boin, Victor. "Graf Baillet-Latour," *Olympische Rundschau, 17* (1942), pp. 6–11.

Diem, Carl. "Die Beisetzung (Graf Baillet-Latour)," *Olympische Rundschau, 17* (1942), p. 24.

Polignac, Melchior Marquis de. "Gedanken über Graf Baillet-Latour," *Olympische Rundschau, 17* (1942), pp. 17–22.

Johannes Sigfrid Edström

Bratt, K. A. *J. Sigfrid Edström - En Levnadsteckning.* 2 vols. Stockholm: P. A. Nordstedt & Söner, 1950 (Vol. 1) and 1953 (Vol. 2).

Bring, Samuel E., editor. *J. Sigfrid Edström: Vänners hyllning på 75–årsdagen 21 november 1940.* Uppsala: Almqvist & Wicksell, 1940.
Edström, Ruth Randall. *J. Sigfrid Edström.* Viisteris: Vistmanlands Allehanda, 1946.

Avery Brundage

Schöbel, Heinz. *The Four Dimensions of Avery Brundage.* Translated by Joan Becker. Leipzig, GDR: Offizin Anderson Nexo, 1968.
Gibson, Richard Lee. "Avery Brundage: Professional Amateur." Kent State University, Unpublished Ph.D. Thesis, 1976.
Guttmann, Allen. *The Games Must Go On: Avery Brundage and the Olympic Movement.* New York: Columbia University Press, 1984.

Lord Killanin

Lord Killanin. *My Olympic Years.* London: Secker & Warburg, 1983.

Juan Antonio Samaranch

Miller, David. *Olympic Revolution: The Olympic Biography of Juan Antonio Samaranch.* London: Pavilion Books, 1992.

OLYMPIC WORKS BY COUBERTIN
(ONLY BOOKS ON SPORT AND THE OLYMPIC MOVEMENT)

Coubertin, Pierre de. *L'éducation athlétique.* Paris: Imprimerie de Chaix, 1889.
Coubertin, Pierre de. *Notes sur l'Education publique.* Paris: Hachette, 1901.
Coubertin, Pierre de. *L'Education des Adolescents au XXe siècle. I: L'Education physique: La Gymnastique utilitaire. Sauvetage—Défense—Locomotion.* Paris: Alcan, 1905.
Coubertin, Pierre de. *Une campagne de vingt-et-un ans (1887–1908).* Paris: Librairie de l'Education Physique, 1909.
Coubertin, Pierre de. *Une olympie moderne.* Lausanne: Olympic Review, 1909.
Coubertin, Pierre de. *Leçons de Gymnastique Utilitaire. Sauvetage—Défense—Locomotion. A l'Usage des Instituteurs, Moniteurs, Instructeurs militaires, etc..* Paris: Payot, 1916.
Coubertin, Pierre de. *Leçons da Pédagogie sportive.* Lausanne: La Concorde, 1921.
Coubertin, Pierre de. *Mémoires olympiques.* Lausanne: Bureau international de pédagogie sportive, 1931.

MISCELLANEOUS OLYMPIC WORKS

Borgers, Walter. *Olympic Torch Relays: 1936–1994*. Berlin: Agon Sportverlag, 1996.

Durántez, Conrado. *The Olympic Flame*. Burlada, Spain: I. G. Castuera, 1998.

Gadoury, Victor, and Romolo Vescovi. *Olympic Medals and Coins: 510 B.C.–1994*. Monaco: Victor Gadoury Publications, 1996.

Greensfelder, Jim; Oleg Vorontsov; and Jim Lally. *Olympic Medals: A Reference Guide*. Saratoga, California: GVL Enterprises, 1998.

Jackson, R., and T. McPhail, editors. *The Olympic Movement and the Mass Media: Past, Present, and Future Issues*. Calgary: Hurford Enterprises, 1989.

Leigh, Mary Henson. "The Evolution of Women's Participation in the Summer Olympic Games, 1900–1948." Ohio State University, Unpublished Ph.D. Thesis, 1974.

Lennartz, Karl. *Bibliographie: Geschichte der Leibesübungen, Band 5, Olympische Spiele*. 2nd ed. Bonn: Verlag Karl Hofmann, 1983.

Mallon, Bill. *The Olympics: A Bibliography*. New York: Garland, 1984.

Moragas Spà, Miquel de; John MacAloon; and Montserrat Llinés. *Olympic Ceremonies: Historical Continuity and Cultural Exchange*. Lausanne: IOC, 1996.

Moragas Spà, Miquel de; Nancy K. Rivenburgh; and James F. Larson. *Television in the Olympics*. London: John Libbey, 1995.

Müller, Norbert. *One Hundred Years of Olympic Congresses 1894–1994*. Lausanne: IOC , 1994.

Pappas, Nina K. "History and Development of the International Olympic Academy, 1927–1977." University of Illinois, Unpublished Ph.D. Thesis, 1978.

Welch, Paula Dee. "The Emergence of American Women in the Summer Olympic Games, 1900–1972." University of North Carolina at Greensboro, Unpublished Ed.D. Thesis, 1975.

Wenn, Stephen Robert. "A History of the International Olympic Committee and Television, 1936–1980." The Pennsylvania State University, Unpublished Ph.D. Thesis, 1993.